To Peter McArdle

Those were the days,
my friend!

Affectionately

Gerry Loughran

Newcastle on Tyne

August 2017.

# Birth of a NATION

**Gerard Loughran** spent over a dozen years at the 'Nation' in senior editorial capacities and brings a wide range of international experience to this story. He was Bureau Chief in Beirut, Paris and Moscow for the international news agency, United Press International, and was Foreign News Editor in New York before setting up Compass News Features covering the developing world.

# Birth of a
# NATION

## The Story of
## a Newspaper
## in Kenya

*Gerard Loughran*

I.B. TAURIS

LONDON · NEW YORK

Published in 2010 by I.B.Tauris & Co Ltd
6 Salem Road, London W2 4BU
175 Fifth Avenue, New York NY 10010
www.ibtauris.com

Distributed in the United States and Canada Exclusively by Palgrave Macmillan,
175 Fifth Avenue, New York NY 10010

ISBN: 978 1 84511 838 9

A full CIP record for this book is available from the British Library
A full CIP record is available from the Library of Congress

Library of Congress Catalog Card Number: available

Designed and Typeset by 4word Ltd, Bristol, UK
Printed and bound in Great Britain by CPI Antony Rowe, Chippenham

FSC
Mixed Sources
Product group from well-managed
forests and other controlled sources
Cert no. SGS-COC-002953
www.fsc.org
© 1996 Forest Stewardship Council

## Dedication

To the men and women on the *Nation*'s various publications for their courageous, obstinate and enduring battle for the freedom of speech and expression.

# Contents

*Cleopatra: Thou shalt be whipp'd with*
*Wire and stew'd in brine.*
*Smarting in ling'ring pickle.*

*Messenger: Gracious Madam,*
*I that do bring the news*
*Made not the match.*

*Cleopatra: Though it be honest, it is*
*Never good*
*To bring bad news.*

William Shakespeare,
*Anthony and Cleopatra*, Act II, Scene V

# Preface

When the first issue of *The Nation* rolled off the presses in Nairobi on 20 March 1960, the newspaper industry worldwide, though it did not know it, was on the cusp of revolution. Editors were aware of television's eager encroachment, but free news-sheets were unknown, local radio stations offered no realistic competition and the Internet was unimaginable.

Today, newspapers in their thousands are collapsing, merging and being subsumed by cyberspace, their advertising revenues and readership drained by a young generation more comfortably attuned to screen and keyboard. Only if the newspapers that survive are better than the ones that die will the industry accommodate these changes.

For 50 years, the Nation Media Group has proclaimed a philosophy of self-improvement, believing its commitment to quality would help it harness technological evolution and ride economic turbulence. This book examines the extent to which the group has hewn to this philosophy and, perhaps more important, how far its newspapers have contributed to the social health of Kenya and the wider developing world.

Did they speak out for the innocent, defend the powerless, accuse the guilty, pillory the thieves? Did they ask the awkward question, investigate, press, persist, excavate and discomfort? To do so whilst subjected over many years to serious repression and unremitting official hostility required steadfast courage from the journalistic rank and file, and a dedicated, risk-fraught idealism from the ownership. In the end, did the *Nation* stretch the bounds of freedom? Did it do the right thing? Did it make a difference?

The media group which the Aga Khan founded at a time of deep economic uncertainty in the twilight of empire has grown to be the largest publishing organisation in east and central Africa. Its 50th birthday can be seen as a triumphant affirmation of a courageous and visionary concept. But triumphalism would be offering a hostage to fortune. More likely is a reaffirmation of the self-improvement philosophy, a push for geographic expansion, the embrace of whatever is new in technology and a fearless renewal of its commitment to truth in journalism.

Many *Nation* readers walk to work so as to have money for their newspaper. This is the least they expect in return.

# Acknowledgements

In researching this history, I sought interviews with a great many people. The vast majority responded positively; two Kenyan journalists and a Western diplomat declined, and none of the Kenyan politicians I contacted responded to my requests.

I wish to thank senior management of the Nation Media Group Ltd for commissioning me to undertake this project, in particular Mr Wilfred Kiboro for his encouragement and personal availability and for allowing me unhindered access to company documents. The late Michael Curtis, so crucial in the *Nation* story, opened not only his files but his home to me. In France, Georgina Cochu and Francesca Cossu were particularly helpful, and in Nairobi Wangethi Mwangi opened a path through the thickets of newspaper bureaucracy. There, too, my work was facilitated by the former chief librarian Charles Mallei and in particular by Evans Luvonga Sasakah.

I want to thank also all those current and former *Nation* staffers, and media people outside of the company, who gave generously of their time and hospitality to recall and explain events of the past half-century, along with those who responded with written recollections and in a variety of other ways. Essentially, this is history as seen by contemporary eyewitnesses, and the book could not have been written in this way without their memories. Gerry Wilkinson was particularly generous not only with his time, encouragement and suggestions over the lengthy period of writing and pre-publication, but crucially for his moral support at times when the way ahead looked obscure. If I have missed anyone who assisted me from the following list, please accept my apologies and take my gratitude as read:

Mahmood Ahamed, Dennis Aluanga, Violet Anyango, Allen Armstrong, Olive Armstrong, Robbie Armstrong, Frank Barton, Dick Beeston, Gavin Bennett, Aziz Bhaloo, Peter Biddlecombe, John Bierman, Brian Carter, Peter Chadwick, Alan Chester, Michael Chester, Nick Chitty, Tom Clark, John Collier, Ivor Davis, Paddy Deacon, Stan Denman, Tony Dunn, John Eames,

John and Mary Edwards, Sean Egan, Albert A.A. Ekirapa, Sarah Elderkin, Jack Ensoll, Cyprian Fernandes, Ian Fernandes, Aidan Flannery, Gado (Godfrey Mwampembwa), Dr B.M. Gecaga, Linus Gitahi, John Githongo, Michael Griffin, Desmond Harney, Charles Hayes, Margaret Hayes, Dr Peter Hengel, Richard Henry, Bob Hitchcock, Gloria Hitchcock, Mark Holden, Joe Kadhi, Paul Kalemba, A.R. Kapila, Irene Karanja, Paddy Kearney, Charles Kimathi, James Kinyua, Andrew Kuria, Tony Lavers, John Lawrence, Eric Marsden, Ros Marsden, Joseph Mathenge, Alastair Matheson, Ian Matheson, Julius Mbaluto, Chege Mbitiru, George Mbugguss, Helen Mbugua, Colin MacBeth, Peter McCardle, John McHaffie, Mike Mills, Tom Mshindi, Njonjo Mue, Wamahiu Muya, Mburu Mwangi, Cyrille Nabutollah, Mbatau wa Ngai, Dugal Nisbet-Smith, Mutegi Njau, Bernard K. Njeru, Philip Ochieng, Charles Onyango-Obbo, Albert Odero, Joseph Odindo, Blasto Ogindo, Patrick Orr, Malcolm Payne, John Platter, Ian Raitt, Arnold Raphael, Paul Redfern, Cyrilla Rodrigues, Jim Rose, Nick Russell, Robert Shaw, Mr Justice J.F. Shields, John Silvester, Peter Smith, Roger Steadman, Althea Tebbutt-Berryman, Louise Tunbridge, Errol Trzebinski, Yussuf Wachira, Neema Wamai, Mohammed Warsama, Frank Whalley, Ray Wilkinson, Ali Zaidi, Karl Ziegler.

# List of Acronyms

| | |
|---|---|
| AFP | Agence France Presse |
| AKFED | Aga Khan Fund for Economic Development |
| AP | Associated Press |
| CCM | Chama Cha Mapinduzi |
| CEO | chief executive officer |
| DC | district commissioner |
| EAN | East African Newspapers |
| EATN | East Africa Television Network |
| FERA | February Eighteen Resistance Army |
| FORD | Forum for the Restoration of Democracy |
| GDP | gross domestic product |
| GEMA | Gikuyu, Embu, Meru Association |
| IPS | Industrial Promotion Services |
| IPI | International Press Institute |
| IPPG | Inter-Parties Parliamentary Group |
| KADU | Kenya African Democratic Union |
| KANU | Kenya African National Union |
| KBC | Kenya Broadcasting Corporation |
| KICC | Kenyatta International Conference Centre |
| KNA | Kenya News Agency |
| KPU | Kenya People's Union |
| KTN | Kenya Television Network |
| Legco | Legislative Council |
| LDP | Liberal Democratic Party |
| MD | managing director |
| MPL | Monitor Publications Ltd |
| Mwakenya | *Muungano wa Wazalendo wa Kukomboa Kenya* (Union of Patriots for the Liberation of Kenya) |

| | |
|---|---|
| NAK | National Alliance Party of Kenya |
| Narc | National Rainbow Coalition |
| NDP | National Development Party |
| NMG | Nation Media Group Ltd |
| NNL | Nation Newspapers Ltd |
| NPP | Nation Printers and Publishers Ltd |
| OAU | Organisation of African Unity |
| Opec | Organisation of the Petroleum Exporting Countries |
| PNU | Party of National Unity |
| Unesco | United Nations Educational, Scientific and Cultural Organisation |
| Unicef | United Nations Children's Fund |
| UPI | United Press International |
| VOK | Voice of Kenya |
| YK92 | Youth for KANU '92 |

# List of Illustrations

**Cartoons**

**Mono Plates** (between pages 80 and 81)
Jomo Kenyatta and guards
Kenyatta and Mboya at the independence conference, London
Two front pages: Launch issue and Kenya Free
Michael Curtis; Hilary Ng'weno; John Bierman
The Aga Khan and Kenyatta in a meeting
The Aga Khan and Moi at the general assembly of the International
    Press Institute
Jomo Kenyatta with white farmers

**Colour Plates** (between pages 208 and 209)

# Challenge
# for Control

**1**

*A democracy without the means of public information
is but a prelude to farce or tragedy.*
US President James Madison (1751–1836)

When the $3 million Serena Hotel in Nairobi was opened on 16 February
1976, there came a moment when four men found themselves together: the
president of Kenya, Jomo Kenyatta; the leader of the Shia Imami Ismaili
Muslims worldwide, His Highness Prince Karim Aga Khan; and two Kenyan
businessmen, Udi Gecaga and Ngengi Muigai. According to an executive on
the fringe, Kenyatta addressed the Aga Khan: 'This is my nephew, Mr
Muigai. He has just come back from America and I was wondering if it was
possible to find a position for him in your newspapers.' The Aga Khan
appeared taken aback but replied politely that he was sure that would be
possible, but he would have to make enquiries. Gecaga and Muigai looked
unhappy at this guarded response, but the Kenyan president nodded and the
group split up.

In a dark suit, with an orchid in his buttonhole and a fly whisk dangling
from his wrist, the revered father of the nation unveiled a plaque opening
Nairobi's most elegant hotel, and then at the celebratory luncheon graciously
acknowledged a toast by the Aga Khan to his continued good health and long
life. The chic guests amidst the flowering jacaranda and bougainvillea were
not to know that Kenyatta's twilight years were approaching their end and
that the prospect of his demise had already begun to influence the course of
national politics, to which the cameo on the Serena terrace would add a significant footnote. Indeed, the meeting set in train a course of events which
had an important impact on Kenya's constitutional development and long-
lasting effects on freedom of expression and the future of democracy.

The new 400-bed hotel on the edge of Uhuru Park was an investment by the Aga Khan's Tourism Promotion Services Ltd, an offshoot of Industrial Promotion Services (IPS), which he established in 1963 as a catalyst for Third World development in partnership with private institutions and global agencies. The newspapers to which Kenyatta referred were an earlier Aga Khan personal initiative, a publishing stable named the Nation Group comprising two English-language titles, the *Daily Nation* and the *Sunday Nation*, the Kiswahili daily *Taifa Leo* and *Taifa Weekly*. The group started in 1959 with the purchase for £10,000 of a tiny Kiswahili weekly, *Taifa* (meaning 'Nation'), from Charles Hayes, a former District Commissioner in the colonial administration, and his business partner, Althea Tebbutt. *Taifa* was quickly turned into a daily, an English-language Sunday paper was launched in March 1960 and the *Daily Nation* appeared in October the same year. The first African editor-in-chief, Hilary Boniface Ng'weno, was appointed in 1964. After investing more than £1 million in the venture (at least £12 million at today's rates), the Aga Khan saw the group move into profit in 1968, and just a year later the daily overhauled its long-established rival, the *East African Standard*.[1] In 1973, the group became a public company, with more than 8,000 mostly Kenyan shareholders, reducing the Aga Khan's shareholding to 60 per cent. This was later lowered to 44.73 per cent ownership and in 2003 the founder transferred his 23.9 million personal shares to the Aga Khan Fund for Economic Development (AKFED), which worked to bring jobs and services to poor countries. At the time of the Serena opening, the *Nation* was selling more than 70,000 copies a day, double that of its rival, and the group was the unchallenged industry leader in East Africa. It was easy to see why the *Nation* was an attractive proposition for a young man with commercial or political ambitions in 1976.

The Aga Khan's personal association with Kenya was a long one. During World War II, his father Prince Aly Khan was based in Cairo with the Free French forces and fought the German Axis armies in the North African desert. Prince Karim and his younger brother, Amyn, were sent to safety in Kenya and lived in a house belonging to their grandfather, the then reigning Aga Khan, Sir Sultan Mohammed Shah. The house in suburban Nairobi had a metal roof, and when the boys lay in bed at night they could hear the rain pattering overhead and occasionally the growls of lions prowling outside. Returning to Switzerland, the country of his birth, Karim attended Le Rosey private school for nine years, then began reading for a Bachelor's degree in engineering, switching later to Islamic History at Harvard University in the USA. He was aged 20 and half-way through his course when his grandfather died in 1957. By tradition, the Aga Khan exerts his personal choice to name a successor. When the will was read the day after his death, it stated:

*In view of the fundamentally altered conditions in the world in very recent years, I am convinced that it is in the best interests of the Shia Imami Ismaili Muslim community that I be succeeded by a young man who has been brought up and developed during recent years in the midst of the new age and who will bring a new outlook on life to his office of Imam. For this reason, I appoint my grandson Karim, son of my son Aly Salomone Khan, to succeed to the title of Aga Khan and be the Imam and Pir of all my Shia Ismaili followers.*

Thus, to widespread surprise, the young Prince Karim became the 49th Imam in direct descent from the Prophet Mohammed through his daughter Fatima, and leader of some 15 million Ismaili Muslims in 25 countries.[2]

One of the largest of these communities was in Kenya, and the new Aga Khan broke off his studies to visit the local leaders and take part in his enthronement ceremony in the course of a world tour to meet his followers. Young, handsome and athletic – he skied for Iran at a Winter Olympics and was a member of the Harvard soccer team – the new Imam was received with delight by Ismailis. But already he was looking beyond the ceremonial and pondering the future in East Africa. Independence, he believed, was inevitable. Though by no means imminent, he considered British Colonial Office talk of ten and 15 years as unrealistic, and was already pondering how majority rule, when it came, would affect Ismailis and the other immigrant communities. They were mostly merchants and thus vulnerable to the future entry of African businessmen into their field. How would they integrate into a new type of society? Could he assist in a peaceful transition from colonial rule and if so, how? The Aga Khan returned to Harvard to complete his studies – he received an honours degree in Islamic History – with much to think about. (In 2008, Harvard bestowed on him an Honorary Doctorate of Laws.) Repeatedly, he urged Ismailis to take citizenship in the new African-led nations and participate in the drive for development. He hired financial experts, and on their recommendation formed IPS to assist in industrialisation and thereby demonstrate his commitment to the new Africa in concrete financial terms. Quite unexpectedly, he also announced he wanted to start a newspaper.

Michael Curtis was Fleet Street's youngest editor, aged 34, when he took over Charles Dickens' old chair at the *News Chronicle* in London in 1954. He had been with the newspaper as editorial writer and deputy editor since 1946, but came into conflict with the ownership on two fronts. In the face of weakening circulation, he argued for a change in the paper's format, suggesting, far ahead of current thinking, a restrained tabloid with serious content, as favoured by some European industry leaders. The Cadbury family, which owned the *Chronicle*, was not convinced. More importantly, Curtis disagreed strongly with the British government's policy over Egypt's nationalisation of the Suez Canal and said so in his columns. The proprietors felt he should support the government, and in 1957 Curtis resigned. A family connection put him in touch with the Aga Khan and he accompanied the new Imam on his enthronement tour as his press advisor. Curtis recalled in an interview for this book that

> the Aga Khan was obviously interested in newspapers during that tour but it was only when he got back to Harvard that he raised the idea. I said to him, 'Look, I better go, I don't think this PR stuff is really my métier and I want to get back to journalism.' He then said, 'Well, how about starting a newspaper in Kenya?' This was a complete surprise to me but also an attractive proposition, the prospect of actually starting a newspaper, which a lot of journalists long to do. I made it very clear that I could not be involved if he wanted a newspaper for the Ismaili community and he said immediately, 'No, no, that's the last thing I want. I want a completely independent paper.' He always said that and he stuck to it and some of the community in fact were unhappy that this paper employed no Ismailis. He never used the paper in the Ismaili interest. What he wanted was a newspaper to give a voice to Kenya's nationalists, who were not being heard in the political debate.

On his 1957 tour, the Aga Khan made note of what Curtis called 'the abysmal quality of newspapers in Kenya and Uganda and all these old British Empire places where the papers were quite simply the mouthpieces of the colonial government'. Encouraging him to go into the business were the young African nationalists of the time: 'It was basically his idea but certainly he was pressed in Kenya by politicians, particularly Tom Mboya. They were pushing all the time, saying "Let's open up, this is going to be the new East Africa."' Mboya and colleagues such as Dr Julius Kiano and James Gichuru would occasionally meet with the Aga Khan for lunch or dinner in London or Switzerland as the hectic pace of independence negotiations quickened.

Although Kenyatta at the Serena encounter had referred only to a 'position' for Muigai with the *Nation*, it soon became apparent that the position he had in mind was the top one, chairman of the holding company, Nation Printers and Publishers Ltd (NPP). Albert Ekirapa, a *Nation* manager and former civil servant who was scheduled to take over as NPP executive chairman, was at the Serena opening. In an interview, he recalled, 'Gecaga and Muigai were not satisfied with the meeting with the Aga Khan, who was due to fly out the next day and they wanted an announcement immediately.' The two turned to Peter Hengel, an influential *Nation* director and the man whose financial expertise dragged the company back from the brink when it over-extended unwisely in the early 1960s. Ekirapa recalled, 'They got hold of Peter but Hengel said he wasn't sure that the Aga Khan wanted to make an immediate announcement.' Next day, the Aga Khan met with Muigai and Gecaga at Nairobi International Airport during a VIP lunch when the feasibility, methodology and timing for Muigai's ascent to the chairmanship was broached. According to the memories of participants, the meal was an uncomfortable affair. The Aga Khan said he could not announce a new chairman without warning, since such a move would create a major upset and have a questionable impact upon shareholders. He suggested a meeting between Muigai and Gecaga and NPP's directors in April, in two months' time, and said meanwhile he would write to the President. In other words, he would communicate directly with Kenyatta and not through Gecaga and Muigai. Ekirapa said, 'The Aga Khan had promised the President he would do something', but the precise nature of the commitment was open to question. 'The management view of Muigai at the helm was very, very negative', Ekirapa said, 'and it was my job to tell the Aga Khan so'.

*Nation* managers were worried by what seemed to be a 'company raider' mentality by the two men. They were even more concerned about the political implications. The two had close ties to the 'royal court' at Kenyatta's Gatundu home, a Kikuyu power centre which appeared to wield more power than Kenya's elected cabinet; they were also members of the head of state's own family – Muigai was a nephew of Kenyatta, Gecaga a son-in-law. Gecaga was also chairman of Lonrho East Africa Ltd, owners of the *Standard*, the *Nation's* chief rival. It did not help that his father, Mareka, was a long-serving director of NPP.

On leaving Nairobi, the Aga Khan travelled to Pakistan, where he had the opportunity to observe the deleterious effects of a government-controlled press, while in Kenya, the *Nation's* top people canvassed opinion on the Muigai proposal from a wide range of contacts. On his return to Europe, the

Aga Khan called NPP directors and senior managers to a series of meetings in St Moritz, Switzerland. Ekirapa recalled, 'We expressed our criticism in no uncertain terms.' The view of Editor-in-Chief George Githii was sought. The controversial Githii was a politically-minded editor whose two periods at the helm of the *Nation* made the newspaper as much a topic of public debate as the events it reported. Recalled Ekirapa, 'Githii was very, very forthright, more forthright than any of us. He believed there was no way this merchant group should be allowed to get anywhere near the *Nation*.' The managing director (MD) of the newspaper company, Gerry Wilkinson, was asked to prepare a list of 'banana skins', possible repercussions if the eventual decision was badly received at Gatundu.

After a weekend break, Gecaga and Muigai arrived. Said Ekirapa:

> *They looked surprised to see us there. The Aga Khan turned to Muigai and said words to the effect that 'These are my directors, they are the people who make decisions on my behalf. Perhaps you would like to tell them what role you believe you can play in our group.' They were taken aback. We had heard that they had already been telling people they were going to get part of the* Nation, *it was just a matter of signing on the dotted line. Muigai was so taken aback, he didn't have anything to say. But Gecaga was very smart. He kept saying the* Nation *needed an injection of business acumen, new blood and so on. The Aga Khan said, 'I really wanted Mr Muigai to answer but since you have spoken up, how would you feel if I suggested that I would nominate somebody to the board of Lonrho?' Gecaga said, 'That's different, I am not here as a representative of Lonrho, I'm here in my personal capacity.' The Aga Khan said, 'I don't see where the divide is. Could I also nominate somebody for you?' It became like a game and in the end the Aga Khan said, 'We will discuss with the board what contribution you might make to our group and we will let the President know.' So they left, obviously very disappointed, since this was not what they had expected.*

The Aga Khan and his directors were confronted with an extremely awkward situation. It was impossible to reject President Kenyatta's expressed wishes out of hand without risking severe and far-reaching consequences. But to put Muigai in as chairman would be to surrender the *Nation's* hard-won reputation for independence and label it a blatant sell-out. With Udi Gecaga at the *Standard*, such a move would effectively submit the national print media to the control of a single political faction, and the *Nation* leadership was never in doubt that the Muigai initiative was intended to place control of the domestic editorial output in the hands of the Gatundu circle. One solution would be to sell the newspaper to the government. Such an offer had been made once before, in 1965, when the *Nation* was being given a torrid time by the then information minister, Achieng Oneko. Recalling that period, Director Peter Hengel said, 'It had become increasingly difficult to manage the paper. The government was exceedingly touchy and giving us lots of problems and I recall being at a function when Kenyatta scolded Githii for being too critical of the government. He said, "I know your mother very well and she would not have approved".'

Hengel also said:

> With all these problems, the Aga Khan decided to force their hand and he sent me to Nairobi to see Kenyatta to see if the government wanted to buy the Nation. His reasoning was that either the government should let the press be free and leave us in peace or let them take the paper. When I put the situation to Kenyatta, he said no, no, no, he didn't want to buy the Nation. I think at that time they had in mind to launch their own government paper, but we were relieved because it cleared up the situation. We had loyally offered the government a chance to buy or just take the paper and they didn't want to.

The deal that Hengel offered Kenyatta was an out-in-the-open transaction in which ownership and editorial stance would be publicly acknowledged. To accept, ten years later, factional control as represented by Muigai, while still ostensibly an independent newspaper, would deprive the *Nation* of its credibility and shroud it in public suspicion and ill-will.

The St Moritz meetings pondered the way ahead. The easy option was to accept Muigai as chairman of NPP, though this would destroy the Group's credibility and risk a mass exodus of key personnel; there was also the likelihood that the Gatundu family rule would collapse with Kenyatta's eventual demise and the *Nation* would be exposed to retribution from a new leadership. A second course was to sell off the newspaper company, Nation Newspapers Ltd (NNL), with a management contract going to NPP. The paper's loss of independence would not then sully the group's image. Legally, however, this would be almost impossible; what's more, it would deprive the group of its major revenue source. A third and harder option was to offer Muigai the chairmanship of NNL, perhaps altering the Articles of

Association to limit the appointment to one year. If he insisted on the NPP job, consideration would be given to selling the group. The hardest course of all would be simply to say no to Kenyatta.

The consultations were extraordinary in their thoroughness, including examination of how a Muigai-headed *Nation* would be affected by any change of regime in Kenya. A three-page analysis typed on the notepaper of the Crystal Hotel, St Moritz, was headed 'Plan of action in the event of a sudden transition of power'. There had been no overt moves against the ageing Kenyatta, but the succession issue was an obsession with Kenya's politicians. The St Moritz paper noted that change in Kenya could come in three ways: through a constitutional accession to power by the vice-president (VP), Daniel arap Moi, followed by elections; by the temporary accession of the VP followed by his removal; or by the forced accession to power of a group with the support of the security forces. In the first case, the paper said, the *Nation* would have to cover the run-up to the elections 'and under the new chairman this would be the area of danger with an obvious desire for a bias against the vice-president'. If the constitutional process was halted, criticism by the *Nation* could lead to closure, but since the 'non-constitutional party would likely be the group represented by our chairman, the avenue of attack on the regime would obviously be closed'. In the third case, 'the forced and immediate accession to power by an individual supported by the security forces would come from ... the parties represented by our chairman, or some other section'. If the former, the newspaper would be lined up against the chairman's friends, and if the latter, it would most probably be closed immediately. In either case, the *Nation* would be in the anti-constitutional camp.

After the first round of St Moritz consultations, the Aga Khan sent a letter to Kenyatta saying he had had 'serious second thoughts' since their meeting at the Serena. 'There is no doubt', he wrote, 'that if Mr Muigai were to become chairman of NPP, the press in Kenya would be, to all intents and purposes, under the control of one group of individuals with a consequent monolithic outlook (and) whatever may be the actual facts of the case, public opinion in Kenya would be likely to regard the new chairmanship as an act of government to create a press monopoly'. He added that if circulation declined because the public considered the paper had become part of a state monopoly, the 2,000-plus Kenyan shareholders in NPP would suffer. (The total of shareholders grew to close on 8,000 in 1988 with a second offering.) The letter also pointed to the Gecagas' relationships with the *Nation* and the *Standard* respectively. 'I consider this sort of situation to be potentially very unhealthy', the letter said. 'If, within the next few months, it becomes known that our new chairman is closely related to the controlling interests of the *Standard* group in Kenya, I expect that a number of questions will be raised at our General Assembly [AGM] and that they will have a substantial impact on our readership.'

The Aga Khan added that he had just returned from Pakistan, where he had been dismayed to find the vast majority of the media under government control:

> *The government there itself now feels that this is not a satisfactory situation. Among the many reasons for their dissatisfaction were a substantial deterioration in editorial quality, failure by foreign governments and organisations to give serious consideration to the national media and the latter's considerable financial troubles.*

The letter concluded:

> *I think that it would be in the best interests of Kenya that while NPP clearly remains loyal to you and the government, it also remains independent of Lonrho… I would truly request you to reconsider the suggestion that Mr Muigai become the chairman of NPP.*

What started as a polite response to a request from the head of state – 'a vague promise' as Hengel put it – had somehow become a critical part of the political power struggle. Though entirely unknown to the general public, the implications of the Muigai affair were not lost on leading politicians, particularly those outside the Gatundu circle, and a number of them made personal appeals to the Aga Khan not to proceed with the appointment. They included VP Moi, Finance Minister Mwai Kibaki and Attorney-General Charles Njonjo, who called at the Nairobi home of Sir Eboo Pirbhai, the astute and influential leader of the Ismaili community in Kenya, during a visit by the Aga Khan and put their case directly to him. A witness recalled a number of government limousines flying national flags parked outside Eboo's house.

Over several weeks, in his typically systematic way, the Aga Khan consulted his directors, the *Nation's* top managers, his lawyers and a wide range of Kenyan opinion. The consensus was that he had no other course than to meet with Kenyatta. The Aga Khan was an eloquent and persuasive advocate and Kenyatta was known to be a rational listener. The publisher–investor flew to Nairobi, travelled 100 miles north to Nakuru town and met Kenyatta at the State House there. His argument was simple: he loved Kenya, he said, he had spent his boyhood there; he was a good friend of the country as his extensive investments and welfare initiatives proved. But he did not think it would be in the interests of Kenya if his, Kenyatta's family, should effectively control the two largest newspapers in the country. He believed sincerely that upholding the independence of the media should become part of the Kenyatta legacy. If the President wished, he would sell the newspaper to the government, but he did not wish to proceed with the appointment of Mr Muigai. The two men had met many times and held each other in mutual respect. Kenyatta, pragmatic master of the political terrain, saw no advantage in promoting conflict. No, he said, the government did not want to buy the *Nation*, and as for Mr Muigai, while he found it difficult to go back on his promise, he would accept the Aga Khan's judgment on the matter. They parted amicably and the Aga Khan returned to Europe the same day. The crisis was over.

Just six months later, the crucial importance of the Aga Khan's stand became clear. On 27 September 1976, the *Standard* front-paged a demand by a group of MPs and cabinet ministers at a rally in Nakuru: they wanted Kenya's constitution changed to bar the VP from automatically assuming the presidency when that office became vacant, with elections within 90 days. The Gatundu group had broken cover, moving to keep power in the hands of their ethnic circle. Kenyatta was an old man, increasingly remote and occasionally ailing, and VP Moi stood constitutionally unchallenged as his heir. Ninety days as president *pro tem* would surely suffice to ensure his permanent transition. The royal court wanted one of their own in the supreme office and a change in the constitution could effect Moi's removal. Spearheaded by leaders of GEMA, the tribal Gikuyu, Embu, Meru Association, they suggested that temporary power should be invested in the Speaker of the National Assembly, with Gatundu heavyweight Foreign Minister Njoroge Mungai as their candidate for Speaker.

Sedulously, the Gecaga-controlled *Standard* headlined the demands of the Change the Constitution group and its attacks on Moi, sanctimoniously asserting that no personal ambitions were involved and that the change would simply be for the good of the country. Whenever the campaigners spoke, the *Standard* was there offering page-one treatment, and Mungai in particular seemed to have a hotline to the newsroom. Even when Attorney-General Charles Njonjo declared it a capital offence to speak of the president's demise, the *Standard* responded that this was no more than his personal opinion. The *Nation*, by contrast, gave little coverage to the Change the Constitution rallies and Githii wrote sharply worded editorials in defence of a constitutional succession. Moi's detractors, he warned in one, were on the borderline of treason. Eventually, Kenyatta himself, having tested the political waters, called a cabinet meeting in Nakuru and upbraided those ministers who had joined the anti-Moi campaign. Meekly, they submitted to the *mzee*, the old man, as Kenyatta was respectfully known, and an official, joint cabinet statement supporting the provisions of the constitution was issued, putting an end to a naked move for power.

It is profitless to speculate what might have happened if the Change the Constitution movement had succeeded. One minister suggested there could have been civil war,[3] and certainly many Kenyans were so outraged by the arrogance and corruption of some of those close to Kenyatta that, had their power been perpetuated by illegal means, a violent response was likely. This must have been evident to the *Standard's* managers. That they nevertheless permitted their title to be used as a weapon in a potentially destructive war signalled the vulnerability of a newspaper to the political caprices of a tendentious ownership. It would be foolish to suggest that the power-seekers were disarmed by the opposition of the *Nation*. That was achieved largely through the good sense and strong personality of the head of state. What is clear, however, is the immense monopoly power in terms of exposure and persuasion that would have been available to the Change the Constitution group if the Aga Khan had not resisted the pressures to install Muigai. Kenya would have seen *Nation* and *Standard* joined at the hip in prosecuting the same political agenda with never a dissenting published voice. Thus it is hardly an exaggeration to suggest that, in clinging so stubbornly to its independence, the *Nation* changed the course of Kenya's history.

## Notes

1. During the period covered by this history, the *Nation's* principal rival changed its name from the *East African Standard* to the *Standard* and then back again. For ease of reference, this book generally refers to the *Standard*.

2. The first Aga Khan, Hasan Ali Shah (1800–81), was governor of the Persian province of Kerman and granted the title Aga Khan by the Shah of Iran in 1818. The title was recognised by Britain after the family moved to India. Aga Khan III, the present holder's grandfather, played a prominent role as a world statesman and served as president of the League of Nations.

3. The late Coast Province MP Shariff Nassir, quoted in *Moi, The Making of an African Statesman* by Andrew Morton, Michael O'Mara Books Ltd, London, 1998.

# Birth of a Newspaper

*The newspapers! Sir, they are the most villainous, licen-*
*tious, abominable, infernal ... not that I ever read them.*
*No, I make it a rule never to look into a newspaper.*
R.B. Sheridan (1751–1816), *The Critic*

When Michael Curtis began visiting Nairobi in 1957, Kenya was pronounced Keen-ya, a musical recreation of the jazz age, *The Boy Friend*, was
playing to white audiences at the National Theatre, and the most important
person in the country, the Governor, wore ostrich plumes in his hat to rival
the best tribal headdress. A housewife could buy a tenderloin steak from her
butcher for a shilling and a half (a fraction of a dollar but nearly a day's pay
for an African) and May and Co., retailers on Government Road, sold arms
and ammunition along with fishing rods. Volkswagen Beetles and French
Peugeots parked in neat diagonal rows and the city's roads were immaculately tarmacked. A statue of pioneer settler Lord Delamere stood at the head
of Nairobi's main street, which bore his name, the through highway was
named after the English queen Elizabeth II and the leading hospital after her
sister, Princess Margaret.

This was a rigidly stratified society, with a small, white governing class at
the top, the trading Asian community in the middle and a vast majority of
powerless Africans at the base. Everyone knew their place, none more than
the Europeans, whose community was susceptible to subtle and arcane gra-
dations of class and prestige. There were the clubs, for instance. In upcountry Nakuru, 'capital' of the White Highlands, the top people went to the Rift
Valley Sports Club and lesser whites to the Nakuru Athletics Club. In
Nairobi, the pink stucco Muthaiga Club in the affluent suburb of that name

was mostly for settlers, while Nairobi Club favoured government officers, as well as bankers and businessmen. The animosity between these groups was well documented. The settlers considered the officials to be transient mercenaries with no stake in Kenya, thinking only of promotion and pension, intent on robbing them of the land they had cleared, ploughed and watered, and eager then to scuttle back to retirement in Britain. The officials saw themselves as conscientious administrators of laws which the settlers apparently believed should not apply to them. There was a popular story of a district officer who seduced a settler farmer's daughter and begot twins. Honourably, he offered marriage. Responded the settler, 'I would sooner have two bastards in my family than one official.'

Although the Muthaiga Club barred Jews in the early days, it had nothing in its constitution against Africans or Asians since it was simply inconceivable that they would ever seek to join. But when Curtis – Cambridge graduate, editor of a quality Fleet Street daily, distinguished World War II soldier – sought membership, he was blackballed. 'They believed I was bringing in a left-wing newspaper', he said. 'I certainly wasn't a Conservative, I had opposed the British Prime Minister over Suez, but a story was put about Nairobi that I was a dangerous lefty.'[1] Jack Ensoll, a journalist long resident in Kenya, believed it was simply that Curtis was a newsman. 'They hated the press', he said in an interview. 'They didn't want us in there watching them getting sozzled, they thought we were the lowest of the low. I never applied, I knew they wouldn't let me in.' Charles Hayes, who became a member before he became a journalist, recalled taking Reuter's East Africa correspondent to dinner at Muthaiga one New Year's Eve during the Mau Mau emergency: 'The chairman of the club came up and said to me, "We understand your guest is Ronald Batchelor. We would like you to remove him immediately. The next thing you know there will be a story in *The Times* saying how we are having a party when killing is going on outside the doors of the club".' Hayes refused and was later reprimanded by the committee. 'I was suspect because I was a journalist and because I was in contact with Africans', he said. Although change did come to the clubs, it came slowly. *Nation* managing director (MD) Gerry Wilkinson remembered being taken to Muthaiga on his first night in Nairobi in 1971: 'An old couple sat by the fire and the husband held up an ear-horn which his wife shouted into. When I left several years later, they were still there, except she was shouting into an electronic microphone with a cable attachment.'

Legally, there was no colour bar in Kenya but socially it was inescapable. When Alastair Matheson, a government information officer, asked owner

Jack Block why he barred Africans from his New Stanley and Norfolk hotels, Block replied, 'Because we would be full of bloody taxi-drivers' – all of whom of course were African. Another pub owner would tell his white drinkers, 'I have no colour bar here, any African is welcome – if he can pay a hundred bob for a Pilsner.' Mareka Gecaga, a distinguished Middle Temple lawyer who became the *Nation's* first African director and later chairman of the group, recalled, 'There was a lot of racial compartmentalisation before independence – schools, hospitals, clubs. Even as a lawyer, I could not go into the New Stanley Hotel for a cup of tea.' Richard Cox, correspondent for the London *Sunday Times*, recalled an artist at Ron Partridge's Equator Club, the city's top nightspot across the road from the New Stanley, singing about the much anticipated *uhuru* (independence): '*No more working, no more tax, we'll sit in the sun and just relax.*' And, '*When the money's all finished and the country's on the floor, we'll get the government printing press to turn us out some more.*' Noted Cox, 'The African band looked pretty sick accompanying this song and it was taken off after Christmas 1960.'[2]

Kenya's population in 1959 was 6.4 million, of whom 60,000-plus were whites, officially categorised as 'Europeans' to the bewilderment of visiting Americans,[3] and the population of Nairobi was under 250,000, though it was still the largest city between Johannesburg and Cairo. Racism was institutionalised in government service, with salaries graded by ethnicity: Class A for Europeans, B for Asians, C for Arabs and D for Africans, the latter being mostly drivers, messengers and cleaners. Categories also extended to accommodation, as Alastair Matheson found when he arrived in Nairobi from South Africa to take up a post in the colonial government's Information Service:

> *The government rented a flat for me, a pink-painted place up Valley Road, but unknown to me there was a clause in the lease saying no non-Europeans could enter the premises except for government staff. I held an official cocktail party to introduce the new General Officer Commanding the armed forces in Kenya, General Sir George Erskine, at the time of Mau Mau. I invited six African journalists who were all working for government vernacular newspapers, plus Gama Pio Pinto, who was certainly a radical but also at that time a journalist.[4] The Indian ambassador was also there; he was a personal friend because we shared an interest in model trains but the government believed he was a Mau Mau sympathiser. I later got a note from the landlords*

*saying I had broken the lease and other tenants had complained that it was a rowdy party. Actually it was a perfectly proper party and ended at 9 pm. I leaked all this to the London* Daily Express *and questions were asked in the British Parliament. But I had to leave the flat, I was evicted. My then wife was a Cape Coloured and that might have had something to do with it. I had just left South Africa because I considered it was racist and when I came to Kenya I found it the image of South Africa.*

Nairobi was unofficially zoned by race. Africans lived in 'native locations' such as Pumwani, where the young Tom Mboya had a tiny house; Asians gathered in Parklands and Nairobi West; and whites in Muthaiga, Lavington, Karen, Kitisuru and other upmarket areas. Africans were required to carry around their necks the hated *kipande* (an employment card bearing their fingerprints), were not allowed to grow coffee or other cash crops and, however unlikely the prospect seemed at the time, were barred by law from owning company shares. As late as 18 months before independence, high society was reminiscent of the Raj in India. Ian Raitt, journalist, broadcaster and PR man, wrote in an unpublished memoir:

*I remember a great ball at Government House given by the Governor. There was a British military band in full dress uniform and Gainsborough-like English girls with long blonde hair dancing the Gay Gordons through colonnaded halls and galleries hung with grand portraits of past servants of Empire. It was fin de siècle but they did not know it.*

An eclectic media market included a wide range of ethnic newspapers, mainly Asian: *Goan Voice, Colonial Times* (Gujarati), *The Observer*, a Muslim weekly, but also *Baraza* and *Jicho* (Kiswahili) and *Ramogi*, a Luo publication. But Curtis knew that competition for the Aga Khan's planned newspaper would come from three publishing houses: the Nairobi-based English Press Ltd, which published the *Sunday Post*; the upcountry Nakuru Press Ltd, which put out the *Kenya Weekly News*; and the East African Standard Ltd, whose flagship product was the Nairobi daily of that name. The group also published the *Tanganyika Standard* – characterised by Governor Sir Edward Twining as 'the three-minute silence', that being how long a reader would interrupt his breakfast to get through it – the *Uganda Argus*, a six-page daily in Kampala, and the *Mombasa Times*, edited by a widely admired columnist,

Edward Rodwell. *Baraza* was the *Standard's* Kiswahili weekly. With political awareness growing, there were also increasing numbers of factional political papers put out by jobbing printers in hectic River Road. Charles Hayes recalled, 'They were mostly rags full of lies which existed on political name-calling, but they were dangerous in the excitable climate of the time.' It was his fear that such publications were raising unrealistic expectations for independence and could lead to a reversion to Mau Mau activism that impelled him to start his own Kiswahili weekly, *Taifa*. There were also a large number of vernacular newspapers funded by the colonial government to propagate the official view on national issues.

The *Kenya Weekly News* magazine was founded in Nakuru by Frank Couldrey, and the principal shareholder was his son Jack, a Nairobi lawyer. Wholly devoted to settler interests (its first edition carried an article on the price of maize and so did its last), it became known as the 'pea-green incorruptible' for the colour of its cover and the feisty staunchness in the farmers' cause of its editor, Mervyn Hill. A promotional ditty popular at the time ran:

> *Sam the settler's in despair,*
> *He wrings his hands, he tears his hair,*
> *His temper you will please excuse,*
> *He's lost his* Kenya Weekly News.

Hill's chequered career had included a run-in with the law which barred him from membership of the Rift Valley Sports Club. But he was widely admired as the author of *Permanent Way*, the definitive history of the construction of the railway from Mombasa to Uganda, and according to Ensoll, his Nairobi editor in the late 1950s, he was 'a total amateur but the best journalist I ever came across'. Hill was consulted not only by the colonial rulers in Nairobi but by Whitehall, too, as negotiations on the shape of an independent Kenya gathered pace. Ensoll himself was convinced settler hegemony was over and when later he became editor of the *Sunday Post*, he pressed for a multi-racial, power-sharing arrangement for the Kenya of the future. 'When I started running that policy,' he said, 'invitations poured in from the Muthaiga Club and I would have lunch with the Governor one day and the arch-settler Ewart Grogan the next. The settlers already knew they were on a hiding to nothing.' But when he spoke one day with the nationalist Dr Kiano, Ensoll realised his naive dream of a rainbow-hued Kenya was doomed: 'I put the usual settler argument to him: If we go for one-man, one-vote, the whites will be swamped and we are so important to the economy, run all the business, employ so many Africans, what's going to happen? And he said coolly, "You will have to rely on African good will". That was a big message to me.'

Ensoll's efforts at the *Sunday Post* were not helped by the owners. 'English Press was a twopenny-ha'penny outfit', he recalled. 'We had an old Cosser press and the owner and founding editor, old Jack Rathbone, had newsprint reels stashed away all over Nairobi.' The *Sunday Post* had started in 1933 and changed little in the ensuing years. Dull, grey and slabby, its most popular feature was a social column, 'Miranda's Merrier Moments', which chronicled the doings of Nairobi's glitterati. Miss D.R. (Mugs) Muggeridge, who wrote the column for a time, told researcher Mary Edwards, 'It was a tedious job. We used to call the paper the *Sunday Pest.*' She would get letters saying, 'My wife is grousing because she hasn't been mentioned in Miranda for a long time.' There were also political problems. Ensoll recalled, 'I was carpeted by the board a couple of times for using stories about Tom Mboya. They said, "We're financing this paper and we don't think our editor should be giving publicity to our political enemies".'

The intention of the Aga Khan at that time was to buy an existing newspaper and develop it into a new voice for Kenyans, avoiding the expense of acquiring a building, plant and equipment. Accordingly, Curtis approached Rathbone, the English Press chairman, then well into his 70s, and made an offer for the *Sunday Post*. Later he was called to a meeting of the directors at which Rathbone, who spoke with a strong Yorkshire accent, declared, 'Mr Curtis, I know you represent the Aga Khan so the money is all right. But I 'ave to tell you quite plainly, after very careful consideration, that it would be utterly repoognant, I repeat repoognant, to any of us at this table to sell this great newspaper of ours [long pause] to an Asian!' Ensoll described this remark as 'a voice from the 1920s', but as well as being racist, the decision was economically foolish and it effectively doomed the English Press. The Aga Khan decided to start the *Nation* from scratch, and its verve and professionalism inevitably sent the *Sunday Post* to the wall. When Nakuru Press Ltd subsequently approached the *Nation* to take the ailing *Kenya Weekly News* off its hands, the board could see no economic benefit and declined. The magazine was eventually subsumed into the *Standard* as an agricultural section and lost its identity.

The *East African Standard* was Kenya's oldest newspaper, launched in Mombasa in 1902 as the weekly *African Standard* by an Asian businessman, A.M. Jevanjee, who had become a millionaire as the principal contractor for supplies to the Uganda Railway. It was Jevanjee who donated a statue of Queen Victoria for the eponymous Jevanjee Gardens in downtown Nairobi. Having the epitome of empire in the city centre was seen by visitors in later years as a sign of Kenyans' good-natured tolerance of their former colonial rulers, but an early settler had a different story. Dr Gregory, one-time Mayor of Nairobi and inventor of the 'City in the Sun' slogan, said the statue survived because pious city fathers thought it represented the Virgin Mary. As a newspaper proprietor, Jevanjee became alarmed by the fear of libel suits and sold the paper to the father of Claude B. Anderson, the chairman and MD when Curtis arrived, and to his business partner, a certain R.F. Mayer. The senior Anderson and Mayer had arrived simultaneously in Mombasa to seek their fortunes in December 1900. When Nairobi was named the capital city of Kenya in 1910, Anderson and Mayer changed their paper's title to the *East African Standard* and chartered an entire train to move the machinery upcountry, leaving a small plant at the coast to print the *Mombasa Times*. Once in Nairobi, whose population at that point was 16,000, the *Standard* became a daily, and eight years later a public company, the East African Standard Ltd, was floated 'with a board of directors of distinguished colonists', as the company literature proclaimed. The *Tanganyika Standard* was launched in 1930 and the *Uganda Argus* in 1953.

The long-time editor of the group's flagship daily was George Kinnear, a far-sighted journalist–scholar with a liberal outlook for his era. When Edward Rodwell assumed the editorship of the *Mombasa Times* in 1951, he asked for an outline of editorial policy, and Kinnear sent him a six-page, single-spaced letter which said in part:

> *Encouragement of good human relationships among all races is a broad basis of policy ... there is already a considerable breaking down of residential segregation in the townships and this movement should be allowed to develop at its natural space. Many Asians have already left the bazaars behind them and established high and expensive standards of private life and in time Africans will follow suit.*

Though Kinnear's references to Africans reflected the condescending paternalism of the time, he was in no doubt that

> *there is a duty to point out discriminations which are unfair, unwise and untenable. There will be increasing pressure for the abolition of discriminations based on race and this movement should be*

*recognised and guided ... improvement of the conditions of life of the
African should be constantly stressed ... European and African
partnerships in business enterprises should be encouraged ... the
African should be helped to enlarge his experience especially on local
government bodies [and] there should be a liberal and helpful
attitude towards the African's representatives in government.*

But when it came to African nationalism, Kinnear seemed to believe the less
said the better. Alastair Matheson recalled that in 1951 he was told by an
Irish priest of the White Fathers missionary order, a Father McCourt, that
anti-white oathing was taking place among people in his area.[5] 'The most
that the *Standard* would publish was that somebody had been arrested for
forcible oathing. Cattle had been hamstrung near Nanyuki but they wrote
nothing about it. The government did not want to admit it was Mau Mau.'

In 1956, Kinnear was succeeded by his deputy, Lieutenant Colonel
Kenneth Bolton, who was directed by his board to 'ensure fair and adequate
apportioning of the news columns to all communities and to interpret the
policies of each to the other'. It would be over-generous to conclude that
Bolton followed this directive to the letter. The man who once remarked that
Kenya was run by 'the three B's' – Governor Sir Evelyn Baring, settler-politi-
cian Michael Blundell and himself – found little space in his paper for views
much beyond those of the white settled community and Whitehall. Indeed,
the *Standard* carried Britain's royal coat of arms beneath its title until 11
December 1963, the day before Kenya achieved independence. Many of
Bolton's acquaintances testify that he was at heart a kindly man but shy,
uncomfortable with people, pompous and snobbish. He was awarded the
Military Cross for valour during his World War II service with the Royal
Horse Artillery and made much of his membership of that elite regiment.
'He wasn't an easy person to know', Ensoll recalled. 'I don't think he actually
liked journalists, though he was one himself and a good one.' Arnold
Raphael, hired by Bolton in 1960 to be the *Standard's* first London correspondent – 'I think because my application was on headed notepaper and
the others were not' – gave a considered opinion of his editor in an interview
for this book. He believed Bolton was corrupted by the social climate in
Kenya: 'I don't mean the Happy Valley thing among amoral settlers. He saw
himself as the defender, through his newspaper, of an upper-class way of life,
though he came from a relatively modest background himself of grammar
school and a newspaper in Birmingham. He came to see himself more as a
proconsul than an editor.'[6]

A singular irony about Curtis' appearance in Nairobi was that he and Bolton had both worked for the *News Chronicle* in London: Bolton as a reporter covering such important stories as the Berlin Airlift; Curtis as leader writer, deputy editor and eventually editor. A number of people interviewed for this book believe Bolton resented Curtis' success, but, whatever the reason, the *Standard* editor greeted the prospect of a competing newspaper managed by Curtis with the utmost disdain, telling anyone who would listen that the new paper would not last six weeks. When Frank Pattrick arrived in Nairobi to be the *Nation's* MD, he met with his opposite number at the *Standard*, Charles Thetford, at a cocktail party. Thetford greeted the new arrival with the remark, 'Don't bother to unpack your bags.' A seething Pattrick retorted, 'You are going to regret that remark.' Pattrick said later that this meeting was the motivating factor during all of his years with the *Nation*.

*Standard* chairman Claude B. Anderson lived upcountry in the so-called White Highlands, and stayed largely aloof from Nairobi's social and political milieu. Perhaps because of this, he seemed unable to grasp that fundamental change was not only inevitable but was approaching with the speed of an express train. Said Raphael, 'The proprietors and the editor were in a colonial time warp. They could not or would not take the measure of the forces at work in Whitehall in terms of imperial disengagement. The *Nation* people were coming on the scene free of colonial contamination.' It was the *Standard*, not the *Nation*, whose future was at risk.

Thwarted by racism at the English Press and loftily ignored by the *Standard*, Curtis made contact with Hayes, whom he knew as the *News Chronicle's* Nairobi stringer. In an interview years later, Hayes recalled:

> *Michael was accompanying the Aga Khan on his first visit to Africa as Imam of the Ismaili community, handling press relations, and we talked quite a bit. I took him to dinner and then we went on to the Equator Club. We sat there talking and drinking whisky until three in the morning and I told him about my little weekly paper,* Taifa, *and the stories we were printing about African politics and the fever of independence and things happening in other parts of Africa, stories which the* Standard *and* Baraza *never published. Then suddenly he said, 'I'd like to join you. We'll make* Taifa *into East Africa's best Kiswahili newspaper and we will hive off an English-language newspaper to ride alongside.' I knew Michael was working for the Aga Khan but I thought here he was talking about himself, wanting to make a new career.*

Hayes said, 'I located a small Asian-owned jobbing printer in some back street in Nairobi which had a sheet-fed press. It looked like a cheap solution for our planned endeavours and the next time Michael returned to Kenya, we went to inspect it. In his quiet way, he said, "I think we can do better than that". It was then that he made clear his proposals were on behalf of the Aga Khan and that the target was a newspaper group to cover East Africa.' One other thing Curtis said remained in Hayes's mind: 'We must write ourselves out of our jobs. We must train African editors and managers to take over in 10 years.' In the event, the target was missed by only a few years.

Charles Arthur Andrew Hayes arrived in the Kenya Colony in 1948 with the West African forces of the British Army after war service in Burma and post-war duties in India. He travelled upcountry from Mombasa and said to himself, 'My God, if this is East Africa, I want to stay!' He resigned his commission and became a District Officer in the colonial service in Machakos, southeast of Nairobi, learned the local tongue, Kikamba, and started a vernacular newspaper putting over administration policy. Later he became the Provincial Information Officer for the Rift Valley Province: 'I was head of the African section which contained a number of radio stations in many languages, 26 publications, a photo section and a film section, but by 1956 I was tired of the propaganda.' Tom Mboya was a good friend: 'He came into an Information Service hut I built at Nakuru and he talked so well I did a piece on him for radio and sent it down to John Rice, the Director of Information. It was good and constructive and talking about the future, but Rice wouldn't use it.' Angry, Hayes decided it was time to do his own thing: 'This was 1957. The Emergency to combat Mau Mau had dragged on since 1952 and life was lived under many restraints. Suspicion was everywhere and tribalism heated it. I wanted to interest Kenyans in a new future, put facts before them they could trust.' He resigned from the colonial service, as did a colleague, Althea Tebbutt, and for £10 they bought the articles of association of a company named East African Press Exchange from the widow of the owner. Legend has it that her intrepid husband had gone reporting in the Congo and been eaten by a crocodile.

Hayes' experience of publishing was not extensive, but he had launched a general-interest Kiswahili weekly magazine in 1952 – *Tazama* (Look), which was sponsored by the East African Literature Bureau and managed by the *Standard*. Author Elspeth Huxley was among the contributors and the reporting staff included Musa Amalemba, later to become a controversial cabinet minister. Hayes also wrote for *Drum*, the South African magazine owned by Jim Bailey which was to achieve international recognition under editor Tom Hopkinson.

*Taifa* was conceived out of an evening of embarrassment with Kenya's media establishment. Hayes was appointed stringer for the French national news agency, Agence France Presse (AFP), and set up a small bureau with a teleprinter in what was then Victoria Street, Nairobi. AFP, dominant in Francophone Africa, wanted to extend its reach to the English-speaking regions and sell its service in competition with Reuter, which held sway in the Anglophone countries and funnelled its service to East Africa via the *Standard*. Hayes arranged a cocktail party to show off AFP's Africa service and invited all the leading editors, broadcasters and government press officers. He had arranged with Paris that the transmission should start at 8 pm and, precisely on time, the teleprinter chattered into life. Unhappily for Hayes, the stories were all in French and the guests politely took their leave. But left alone amidst the empty glasses, Hayes checked through the telecast and spotted many stories he believed would interest Kenyan Africans. Human interest stories and accounts of political developments in West Africa, they were not the sort of thing that Reuter carried and they never appeared in the *Standard's* stodgy government-supporting *Baraza*. Kenyans were eager to hear about other African countries heading for independence, and here was a story from the Congo about a young political firebrand and postal clerk, Patrice Lumumba, who had been jailed for stealing from his employer. 'Nobody else in Kenya was carrying this sort of story and I was convinced they would be winners with an African audience', Hayes said. 'I decided the only way to get them out was to start a new paper myself.'

But when Hayes and Tebbutt launched their weekly *Taifa* in 1958, it proved tough going. Hayes recalled:

> We did not draw any salary for three months and then we tossed up to see who would get paid. We were putting the paper on buses and we never knew if it got there and collecting payment was horrendous. English Press did the printing and our first print order was 10,000 and we got plenty returns. It was eight pages and the cover price was only 25 cents but money was scarce and there was a limit to literacy. We had real trouble getting advertising. But I knew we were on the right track. We filled a gap that the Standard and Baraza were leaving. Taifa *was brighter than anything else on the market and our policy was to support Kenyan independence in a reasoned way and to show a new way of living was possible. Our first headline was, 'When*

*shall we see freedom?', something Tom Mboya said in Kaloleni* [venue
for political meetings]. *He had just started a political party but you
never heard of him in the establishment press.*

A story persists that Claude Anderson ruled there should be only one picture of an 'African nationalist' on the *Standard's* front page in any one issue,
but that Mboya should never appear.

Hayes and Tebbutt eked out a living by stringing for AFP and British and
American newspapers, and by publishing magazines for the Tea Board and
the Coffee Board. 'That was our bread and butter', Mrs Tebbutt recalled in
an interview. 'The English Press wanted to buy us out so they sent a demand
to pay their printing bill and to avoid selling up we sank everything we had
into paying their bill.' When there was not enough money to pay the staff,
Hayes managed to secure an overdraft with his bank. *Taifa's* editorial staff
was tiny but included John Keen, running the news operation, who became
a prominent MP and cabinet minister, and W.W Awori, who came from a
family of writers and politicians, one of whom became a VP of Kenya and
another chairman of the *Nation* group. One of the little group's greatest tri-
umphs was its choice of title. *Taifa*, meaning *Nation*, caught perfectly the
growing consciousness of Africans as a sovereign community. Said Mrs
Tebbutt, 'We had a brainstorming session before we launched and *Taifa* was
suggested by our bookkeeper, an Asian man called Thakrar, and it seemed
entirely appropriate for what we were trying to do, bring the races together.'

This was the newspaper which was the sole item on the agenda when the
Aga Khan's new company, East African Newspapers (Nation Series) Ltd
(EAN), formed on 2 April 1959, held its first meeting at Mercury House,
Victoria Street, one month later. Present were Curtis in the chair and Hayes,
with J.P. Ord, accountant, in attendance. The meeting approved the purchase for £10,000, payable in cash, of 'the newspaper *Taifa* together with
certain photographic equipment'. The Hayes–Tebbutt company took £6,500
in shares in EAN and used the remaining £3,500 to pay off outstanding
printing bills.

There then ensued as frantic a development programme as any publishing company could have known. The targets were to acquire staff, premises
and a printing plant, turn *Taifa* into a daily, launch a weekly English-language newspaper and then add an English daily. As the *Nation's* first editor
John Bierman agreed in retrospect, 'It was inordinately ambitious to start a
daily Swahili, an English Sunday and an English daily all in one year, especially since we were using a revolutionary method of production, the offset

press. But we were all young and we thought we could do anything.' The first weekly *Taifa* under the aegis of EAN appeared on 28 April 1959, and Curtis put his Fleet Street experience to use in considerably less sophisticated conditions than the panelled halls of the *News Chronicle*. 'I was up all night seeing it printed and distributed', he reported to the Aga Khan. 'The editorial was my own work. Sales are doing well considering there is no organisation behind it at all.' The first Curtis issue sold out at 15,000 copies and carried 'a record £200 advertising'. But the accountants estimated it would run at a loss of £1,000 a month for the foreseeable future. The paper carried the title *Taifa the Nation* and must have impressed the colonial administration because the powerful Chief Secretary, Sir Walter Coutts, asked Curtis if he would be interested in government sponsorship. 'I told him quite impossible', Curtis noted at the time. '*Taifa* must be independent of government funds and influence.' It was an early example of a Kenyan government trying to manipulate an independent newspaper in its own interest.

The Aga Khan had by then acquired a printing company, W. Boyds and Co. Ltd, which became East African Printers (Boyds) Ltd. It cost £72,000, including stock and equipment. But the plant was antiquated, limiting circulation potential. The company promptly ordered a £36,000 rotary press from Copenhagen and soon afterwards placed an order for an American typesetting machine that was then the marvel of the printing world, the multi-font Photon. It cost £21,000, with £3,500 worth of ancillary equipment. At the same time, Curtis rented for £5,000 a year the former Elliott's bakery in Victoria Street, a modest two-storey building which had burned down and been refurbished, to be the new company's headquarters, Nation House. A financial statement dated November 1959 added £8,000 for vans and cars and £1,500 for alterations to Nation House. At this point, the Aga Khan had committed something like £200,000 to Boyds and £75,000 to EAN.

These figures should not suggest that Curtis had money coming out of his ears. The Aga Khan, at that point still a student at Harvard University, was in the process of settling his late grandfather's estate (and soon afterwards the estate of his father, Prince Aly Khan, who died in a car crash in Paris in May 1960). With the settlement of onerous death duties, the flow of cash to Nairobi was restricted and efforts to find co-investors for his publishing ventures were proving difficult. At one point, Curtis reported, 'The cheque from Switzerland (the Aga Khan's monthly contribution) was four days late. I had a very awkward time with the vendors. There was simply not enough in the kitty to hand over the money when I had promised. I managed to get a temporary overdraft from the bank.' A widely held view in Kenya and elsewhere that the *Nation* succeeded because it had access to an unceasing river of gold could not be farther from the truth. Funds in the early days were extremely tight except for essential capital expenditure, and the Aga Khan demanded the strictest financial control.

Building a staff was the next priority. The ideal was to create a newspaper that would be written and managed by Africans for Africans, but the reality of 1959/60 was that there were very few African journalists in Kenya and even fewer African managers. Curtis had to look to Britain. Seeking a managing editor, he first approached Michael Randall, then assistant editor of the *Daily Mail*, but Randall had other things on his mind (he eventually became editor of the *Mail*) and suggested Bierman, one of his sub-editors. Bierman, with experience at two other UK nationals, the *Daily Express* and the *Daily Mirror*, was then aged 30, bored with his London job and ready to change his career path: 'I was young and idealistic and when Michael Curtis explained to me what the *Nation* was to be all about, which accorded with my views about the end of colonialism, well, that was it, I had to take the job.' To staff the new *Taifa*, Hayes brought to Nation House most of his editorial staff and ruthlessly poached others from *Baraza*, including an outstanding trio of Joram Amadi, John Abuoga and George Mbugguss. There was also a young trainee, Francis Masakhalia, who soon decided his talents lay in other directions – good thinking, for in 1999 he was appointed Kenya's minister of finance. Sammy Githegi, Harry Sambo, Moses Mumbo and Henry Gathigira were later joined by another young Kenyan who proved to have editor qualities, Joe Kadhi.

For the planned English-language papers, Bill Harris, a volatile, baby-faced Scot, was hired from the *Standard* to be the first chief reporter, and Ron Jones, a controversial political writer, joined from the *Sunday Post* – to the relief of editor Jack Ensoll, who recalled, 'Ron was always digging up exclusives which were great stories but very dangerous to use.' Ted Mullis, Eric Meacher, Sashi Vasani, Akhtar Hussein and the diminutive but combative Caleb Akwera were the first photographers. Reporters included David Barnett, an acerbic Australian who became speech-writer for an Australian prime minister, the laid-back John Fairhall, later education correspondent for the *Guardian* in Britain, Dick Dawson and Chhotu Karadia, both Kenya-born, and Mike Harris from the Kenya Police. The first sports editor was John Dunn, followed by Tom Clarke, who went on to be sports editor of *The Times* of London. A jokey Welshman with immaculate Kiswahili, David Price, left the *Standard* to become assistant sports editor, and a much-loved and entirely feckless South African, John ('me old buck') De Villiers, wrote features when he remembered. Recruits from Britain included Peter Moss from the Press Association to be Managing Editor of the *Sunday Nation*, this writer and Roy Anderson, sub-editors from the Newcastle *Evening Chronicle*, and David Levine, a sports sub from Grimsby. The *Nation* set up editorial offices in Mombasa (Francis Raymond, Neta Peale, Adrian Grimwood), Dar es Salaam (Tony Dunn, Robert Makange) and Kampala (Manning Blackwood, a portly scion of the *Blackwood's Magazine* publishing family, and Rex Brindle).

Mostly in their 20s, the newly recruited employees brought a fresh, aggressive style to Kenyan journalism, and, lacking colonial attitudes, they considered it perfectly normal that Kenya should receive its independence on a one-man one-vote basis as soon as possible. There is little doubt those political perceptions were shared by many in the *Standard* newsroom, but senior management was blinkered by settler politics and ingrained paternalism. Alastair Matheson's son, Ian, joined the *Standard* in 1959 as a trainee reporter, along with *Nation* editor-to-be George Githii. He recalled:

> In those days at the Standard, *Tom Mboya's press releases were thrown in the dustbin. The paper was all settler stuff and white politicians. Lord Delamere would come in with his florid face and big Stetson hat berating the newsroom because they hadn't done enough on his speech at the Farmers' Union. The paper recognised there was such a thing as African nationalism but there was just some small story occasionally. It was as if they lived in another world.*

As well as editorial staff, Curtis had to fill the many positions that the complex organisation of a newspaper requires, and getting the technical side right was the first priority. Stan Denman was a young, former Royal Marine Commando working as a printing engineer as well as a print salesman for John Bull, who ran Boyd's printing works in Nairobi's Industrial Area. Denman recalled:

> *I was out selling print when I got a message to meet Harry Smith at the Norfolk Hotel. Harry was head lecturer at the prestigious London School of Printing and he outlined this idea that I should go to America to study electronics and printing. Michael Curtis then walked in and said the plan was that I would come back as head printer for the Nation. I said, 'Fantastic but I don't want to leave Boyd's, I'm doing very well.' They said, 'Don't worry, we've just bought Boyd's!' From that moment, I was 100 per cent involved in the Nation.*

Denman redesigned an old bakery on Victoria Street to accommodate the flow of copy from teleprinters and reporters to sub-editors and thence to Linotype operators. To streamline the process, a hole was bashed through the floor next to the chief sub-editor's desk and an aluminium tube inserted, down which stories were dropped to the printers on the floor below – speeded on their way by lead weights when the folios stuck. Denman subsequently moved into top management, but in 1959 he was key to the *Nation's* most critical task – setting up an efficient printing operation. 'The Aga Khan wanted the very highest standards using the newest technology, which meant web offset', Denman recalled:

> *I first joined a printing company at the age of 14 and I knew offset printing had been around for years but web offset was new and really known only in America. I flew to Cambridge, Massachusetts, and studied electronics for three months and I got nervous about what we were planning back in Nairobi. It was visualised that everything the Photon produced would be on film, that was the newest technology, and I had nightmare visions of teaching people to patch up film. I went to see a good local paper, the* Quincy Patriot Ledger *near Boston, which was producing on web, and decided there was no way we could do that back home and we had to go to paste-up, that is, paper. I telephoned Harry Smith, it was the longest international call I ever made, and he said, 'You can't change now, all the equipment we have ordered is for film.' But I was right. They altered the Photon to produce paper and everyone in the world is now using it.*

Returning to Nairobi, Denman entered what he remembers as a madhouse: 'We had new people in, technical people, an engineer, experts all over, and there was an Australian called Elliott who had bought thousands and thousands of pencils with EAN on them. Everywhere you looked, there were piles and piles of these bloody brown pencils.' Denman brought Linotype operators and compositors – all Asians, there were no trained Africans – from Boyd's to Nation House and started printing *Taifa* on sheet-fed offset machines. One night two presses broke down. Denman said, 'I had no keys to the Boyd's plant so I physically smashed in the front door and managed to print the paper there, 2,000 copies. I still have a letter from Michael Curtis thanking me and giving me a bonus of a hundred shillings', a couple of dollars.

The early workers at the *Nation* coalface secured a niche in printing history. Several newspapers in the United States were using web offset, but

Harry Smith believed the *Nation's* was the first combined photosetting and web offset daily newspaper operation in the world. Writing many years later in *Printing World*, Smith recalled how the Nairobi link was established. He published an article in *The Times* of London about photographic typesetting which Curtis spotted and read in New York: 'Michael telephoned: Would I act as consultant? To produce a newspaper in the heart of Africa via photo-setting/offset was a long shot but I had to accept. Fourteen months after my first meeting with Michael, two daily papers and a Sunday were being pro-duced, followed by several others.' Within 18 months, production had risen to more than 4 million eight-page units per month and by late 1961 Curtis was telling the Aga Khan, 'The offset system is spreading like wildfire all over the world and paper manufacturers, platemakers and ink suppliers are falling over themselves to come and visit our works.'

It was on 15 January 1960 – a huge year for the company – that *Taifa* went daily, sporting the cumbersome title of *Habari za Leo TAIFA* (News of the Day TAIFA), later changed to *Taifa Leo*. It was the first Kiswahili daily newspaper in East Africa. The lead story concerned the black American chief justice, Thurgood Marshall, commenting on Kenya's prospects for *uhuru*, and the front page carried a photograph of Kenyan politicians C.B. Madan, Musa Amalemba, Michael Blundell and Wanyuti Waweru arriving in London for the first constitutional conference on Kenya. The launch issue sold a modest 4,000 copies, but next day sales shot up to 11,000 and three weeks later the figure was 18,000. Curtis cabled the Aga Khan: 'The paper has been a tremendous success with Africans, although sales are certainly stimulated by excitement over the London constitutional talks.'

Much effort at this time was going into securing additional investment for the *Nation*, but overseas publishers foresaw little return from a newspa-per in Africa and local businessmen were nervous about an economy which was slowing dramatically in the face of political uncertainty. Curtis told the Aga Khan:

> *Europeans here are in rather a jittery state of mind as a result of*
> *reports from London that Iain Macleod [Britain's Colonial Secretary]*
> *is going much further in Mboya's direction than anyone had any idea,*
> *even a few weeks ago. Public opinion here has simply not been in tune*
> *with public opinion in the UK ... our chances of getting further*
> *capital locally are not very bright this year.*

Approaches to the *Christian Science Monitor* in the United States were turned down and, when the Aga Khan met the money men at *The Observer* in London, he found them 'very sticky about the whole thing'. Boston businessmen were canvassed and a meeting was planned with Germany's Axel Springer group. A cable from Rupert Murdoch, Australia's super-tycoon in the making but then only proprietor of the *Adelaide News*, said, 'Fascinated by your plans, would like to hear more.' But nothing further developed. Finnish, Swedish and Norwegian newspapers were offered participation, as were Associated Newspapers of Ceylon, the *Washington Post*, the *Miami Herald* and the *International Herald Tribune*, as well as the Ford Foundation.

The Aga Khan was keen to secure outside participation in East African Newspapers because he felt links to internationally known newspapers would add gravitas to the *Nation's* image and help alleviate suspicions in Kenya about his own role as head of an Asian community. Clearly, too, injections of capital would be critical to create newspapers of the highest editorial and technological standards. In the event, only a few investors were brought aboard. Debentures went to Thomson Newspapers of Canada and Britain for £25,000, the Toronto *Globe and Mail* (£20,000), Rothschilds bankers (£5,000) and Warburgs bankers (£2,500). The Hon. John Jacob Astor invested £5,000 and Esmond Wickremsinghe of Ceylon's Associated Newspapers a like amount. Roy Thomson, the world's leading media magnate, agreed also to help with recruitment. While this assistance and his cash injection were welcomed, there was a feeling at Nation House that his real interest was in the company's new technology. Interestingly, Thomson visited the *Nation* late in 1961, and at a cocktail party for local media managers offered to buy the *Standard* from Claude Anderson. Curtis reported that 'Anderson responded with a wintry smile'.

With the *Nation* failing to generate significant outside investment, a certain asperity began to greet Curtis' continual requests for funds, although the Aga Khan did acknowledge that EAN was 'living on a shoestring'. When Curtis reported plans to buy a factory site to extend Boyd's, which the *Standard* was also pursuing, the Aga Khan replied, 'I entirely agree, but *don't* expect more capital from me.' In August 1960, in response to a request for £27,500 'to see us through to the end of September', the proprietor replied, 'I have already put a huge amount of money into EAN and Boyd's. I will come through for the last time on condition my loan is reimbursed before January 1 1961.' He softened this response by adding, 'I do not mean this letter to sound harsh, it's always thumbs up.' By late 1961, the Aga Khan was expanding his Ismaili community welfare activities in Kenya, including extending the open-to-all-races Aga Khan Hospital, and he warned Curtis it would be 'extremely difficult' for him to continue supporting the *Nation* as in the past. In fact, the records show the Aga Khan invariably came through in a crisis during the difficult early years, a confidence which was repaid in kind when his venture eventually reached and passed break-even.

Constant dialogue between Curtis and the Aga Khan was the nexus of the *Nation's* early years. Scarcely a day passed without the two exchanging telegrams, letters, tapes, telephone calls or Telexes. The exchanges were generally businesslike but often ended on a personal note, as when Curtis added, 'I am taking flying lessons and hope to do my first solo this weekend', or when his correspondent scribbled a weary postscript, 'I now have two 30-page papers to write for Harvard for my MA next year.' The modes of communication reflected the young leader's life-long interest in technology. When he did not write by fountain pen in an elegant forward-sloping hand ('My dear Michael ... as ever, K') he liked to use audio discs. These were less than saucer size and played on a gramophone. Later he sent what were known as 'dictabelts', announcing happily, 'This letter has been dictated on my new Dictaphone. I recommend it to you.' The record suggests Curtis was less enthusiastic. Notably, the proprietor's views were almost always conveyed as recommendations. He knew he was operating at a distance, and direct instructions, except very occasionally when Ismaili affairs intruded, usually came only when Curtis sought a specific decision.

With the major printing problems solved and the editorial department running smoothly in Nation House, *Taifa Leo's* circulation began to rise: 21,000 in March 1960, 22,000 in June, 24,000 in July, 30,000 in August, 35,000 in December. The figures were boosted when Hayes' staff launched a feature-focussed *Taifa Weekly*, which caught on immediately and consistently sold around 43–45,000. By now Bierman and his staff were putting out dummies for the first issue of *The Nation*, the English-language Sunday paper whose debut was set for 20 March, with a print order of 20,000. The first issue of the new paper arrived on time and, unusually for a new publication, without serious problems – something the daily failed to replicate when it appeared in October. *The Nation* led with gloomy news of arrests of opposition politicians in Ghana, the first of Africa's independent nations. A cartoon on the editorial page showed Kenya's black and white leaders gathered round a new-born infant in a pram marked *Nation*. They are saying, 'He's a cute little fellow, but will he behave?' It was a cogent caption considering the many painful conflicts that lay ahead between the paper and the politicians. The editorial promised readers 'a vigorous, inquisitive and cheerful' newspaper, expressed support for the transfer of power to the African majorities in the region within the next few years, and declared that Europeans and Asians should still have a role to play. *The Nation* also told the coming African rulers, 'The old carefree days of frivolous opposition, personal jealousies and tribal rivalries are, or should be, over. There is a crying need for efficient leadership and a sense of unity.' It is unlikely the writer expected those words would remain as relevant nearly half a century later.

A story that quickly won the paper wide attention, as well as considerable hostility, was an exclusive photo-spread on Jomo Kenyatta, Kenya's most talked-about and least-seen politician, who lived under restriction at distant Lodwar in the Northern Frontier Province, having recently been released from prison in Lokitaung. Bierman told the story of the scoop:

> *Charles Hayes had got wind that Margaret Kenyatta was being allowed to visit her father and suggested we get her to take some photographs. I jumped at the idea. No pictures had been seen of the old man since he was convicted years before and there were many gossipy stories that he was in ill health, drinking heavily and so on. Margaret used her own little camera and we gave her a couple of rolls of film. I told her to shoot them all off in the hope that we might get one or two useable prints. I remember she was eking out a living as a bookbinder with a small Asian-owned firm and I personally collected the film from her at her workplace just down the road from Nation House. What she brought back far exceeded my expectations and made a massive impact.*

*The Nation* of 19 June 1960 carried a front-page picture of Kenyatta in shorts and sandals, describing him as 'corpulent but as vigorous as ever', with another five photographs inside under the headline, *The Old Man Who Waits at Lodwar*. There was also an editorial saying for better or worse he must be released, and there would be no peace and progress until he was. 'This story was a sensation and the papers sold like hot cakes', Bierman recalled. 'It caused consternation at Government House. The settlers hated us for it, they felt Jomo should be buried in some distant prison and never seen again. I got a lot of nasty phone calls. One chap actually threatened to horsewhip me. But it was a brilliant editorial success.' When two African politicians, Ronald Ngala and Masinde Muliro, were permitted to visit the *Mzee*, Ivor Davis, who ran the Africapix photo agency with Mohinder Dhillon, gave a loaded camera to Muliro and his pictures appeared in the *Nation* and the *Standard*.

In a telegram to the Aga Khan on 23 March, Curtis reported, 'First issue *Nation* great success, sales estimated at 17,500.' After the fourth issue, he followed up, 'More advertising than the *Sunday Post*, searching everywhere for newsprint.' On 11 May, circulation reached 18,500, on 24 July, 24,000. A telegram of 10 August reported: 'Progress on all the papers continues to be almost too good to be true. *Nation* print order 35,000, returns under 10 per cent.' The Aga Khan replied, 'I am thrilled.'

As late as June 1960, the precise nature of the projected *Daily Nation* had not been decided. Curtis wrote, 'My plan at present is to make it an afternoon paper in Nairobi and district, replating in the early evening and selling as a morning paper in Mombasa and upcountry.' That never happened, but the proposal must have leaked and, when the daily came out as a morning paper, the *Standard* was taken by surprise. Bierman was the only senior executive at Nation House versed in all areas of journalism and newspaper production, and was crucial to planning. 'Some of those preparatory meetings were fraught', he recalled. 'There were endless arguments about morning or afternoon papers, what type of vehicles we should have.' *The Nation* was Kenya's first truly national newspaper. Said Bierman, 'The *Standard* had never trucked papers to the Coast, they had their *Mombasa Times* for that area, and we were considered insane for even thinking about driving overnight down 300 miles of dirt road which could easily be cut in three places in the rainy season.' When the dreaded Mombasa run started, one van was charged by a rhino, and on two successive nights vehicles ran into herds of elephants. One driver was swept five miles downstream in a flood but survived, though over the years several *Nation* workers lost their lives in the high-speed charge to the Indian Ocean.

Issue No. 1 of the *Daily Nation* (*The Nation* had earlier changed its name to *Sunday Nation*) came out on Monday 3 October 1960 and upheld the tradition in publishing that 'the first's the worst'. One point that had evaded the planners was that a Monday paper carries Sunday's news and there is often not much of that. So it proved with the inaugural issue, and Curtis confessed to the Aga Khan, 'I'm afraid the first issue was not a particularly brilliant effort. There was almost nothing to print except our own launching ceremony. Dr Kiano, Minister of Commerce and Industry, pressed the button.' Even the lead story – *Fit as a Fiddle Sultan is Back* – proved an embarrassment when the 81-year-old Sultan of Zanzibar, newly returned from a visit to doctors in Europe, went to his reward six days later. A front-page statement by the Editor outlined the newspaper's policy: 'To do our utmost to help Kenya and the other East African territories make the perilous transition to African majority rule and full independence as peacefully and constructively as possible.'

The print order for the inaugural *Daily Nation* was 15,500, and it sold 13,000. If the *Standard's* senior management disdained the *Nation* as, in Bierman's words, 'a bunch of ignorant parvenus', the same could not be said for that paper's circulation department. Denman remembered, 'We had a terrible time with the *Standard* when we started. They messed up all our vendors and their vendors threw our papers into the gutters. They gave us hell.' Curtis noted, 'The *Standard* was very strong indeed in Nairobi and we wanted to make an impression in the rural areas. On the day we first came out we heard that a large Buick saloon with two portly Europeans was seen distributing the *Standard* in Kisumu.' As with all new papers, the original curiosity sale dropped after the first day and come November the paper, selling at 25 cents for 24 pages, was down to 12,000, though putting back sales at a modest 200 per week. By the end of the year, the figure was 14,000, at which point the *Sunday Nation* was a 48-page paper carrying 50 per cent advertising and selling 35,000. Unlike its Sunday stablemate, which romped ahead from the day of its birth, the daily was to face a long, uphill circulation battle, taking more than five years to cross the 20,000 barrier, which the *Sunday Nation*, facing less significant competition, achieved in four months.

Editorially, however, the new baby quickly showed its paces and in short order carried a series of page-one exclusives which left the *Standard* reeling. A report that an East African Airways passenger airliner had tried to land in Nairobi National Park short of the runway at Embakasi Airport was vigorously denied, until the *Nation* printed John de Villiers' photos, shot from a chartered light plane, showing the wheel marks in the earth. The newspaper also reported an 'alarming drop' in private building investment in Nairobi, from £680,000 in July to £15,000 in October. Bierman's team correctly predicted that an important political detainee, Walter Odede, would be freed from restriction, that Humphrey Slade would be made Speaker of the Legislative Council that governed Kenya, and that Britain and the colonial government would announce guarantees of land titles. John Fairhall filed a vivid interview from the hospital bedside of a white hunter who had survived a physical tussle with a leopard.

What surprised and dismayed the journalistic pioneers was the critical attitude of African politicians, who had received from the new paper qualified but consistent support for their demands for the early release of Kenyatta and a speedy move to independence. Just 14 days after the *Daily*

*Nation* hit the streets, a statement from the Kenya African National Union (KANU), signed by its president James Gichuru, VP Oginga Odinga and general secretary Tom Mboya, accused the paper of seeking 'to use rumours from every source to vilify and discredit KANU, its leaders and activities'. The *Nation* had not expected gratitude from politicians for its forward-looking stance, but the hostility was surprising. The reason for the nationalists' anger was a story which claimed Odinga was bidding for the leadership of KANU. Standing by its account, the newspaper replied on its front page, 'It is right and proper that Nation Newspapers should report and comment on these differences [within the party].' It would, it warned, continue to do so. The KANU statement was the first shot in a battle between successive Kenya governments and the *Nation* that was to become the leitmotif of the newspaper's history. The cute little fellow in the pram simply would not behave.

## *Notes*

1.  Curtis did eventually become a Muthaiga member, in 1964, and listed the club in his *Who's Who* entry alongside the Garrick and the Travellers in London.
2.  *Kenyatta's Country* by Richard Cox, Hutchinson, London, 1965.
3.  Race categories were highly specific. I once asked a house servant if the people next door were Asians, to which he replied, 'No, they are Japanese.'
4.  Pinto was a Goan socialist, active in the African cause, a friend of the Marxist nationalist Oginga Odinga and an occasional journalist. He edited a short-lived paper, *PanAfrican*, and worked with Kenya's Gujarati newspaper, the *Daily Chronicle*. He was shot dead in the driveway of his home on 24 February 1965, becoming the first of Kenya's high-profile political assassinations, to be followed by Tom Mboya, J.M. Kariuki and Robert Ouko. Two teenagers were found guilty of Pinto's murder. One was sentenced to death, later commuted to life imprisonment, and spent more than three decades in jail; the other was acquitted.
5.  The Mau Mau rebellion, which lasted actively from 1952 to 1956, though a state of emergency continued until 1960, grew out of long-standing resentment of British occupation of Kenyan land and oathing was a crucial component of participation. Its rituals, traditional in Kikuyu culture, symbolised the solidarity that bound oath-takers in opposition to the colonial regime.
6.  The British government saw nothing unusual about Bolton's perception of his role and appointed him an OBE.

# CHAPTER 3

# Birth of a Nation

*Freedom of speech is a right to be fought for, not a blessing to be wished for.*
Former UN Secretary-General Kofi Annan

The first issue of *The Nation* carried a letter from a certain Arnold Bradley that declared, 'I wish you all the best in your uphill struggle for *Uhuru ya Pressi*. After nearly 40 years in East Africa, I have yet to see a paper that is not suppressed or under some form of government control. There is no such thing as freedom of the press here.' In the second issue, a member of the ruling Legislative Council (Legco), Air Commodore E.L. Howard-Williams, concurred, 'Our newspapers do what they dare but no newspaper is allowed to tell the truth about much. Propaganda is the order of the day.'

Whether *The Nation* saw these comments as a challenge to its virility or was displaying a swiftly developed instinct for self-preservation, it charged full tilt at a dragon immediately to hand, the Books and Newspapers Bill 27 of 1960, which had just been tabled in the ruling Legco. This legislation provided for the appointment of a Registrar of Books and Newspapers by the relevant minister and for bonds of £500 'as security for the payment of any monetary penalty which may at any time be imposed against any person upon his conviction for any offence relating to the printing and publication of that newspaper'. Printing without a bond made an offender liable to a fine of £500 or one year in jail, or both. These regulations covered the publication of everything from a church magazine to a daily newspaper, but generously exempted business cards, price lists and trade advertisements. The legislation also provided that any police officer could seize any book or newspaper if he suspected it was publishing in contravention of the Act, and could make a search without a warrant if he thought delay would defeat the purposes of the Act. In a thundering leader-page article, 'Why we fight this bill', the *Nation* denounced the good-behaviour bond and declared:

> *If taken to its logical conclusion, it could mean that every person capable of speaking is capable of slander and must deposit £500 ... it departs from Common Law and from the press laws in free countries ... a future attorney-general could increase the bond to £5,000 or even £50,000 and order a police officer to seize an entire edition of any newspaper. This newspaper profoundly hopes that the proposed legislation will not become law in its present form.*

In his combative 'Keeping Up With Jones' column, Ron Jones expressed shock at 'the surprising degree of latent hostility towards the Press' displayed by European members when Legco debated the Bill. Suspecting that this stemmed from the media's role in exposing administration lies about the 1959 Hola Camp massacre, when 11 Mau Mau prisoners died from ill-treatment, Jones pointed out, 'No newspaper or journalist can make a government look sillier, more inept, more bigoted, more tyrannous, more ham-handed, more blind or more stupid than its performance warrants.' A *Nation* cartoon showed a traffic cop telling a motorist at a 60-minute parking place, 'Just in case you park longer than an hour, here's your ticket for 50 bob', and a dentist proposing to take out a patient's teeth because 'they might go bad'. A letter from a lawyer said the Bill implied that 'only a man with £500 in his pocket may put his views before the public'. He said, 'One of the most important functions of the Press is to draw public attention to any attempts by the Executive to diminish our freedom. In Kenya, you have a wide field open to you.' *The Nation* did not have to be told. In a page-one piece, 'World Press Groups to Oppose Kenya Bill', it said the Commonwealth Press Union was vetting the legislation, and it quoted Jim Rose, Director of the International Press Institute in Zurich, as saying, 'There is nothing to justify, in normal periods, the seizure of a newspaper. Editors and journalists should bear the responsibility for what they write or do in a court of law.'

Unhappily, the battle was lost, with dire consequences for freedom of speech in Kenya. When the legislation was enshrined in the statute book, it became a law which authoritarian post-colonial governments implemented with enthusiasm – as they did much other repressive colonial-era legislation – banning titles, searching and seizing with zeal, confiscating and destroying the printing machinery of so-called seditious publications and sending editors to prison.

*The Nation's* spirited defence of individual liberties made no impression on Mrs M. Boardman of Limuru, who wrote, 'Frankly, I do not like your paper but I buy it because there is little else available for Sunday reading. From page 1 to page 40, your paper is one breathless rush of sensationalism, unalloyed by anything that could be called serious reading. Throughout, there is an element of deep salaciousness. In a developing country like this, there is a very real need for a sober, informed journal, but that description could not be applied to the *Nation.*' Bierman must have wondered if Mrs Boardman was reading the same paper he was editing. True, the *Nation* adopted the tabloid technique of personalising its reporters. 'I fly in and the band strikes up – They thought I was Patrice Lumumba' declared a front-page headline over Mike Harris' description of his arrival at Stanleyville Airport to cover troubles in the Congo. And when Althea Tebbutt, by then advertising manager of Nation Newspapers, encountered street demonstrations during a business trip to Salisbury, Rhodesia, the paper bannered her account, 'I drive through rioters'. This form of news presentation was foreign to the *East African Standard* and thus to residents of Kenya. However, the stories by Harris and Tebbutt were accurate and exclusive, and, like the British tabloids of that time, addressed serious issues.

As for Mrs Boardman's sensationalism, this was hard to find. The newspaper introduced a leisure section, *Time Off,* which was a novelty to Kenyan readers and contained two comic strips in colour, a page of pocket cartoons, chess and gardening columns, a crossword and book reviews. Daringly, it also ran a pop music column plus the sort of women's features current at the time ('Cooking the perfect omelette' and 'Does your man work too hard?'). Had Mrs Boardman looked closer, she might have found the sober information she wanted in a serialisation of *My Suez Memoirs* by Sir Anthony Eden, foreign news stories on the shooting of South Africa's white leader Hendrik Verwoerd, the aftermath of Sharpeville and the race crisis in the US Deep South, in a review of *The Winter's Tale* and in an interview with England's classical actor, John Gielgud. There were local columns such as Tony Lavers' 'Karen Diary', a weekly account, under the name James Shelley, of life in a rural suburb and the doings of whites and blacks in a tolerant and friendly community.

There were numerous stories on Kenyan politics and a report that crimes in Nairobi in March 1960 totalled 1,142, the highest monthly figure on record. An editorial linked the crime rise to high unemployment. *The Nation* also published the first opinion poll in East Africa. It contained the startling conclusion that among nationalist politicians, Tom Mboya was placed far

ahead of Jomo Kenyatta in popularity – 41 per cent and 24 per cent respectively. Behind these two were Julius Kiano (11 per cent), Ronald Ngala (7 per
cent) and Oginga Odinga (3 per cent). The polling was restricted to Africans
and done by the Market Research Company of East Africa. The evidence for
salaciousness in the new paper had to lie between an article about geisha
girls (pictured clad from top to toe), a sultry London showgirl who was in
Nairobi to marry her Asian lawyer fiancé, and the then pop icon, Bobby
Darrin, singing in his bath.

In what the more censorious readers doubtless took as an example of *lese
majeste*, the newspaper published a verbatim account of an airport news
conference with Dr Hastings Banda, the eccentric African leader in
Nyasaland, later Malawi:

> Q: *Dr Banda, you are having talks with Kenya and Tanganyika
> leaders. Can you tell us the basis of these discussions?*
> A: *That's my business.*
> Q: *Dr Banda, how soon will it be before Nyasaland leaves the Central
> African Federation?*
> A: *Go and ask Mr Butler [R.A. Butler was Britain's Colonial
> Secretary].*
> Q: *Dr Banda, have you any new comment on the Federation?*
> A: *I have made enough comment about the stupid Federation.*
> Q: *Dr Banda, who will you go to for financial help after Nyasaland
> becomes independent?*
> A: *Do you think I would go to you? I have never applied to you.*
> Q: *Dr Banda, don't you think you could be as polite in replying as we
> are in asking you questions?*
> A: *Do you call that a polite question? If a reporter asks me about
> Federation I do not call him a polite journalist. Why do you ask me
> these stupid questions? I did not ask to see you. You asked to see me.*

*The Nation* added, 'With Dr Banda still in full spate, the reporters emptied
the room. As he left the airport, Banda was greeted by a crowd of Kanu supporters singing *uhuru* songs. Tom Mboya led the singing. Dr Banda was
chaired shoulder-high to his car.'[1]

The journalist's long-held suspicion that some readers judge a newspaper by whether they *like* the news it contains received support with a letter
that denounced *The Nation* as 'extremely distasteful' for reporting that a
colour bar existed in hotels at Malindi on the coast. Another reader added

that it was 'worse than distasteful, it stinks'. It would have been interesting to hear their views on an early stunt by Ron Jones, who blacked up as 'a kind of westernised Somali in patterned cap' and walked the streets of Nairobi looking for racial insults: 'I got smiled at by an African girl, had a drink at the Garden Hotel, was given directions by both African and European policemen, was given terms to join the Macmillan Library and had a beer at the Thorn Tree Café at the New Stanley Hotel. My search for humiliation was in vain.' Political news was not hard to find. Groups of self-appointed leaders, invariably flourishing Kenyatta-style fly whisks, trudged up the stairs of Nation House in droves demanding to be inter-viewed. This would depend on whether they got past Marina, the formidable African receptionist. Second in number were Asian boy scouts who had climbed Mount Kilimanjaro and wanted their achievement immortalised in print. Since they usually asked to see 'the person in charge', reporters mischievously directed them to Curtis' office. The contempt in which the media were held by the ruling classes is well documented. A journalist remembered being at Embakasi Airport when the Governor, Sir Patrick Renison, returned from a London trip. 'We were kept behind this wire fence and doubtless we looked like some species of monkey in a zoo', he recalled. 'Renison glanced over and remarked, "Ah, the *gentlemen* of the press".'[2] Charles Hayes recalled seeking an interview with Renison at his London apartment during the constitutional talks. When he introduced himself as 'Hayes from the *Nation*', the Governor's daughter inquired waspishly, 'Do you know what we call your paper in Government House? The Daily Filthy.'

There can be little doubt that the charges of sensationalism which were levelled at the *Nation* in its early years stemmed not so much from its con-tents as its appearance, its tabloid size. The mostly British white population of Kenya knew only one tabloid, the London *Daily Mirror*, which was widely perceived as vulgar and trashy, though it had its own foreign correspondents covering global issues and was a model of propriety when set against, say, today's UK *Sun*. The newspaper-reading public in Kenya knew nothing of France's *Le Monde*, the *Tribune* of Geneva, nor of the influential American daily the *Christian Science Monitor*, tabloids all. The establishment newspa-per in Kenya was a broadsheet and Kenyatta himself, according to Hayes, preferred the large-size newspapers which he had become accustomed to during his years in England. That it was impossible to open a broadsheet in a crowded bus or *matatu* (minibus) was not relevant to most of those liter-ate enough to read newspapers in the early 1960s.

When Curtis first discussed the *Nation* with the Aga Khan, the word 'tabloid' was not synonymous, as it later became, with 'sleazy', 'downmarket' or 'sensational'; it referred simply to size, a half-sheet newspaper, indeed anything in compressed form. A further advantage was the substantial saving a tabloid brought in swingeing newsprint costs, while research indicated that the advertising impact of the compact was at least equal to if not greater than that of a broadsheet. 'A page is a page' became the slogan of the department. Curtis proposed a tabloid based on his conviction that an upmarket redesign in such a distinctive new format would have saved his own previous newspaper, the *News Chronicle*, when it was facing the financial and circulation problems that eventually killed it. 'There's no reason a tabloid should look like the *Mirror*', Curtis argued at the time. 'A tabloid can be as brash as the *Mirror*, as middle-brow as the London *Evening Standard* or as austere as *Le Monde*.' The Aga Khan didn't argue, though he went on record as stating, 'I am keen on trying to avoid big, flashy headlines', and regularly protested about frothy coverage of film stars and celebrities. In practice, the *Nation's* sub-editors tended to make the paper more jazzy than it needed to be and Curtis often pondered introducing a rule, as the British press magnate Cecil King had done with his newspapers in West Africa, to limit the size of headlines. Not being a trained production man, however, he was reluctant to intervene, and without design guidelines later sub-editors freely embellished Bierman's handsome but restrained early issues with often disastrous consequences. Only when the Group introduced its regional weekly, *The EastAfrican*, in 1994 under the guidance of Joseph Odindo, a talented editor with a fine eye for design, did the Aga Khan finally see the physical realisation of his dream – a good-looking, sober, upmarket product that discreetly murmured authority from every page. Ironically, by then the Kenyan public had long been converted to tabloids – the *Standard* finally changed its format in 1977 – and *The EastAfrican* actually encountered some consumer resistance, not to mention considerable in-house opposition, to the modest size of its headlines and the breadth of its columns.

When Althea Tebbutt took charge of advertising, she knew she had to provide the financial lifeblood of the company while the newspapers fought to push up their circulations. She said in an interview:

> *The establishment thought we were a joke, that we would never last, but I felt confident when I looked at the* Standard's *space sellers, men with cigarettes in the corner of their mouths, and I picked my team*

*very carefully. They were all women and frankly I chose them for their*
*sex appeal as well as personality and brains. There was Nicole*
*Gavaghan, Errol Trzebinski, Leila and 'Baby Leila'. Several were*
*blondes but there was a redhead, too. And I was keen to get women*
*whose husbands were managing directors of local companies; that*
*didn't hurt.*

An advertising department of women would cause little comment today, but was exceptional in the conservative Nairobi of the time. Errol Trzebinski, later to achieve distinction as a writer and historian on Kenya, said in an interview, 'In 1963, when trouser suits for women were becoming popular in Europe, I was actually interviewed by our fashion editor and asked if I would dare to wear one to the office in Nairobi.'[3] Mrs Tebbutt said, 'Another advantage we had was the ad agencies were terribly lazy. We were so far ahead with our offset printing, we did a lot of the artwork the agencies should have done.'

Mrs Trzebinski said:

*We used to report to Althea every morning and then go out on foot*
*from office to office. With the Lancaster House talks on independence*
*getting a lot of attention, many people had lost confidence in Kenya*
*and money was short. I did a lot of selling along Government Road, in*
*the dukas and bookshops. There were quite a lot of mzungus, white*
*people, who owned or worked in shops in those days and one of them,*
*a chemist, said, 'I never read the* Nation, *it's disgusting, we don't want*
*tabloids in this country.' They were terrible snobs. All the MDs*
*pretended they didn't read the* Nation. *They were suspicious about*
*our printing process, they were even suspicious because we charged*
*less than the* Standard. *The job wasn't just tough, it was*
*overwhelming.*

Companies were sensitive about editorial content and Jack Block cancelled his hotel advertising in *African Life* after the magazine published a photo-feature of lions mating. Mrs Trzebinski said, 'The Ron Jones column in the Sunday paper was extremely popular and people used to ask for ads on his page. Supplements were very important and Althea was always dreaming up supplements to bring in more cash, even travelling overseas.' One trip to Europe brought in £3,500 in advertising at a cost of £500. There were eight people in the display advertising department when Mrs Trzebinski arrived just before Christmas 1960 and 18 when she left – by then deputy advertising manager – in 1966. At that point, EAN was handling more than a dozen publications, including several trade papers.

What seemed to put off some advertisers was the *Nation's* refusal to conform to the white establishment. If the *Standard* sometimes acted more like a participant in government than a recorder of it, the *Nation* was cast increasingly as the opponent of authority. This was not bloody-mindedness, reverse snobbery or sycophancy towards the African rulers-to-be; least of all was it calculated policy. Simply, Bierman, by nature a radical, and many of his bright young imports found so much that they abhorred in Kenyan society, from the institutional racism to the unfeeling complacency of many individual whites. It was Bierman's anger at the authoritarian stance of the colonial government that informed the photo story of Kenyatta at Lodwar. He published the pictures to give the lie to administration-fuelled rumours that Kenyatta was drinking heavily, and to raise a finger to the authorities who had refused to let reporters visit the old man. Bierman, strictly speaking, was managing editor, while Curtis assumed the role, though never the title, of editor-in-chief. 'Michael allowed me enormous latitude (sometimes I think too much given how brash and pugnacious I was in those days) in setting day-to-day policy and writing leaders and running campaigns such as the one against the Press law', Bierman recalled, 'but every time I stuck our collective neck out, he backed me to the hilt, as did the Aga Khan'.

The irascible Jones was another who sniped constantly at authority, particularly the police force of which he had once been a member. One column said:

> *The other day a policeman told a* Nation *photographer that he was not to take a particular picture and that if he did, the film would be confiscated. I take pleasure in informing all members of the police that they have no legal right to take such action. A photographer can be rightfully arrested for obstructing a police officer or refusing to obey a lawful order but that gives the policeman no right to interfere with the contents of a camera. This assertion is made as a result of legal advice.*

Within three years, the *Nation* seemed to have established a firm reputation for iconoclasm. In 1963, with independence fast approaching, waggish students hung a sign outside Government House: 'This desirable residence for sale, owner going overseas very shortly.' The board was taken down and put in the office of the Governor's private secretary. A visitor to this functionary advised, 'I should turn it to the wall or those *Nation* people will see it and plaster it all over their front page.'

Where hindsight shows the *Nation* got it wrong in the early days was in the largely Eurocentric nature of its perceptions. In the view of director Peter Hengel, 'the paper was almost, in a sense, imitating the *Standard* and addressing their buyers'. It seemed to speak to a white audience rather than an African or even a multiracial one, and while its coverage of Kenyan politics was sharp and comprehensive, the choice of many other stories was often made through a British lens. There seemed to be an obsession with Princess Margaret, newly engaged to society photographer Tony Armstrong-Jones. The first issue of *The Nation* showed them at a theatre in London ('*Follow That Girl*') and so did the second ('*Flower Drum Song*'). There followed stories on her wedding dress, the wedding in Westminster Abbey and finally an oleaginous caption to a honeymoon picture: 'Hair tousled by the soft Caribbean winds, skin golden-tanned from long days in the sun, Princess Margaret drives in an open car through the island of Dominica with her husband.' The American statesman, Adlai Stevenson, once memorably observed, 'An editor is one who separates the wheat from the chaff and prints the chaff.' The problem of course was that one man's wheat was another man's chaff. Foreign reporting by the Western news services also reflected developed-world preoccupations, and it was only when Hilary Ng'weno took over the editorship in February of 1964 that an African relevance was properly addressed. Sub-editors remember the *Nation's* first African editor exploding wrathfully over wire-service coverage of the horrors in the Congo: 'Africans are dying in droves and all we get are heroic Paras rescuing beleaguered Belgians!'

Bierman frequently sent the *Nation's* own reporters on foreign assignments, particularly to the chaotic Congo, and he said later that he recalled no budgetary restraints on such travel. The enthusiasm of the Press corps was dampened, however, when three photo-journalists working out of Nairobi – an African, an Asian and a European – ventured into the Congo and never returned. Foreign news was something of an *idée fixe* with the Aga Khan. He believed African readers were interested in the world beyond Kenya, indeed beyond Africa, and when a research team investigated the market in 1963, that is precisely what it found. It was probably expecting too much for white British journalists of the time to see through African eyes, but the problem of copy-tasting, deciding just what really interested the Kenyan reader, was to persist until the late 1970s, when there were finally enough trained African sub-editors to supplant their expatriate colleagues.

What has receded into the mists of time was the effect that the Cold War had on the politics and therefore the media of the early 1960s, and the extent to which Kenya's geopolitical alignment with the West influenced the future of the country. 'In those days the papers were full of the Communist menace, how they were going to take over Africa', recalled government information officer Matheson. The *Sunday Nation's* lead story of 5 February 1961 shouted, 'Red bid to sway voters'. It said:

> *Communist sources are trying to interfere in Kenya's general election. Red intervention has come into the open with the circulation in Kenya of a pamphlet entitled 'The great conspiracy against Africa', which purports to be an annexe to a British cabinet paper. This astonishing pamphlet, which aims at discrediting British and American policy in Africa, and which is also directed to trying to prove that certain African politicians are 'stooges', is yet another product of the East German Communists' propaganda factory in East Berlin.*

The pamphlet apparently named the 'stooges', but the *Sunday Nation* did not. However, it can be safely assumed that Tom Mboya's name was listed. His contacts with the West-backed International Conference of Free Trade Unions and with the US labour movement made him a frequent target of African leftists. In a letter quoted by the *New York Times* shortly before his murder in 1969, Mboya said, 'Ironically, people who receive money from foreign sources have levelled accusations against me. I have lived with a label of help from America. Sometimes I wish this were true.' The accusers Mboya had in mind doubtless included his fellow Luo, Oginga Odinga, who in turn was pilloried as a Communist stooge for his frequent trips to China. Just as Mboya organised airlifts of Kenyan students to universities in the USA, so Odinga arranged scholarships for bright young Kenyans in Cuba, East Europe and the Soviet Union. The American poet Ogden Nash expressed the anti-Marxist view in the ideological war with a contribution to *New Yorker* magazine:

> *Oginga Odinga, Oginga Odinga,*
> *In Kenya's black pie*
> *He's Mao's Red Finger.*
> *Let's hope that old Jomo,*
> *The Lion of Kenya,*
> *Will settle the hash*
> *Of this scheming hyena.*

It was difficult, even then, to believe that Odinga was a convinced Communist. He took funds from Communist regimes but his personal beliefs were unashamedly capitalist. He owned and ran transport and printing businesses in Kisumu and participated enthusiastically in the personal acquisition of property. As for atheism, pictures of Jesus, with heart aflame, hung on the walls of his Kisumu home.

Almost from the day the *Daily Nation* was launched, politicians complained that the new paper supported their opponents, was bent on undermining African unity or was following a secret colonial agenda. In a message to Curtis only three weeks after the launch, the Aga Khan cautioned, 'We cannot weather these sorts of attacks too often in our formative years. We have to be careful not to get on the wrong side of either the Kenya African National Union or the Kenya African Democratic Union.' He was referring to KANU's anger over the *Nation's* story about splits in the party. Curtis explained, 'Mboya's reason for attacking us was that he in turn had been attacked by Odinga and Co. as being "in the pocket of the *Nation*". He was mainly concerned to establish his independence.' This may have been the first occasion, but certainly it was not the last, when an African politician sought to use the *Nation* in his own interest. Some five months later, the proprietor seemed to have heard that the paper was hostile to the Kenya African Democratic Union (KADU). Curtis responded, 'I don't think this criticism is justified at all. The secretary of KADU, John Keen (Hayes' old *Taifa* news editor) has taken it into his head that we are against his party. This is simply not borne out by the facts.' He added that 'KADU leaders are pretty dim figures compared to their opposite numbers in KANU. They very rarely have anything original, constructive or even provocative to say.' As to complaints of excessive exposure for Mboya, Curtis noted, 'The trouble is this man has an instinctive news sense and when he opens his mouth, he invariably has something to say – a rare quality among politicians of any race in Kenya.'

After further political pressures in 1961, Curtis wrote to the Aga Khan: 'We shall never satisfy either KANU or KADU so long as they are jockeying for power and so long as we remain independent of both. Our editorial line has been to advocate a coalition.' This was not at all to the liking of KANU, which preferred the biblical approach: 'He who is not with me is against me.' In hindsight, this attitude to the *Nation* might be said to prefigure the party's stance in government, which at its most extreme led to critics, however loyal and patriotic, being equated with traitors. When the Aga Khan wrote to Jomo Kenyatta later that year suggesting a meeting, the KANU leader replied, 'I would very much like to meet with you... *Nation* and *Taifa* are not helping to bring unity among the races in Kenya. Through their sensational stories and taking sides, they are doing more harm than good.' Bierman also recalled Kenyatta telephoning: '"You are causing splits, Mr Bierman" – because we would report on differences within KANU.' When Mboya, too, protested, Bierman said, 'Do you not realise we are on the African's side, that we want basically what you want for this country?' Said Mboya, 'John, if I didn't believe that, I wouldn't bother to talk to you.' Odinga's approach was simpler. 'He was invited to China to make a speech', Bierman remembered. 'The Americans monitored it and slipped me a transcript and it was pretty hot revolutionary stuff. After we printed it, he said to me over the phone, "Oh Mr Bierman, we will settle with you after *uhuru*".'

The pressures worsened when independence neared under a KANU administration. Mboya, the Minister of Justice and Constitutional Affairs, ordered the burning of the *Sunday Nation* and the *Mombasa Times*, in the *Nation's* case apparently because it gave greater prominence to his own remarks than to Kenyatta's when Kenya's first prime minister made a triumphal visit to Mombasa. Mboya declared that if newspapers thought freedom of speech meant licence to write destructively about the country, then independent Kenya would have to do without any newspapers at all. At one point, the *Standard* remarked mildly that 'KADU seems to know where it's going'. Mboya shot back, 'The Press must be aware ... freedom does not mean irresponsibility.' Minister of Information Achieng Oneko, who was to prove the hammer of the media, warned that 'any attempt to provoke disunity, to slight our prime minister or other members of the government in any way will not be tolerated by the government'.

Curtis suggested that an Editorial Advisory Board with in-house and outside members could form a useful line of defence. At first, the idea was confined to *Taifa Leo* and the outsiders suggested included Mareka Gecaga, Kenyatta's friend Peter Mbiu Koinange, an up-and-coming politician named Mwai Kibaki, as well as John Seroney and Moody Awori. Such a board was eventually established, responsible for all of the Group's titles. Its weakness was that it depended upon the enthusiastic co-operation of the editorial chief and, during some crucial periods in the *Nation* story, this was notably lacking. Putting its bona fides on the line, the *Nation* also in later years drew up a Code of Ethics for its journalists, and published a statement of editorial policy and a list of editorial objectives which were approved by shareholders. The clear intention was to make the board of directors responsible for ensuring the guidelines were followed as part of corporate policy and protected from editorial whim or negligence – the only way quality control could be assured. Since the Board was not wholly Kenyan by membership or residence, however, there was need for an oversight body to monitor the papers' independence, balance and quality.

What dominated life in Kenya at the time of the *Nation's* gestation was the issue of independence, an event some whites secretly believed, and certainly hoped, would never come to pass. They had reason to think so. In 1950, Britain's then Secretary of State for the Colonies, James Griffiths, said after a visit to Kenya, 'This is God's own country with the Devil's own problems.' Two years later, another colonial secretary, the anti-colonialist Arthur Creech Jones, was asked by a Labour party colleague, Denis Healey, about the prospects of majority rule. He replied, 'Denis, Kenya will not be independent in my lifetime or yours.'[4] As late as January 1959, the then Colonial Secretary Alan Lennox-Boyd hosted a conference of the three East African governors at which it was decided that Tanganyika might achieve independence by 1970, Uganda soon after and Kenya by 1975. Thus when the colony's delegates returned home from the January 1960 constitutional conference in London with a firm promise of independence, the sense of shock among Kenya's whites was palpable. Even the African leaders were astounded. A.R. Kapila, the Kenyan lawyer who defended Kenyatta at his Kapenguria trial for managing Mau Mau, remembered meeting Tom Mboya when the delegation returned: 'He was jumping up and down and shouting, "They've given in, they're giving up". He couldn't believe it. It was like a man asking for a pound and being told, take five.'

So what happened between January 1959 and January 1960 to bring about such a radical change in British policy? In short, an election. Prime Minister Harold Macmillan's Conservative government was returned to power in October 1959 with a 90-seat majority, large enough to assure passage of legislation severing the African colonies from the mother country. These overseas territories were seen as expensive and potentially involving – agitation was increasing and delay was the riskier option. Iain Macleod, the Tory radical who succeeded Lennox-Boyd, wrote later in the *Spectator* weekly, 'It has been said that after I became Colonial Secretary there was a deliberate speeding-up of the movement towards independence. I agree. There was. In my view, any other policy would have led to terrible bloodshed in Africa … the march of men towards their freedom can be guided but not halted.' In Nairobi, Bierman saw it in less elevated terms: 'The British no longer had the political will or the economic wherewithal to hold down an empire, so the best thing was to get out in good order and as decently as possible.'

It was at the time of the first Lancaster House conference on Kenya that Macmillan, during a visit to Africa, made his first public allusion to Britain's dramatic change of course. He told guests at a state banquet in Accra, Ghana, 'The wind of change is blowing through Africa.' The significance of his statement was not immediately grasped and in Cape Town, on 3 February, he spoke at greater length, sending a direct message to the apartheid regime of South Africa: 'The wind of change is blowing through this continent and whether we like it or not, the growth of national consciousness is a political fact. We must accept it as a fact and our national policies must take account of it.' The liberal Kenyan leader, Michael Blundell, who played a significant role in the independence negotiations, later wrote that contributing to the decision to get out of Africa were Britain's diminished post-war strength, a growing public distaste for imperial adventures and the reluctance of UK voters to send their sons to remote places to maintain law and order. There was also an official 1957 analysis which showed the colonies to be costing Britain £51 million per year. Realists had long acknowledged that once India received its independence the African colonies were bound to follow.

By 1960, the key questions were how soon Kenya would become independent, what form of government it would have, and to what extent, if any, whites would share power. The settlers' strength, rooted throughout the halcyon days of colonialism in family connections with the politically powerful in Britain, was eroding fast, and the days when they could defy imperial policy whilst loyally singing 'God Save the King' were over.

At the 1960 talks, the settlers' political position was informed above all by a sense of betrayal. Many of them had come to Kenya as ex-World War II servicemen, mostly officers, under a settlement scheme designed to run for 44 years under British administration, and they had worked mightily to establish farms in areas which were bush or grass. For the British government to renege on its promises after a mere 15 years was, they believed, the vilest treachery. The Africans, for their part, remembered the political parable that Kenyatta enjoyed telling about the wily camel which prevailed upon a kindly tent owner for shelter from the storm and gradually pushed the owner out. The camel was clearly the settler and the tent-owner was the Kenyan African. In African eyes, a settler was a settler, though many of the post-war arrivals had little in common with the freebooters of the early 1900s.

The original settler Delamere (1870–1931) wrote in 1903 that he took 100,000 acres on a 99-year-lease at a halfpenny per acre per annum, adding, 'Land here seems to me absurdly cheap.'[5] By contrast, the later settlers sank their life savings into their ventures or took onerous loans to back their risk. But history was against them. As far back as 1923, the British government, in a far-seeing White Paper issued by the then Colonial Secretary the Duke of Devonshire, had proclaimed that the interests of the African in Kenya were paramount. It stated, 'Primarily, Kenya is an African territory and His Majesty's Government think it necessary definitely to record their considered opinion that the interests of the African natives must be paramount and that if and when those interests and the interests of the immigrant races should conflict, the former should prevail.' It went on, 'In the administration of Kenya, His Majesty's Government regard themselves as exercising a trust on behalf of the African population, and they are unable to delegate or share this trust, the object of which may be defined as the protection and advancement of the native races.' By 1960, those paramount interests had coalesced into one burning objective: sovereignty.

But if independence in principle was one thing, the modalities were another, and the first conference, which opened in the Music Room at London's opulent Lancaster House on 18 January 1960, lasted a long and difficult five weeks. Kenya's 50 delegates flew to Britain at a discount by block-booking on East African Airways at the tourist rate, though it is unlikely that the settlers and the Africans sat together. The African team included Tom Mboya, Oginga Odinga, James Gichuru, Ronald Ngala and Daniel arap Moi, a young emerging politician representing smaller upcountry communities. Michael Blundell led the moderate New Kenya Group of Europeans with Bruce Mackenzie, Peter Marrian and Wilfred Havelock, and the settlers were represented by the United Party under Group Captain 'Puck' Briggs. When proceedings opened, the African group immediately demanded the release of Kenyatta, but Iain Macleod refused to discuss it. They then requested that Jomo Kenyatta's personal friend, Peter Mbiu Koinange, currently working as a milkman in Watford, should be admitted as an adviser. When this, too, was refused, the Africans boycotted the talks until a blank pass was produced on which Koinange's name could be written, admitting him to Lancaster House but not to the conference room. A British civil servant commemorated the affair in a quatrain after the English nursery rhyme, 'Baa Baa Black Sheep', which the Kenyans did not care for:

> *Mau Mau milkman, have you any pass?*
> *Yes sir, yes sir, but only second class.*
> *Good for the cloakroom and good for the loo,*
> *But not for the Music Room among the chosen few.*[6]

On the table was a proposed multiracial constitution giving Kenyan Africans 35 of the 66 seats in the Legislative Council, four government ministries to the whites' three and making provisions for a wider franchise – in effect conceding African majority rule and an African government after elections. Predictably, the right-wingers rejected the proposal out of hand. The Africans accepted it despite fears that it was meant to delay full independence, and crucially Blundell's group accepted it, too, forging an important first link between white and black. In his memoir, *A Love Affair with the Sun*,[7] Blundell wrote that 'we accepted because we believed that we must move to the concept of one nation and abandon the racial tensions of the past'. The decision was to bring him much grief.

When Blundell returned to Nairobi, a settler at the airport famously threw a small white bag at his feet. It burst open and 30 silver *simunis*, sixpence pieces, flew in all directions as the man cried dramatically, 'Judas, you have betrayed and left us.' In the election campaign, Blundell was spat at in upcountry settler strongholds Njoro and Nakuru, and when he spoke at Londiani he was pelted with missiles. He recalled in *So Rough a Wind*, his account of the movement towards independence,[8] that 'a man got up and asked me, "Mr Blundell, don't you agree that you are a traitor to the European community?" Immediately 12 men and women arose, including a beautiful blonde, and bombarded the chairman and myself with eggs and tomatoes ... the missiles burst and plopped all round and an egg landed and broke on my cheekbone.' Blundell returned fire with a glass of water but only splashed one of his own campaign workers, and he later found that the tomatoes had been bought from another of his supporters, albeit unwittingly. On election day, Blundell visited a polling station and was cheered by a large crowd of Africans. He wrote, 'A European woman pushed her way up to my small party and spat in my face, rasping at me, "Why don't you let them kiss you, Judas Iscariot!"' For nearly three years, Blundell did not enter any Kenyan club because nobody would speak to him or his wife.

Though the result of Lancaster House had long been anticipated by the politically aware, it came as a stunning blow to the settled Europeans, and Blundell recalled, 'Many farmers abandoned all development, fine dairy herds were sold off as beef, workers were dismissed and an air of gloom was prevalent. The road from Nakuru to Nairobi was almost empty of vehicles, only forlorn numbers of African workers who had lost their jobs were to be seen trudging hopelessly along the roadside.' Within the year, settler leader Ewart Grogan had sold his 120,000 acres, saying Kenya was no place for his family, another European took £5,000 for a farm valued at £35,000 and a third, Peter Bibby, moved to South Africa because 'I was damned if I was going to take my hat off and say Sir to Kenyatta'. The exodus of whites was to reach 7–10,000 by early 1964, probably peaking at 28 per cent of the 60,000-strong community in 1966. An Asian businessman, J.B. Ahamed, bought the £20,000 Highlands Hotel in Molo with a nine-hole golf course and a 300-acre farm for £3,000, stating, 'I have every confidence in the future of Kenya.' He was an exception. Capital outflow accelerated and, though the commonly quoted figure of £1 million a week was described by the Kenya government as 'highly exaggerated', Finance Minister Kenneth Mackenzie admitted that £3.4 million left the country in the first three months after the London conference. The economy slowed markedly, unemployment escalated and inward investment was a mere trickle.

Still the Aga Khan was optimistic. In June 1959, Curtis had reported that 'there is every prospect that the company will be earning a respectable profit within two, or at the most three, years'. But that was when *Taifa Leo* was the only title. It was never in doubt that the Aga Khan wanted to extend his reach beyond the borders of Kenya, and although his papers were losing £15,000 per month in May 1960, expansion was the codeword. By early 1961, the *Sunday Nation* was being distributed in British-ruled Aden, and the Aga Khan suggested grandly, 'At some future date, we might move south into Northern Rhodesia and Nyasaland and west into Rwanda, Burundi and the ex-Belgian Congo. I hope EAN will one day have its own company flying newspapers over half the continent.' The proprietor directed that publishing opportunities be explored in Uganda and Tanganyika. Curtis said he would look at the printing plant of a Mr Mulira in Uganda, but added sadly, 'The last time I saw this, there was a hen laying eggs on one of the flat-bed presses.' In Tanganyika, most printing equipment was about 90 years old. Expansion did take place, however.

In addition to the two *Nations*, *Taifa Leo* and *Taifa Weekly*, Hayes's Kiswahili journalists spun off *Taifa Uganda* and *Taifa Tanganyika* weeklies, and EAN bought interests in two more dailies with local African editors, *Mwafrika* in Tanganyika and *Taifa Empya*, a Luganda-language daily in Uganda, to which was added a Sunday version. In October 1962, Kenya-born Roger Stovold directed the launch of the English-language *Uganda Nation*, an eight-page paper raised to 12 by using four centre pages of the *Daily Nation*, paste-ups and negatives being freighted to Kampala. Initial sales were an encouraging 4,000 a day against 12,000 for the well-established *Uganda Argus*. EAN also bought the English-language monthly *African Life* and paid £1,000 for the Tanganyika Kiswahili magazine *Mambo Leo*, adding a Kenya/Uganda edition titled *Maisha* (Life). But when Charles Hayes reported an offer from the *Colonial Times* to sell their two vernacular newspapers, Curtis gave a firm 'no'. The new publications were being managed by two new *Nation* companies, Tanganyika African Newspapers and Uganda African Newspapers. In November 1961, the EAN board of directors agreed to pump £30,000 into the Tanganyika company and £25,000 to Uganda. Although some of the circulation figures looked promising, sales fluctuated, and the Dar es Salaam company lost £8,615 over the first ten months of 1961, a loss which soon increased to £1,000 per month.

These ventures sometimes proved self-defeating. When the *Uganda Nation* started, the Nairobi *Daily Nation's* sales in Uganda dropped from 1,000 per day to 200. Because Kampala had a bigger printing workload, it received a rotary press originally destined for Dar es Salaam, while Dar es Salaam got Kampala's plant to print *Mwafrika*. Nevertheless, distribution was costing £3,600 per month and the financial picture was not helped by a printers' strike in Nairobi. This led to recognition of the Printing and Kindred Workers Union, and to pay increases and backdating that put £3,000 per annum on the wages bill. The *Uganda Nation* performed poorly and when sales dropped to 3,000 against a 5,000 break-even point, Curtis warned that consideration must be given to abandoning the project. The expansion across East Africa had been eagerly canvassed by African leaders and in Tanganyika by Julius Nyerere personally, but clearly EAN was overextended. There was no way executives in Nairobi could ride herd on editors hundreds of miles away, as Curtis discovered when President Milton Obote summoned him to Kampala and lectured him about 'irresponsibility and sensationalism' in the *Uganda Nation*. What's more, largely due to lack of advertising, all the far-flung publishing ventures were losing money. Fortunately help was at hand – from Germany, of all places.

A single paragraph in the minutes of the EAN board meeting of November 1962 stated that a Doctor Wolff, business consultant, had been invited to 'look into the affairs of the company and advise on any problems'. Wolff was head of the German Kienbaum company of financial consultants and Dr Peter Hengel was one of its directors. Hengel had already carried out an economic analysis of the Ismaili community in East Africa at the request of the Aga Khan, which had resulted in the establishment of Industrial Promotion Services, an early form of what today would be called a venture capital company. Now the Aga Khan wanted a similar investigation of EAN. 'There was a cash-flow problem at the time', Hengel recalled in an interview:

*The chairman of Lloyd's Bank had written saying the bank could no longer support the newspapers' situation. The Aga Khan wrote back saying this analysis was going to happen and he expected improvements pretty soon. But there was definitely a squeeze on and this made it difficult for Michael Curtis. He had no long-term plan to work from and he simply had to ask for money all the time and no financier likes to be told, 'We're out of money, send another million tomorrow or we'll have to close.' He needs to see light at the end of the tunnel or at least a concept about how to improve the situation. Also this was the Aga Khan's first large commercial venture and he naturally wanted it to succeed. All these things impelled him to commission an in-depth analysis.*

The financial picture that Hengel uncovered in 1963 was a sorry one. The Group had total fixed and current assets of £659,000 and the accumulated total loss was £778,000. Turnover for the year 1962/63 was £717,000, less than the accumulated loss, while the loss for the last year was £184,000, or 26 per cent of turnover. By that time, the Aga Khan had invested £766,243 in share capital and £461,698 in loans, a total of £1,227,941.[9] Hengel recalled:

*There was no real management structure and the first thing we did was to rearrange the cost accounting so we could see loss or profitability per newspaper and per area, where money was being made and lost, what the freight costs were and so on. We also did some improvements in internal material flows such as the dispatch of the papers, packaging and so on. To address a problem, you have to know the facts. The finance people were book-keeper types who could tell you exactly how much a chair cost but who had no controller's education or instinct; they were running after figures when everything had already happened whereas they should have devised a system towards which they could work. By seeing where you depart from your goals, you can devise measures to counteract it.*

Hengel's investigation was complemented by a time-and-motion study of work habits. This did not always go down well in the newsroom. On one occasion, an expert stood for several moments, stop-watch in hand, scrutinising the immobility of columnist Jones. Trademark cigarette-holder clenched between his teeth, Jones sat motionless before his typewriter, fingers poised over the keyboard. Finally, the investigator spoke: 'Er, Mr

Jones, what are you doing?' Jones favoured the man with a bleak look: 'Bloody *thinking*.'

The financial investigators set out their conclusions in a study that became known as the Kienbaum Report. It stated in part:

> *The group has continuously expanded into new activities instead of consolidating at each stage. There is no long-term consolidation plan. The financial position is dangerous and will get worse if the group carries on in this way. There is a lack of company thinking and sometimes departments even work in opposition to each other. There are no managerial instruments and insufficient systems of information such as costing and statistics.*

All this was hardly surprising. The *Nation* had been started by a tiny group of enthusiastic and talented people, but over four years they had not been joined by a necessary number of knowledgeable commercial staff; often they found themselves working outside their areas of expertise in straitened economic circumstances, not to mention basic if not primitive office conditions. The pressure for expansion was beyond their ability to restrain.

The Kienbaum Report was the first step towards professionalising the *Nation*. Hengel and his colleagues made nine major recommendations: (1) implement a new organisational structure; (2) close the *Uganda Nation*; (3) cancel the first edition of the *Daily Nation*; (4) cancel the second edition of the *Sunday Nation*; (5) formulate a new system of deadlines; (6) reduce personnel; (7) implement market promotion for sales as well as advertising; (8) institute a work study programme; and (9) set up a costing and control system. If these measures were accepted, they said, the annual loss could be cut from £184,000 to £90,000 in the first year and to £70,000 in the second, with the break-even point reached in five years. The report also urged a massive campaign for classified advertising. What Hengel stressed was that cost-cutting and staff rationalisation would not in themselves rescue the company; the crucial factor would be a quantum leap in circulation through a stronger identity with African readers. A deeply relieved Curtis moved eagerly to implement the recommendations, though Hengel recalled, 'There was massive resistance from the staff and the trade unions. Each time you moved a worker from here to there, you had trouble.' EAN owned or managed 18 publications. These were reduced to ten. Editorial numbers were cut from 63 to 49 and 15 jobs were rationalised in the production department. Curtis wrote later that 'by cutting back the offshoots and concentrating on really healthy growth at the centre, the haemorrhage of funds ceased almost immediately'. In the six months from October 1963 to April 1964, costs dropped by £12,000 and in the next six months by £21,800. This reduced the monthly cash requirement from the Aga Khan to a relatively modest £5,350. Some changes were rescinded as the *Nation* grew in strength, but there is no doubt the programme was a crucial turning point in the company's history. The magic moment of break-even actually came a year earlier than Kienbaum predicted.

The Kienbaum Report was not infallible – it predicted wrongly that major growth would come in the Kiswahili newspapers – but Hengel laid down a clear vision for the future. He strongly supported the Aga Khan's stated intention eventually to float the *Nation* as a public company and offer Africans their own stake in his venture. Such a move might also safeguard the company against nationalisation, then very popular with new African governments. All of this, Hengel stressed, depended upon the English-language newspapers building a strong African identity, in contrast with the *Standard's* British image, and surpassing their rival in circulation. At that point, the daily was still selling only 17,000, but the Christmas 1962 edition of the *Sunday Nation* had a print order for 38,000 and advertising at 50 per cent – 300 column inches – beating the bumper Friday issue of the *Standard* for the first time. When this writer, then assistant editor, described the *Sunday Nation* as the biggest newspaper in East Africa, Colonel Bolton wrote to claim this honour for the Friday *Standard*. He copied his letter to every advertising agency in Nairobi. In Curtis' absence, Hayes replied, 'Dear Ken, Dear oh dear. Yours ever, Charles.' He copied his letter to the same agencies and added a final line, 'cc God'.

On the political battlefield, the rival papers had plenty to report. KANU, effectively the successor to Kenyatta's Kenya African Union, was formed in May 1960, following the first constitutional conference; Kenyatta, still in detention, was elected president in absentia, and Mboya, Odinga and Gichuru were the leading lights. The following month, politicians fearful of Kikuyu-Luo domination formed KADU, which favoured a federalist government; Ronald Ngala became president, Masinde Mulriro VP and Daniel arap Moi chairman. In February 1961, KANU won the first general election under the new constitutional arrangements, taking 16 seats in the 53-member Legco to KADU's ten. But it refused to form a government until Kenyatta was released, so KADU put together an administration with the help of European and Asian poll winners. It was soon after the constitutional conference that Governor Renison enraged Africans – and, it was later to become apparent, wrecked his own career – by describing Kenyatta as 'an African leader to darkness and death' and by refusing all appeals to free him. But in March 1961, clearly directed by Whitehall, he announced the *Mzee* would be moved from restriction in Lodwar to a halfway house at Maralal. Five months later, he was set free and allowed back to his Gatundu home area, where the KADU government built him a house and Asian merchants donated the furniture.

The government coalition was a shaky arrangement and brought new pressures upon the media. The luxuriously moustached, South African-born cabinet Minister Bruce Mackenzie invited Hayes and Bierman, and warned that the Press must 'discipline itself' and not print anything that would destroy what little remained of the multiracial coalition. In a letter to Curtis, who was out of the country, Hayes wrote, '[Mackenzie] says that if this doesn't happen, then we are heading for suppression or censorship. He said, "If you go on as you are doing now, you are having your last fling".' Hayes went on, 'John and I pointed out that if political speeches were made and not fully reported, the crowds who listened to the words would suspect the reputation the Press has tried to build. Equally, what a wonderful opportunity we hand to the agitators who, knowing they will not be reported, could get away with murder.' Bierman reluctantly agreed to place a three-month moratorium on all political news if every other paper did the same, and provided the *Nation* could tell its readers that this was a voluntary discipline at the request of the government. Hayes added, 'Heaven knows what such a situation would do to our sales, and to our consciences, but Brucey Boy is deadly serious in issuing his threats.' The moratorium idea was clearly a non-starter and no news blackout ever happened. What Mackenzie's strictures demonstrated was the wish of national rulers from the earliest days to decide what the Press should print and what it should omit.

It was during his brief stay at Maralal that Kenyatta made his first appearance before the world's media after nine years locked away from public contact, allowing outsiders to see and hear for the first time the man many Kenya whites considered to be the devil incarnate. In fact, Kenyatta was infinitely more subtle and complex than the colonial demonology suggested. Terence Gavaghan, District Commissioner (DC) in Kiambu in 1951 (and husband of Nicole, who was later to sell advertising for the *Nation*), recalled a remark by Kenyatta during a discussion in his DC's office about the Kikuyu Peace Front, headed by nominated Legco member Eliud Mathu. Kenyatta chuckled and said, 'Mr Mathu does not have the common touch. I have the common touch.'[10]

The Maralal Press conference was attended by 120 reporters, mostly foreign correspondents who flew 160 miles from Nairobi in light planes. But Kenyatta demonstrated he had not lost that common touch he boasted of. In his book *States of Emergency*,[11] Alastair Matheson, who organised the event for the government, wrote:

> *The small trading post of Maralal had no facilities for visitors but it did have a club for the white cattle ranchers and I approached the club secretary to ask if the government could use the club for Kenyatta's press conference. The answer was a blank refusal. 'We won't have that man on our premises, no, no, no' was all the European secretary would say.*

A large marquee was borrowed from the army instead. Matheson sat to the right of Kenyatta, who was wearing his trademark leather jacket, with A.R. Kapila, his trial lawyer, to his left. Matheson added, 'Presumably Kapila briefed Kenyatta beforehand and the lawyer came well armed with notes as well as his memory, but Kenyatta seldom had to consult him. He gave a magnificent performance, sharp-witted and articulate' that lasted three hours. Kapila himself recalled in an interview, 'He had been in custody all that time but didn't give the impression of a man who had been broken. He handled all the questions from sharp reporters on any level. It was the same at his trial, he always got the better of the exchanges and often brought the house down in laughter.'

Bierman himself covered the story for the *Daily Nation*, characterising Kenyatta's marathon as 'a display of verbal eloquence and political one-upmanship which would have been remarkable in a man half his firmly declared age of 71'. In a story that covered most of page one and all of page two, Bierman added, 'If one were asked, Has the leopard changed his spots, one would have to answer that he claims most forcefully that he was never a leopard at all.' A carefully worded editorial suggested that Kenyatta might just be the man to create the conditions necessary for a properly timed handover of power.

A second round of constitutional talks in London in 1962 took place against a background of growing political and economic instability in Kenya. The conference was marked by the first appearance of Kenyatta at Lancaster House at the head of a team from the two African parties. But unity was fragile, with KANU men pressing for centralism and KADU for regionalism. William Murgor from the Eldoret area warned that if KADU's plans were not accepted, he would tell his Kalenjin people 'to sharpen their spears and poison their arrows'. The *Nation* was never convinced of the merits of regionalism and an editorial spoke warmly of KANU's constitutional proposals. It added, however:

> There is one omission from the list of fundamental rights, which may or may not be an oversight. This is the question of freedom of the press. Freedom of the Press (and we mean not licence but freedom to perform our democratic task of informing the public and protecting them against overbearing officialdom, corruption and graft) is certainly one right which should be protected.

But KANU never did press for a specific clause on Press freedoms being written into the constitution and its absence has caused grief to journalists ever since. The *Daily Nation* marked the opening of the conference by adopting a new look for page one. The red-top, *Mirror*-style corner title was banished in favour of one stretching across the page, and a burning torch emblem was introduced with the Biblical slogan 'The truth shall make you free'. The editor explained, 'These words and this symbol sum up the aspiration of this newspaper to bring about fruitful independence [and] safeguard the freedom of the millions who live here, by the relentless pursuit of truth.'

The conference started on 4 February and after many deadlocks the new Colonial Secretary, Reginald Maudling, produced a framework constitution to be refined by the coalition government back in Nairobi. He said the document provided for 'a strong and effective central government responsible to a parliament of two chambers'. At the same time, it aimed to protect the smaller tribes by extending powers to the regions. An agreement was signed on 6 April and KADU's Ronald Ngala said regionalism had been achieved. No such thing, said Kenyatta. Subsequent party wrangles over the constitution became so bitter that the coalition government came to be known as the collision government and, in the event, the so-called *majimbo* (federal) constitution was comprehensively rewritten. Looking back on the negotiations, Blundell recalled:

> Kenyatta was making his views known for the first time and in the course of his speech he said that Kikuyus must be allowed to take up land in the Rift Valley. Immediately there was a long-drawn-out 'Aaaah' from the Kalenjin and Maasai representatives and Willie Murgor produced a whistle and blew a long note of alarm on it.[12]

This was an issue which was to reverberate down the years, leading to bloody ethnic cleansing of the Kikuyu from parts of the Rift Valley in the early 1990s.

Blundell also recalled an impressive performance by the man who was to become President of Kenya many years later, the then little-known Daniel arap Moi: 'Moi stood up and spoke to the relevant points, introducing them with an immense snap of his fingers ... which penetrated the room like the crack of a whip.' Moi was clearly beginning to make an impression and, after the conference, Ron Jones, writing under his political nom de plume Paul Pry, published a lengthy interview headed, 'The formidable Daniel arap Moi'. The story, perhaps the first and last face-to-face interview Moi ever gave the *Nation*, described him as 'a proud man, perhaps an autocratic cum aristocratic man'. It added, 'What is striking about Moi is the manner in which there comes through his conversation on politics his own clear-cut conviction that he knows where he and his Kalenjin people are going and on that basis will be decided Kenya's future.' A wider view was that Mboya was the crucial figure at the London talks in both 1960 and 1962. Jack Ensoll, who covered the conference for the *Sunday Post*, said:

> *Tom was the hard man. He would not join in the joint Press conferences which were actually Colonial Office briefings and were pathetic. We all knew where to go the following morning, Dean Street in Soho, some office where Tom was a friend and we all used to pour in there at about 7.30 am and get the word. He was such a good operator and a good politician. He was extremely clear-sighted, he was going to have none of this multiracial stuff. [Kwame] Nkrumah influenced him and the Yanks financed him. The Colonial Office couldn't stand up to Mboya.*

With independence over the horizon, emotions in Kenya were reaching fever pitch. The settlers were angry, either packing to leave or trying to decide; non-settler Europeans and many Asians were apprehensive; Africans were frantically excited. Peter McCardle, a young British police inspector, recalled in an interview, 'As independence approached, you would sometimes see Africans on bicycles holding cockerels by the legs and shouting, "*Moto moto*". (The cockerel was the KANU symbol and *moto* meant 'hot' or 'fire'.) McCardle said:

> Moto moto *could actually mean a hell of a lot of things but to me it*
> *meant, 'We've got the power, we're the lads.' But I recognised they*
> *were happy. After the big rallies, the police were sent down on*
> *motorbikes to sit at street corners in pitch blackness when people were*
> *going home happy, back to the locations. If there had been any*
> *ugliness we would have revved out of there but I never remember a*
> *single occasion being threatened by the enthusiasm that came when*
> uhuru *was creeping up.*

Lorry-loads of ululating women or chanting men would sweep past the Thorn Tree Cafe after Sunday rallies, and Europeans at the tables would raise fist or finger to return whatever was the appropriate party symbol (finger, KANU; fist, KADU). The atmosphere was nevertheless combustible and there came two defining moments: separate appearances by Mboya and Kenyatta in front of settler audiences at Eldoret and Nakuru respectively.

Speaking in the lions' den of settlerdom on 23 July 1962, Mboya referred to a remark that had dogged him for years. In 1958, as chairman of the All African People's Conference in Accra, Ghana, Mboya told the white man to 'scram out of Africa'. The text makes plain that he was referring not to individuals but to colonial rule. In Eldoret, he said:

> *Sometimes I get it thrown at me that when all the Europeans have*
> *'scrammed out of Africa', these farm workers will simply join the*
> *queue of unemployed and how do I like that? Others tell their*
> *discharged workers to 'go and get a job from Kenyatta or Mboya'.*
> *People who say this kind of thing seem to me to combine vicious*
> *irresponsibility with a peculiar kind of despair. It is an odd moral*
> *outlook that would use unemployment as the currency in a game of*
> *politics and people of this kind are beyond any reach of sympathy*
> *from me.*

Mboya told the settlers, 'Your security fears will disappear when the people can see that you are working towards a goal that everybody wants to reach, for rewards we can all share. If you accept us, you are with us.' But it was his next remark that made the headlines: 'On the attainment of our independence, all who were formerly non-Africans must become full citizens of Kenya … if you are not prepared to be citizens of Kenya, there will be no place for you here, except as aliens.' Many Europeans saw this statement as a sign of their future subjugation. Mboya ended, 'To date, our people have been dragged through history. Henceforth we will write our own history.'

It was Kenyatta, a year later in the Town Hall at Nakuru, unofficial capital of the White Highlands, who delivered the assurances the Europeans had been looking for. By then prime minister, he told 500 white farmers and their families, 'We want you to stay and to farm and to farm well in this country. I beg you to believe that this is the policy of the government.' Reminding his audience that he, too, was a farmer, he said, 'We have something in common, the soil. The most dangerous thing for Kenya is suspicion and fear. We must learn to forgive one another.' He also alleviated fears about citizenship. It would be open to anyone, he said, and there would be a two-year period for people to make up their minds. (Mboya had later described Britons as a special case and in the event, no non-African was ever required to take up citizenship.) The audience repeatedly applauded and joined Kenyatta in the 'pull-together' dockers' chant of *Harambee!* The correspondent of *The Times* of London reported, 'The Prime Minister succeeded in putting himself across so well, the farmers complimented him with prolonged applause.' Reuter's story said, 'Five hundred white farmers stamped, clapped and cheered as Mr Kenyatta said, "I am sincere when I say we want you to stay. I was imprisoned but I forgive you. Please forgive me, too".' Ensoll commented in an unpublished memoir, 'What Jomo Kenyatta said that day changed the course of Kenya's history and won many European converts.'

With Whitehall and the Nairobi politicians negotiating feverishly on crucial issues such as the final form of the constitution and compensation to white farmers, there was one awkward figure on the landscape – Sir Patrick Renison. The Governor's description of Kenyatta as 'an African leader to darkness and death' had angered not only Africans but Iain Macleod, who considered sacking Renison at the time but did not want to antagonise the Europeans further. It was not the first time Renison and Macleod had been at odds. Alastair Matheson recalled getting a telephone call at three o'clock in the morning: 'I'm Sir Patrick Renison, I want to know if that press release I gave you has been published.' Matheson told him, yes, that the Nairobi papers had gone to press long ago. The Governor commented, 'I'm glad. Iain Macleod didn't want it in but I wanted it in.' Renison, a one-time district commissioner and a dyed-in-the-wool civil servant (he would refer to 'my service' and 'you politicians'), had a good record as a governor in the Caribbean and was admired as a person of utmost integrity. But he was now clearly the wrong man in the wrong place at the wrong time. When he was finally eased out, the coverage of his departure reflected intriguing differences between the *Standard* and the *Nation*.

Arnold Raphael, the *Standard's* London correspondent, said:

> *To give you an example of the positive approach by the* Nation *and the* Standard's *crippling timidity, I was told by highly reliable official sources that the Macmillan government was going to sack Renison. He was quite unsuited to the turbulence of constitutional politics in Nairobi and if anything, he was retarding the independence process. London had lost patience. It was past my deadline when I got wind of this in Whitehall. I sent an immediate Telex to Nairobi and followed it up with a telephone call. By Fleet Street standards, it was no great scoop but in Nairobi it ranked second only to Kenyatta's release. But Kenneth Bolton, hard as it is to believe, absolutely refused to run the story, even on a watered-down basis. Bolton was very close to Government House, indeed a friend of Renison, and he couldn't believe he would not have heard of this development. The* Standard *had good people like Ken Meadows and Eric Marsden but the story didn't fit for Bolton. He could not bring himself to accept that London was quite simply giving the Governor the push. I gather there was near mutiny on the* Standard *news desk when the editor spiked the story. Of course it got out, probably when the* Standard *reporters vented their frustration over late-night drinks, and the* Nation *replated with Renison as the lead story. Where the* Standard *hesitated, the* Nation *acted. It was entirely in character for both papers and encapsulated the difference between them.*

John Bierman's was a different version, but it confirmed Raphael's perception of the two papers' attitudes:

> *I got a tip, I think from Richard Kisch who was our London correspondent, that Renison was going to be replaced. He was in London to confer with the Colonial Secretary and we sat up all night waiting for confirmation and it never came. I had arranged to do a special edition and we had the front page all set up and I was waiting for the phone call to say it had actually happened but it never came. But I was so sure it was going to happen and happen that day that I went out on a limb and said, Print. We put out four or five thousand copies and they were on the streets of Nairobi by mid-morning, a*

*Saturday. And we were right, it was true. It was an incredibly rash*
*and chancy thing to do and I would never dream of doing it now, but*
*we looked really good and stuck it to the* Standard. *That was half my*
*motivation, to stick it to those pompous bastards.*

The *Standard* did carry a brief item in its Stop Press column, but when *The Times* put out its own story, it quoted 'reports in the *East African Standard*'. (*The Times* habitually referred to the *Standard* by its title, while describing the *Nation* as 'a Nairobi morning newspaper'.)

Considering the hauteur which had always been directed towards the *Nation* by the occupants of the Palladian-style mansion known as 'GH', the paper was generous about Renison's dismissal and carried a sympathetic editorial, saying, 'We offer sincere condolences for the abrupt and ungracious way in which his loyal and steadfast services have been terminated.' In announcing that Renison would be replaced by Malcolm MacDonald, Colonial Secretary Duncan Sandys sought to rationalise the change by saying the Governor's duties henceforth would 'assume more of a political and diplomatic than an administrative character'. It was the end of Renison's career. Back in London he became vice-chairman of the British Red Cross and an adviser on sport and physical education to the Conservative Party grandee Lord Hailsham. He retired soon after and died in 1965, aged only 54.

On the final lap to *uhuru*, Sandys' appointment of MacDonald as Kenya's last governor was a brilliant one. Son of Britain's first Labour Prime Minister, Ramsay MacDonald, Malcolm had entered Parliament in 1931, been Colonial Secretary in his 30s, and held high diplomatic posts in Canada and East Asia. He was short, buck-toothed, a known womaniser, an easy and congenial mixer and a brilliant talker. He arrived in Kenya in January 1963 with instructions to get a final constitution hammered out and open the way to independence. Raphael observed:

*He was given a knife and he put it to the throats of the Africans and*
*the Europeans. As soon as he got off the plane, he ordered suppers to*
*be laid on at Government House and he kept all the politicians there*
*working on the constitution and wouldn't let anyone leave until the*
*work was done. He got independence through by force of his*
*personality and his pushing and shoving.*

The plan was for an election in the autumn of 1963, internal self-government immediately afterwards and full independence by the end of

1964. Fearing African impatience and probable extremism, MacDonald persuaded Sandys to speed up the timetable, with elections set for May 1963, internal self-rule on 1 June and independence in December. He organised meetings of the Council of Ministers at Government House three days a week, with three sessions a day, instead of one morning a week under Renison. 'Our toil was long and hard', MacDonald wrote in his book *Titans & Others*.[13] Lunch was served after the morning meeting, tea in the afternoon, and a buffet supper was set out before the evening meeting at the table where the negotiators worked. Drinks were also served. MacDonald wrote:

> *Only once did a solitary African minister imbibe too much and I received the unanimous support of all his sober colleagues when I ruled him out of order every time he opened his mouth to make a sozzled contribution. After three attempts, he lay his head on his arms and fell asleep. Otherwise, whisky, gin and liqueurs were consumed, but Kenyatta never took anything except an occasional cup of tea or a glass of Coca-Cola. As for drinking himself to death, I had never known any judge who stayed more sober.*

The 248-page constitutional instrument, which weighed 14 ounces, was tabled as an Order in Council in April. The *Daily Nation* described the document as 'the most complicated colonial constitution ever produced' and welcomed it for its 'built-in safeguards for individual liberty and positive brakes upon the ambitions of a dictator'. But the leading article cautioned, 'Just as constitutions can be written on paper, they can likewise be torn up and we place our ultimate trust upon the character of the men who will assume power.' This trust was soon and consistently to be betrayed. The regionalism of the constitution was watered down both then and at a final constitutional conference in September and October, when the powers of the centre over the police and the civil service were strengthened. Mboya made his own views clear when he remarked caustically, 'Regional authorities will have a status inferior to that of Nairobi City Council.' Indeed, less than a year after independence, constitutional amendments transformed the prime minister into a strong executive president and turned the regions into provinces headed by colonial-style provincial commissioners – even down to the green-lined solar topees – appointed by the President. *Majimboism* was no more.

Mboya was by now married to Pamela Odede, the beautiful daughter of Walter Odede, a comrade-in-arms of Kenyatta (up-and-coming lawyer-politician Charles Njonjo was best man), and had moved from his small house in Pumwani to a handsome new residence in Nairobi's Lavington sub-urb. At a cocktail party there shortly before the 18 May election, the *Nation's* chief reporter Bill Harris, like many Europeans sympathetic to KADU, ven-tured the opinion that Ngala's party would win. Mboya looked at him under lowered eyelids – a habit that helped give him his reputation for arrogance – and said, 'Bill, it will be a KANU landslide.' It very nearly was. Paul Ngei, another of the accused Mau Mau hardcore, had defected from KANU to form his own African People's Party in alliance with KADU (he was soon to return), but, even without the support of Ngei's Kamba people, KANU won a decisive two-thirds of the vote. Kenyatta formed a strong government with wide tribal representation and became Kenya's first prime minister on 1 June, Madaraka Day, ushering in self-rule. The political pundits peered into a glass darkly and saw little more than their own reflection. In a leader page article in the London *Daily Telegraph* titled, 'Kenya after Kenyatta', Nairobi correspondent John Osman declared, 'The first problem facing the victors in Kenya's election is to decide on a successor to their 73-year-old Prime Minister.' He favoured Mboya or Odinga. It was a classic case of the outsider misreading Africa and its political and cultural dynamics, further fuel for Ng'weno's despair over Western coverage of the continent.

The election was a landmark for the *Nation*, too. It marked the only time in its history to date that the newspaper endorsed a political party. On 25 May, the eve of polling for what would be the Lower House of the National Assembly, an editorial in the *Daily Nation* bore the headline 'KANU for Kenya!' It gave four reasons: KANU had better leaders; they would be more successful at achieving an East African Federation; internal security would be more likely with KANU in power than in opposition; and KANU's cen-tralist approach to government was more realistic than KADU's reliance on ever more regionalism. The editorial explained, 'We believe it is the duty of an independent newspaper in a free society to make its views known. The *Nation* believes that editorial fence-sitting at such a vital moment is the negation of a true newspaper's function. It therefore urges its readers this weekend to support the Kenya African National Union.' The editorial warned, however, 'Our preference for one party at this moment in 1963 does not imply that this support will be maintained indefinitely.' Given the *Nation's* oft-reiterated concerns about quality leadership, it is unsurprising that Michael Curtis plumped for KANU (even if the edito-rial predicted only a narrow win). That the paper never again endorsed a particular party clearly has more to do with the dismal record of

Kenya's political operatives than with any principled reluctance to follow the 1963 precedent.

As the last problems concerning the handover of power were ironed out, including the setting aside of large sums of money to buy out the European farms for sale to Africans, Kenya began to take on a sense of black nationhood. Ian Raitt, who was doing public relations for the Pyrethrum Board, remembers organising a function at City Hall attended by Kenyatta: 'There were four or five old African women in bare feet and some expatriate official at City Hall wanted me to throw them out. I'm glad I didn't because one of them was a member of Kenyatta's family. I learned a lesson that day: everyone is important in the new Africa.'

By then, Charles Rubia had become the first African Mayor of Nairobi, the Nairobi Club opened its doors to all races and Secretary F.J. Hollister announced that the Muthaiga Club would rewrite its constitution to do the same. Lord Delamere's statue disappeared quietly from Delamere Avenue, which was renamed Kenyatta Avenue; 20 October was proclaimed Kenyatta Day to mark Jomo's arrest 11 years earlier; Charles Njonjo was appointed Attorney-General; and the *Nation* had already recruited its first African director, Mareka Gecaga. The national flag was unveiled – a shield and crossed spears on a red, black and green background – and Mboya said, 'We appeal to the public not to fly the national flag on bicycles and so forth, we do not want to see it made of some cheap material in River Road.' Waiters swapped their kanzus, cummerbunds, tarbooshes and brocaded waistcoats for jackets, trousers and bow ties; nobody said 'Boy' any more and Britain's Prince Philip accepted an invitation to preside over the lowering of the Union Jack on 12 December 1963.

Of the many African nations that won their independence in the 1960s, Kenya was the star in Western eyes. This was, after all, the country of Mau Mau, Jomo (Burning Spear) Kenyatta as Fleet Street always named him, the Lord Erroll murder, Elsa the Lioness and the maneaters of Tsavo, the 'Lunatic Line' between Mombasa and Uganda, aviatrix Beryl Markham, white hunters and the Happy Valley crowd. Little of this was germane to the reality of Kenya in 1963 but nobody cared. Harry Belafonte and Miriam Makeba sang, 1,200 dancers danced, the Corps of Drums of the Kenya Army drummed (24 hours earlier they had been the King's African Rifles) and the lights at Uhuru Stadium dimmed at midnight. Prince Philip reportedly whispered to Kenyatta, 'Are you sure you won't change your mind?' The Prime Minister declined and two British officers lowered the Union flag in total darkness. According to David Barnett's report, 'a moment later the lights blazed on again and the Kenya flag was slowly raised in its place'. 'Kenya free' trumpeted the 72-point headline on the *Daily Nation's* front page, issue number 791. The founder and proprietor celebrated his 27th birthday the following day.

## *Notes*

1. Much of the negotiation concerning Malawi's independence took place between Banda and Butler's successor, Iain Macleod. When a reporter told Macleod's wife that Banda was to make another of his then frequent visits to Britain, she commented, 'Oh, dear Dr Banda!' Unfortunately, the British newspaper transposed the comma, so her remark read, 'Oh dear, Dr Banda!'
2. A distinguished BBC correspondent, Gerald Priestland, once wrote, 'Reporters are addressed as Gentlemen of the Press in the vain hope that they will behave as such, rather than as a statement of fact.'
3. Fashion attitudes seemed not to have changed much 15 years later when Violet Anyango joined the company as personal assistant to Albert Ekirapa. She said, 'I liked to put on trouser suits but they said, Not for an executive's office. Mr Ekirapa found it very difficult to talk to me about it, so Vic Onan, MD of our company, Kenya Litho, did, in a very nice way. After that, I went about in very long skirts.'
4. *The Time of My Life* by Denis Healey, Michael Joseph, London, 1989.
5. *White Man's Country* by Elspeth Huxley, Chatto & Windus, London, 1935.
6. *Iain Macleod* by Nigel Fisher, Andre Deutsch Ltd, London, 1973.
7. *A Love Affair with the Sun* by Sir Michael Blundell, Kenway Publications Ltd, Nairobi, 1994.
8. *So Rough a Wind* by Sir Michael Blundell, Weidenfeld and Nicholson, London, 1964.
9. These were large sums for the place and time. The approximate equivalents today can be found by multiplying by ten.
10. *Corridors of Wire* by Terence Gavaghan, A.H. Stockwell Ltd, Ilfracombe, North Devon, 1998.
11. *States of Emergency* by Alastair Matheson, Media Matters, Nairobi, 1992.
12. *A Love Affair with the Sun.*
13. *Titans & Others* by Malcolm MacDonald, William Collins & Co. Ltd, London, 1972.

# Squeeze on Democratic Space

*Were it left to me to decide whether we should have a government without newspapers or newspapers with-out a government, I should not hesitate a moment to prefer the latter.*

US President Thomas Jefferson (1743–1826)

It was in Tel Aviv, with independence back home still two-and-a-half years off, that Michael Curtis made a prescient statement about the problems Kenya's newspapers were likely to face. Addressing the annual assembly of the International Press Institute, he said, 'I am under no illusions that the toughest pressures will come when Kenya and the rest of East Africa are free of colonial rule and when relatively young and inexperienced politicians will expect the newspapers to support them in all circumstances in the interests of national solidarity.' The flak he was already receiving from Kenya's African politicians left him in little doubt about what to expect when they assumed power. Within months of the three nations securing their independence, Uganda established a Press Censorship Board, Tanganyika deported a *Nation* journalist and banned the paper, and Kenya expelled a stream of journalists, as well as the Kenya-born Asian manager of a Mombasa cinema, who was sent packing to India, a place he had never been, because he failed to show a film of the independence celebrations. In his speech in Israel, Curtis expressed sympathy for the new African leaders, 'unaccustomed to their authority, uncertain of the extent or limitations of their powers and trying hard to create a sense of national unity'. Aggrieved deportees, how-ever, saw no reluctance by the new ministers to use their power, perceiving it as simple retribution, official bungling or muzzling of the truth. Sometimes, the authorities simply got the wrong person.

Best remembered by journalists of the time was the famous 'trick that hastened independence'. At a rally in Kisumu on 2 August 1964, Kenyatta, speaking in Kiswahili, said sources had told him that if Kenya federated with Uganda and Tanganyika, she would assuredly get her independence from Britain. So he invited Presidents Nyerere and Obote to Nairobi on 5 June 1963, and within an hour they signed an agreement to federate on condition Kenya got its independence before federation came into being. The official Kenya News Agency quoted Kenyatta further: 'The British, not knowing the trick to this, invited me to London for talks on independence and that's why independence was accelerated.' When Nyerere learned of this speech he protested that he had signed the declaration 'in all honesty'. The Nairobi government thereupon denied the agreement was a ruse, reaffirmed faith in the federation and said the word Kenyatta used was not trick, 'a malicious fabrication by mischief-makers', but 'ingenuity'. Kenyatta's comments made little sense anyway, since it was always intended that the three territories would only join in a federation as independent nations.

On 5 August, the Minister for Home Affairs, Oginga Odinga, ordered Richard Kisch, formerly the *Nation's* man in London but now the Nairobi correspondent of the Tanganyika government daily, *The Nationalist*, to leave the country within 24 hours for 'misreporting the Prime Minister's speech'. Many newspapers had used 'trick', including the *Daily Nation*, which put the word in its headline, 'PM tells of trick'. Nyerere's reaction had embarrassed Kenyatta, but singling out Kisch was baffling and most journalists saw the hand of Information Minister Achieng Oneko in the affair, firing a warning shot across the bows of the entire Press corps. Simultaneous with Kisch's expulsion, Odinga ordered out Ian Henderson, a third-generation Kenyan who had hunted down Mau Mau forest leader Dedan Kimathi, and two British civil servants, Walter Whitehead and Gordon Hender, on grounds that their continued presence was 'contrary to the interests of national security'. In a *Nation* commentary, James Ngugi, who later achieved fame as the radical novelist Ngugi wa Thiong'o, said the government had every right to deport undesirables, but any failure to give an explanation would start a whispering campaign that could damage the country's image.

The dubious honour of being independent Kenya's first deportee, on 22 January 1964, just 41 days after *uhuru*, went to the *Nation's* Tony Dunn. He was followed by Richard Cox of the London *Sunday Times*. In July, while Kenyatta was out of the country, Odinga expelled the Assistant Police Commissioner, Leslie Pridgeon, as 'the beginning of a clearout of ill-intentioned imperialist elements'. His boss, Inspector General of Police Sir

Richard Catling, and 30 of his fellow officers gathered defiantly at the airport to bid Pridgeon an ostentatiously public farewell, and Catling's job was Africanised shortly afterwards. Richard Beeston and Douglas Brown of the *Daily* and *Sunday Telegraph* were respectively expelled and barred just before Christmas, taking to nine the number of Britons made *persona non grata* in the first year of independence.

Ironically, Dunn was kicked out for reportage that had nothing to do with Kenya. The part Arab/part African island of Zanzibar became independent two days before Kenya itself and was soon in turmoil. Dunn was the *Nation's* bureau manager in Dar es Salaam and blamed the Tanganyikan politician Bibi Titi Mohammed: 'She went to Zanzibar and made a speech saying the Arabs had a history of slitting open the bellies of pregnant African women and murdering the babies. It was rabble-rousing hysterical, insurrectionist rubbish. She was dropped by Nyerere straight away but the damage was done, she had inflamed African passions and they were inflamed enough anyway.' Sporadic violence against Arabs and Asians was reported, then rumours reached Dar that armed men had landed on the island. Dunn recalled in an interview:

> This was the infamous 'Field Marshal' John Okello, a Ugandan. He led a landing party of just six men with rifles (other accounts say 20) and they attacked the Central Police Station. The British Commissioner of Police panicked. If he had known the scale of the enemy, he could have arrested the lot of them in half an hour but by then Okello had the African mobs marching and they turned on the Arabs.

Dunn discounts reports of thousands killed: 'I was there and it was more like tens than thousands. They seem to add a nought every year.' The upshot was that the new Sultan of Zanzibar, whose father had died a few months earlier, fled to Dar on his yacht and the African politicians seized control of the island, proclaiming the People's Republic of Zanzibar.

Dunn raced back to Dar es Salaam in time to cover Okello's arrival there to a hero's welcome. Tanganyika had become independent in December 1961 and had rapidly Africanised its police force, but not yet its military. 'The army was seething with discontent', Dunn recalled, 'and Okello latched on to this and went round the barracks making speeches. The army mutinied, arrested their British officers and held them in the barracks. The soldiers then went for Nyerere at the old Governor's House but his security men smuggled him out of the back door and the American embassy hid him there for three days.' Dunn said, 'I was the only journalist living on the mainland. All the other hacks were over the bridge in Dar and couldn't file, so I had the story to myself. I was reporting for the *Nation* and for our Kiswahili daily *Mwafrika* and filing for the BBC as well. I was jumping from house to house wherever there was a telephone.'

Dunn recalled:

> *I managed to get into the office and got a teleprinter up. We did a special edition for the* Nation *which hit the streets in Nairobi and also got to Moshi and Arusha. Derek Bryceson, who was the only white minister in the cabinet, warned me that I was skating on very thin ice. There were rumours Nyerere had been assassinated and I said I knew he had not been, that he was in the American embassy and the best thing he could do was make a broadcast. We agreed that I should try to put out a proper accurate account of the mutiny on the BBC, so I went to the radio station. It was being held by the rebels but they let me in and let me do a piece which specifically said Nyerere was alive and well and in command, which was a direct quote from his spokesman ten minutes earlier. I thought I had been great doing all this but when I got back to my house, the gendarmes were waiting for me. Minutes later, I was banged up in the police station. They said I had to be out of the country in 12 hours because I had reported Nyerere was assassinated. I had said exactly the opposite and I showed them my cables, but they wanted me out. I was the only one with filing facilities and direct access to the BBC. They just wanted to shut my voice.*

Since there were no scheduled flights, Dunn chartered a plane to Nairobi. But he said, 'The minute I got off at Embakasi airport, the Kenyans arrested me and I was back in pokey. I had planned to report to Michael Curtis for reassignment and here I was deported twice from two different countries.' Curtis and Hayes drove to the airport but were not allowed to speak to Dunn. All they could do was stand unhappily on the departure balcony and wave. Dunn was being deported to a British winter clad in shorts and a shirt with only East African currency in his wallet. General Manager Bob Petty gave some sterling to space saleswoman Hilda Bell, with instructions to get into the transit lounge and pass it on. She recalled, 'I had to charm my way into transit and hug and kiss this man I had never seen before just like he was an old friend and slip the money to him.' Before embarking, Dunn opened his portable typewriter and tapped out a final dispatch:

> *My Dear Michael, I am writing this at the airport where the*
> *Immigration chaps have taken me under their wing ... I am most*
> *sincerely sorry this has happened, not just from my own point of view*
> *but because of the effect it has on our standing with the government*
> *... I think they simply decided I had been there too long and knew too*
> *much ... I want to thank you very much for all you have done and*
> *tried to do on this black day. My friends were marvellous and the*
> *German, French and American ambassadors all made*
> *representations, plus of course Britain ... Nyerere knew nothing of the*
> *decision until after it had been taken.*

In the obsessive way of editors, Dunn added, 'Tell Muthusi that all the copy for the next edition is on the table opposite my desk and that the annual meeting of the Plantation Workers' Union should be the splash.'

Dunn was expelled from Kenya under an inter-government agreement that any person deported from one of the three East African nations was automatically *persona non grata* in the others. The *Nation* Board of Directors sent a strong protest to the Tanganyika government and the daily reproduced a BBC cable which said, 'BBC deny any broadcast reporting Nyerere dead and therefore exonerate Dunn all blame alleged misreporting stop Director General BBC cabling denial to Nyerere personally and asking revocation expulsion order.' The order never was revoked and Dunn went on to become a senior editor with the BBC World Service, as well as the *Nation's* London correspondent under the name Anthony Denton. But problems with Tanganyika were far from over.

Six days after the expulsion, Nyerere banned the *Nation* for 'distorting the news about Tanganyika', and Home Affairs Minister Job Lusinde said anyone found with copies of the paper would be prosecuted. The daily was then selling 3,000 in Tanganyika and the Sunday 5,000, and the accountants predicted a monthly loss of £1,000, a severe blow to a heavily loss-making company. What's more, advertising had to be reduced by two shillings per single column inch. The ban had nothing to do with Dunn. When Curtis managed to secure a meeting with Nyerere, the President explained that Lusinde had brought him a *Sunday Nation* with an article by Dunn which they both agreed was excellent and very fair. Nyerere said he had always liked Dunn, 'though he did make some enemies in my cabinet'. However, Nyerere then leafed through the paper and was angered by the editorial which, in essence, abrogated higher pay for the army at a time when the issue still had not been settled with the mutineers. Curtis recalled, 'We were not aware of this at the time, since Tony had been deported two days earlier, and the general impression in Nairobi, where the editorial was written, was that Oscar Kambona, the minister, had conceded the demands and the issue was out of the way.' Curtis tried to explain the problems of reporting on complex events 600 miles away without your own correspondent, and Nyerere gave the impression that he regretted the whole business. But he felt 'tempers must be allowed to calm a little' before the ban was lifted, which happened six months later.

When the Zanzibar and Tanganyika troubles broke out, the *Nation's* editorial of 23 January spoke of a 'wave of fear throughout East Africa' and said, 'The question on every tongue is, "Can it happen here?" ' The answer came in the next two issues, 'UK troops fly to Uganda' and 'Shooting at KR Camp'. In Uganda, Interior Minister Felix Onama was taken prisoner by men of the Uganda Rifles at Jinja Barracks demanding a pay increase, and at President Obote's request seven planeloads of British soldiers flew in from Kenya and secured the country, releasing the minister. In Kenya, shooting broke out at the Lanet Barracks of 11 Kenya Rifles on the outskirts of Nairobi, and men from Britain's 3rd Royal Horse Artillery, stationed nearby, were marched at the double into the KR lines while guards were placed on Embakasi Airport and the Kenya Broadcasting Corporation building. Tanganyika, too, sought and received British military help, and order was soon restored in all three countries. In none of the mainland countries was the military unrest in any sense an attempted coup d'etat. Only on Zanzibar was a change of rule effected, and that in an unpremeditated fashion. But the African leaders were embarrassed at having to call for help from the old colonial power so soon after independence – Nyerere called it 'our national humiliation' – and, with the Congo currently aflame, the mutinies dented confidence in East Africa at a time when nation-building and inward investment were priorities.

On 16 April, the *Daily Nation* reported one of those statements, akin to a football chairman's vote of confidence in his manager, that makes the blood of journalists run cold: 'I wish to state that the Press as a whole will continue to enjoy their freedom, as has been shown since we took over the government. The government will *never* change its policy of freedom of speech and the Press.' The speaker was Information Minister Oneko and the occasion was the takeover by the government of the Kenya Broadcasting Corporation

(KBC), to be known in future as the Voice of Kenya (VOK). Inevitably, the statement coincided with government moves to tighten its control over the media, a policy which was pursued with single-minded intent and increasing success over the years. The *Nation* had connections with KBC going back to the days when it was the Kenya Broadcasting Service (KBS) and heavily reliant on the BBC for management and programming. The relationship was not always a happy one. Because KBS had no news-gathering operation of its own, it bought local coverage from the *Standard* and the *Nation*. What irked Curtis was that the *Standard* received £2,000 per annum for a six-day service (having no Sunday paper at the time), while the *Nation* got £1,200 for a seven-day service. When Curtis protested, KBS Director Patrick Jubb assured him the *Nation's* fee would be increased to £2,000 by the end of 1963. In fact, the *Nation's* fee increased to only £1,500, while the *Standard's* went up to £2,350. Shortly afterwards, Jubb cancelled the *Nation* service. The *Nation* thus greeted the announcement that KBC would become a department of government without regret, noting that its financial problems – a deficit of £71,000 on the television service which started only in 1962 and one of £21,000 on radio – made such a move inevitable. The newspaper only hoped that VOK would be amenable to public opinion. It was not to know that the national broadcaster would turn into a sycophantic handmaiden of government, an obstacle to democracy and at times a vituperative enemy of the Press itself.

What concerned the *Nation's* managers more at this time was that Reuters news agency had removed the rights to receive and retransmit its service from the *Standard* and sold them to the recently formed government-controlled Kenya News Agency (KNA). Curtis reported to his board that the government had asked the *Nation* to subscribe to the Reuter service at a cost of £2,160 per year. The paper was already taking the Associated Press world wire, but he felt the company could not refuse. It would also get the Tass report from Moscow free – not a particularly generous gesture since the Soviets were not charging the government in the first place. The *Nation* asked only for guarantees that the two services would be clearly identified. Under the new deal, the Reuters file of international stories was transmitted to KNA which distributed it, after editing, to subscribing newspapers and radio stations. Eric Marsden, who ran the *Standard's* syndication department, recalled:

> *The government promised that the changeover wouldn't affect coverage, but it did. KNA held everything up and rewrote stories.*

*They looked for anything political like Moise Tshombe in the Congo –*
*he was their arch-traitor – and they inserted things about Ian Smith,*
*'racist' and so on, and then they crossed out Reuters and put KNA*
*and eventually you would get it. I complained that we could not get*
*our early pages done, non-controversial stuff, features and so on, and*
*could we get that direct? But no, it all had to come through KNA. We*
*had a real rebellion in the office over this. The* Nation *was also taking*
*AP so they had an alternative.*

Reuters, later to become a massively profitable provider of financial information, was making a concerted drive for clients in Africa at the time, and
by 1965 had contracts with many independent states, earning £175,000 per
year from English-speaking Africa. General Manager Gerald Long said the
governments were required 'to preserve the integrity and identity of the
Reuter news service when issuing it internally'.[1] Whatever attempts were
made to enforce this policy certainly did not work in Kenya. Marsden said,
'We felt we had been sold down the river by Reuters. I never had any regard
for them after that.'

Alastair Matheson, who had transferred within the information ministry
to the VOK, remembers Oneko 'breathing down our necks to use as much
Tass as possible', even when it was a day late reporting its own sputnik space
triumph. There was also a list of epithets to denigrate white-ruled South
Africa and Rhodesia, with 'racist-minority' required to precede both.
Matheson insists he heard a newsreader say, 'In Salisbury today, rebel leader
Ian Smith declared, "My racist-minority government will not tolerate..."' On
the day Belgian paratroops were dropped into Stanleyville (Kisangani) in
the Congo, KNA withheld all of Reuter's incoming accounts of the Paras'
clash with the Simba guerrillas and a subsequent massacre of white
hostages. Bravely, the Kenya Union of Journalists deplored the 'flagrant contravention by the government of the Bill of Rights and its provision on freedom of expression in deliberately suppressing Reuters' news on the
paratroop landings'. It added that the union 'once again affirms its belief that
the sale by an international news agency of its news service with the sole
rights to government is bad in principle and in practice, as these events have
proved'. That same month, Oneko tightened his grip on VOK by setting up
an editorial board with himself as chairman 'to advise the newsroom staff on
Kenya's policy'. According to a diplomat then serving in Nairobi, Oneko
decreed that the name of the country should be pronounced over the air as
Ken-ya, not Keen-ya, and when a popular broadcaster, David Dunlop,

refused he was deported. Meanwhile in London, Kenya's High Commissioner, J.N. Karanja, said, 'There is no Press censorship in Kenya. We have one of the freest Presses in the world.'

Dick Beeston, the *Daily Telegraph's* man in Nairobi, got hold of instructions which had been issued to KNA journalists on how to process Reuter copy. They included a directive that any story critical of Kenya had to be referred to the chief editor, who normally killed it. The *Telegraph* published the entire memo. A few months later, Beeston was leaning over the KNA teleprinter when he spotted an item saying he had been given 24 hours to leave the country. It was the first he had heard of it. The reason was a story in the *Sunday Telegraph* which had been written by his colleague, Douglas Brown, while Beeston was in Ethiopia. It claimed that Odinga was receiving weapons from Communist China and hiding them in the basement of the Interior Ministry. Oneko described the *Telegraph* as 'a dirty paper' and said, 'When the time comes to exercise control over the Press, no-one should come weeping and crying that the country was tough.' Brown, who had already left Kenya, was refused re-entry, and Beeston said, 'I was deported for an article I didn't write.'[2] It is difficult to believe his disclosure of KNA's editorial practices was not a factor.

At Nation House, things were changing. The Earl of Portsmouth had early taken a seat on the board of directors alongside Mareka Gecaga, adding aristocratic respectability to indigenous representation, while the drive for ever more Africanisation and the end-of-an-epoch feeling brought about by *uhuru* saw the departure of several pioneers. When Chhotu Karadia wrote a positive review of J.M. Kariuki's book, *Mau Mau Detainee*, his fellow reporters Mike Harris and Meinard Donker, both of whom had served in the Kenya security forces, protested angrily and asked to be released from their contracts. Their resignations were accepted. Bill Harris and Ron Jones departed without warning for South Africa and Bierman accepted an editorship in Trinidad. 'The *Nation* by then was firmly established', he said, 'and I felt that after independence I would come under, to me, unacceptable though probably necessary, pressure to curb my professional pugnacity'.[3]

Curtis was determined to appoint an African editor and set off on a talent-spotting trip to Harare (then still Salisbury), Johannesburg, Accra, Lagos and London. A Sierra Leonean in London was offered the post but wanted more than two years – by which time Curtis hoped Kenyans would be clamouring for the job. An offer was made to a Ghanaian but he failed to respond, and eventually a Briton, Graham Rees, was recruited from a newspaper in West Africa. An accomplished and mild-mannered journalist, Rees held the fort until Hilary Ng'weno joined in 1964. Charles Hayes, worried that the *Nation* was following too radical a path, moved to African Life Publications as managing editor and founded and edited the glossy *Africana* magazine. Later Hayes quit and bought an island in Lake Naivasha, and in the late 1970s he emigrated to Canada with his writer–photographer wife, Margaret, formerly the *Nation's* stringer in Nakuru. There they returned to journalism, running their own weekly newspaper in British Columbia, the *South Okanagan Review*, for 16 years.

Already on board in Nairobi were three major players – Boaz Omori, Jack Beverley and Joe Rodrigues. Hayes had spotted Omori clerking for the Kenya Dairy Board in Thomson's Falls (Nyahururu) in 1956 and brought him into journalism. Between spells with *Baraza* and VOK, he was a widely admired editor of *Taifa Leo* and became Editor-in-Chief of Nation Newspapers, the first to hold this title. Beverley, who had been Curtis' assistant editor at the *News Chronicle*, was hired as managing editor of the *Sunday Nation* and ran the paper with extraordinary vigour and a stream of innovative ideas, one of which secured him a niche in *Nation* folklore. When the first photographs were taken of the moon's surface and a promised wire-service picture failed to arrive, Beverley used a close-up of a Ryvita biscuit. The image was infinitely sharper than the blurred lunar pictures used by the rest of the world. Rodrigues, who was to become a pivotal figure in the *Nation* story, was a Mumbai-born Kenyan Goan, actually named Jawaharlal after India's Prime Minister Nehru. His father, an editorial executive with the *Times of India* and the *Indian Express*, was a committed nationalist, and when he requested that the boy be named Jawaharlal, his shocked parish priest, the Jesuit Father Ghazzie, refused. Goans, after all, were Christians and their names should be Christian, too. After a five-month standoff, the priest backed down, a new baptismal ceremony was arranged, and thus did the future Editor-in-Chief of Nation Newspapers become Jawaharlal Joachim Joel Rodrigues. Bierman knew none of this when Rodrigues joined the *Daily Nation* sub-editors' desk, only that he would never get his tongue round Jawaharlal. 'We'll just call you Joe', he said. The name stuck.

The company's commitment to Africanisation was a serious one, reflecting Curtis' determination that the whites should write themselves out of their jobs. In 1961, he told the Board that 'every effort is being made to give responsible positions to Africans and every department except Accounts has been requested to terminate the services of one European during the coming year'. By 1964, he was able to state that 'the reporting staff has been more or less Africanised but this is more difficult on the sub-editing side of the

*Jomo Kenyatta shortly before his release from detention in remote northern Kenya in 1961*

*Kenyatta and Tom Mboya share a joke at the 1962 independence conference in London*

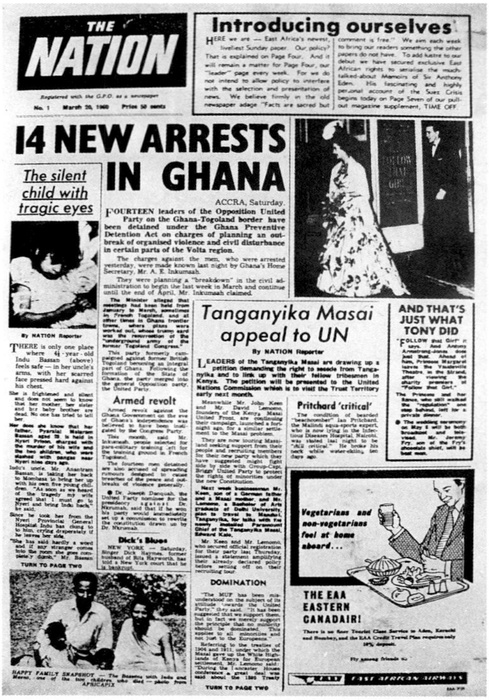

THE NATION

Registered with the G.P.O. as a newspaper

No. 1 March 20, 1960 Price 50 cents

## Introducing ourselves

HERE we are — East Africa's newest, liveliest Sunday paper. Our policy? That is explained on Page Four. And it will remain a matter for Page Four, our "leader" page every week. For we do not intend to allow policy to interfere with the selection and presentation of news. We believe firmly in the old newspaper adage "Facts are sacred but comment is free." We aim each week to bring our readers something the other papers do not have. To add lustre to our debut we have secured exclusive East African rights to serialise the much-talked-about Memoirs of Sir Anthony Eden. His fascinating and highly personal account of the Suez Crisis begins today on Page Seven of our pull-out magazine supplement, TIME OFF.

## 14 NEW ARRESTS IN GHANA

ACCRA, Saturday.

FOURTEEN leaders of the Opposition United Party on the Ghana-Togoland border have been detained under the Ghana Preventive Detention Act on charges of planning an outbreak of organised violence and civil disturbance in certain parts of the Volta region.

The charges against the men, who were arrested yesterday, were made known last night by Ghana's Home Secretary, Mr. A. E. Inkumsah.

They were planning a "breakdown" in the civil administration to begin the last week in March and continue until the end of April, Mr. Inkumsah claimed.

The Minister alleged that meetings had been held from January to March, sometimes in French Togoland, and at other times in Ghana frontier towns, where plans were worked out, whose trump card was the resurrection of the "underground army of the former Togoland Congress."

This party formerly campaigned against former British Togoland becoming an integral part of Ghana. Following the formation of the State of Ghana, the party merged into the general Opposition party, the United Party.

### Armed revolt

Armed revolt against the Ghana Government on the eve of Ghana's independence was believed to have been instigated by the Congress Party.

This month, said Mr. Inkumsah, people selected for para-military training left for the training ground in French Togoland.

The fourteen men detained are also accused of spreading rumours designed to cause breaches of the peace and outbreaks of violence generally.

● Dr. Joseph Danquah, the United Party nominee for the presidency against Dr. Nkrumah, said that if he won his party would immediately set up a commission to rewrite the constitution drawn up by Dr. Nkrumah.

### Dick's Blues

NEW YORK — Saturday. Singer Dick Haymes, former husband of Rita Hayworth, has told a New York court that he is bankrupt.

## The silent child with tragic eyes

By NATION Reporter

THERE is only one place where 4½-year-old Indu Bassan (above) feels safe — in her uncle's arms, with her scarred face pressed hard against his chest.

She is frightened and silent and does not seem to know that her mother, her sister and her baby brother are dead. No one has tried to tell her.

Nor does she know that her father, Pyaralal Malaram Bassan aged 29 is held in Nyeri Prison, charged with the murder of his wife and the two children, who were slashed with pangas near Nyeri nine days ago.

Indu's uncle, Mr. Anantram Bassan, is taking her back to Mombasa to bring her up with his own five young children. "As soon as we heard of the tragedy my wife agreed that I must go to Nyeri and bring Indu back," he said.

Since he took her from the Nyeri Provincial General Hospital Indu has clung to to him, crying desperately if he leaves her side.

"She has said hardly a word and if any stranger comes into the room she goes completely dumb," Mr. Bassan

TURN TO PAGE TWO

HAPPY FAMILY SNAPSHOT — The Bassans with Indu and Meena, one of the two children who died — photo from AFRICAPIX

## Tanganyika Masai appeal to UN

By NATION Reporter

LEADERS of the Tanganyika Masai are drawing up a petition demanding the right to secede from Tanganyika and to link up with their fellow tribesmen in Kenya. The petition will be presented to the United Nations Commission which is to visit the Trust Territory early next month.

Meanwhile Mr. John Keen and Mr. David Lemomo, founders of the Kenya Masai United Front, are continuing their campaign, launched a fortnight ago, for a similar settlement to the Masai problem.

They are now touring Masailand seeking support from their people and recruiting members for their new party which they have suggested might fight side by side with Group-Capt. Briggs' United Party to protect the rights of minorities under the new Constitution.

Next week businessman Mr. Keen, son of a German father and a Masai mother, and Mr. Lemomo, a Bachelor of Arts graduate of Delhi University, plan to travel to Manduli, Tanganyika, for talks with the newly installed Paramount Chief of the Tanganyika Masai, Edward Kalo.

Mr. Keen and Mr. Lemomo, who secured official registration for their party last Thursday, issued a statement amplifying their already declared policy before setting off on their recruiting tour.

### DOMINATION

"The MUF has been misunderstood on the subject of its attitude towards the United Party," they said. "It has been suggested that we support them, but in fact we merely support the principle that no minority should be dominated. This applies to all minorities and not just to the Europeans."

Referring to the treaties of 1904 and 1911, under which the Masai gave up the White Highlands of Kenya for European settlement, Mr. Lemomo said: "During the Lancaster House conference a great deal was said about the 1899 Treaty

TURN TO PAGE TWO

### Pritchard 'critical'

The condition of bearded "beachcomber" Ian Pritchard, the Malindi aqua-sports expert, who is now lying in the Infectious Diseases Hospital, Nairobi, was stated last night to be "still critical." He broke his neck while water-skiing ten days ago.

### AND THAT'S JUST WHAT TONY DID

"FOLLOW that Girl" it says. And Antony Armstrong-Jones does just that. Ahead of him, Princess Margaret leaves the Vaudeville Theatre, in the Strand, after viewing the charity premiere of "Follow that Girl."

The Princess and her fiance, who still walked the "regulation" one step behind, left for a private dinner.

● The wedding ceremony on May 6 will be both broadcast and televised. Mr. Jeremy Fry, son of the Fry's chocolate chief, will be best man.

Vegetarians and non-vegetarians feel at home aboard...

THE EAA EASTERN CANADAIR!

There is no finer Tourist Class Service to Aden, Karachi and Bombay, and the EAA Credit Travel Plan requires only 10% deposit.

Fly among friends on

EAST AFRICAN AIRWAYS

24 PAGES TODAY

TOYS 1ST FLOOR Nairobi Emporium

DAILY NATION

No. 993 Thursday, December 12, 1963 30 Cents

Mekay QUALITY SHIRTS Made in England

## MIDNIGHT—and up goes the flag

# KENYA FREE!

A VAST crowd at Nairobi's Independence Arena last night roared a welcome to the newest nation of Africa.

Kenya joined the councils of the world at one minute past midnight, as the green, red, black and white standard broke where, a moment before, the Union Jack had flown.

By DAVID BARNETT at Uhuru Stadium

The lights dimmed suddenly at midnight in the arena.

Then two officers lowered the Union Jack, in total darkness. A moment later the lights blazed on again, and the Kenya Flag was slowly raised in its place.

### Seventh

Kenya had become the seventh country of the British Commonwealth to achieve Independence in Africa since the end of the war.

She is the 34th independent country of Black Africa. Twenty years ago there were only Liberia and South Africa.

Kenya and Zanzibar will bring the number of United Nations member-countries to 111.

Rain had made life miserable in Nairobi for days but the afternoon was warm and sunny, and the grounds around the stadium had begun to dry out.

The evening programme began with a mammoth display of tribal dancing.

More than 1,200 dancers from all over Kenya kept the crowd entertained for the first two hours and 45 minutes.

The climax came with all 1,200 dancers in the arena at one time, with their shields, feathers, skins, beads, masks, cloaks, spears, kilts, robes and ornaments in a bewildering display of colour, sound and movement.

About 150 Asian dancers performed one of India's most popular folk dances — Dandiya Ras, based on the story of Lord Krishna and Radha.

### Tribute

Another Indian dance was "Uhuru," based on a Gujarati folk-tune, with words by the Nairobi poet, Suswaran (Mr. R. Patel).

The words recalled highlights of Kenya history and paid tribute to Mr. Kenyatta and other Kenya leaders.

Two hours after the dancing began with the crowd now

TURN TO BACK PAGE

Heartiest Congratulations to the Government and people of Kenya from L. G. Harris & Co. Ltd. the home of Harris the paint brush with a name to its handle

We are proud to have been associated with the progress of Kenya in the past and we hope to serve the new Kenya for years to come.

Sole Agents in East Africa: UNITED MARKETING INTERNATIONAL LIMITED

World-wide Marketing - Sales Promotion and Distribution Organisation, P.O. BOX 579, SHAMAS HOUSE, LATEMA ROAD, NAIROBI, KENYA.

## 5 babes born at stadium

FIVE babies "arrived" at the Independence Stadium, Nairobi, yesterday — just in time for Uhuru.

They were born at a temporary maternity hospital set up by the Red Cross at the KAR barracks near the Independence Stadium.

Their mothers had come to Nairobi — despite their pregnancies — to see the celebrations at the birth of the new nation.

The hospital, which has another five expectant mothers in confinement, is being run in liaison with St. John Ambulance Brigade posts and is open 24 hours a day.

PICTURES OF ALL THE UHURU EVENTS ON INSIDE PAGES

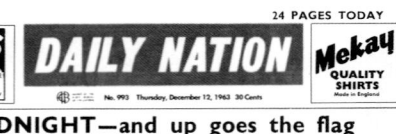

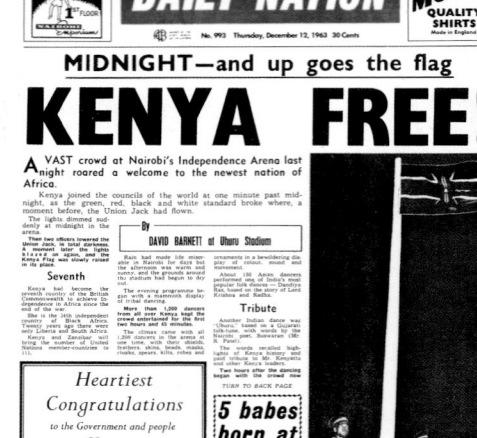

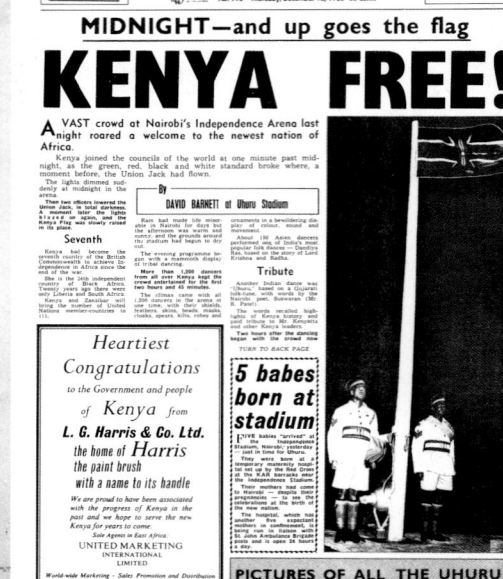

*Launch issue of* The Nation *and the* uhuru *front page*

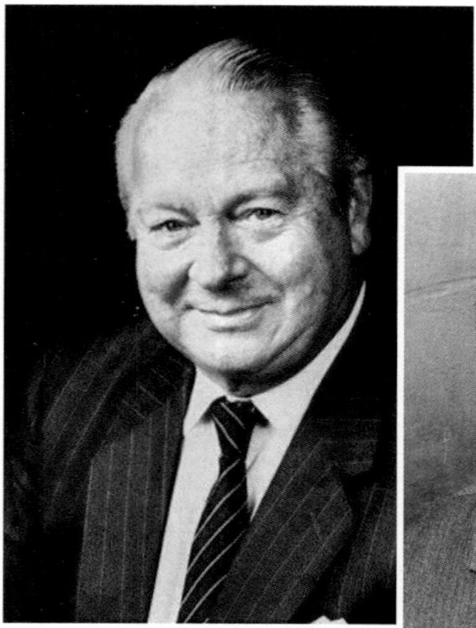

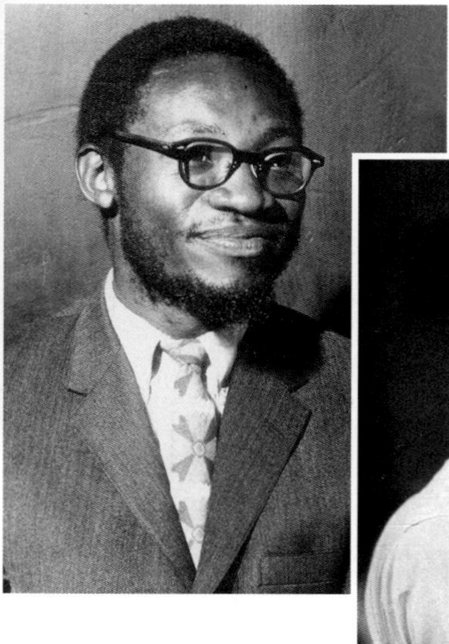

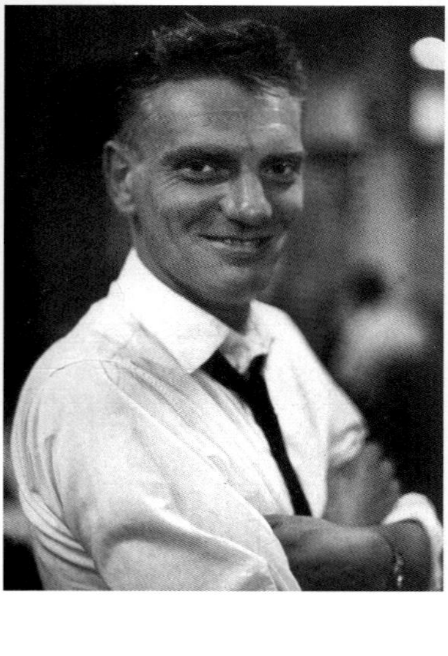

*Left to right, founding chief executive Michael Curtis, first Kenyan editor Hilary Ng'weno, founding editor John Bierman*

*The Aga Khan and President Kenyatta in an early meeting*

*President Moi and the Aga Khan at the 1981 general assembly of the International Press Institute in Nairobi.*

*Thomas, Lord Delamere leads Jomo Kenyatta into the celebrated 1963 crisis meeting with settlers in Nakuru*

*Kenya's newspaper vendors are renowned for the enthusiasm of their sales efforts*

Typewriters were
chained to desks
in crowded, chaotic
Nation House

The Aga Khan meets
editorial staff in 1961.
Joe Rodrigues to his
right, the author
to his left

The Aga Khan checks
production quality
with executives
Stan Denman and
Vin Durnan

*When Tom Mboya was assassinated, his fellow Luos mourned in paroxysms of grief*

## DAILY NATION

RADO
WATCHES
The First "SCRATCHPROOF"
Watch in the world
DIAMOND WATCH CO.

No. 2718   Saturday, July 5, 1969   40 Cents
Uganda 50 Cents

# TOM MBOYA SHOT DEAD

## Killer at city shop escapes

AN ASSASSIN gunned down Mr. Tom Mboya at lunchtime today in the crowded city centre of Nairobi.

The Minister for Economic Planning and Development died minutes later while being rushed to Nairobi Hospital.

The assassin, described as a young African, made his get-away in a car after the shooting, which occurred about 1.15 p.m. outside Chaani's chemist shop in Government Road. The most massive police hunt in Kenya's history is now under way for the killer.

Mr. Mboya, who was aged when the attack occurred. T ing the Minister in the chest.

Mr Mboya fell to the ground and apparently slipped breathing immediately. From tir shop assistants and passers-by stopped to give help. A doctor and an ambulance were called, but evidently, nothing could be done to revive Mr. Mboya.

Mr. Mboya was alone when he went into the shop. His Mercedes, with its Cabinet Minister's pennant, was parked at the curb outside the shop.

Police threw a cordon around the area and began to question all eye-witnesses to the shooting. Mrs. Chaani, who had served Mr. Mboya in the pharmacy, sobbed bitterly in top CID torn took her description of the incident.

A witness who travelled with Mr. Mboya in the ambulance to Nairobi Hospital and later: "The Minister did not speak. He was unconscious. The ambulance got there as quickly as possible, but he did not speak."

Thousands of shocked Kenyans gathered in Government Road as police began continuing. More than 1,000 people crowded into Nairobi Hospital and broke through the main entrance as staff battled to keep them out.

The crowd struggled to get into the emergency ward where Mr. Mboya's body was lying. Thirty police were rushed to

*Riots broke out in Kisumu and police moved against crowds who stoned Kenyatta's motorcade when the President visited*

COURT CLASH IN ANYONA CASE–BACK PAGE

Daily **NATION**

No. 5871, Wednesday, October 17, 1979 Kenya 1/20, Tanzania 1/40, Uganda 1/40

Announcing the new Sunday daylight flight to ZURICH COPENHAGEN With connections everywhere. SAS

# PRESIDENT HANDS IN PAPERS AS SOLE CANDIDATE

MASSES, demonstrating their support for the President, march along Moi Avenue, Mombasa.

THE Supervisor of Elections, Mr. Norman Montgomery, congratulates President Moi on his nomination unopposed as President of Kenya.

# MOI'S THE ONE

By NATION Reporter

**PRESIDENT Moi has been declared the sole candidate for the presidential elections.**

He was proposed yesterday by Vice-President Mwai Kibaki and Kanu chairman Isaac Omolo-Okero.

Nomination papers were presented to the Supervisor of Elections, Mr. Norman Montgomery, at the Attorney-General's Chambers shortly before noon.

As the President was handing in his papers, there were massive demonstrations of support for him, as crowds gathered outside the Attorney-General's Chambers and lined the streets of Nairobi and Mombasa.

Mr. Kibaki said: "On behalf of the Kanu governing council and all wananchi of this republic, I am honoured to present the nomination papers of Mr. Daniel arap Moi to contest the presidency."

He announced that the nomination papers had been signed by 1,000 registered voters from all parts of Kenya.

Attorney-General, Charles Njonjo, who sat next to the President at the nomination table, then said: "The Constitution requires that we wait until noon before we declare Mr. Moi the sole candidate, just in case someone springs up out of the blue to present his papers as well."

It was then 11.50 a.m. and the Cabinet Ministers, Kanu officials and well-wishers in the room burst into laughter.

There were shouts of "Nyayo, Nyayo" as a huge crowd outside the chambers clapped and chanted Kanu and Nyayo slogans.

Then there was silence for a few minutes as all present fixed their eyes on their watches.

"We not need to check our watches since the only watch that will determine the time is that of the Supervisor," Mr. Kibaki said, whereupon everyone stared

PAGE 1 — Col. 4

## Civic papers to be handed in today

By NATION Reporter

MORE than 6,000 candidates for civic seats are expected to present their nomination papers at their respective District Commissioners' offices between 8 a.m. and noon today.

Local Government Minister Robert Matano, who is Kanu Secretary-General, announced the figure yesterday.

He also said that about 800 candidates for the Parliamentary seats were expected to present their nomination papers tomorrow during the same hours.

In Nairobi yesterday, PC Paul Boit issued candidates with their election symbols. Only former MPs will retain the symbols they used during the 1974 elections.

Mr. Boit, addressing the candidates at the Kenyatta Conference Centre, warned against illegal meetings or turning of licensed meetings into demonstrations. "You will not be allowed to hold illegal meetings in social places like bars," he said.

Saying that campaign meetings should be held in places where they had been licensed, the PC said no one would be allowed to change the venue of meetings.

Mr. Boit said there would be 45 polling stations and the number of clerks at the stations had been increased. He said there were 365,000 registered voters in Nairobi.

In Mathare, where there were more than 92,000 registered voters, arrangements had been made to have about 20 rolls in each polling station, he said.

The PC warned all can-

PAGE 4 — Col. 5

**INSIDE**

- El Salvador leader ousted — Page 2.
- Firearms dun "was given pistols by Ugandan" — Page 3.
- People stage demos to support Moi — Page 4
- Rioting students sent down — Page 5.
- Man gets 2½ years for killing girlfriend — Page 12.
- It's make or break for Luo tonight — Page 30.



Daily **NATION**

No. 5610, Wednesday, December 13, 1978 Kenya 1/20 Tanzania 1/40



# MOI FREES DETAINEES

## Jubilation over Jamhuri amnesty

By NATION Reporter

**PRESIDENT Daniel arap Moi yesterday announced the release of all Kenya's detainees in his Jamhuri Day address to the nation.**

The huge crowd erupted into wild cheers and a frenzy of hand shaking, back-slapping, shouting, dancing jubilation.

But while parents, children and the jobless rejoiced at these moves, the release of detainees sparked off the greatest instant response.

President Moi said he had released the 26 detainees "to show all Kenyans I have faith... I have confidence in their determination to respect and promote our unity and stability."

As he spoke, the prisoners, some of whom had been detained for nearly a decade, were already back with their families.

"They had breakfast at home this morning," a police source said.

The detainees included 11 political prisoners, a group associated with a subversive publication and shifta (bandits) from Somali. (**Detainees — See Page 3**).

### Great tribute

LADIES and Gentlemen, this ... Jamhuri Day we are celebrating without Mzee Jomo Kenyatta, the Father of our Nation and First President of the Republic. I therefore ask you all to stand up for a minute's silence in his memory.

Brothers and Sisters, the minute's silence we have just observed should be regarded as renewing publicly our commitment to work for this country with the same dedication as Mzee Jomo Kenyatta did. Indeed, the biggest tribute we can pay to his memory is to steadfastly uphold the principles of Love, Unity and Peace, and to sustain our efforts to develop a united Kenya for

PAGE 4—Col. 1

PRESIDENT Moi and Lt.-Gen. J. K. Mulinge salute the crowds from a ceremonial Land-Rover.

SERONEY ... was Deputy Speaker in Parliament.

SHIKUKU... one-time Chief Whip.

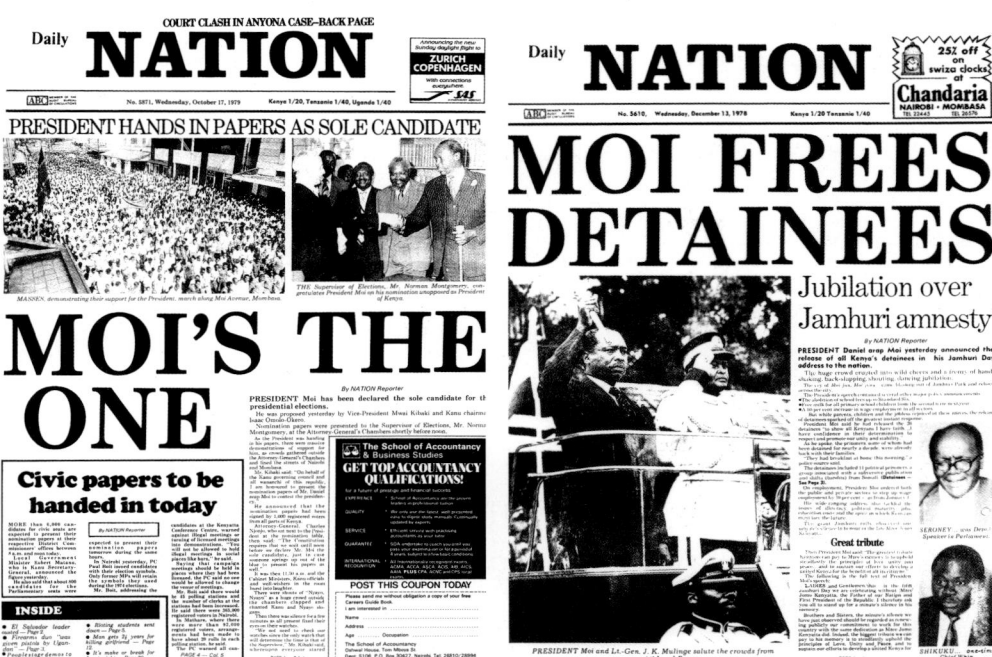

Nation *reflects euphoria of President Moi's early days in office*

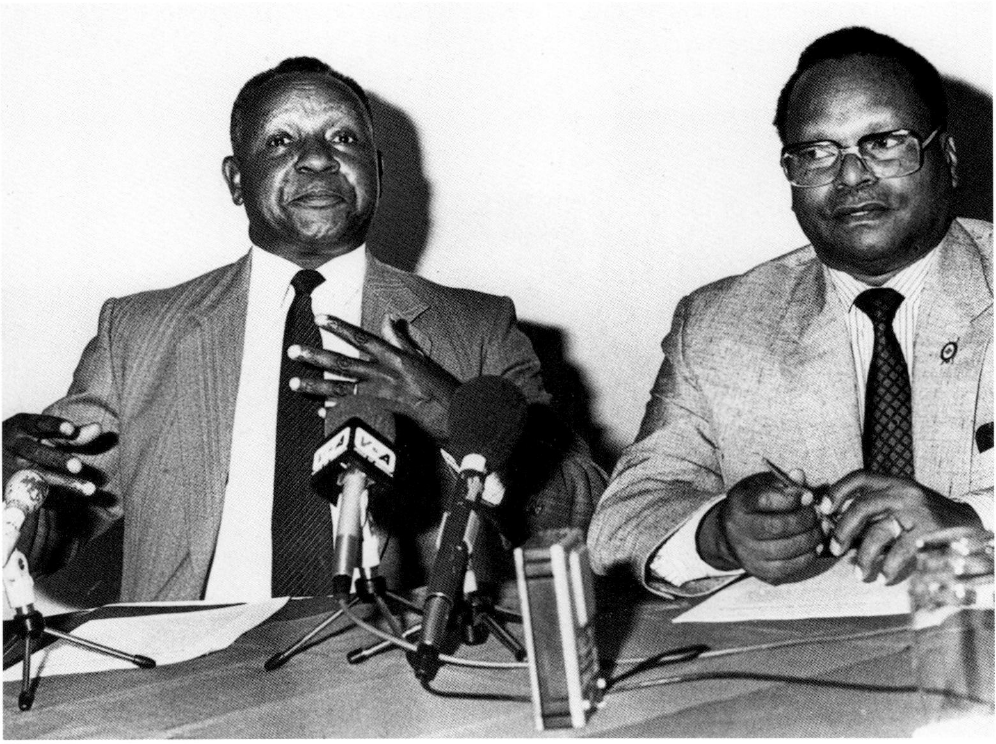

*Kenneth Matiba (left) and Charles Rubia launch the drive for multipartyism*

*Five of the Nation Six in the newsroom after three days in custody. Left to right, Philip Ochieng, Joe Kadhi, Gideon Mulaki, Pius Nyamora and John Esibi. Editor-in-chief Joe Rodrigues had been released earlier*

*Three outstanding early editors, left to right, George Githii, Joe Rodrigues and Boaz Omori*

*Deputy Speaker Kalonzo Musyoka denounces the* Nation *ahead of its banning from Parliament*

---

DAILY **NATION**

The newspaper that serves the nation

For Fax, Telex, Photocopying Services and Urgent Typing

**COPYCAT BUREAUX**
Sarit Centre

FOR THE DYNAMIC OFFICE

No. 8886, Nairobi, Thursday, June 29, 1989          Price KSh4/50

★ ★

# 'Nation' barred from Parliament

DAILY
NATION
Inside

By NATION Reporters

**Parliament yesterday barred reporters from the Nation Group of Newspapers from covering the proceedings of the House indefinitely.**

The historic measure was taken against the newspaper group through a motion of censure moved by the Deputy Speaker, Mr Kalonzo Musyoka.

The motion, which formed part of the day's order of business, read: "That in accordance with the provisions of the Standing Order number 170, this House resolves that representation by the Nation Group of Newspapers be excluded from the Press gallery for an indefinite period."

The House had to interrupt its business to accommodate Mr Musyoka's motion. It was scheduled to debate a motion on the Sessional statement. This debate

**Petition**
Recount ordered in Saboti case against Wamalwa
– Back page

**Broadcasting**
KBC to get Sh2.3b loan from Japan
– page 11

**Customs**
Officials prepare seizure of KTDA containers
– Back page

**Athletics**
Ereng' still unbeaten
– page 39

President Moi poses for a photograph with senior officers in the Kenya Armed Forces at State House, Nairobi, yesterday.

**Military Kuria to manage**

The queue-voting election of 1988, this line headed by KANU's then secretary-general, J.J. Kamotho

Rescue workers scrabble through the wreckage of the US embassy in downtown Nairobi, destroyed by an Al Qaeda bomb in 1998, three years before the Twin Towers catastrophe

*Television joined Nation's front-line media in 2000*

*Flat-screen technology dominated the new Nation Centre newsroom*

*Frightened Kenyans hold their ID cards high following a failed coup attempt by elements of the Kenya Air Force 1982*

*Many shops were looted before order was restored*

English papers'. In 1960, EAN employed 265 people, of whom 37 per cent were expatriates and 63 per cent Kenya citizens. In 1971, there were 41 expatriates; by 1979, just 11. The 2007 payroll of 1,000-plus contained only a handful of foreign specialists, less than 1 per cent, all on contract. There was also a constant search for Africans to take a place on the Group's various boards. When the Earl of Portsmouth proposed James Gichuru, the perennial finance minister, for the board of directors of Boyd's, the printing company, Curtis demurred because he felt politicians should not be involved. He admitted, however, that outside of politicians there was a serious dearth of African prospects. There was no shortage of Ismaili candidates, but the Aga Khan wrote to Curtis: 'It has always been my policy that no member of my community should be directly involved with East African Newspapers or East African Printers (formerly Boyd's) and it would be unwise to change this policy at the present time.' It was 1989 before the first Ismaili, Anwar Poonawala, joined the Group Board.

Minutes of the directors' meetings in the early years depict a small and cosy company unrecognisable from the large, professional organisation that grew from the Kienbaum recommendations. There were constant appeals for staff loans and donations to charity, usually granted: £80 to Meinard Donker to replace his car stolen in Kampala, £20 to Leonard Karori to purchase a bicycle, K7,000 shillings to H. Ng'weno to replace clothing after a burglary, £50 to Ramanlal Patel on compassionate grounds, four loans for school fees, and five loans for hospital bills. The Board agreed to spend £150 decorating Nation House for the *uhuru* celebrations and £150 for a staff Christmas party – hall, band and buffet supper. The paper donated the Nation Cup and £100 for a race for apprentice jockeys at Ngong racecourse and provided a Tail End Charlie award in the East African Safari motor rally. When a suggestion was made that the Aga Khan should donate two two-year-old fillies to the Jockey Club of Kenya, Curtis cabled, 'All I ask is that if you decide to call them *Nation* and *Taifa*, they should move reasonably fast.' Donations over the years went to the Starehe Boys Centre, Gertrude's Garden children's hospital, the Red Cross, the Flying Doctors Service, Dagoretti Children's Centre and numerous other charities. But the *Nation* turned down an appeal to support the Kenya beauty contest as bad for its image.

Easy camaraderie among a group of unprejudiced and talented enthusiasts had got the *Nation* off to a flying start. Now a long grind lay ahead to build circulation, particularly for the *Daily Nation*, battling the entrenched *Standard*, and for *Taifa Leo*, which was vulnerable to economic conditions. The enormity of the task seemed to overwhelm some of the participants at a May 1964 meeting of managers. Circulation chief F.D. Gove reported that the future for Naivasha and Gilgil townships was very poor: 'With the withdrawal of the [British] army and the loss of the European settler due to settlement schemes, the people moving in are mostly peasant farmers and in the main illiterate.' An aide-memoire reported, 'With regard to the editorial content of the paper, Mr Gove said reporting should be aimed more at the Kikuyu and the Luo as they formed the majority of readers of the Kiswahili newspapers … Mr [Gerry] Reilly [Chief Accountant] agreed and said they were also the most literate tribes and the wealthiest.'[4] In what seemed like a counsel of despair, the circulation manager suggested that the *Daily Nation* should be turned into a Mombasa/Nairobi-only paper, and *Taifa Leo* should be confined to Central Province and Nyanza, respectively Kikuyu and Luo areas. The idea was clearly tempting and provoked long discussion, but the problem was that advertising rates would have to be lowered. The meeting decided to commission researchers to survey readers on these options.

Although the *Standard* appeared an opponent of monolithic proportions, its supremacy was rooted in inertia. Circulation reps fought hard on the ground, but no battle plan emerged from the board room. London correspondent Arnold Raphael believed the 'political myopia' of the *Standard's* owners gave the *Nation* a psychological advantage and, though the senior paper had an excellent editorial staff, it was shackled by inert management. 'The *Standard* never really mounted a counter-attack against the *Nation*', Raphael said. 'It seemed paralysed by the competition.' The reality was that, at an early stage, the Anderson family considered surrender rather than fight. In the slump that followed the first constitutional conference, the *Standard's* principal shareholder offered his stock to EAN. The idea of a buyout or a merger appealed to the weakly *Nation*: the political future was uncertain, advertising was down and, with the excitement of Lancaster House subsiding, sales were unstable. *Taifa Leo* had been cut from eight pages at 20 cents to four pages at 10 cents and the *Daily Nation* shrunk from 16 to 12 pages on Mondays. The tentative plan in a takeover was to print a broadsheet daily on the *Standard's* presses, possibly called the *East African Nation*; it would have a circulation of 35,000 and advertising rates would be raised immediately; *Baraza* would be closed and the venture could be in the black in 12 months. EAN duly made an offer for the stock with the proviso that the holdings represent 51 per cent of the total issued capital. The offer and the proviso were both rejected, largely because of opposition from MD Thetford, and the courtship expired. The *Standard* remained with the Andersons until they sold out to Lonrho in 1967.

The *Nation's* other early opponent, Nakuru Press, also came cap in hand. For years, the *Kenya Weekly News* had chronicled the problems of the settler farmers, faithfully printing crop and cattle prices, usually to the sound of loud lamentations. The following verse became the farmers' anthem:

*Maize, maize, maize,*
*How odd that it never pays,*
*Despite all our toil*
*And magnificent soil*
*And the most scientific of ways.*

As the reality of approaching independence dawned, the Nakuru magazine's focus moved from maize and pyrethrum prices to Nairobi and politics. But history was already passing the settler by. The *Kenya Weekly News* lost its core readership as the whites departed and Africans moved onto their farms. When the editor, Mervyn Hill, collapsed and died at his desk in December 1965, chairman of the board Jack Couldrey asked Curtis if he was interested in buying the magazine and/or the Nakuru printing works. It was not an attractive proposition. The plant was entirely letterpress and the paper was losing both readers and advertisers. *Nation* executives pondered turning the magazine into a business-oriented regional product called *East Africa*. They decided against it and the 'pea-green incorruptible' died in the arms of the *Standard*.

When Ng'weno took the helm of the *Nation* three months after independence, a growing political authoritarianism was already evident, and journalists were frequently warned they must see their work as part of nation-building. Kenneth Bolton was shrewd enough to mend the *Standard's* fences with the African leadership, cultivating Kenyatta and making a friend of the up-and-coming Charles Njonjo. Ng'weno took immediate steps to identify the paper more closely with a black readership. Partly this was achieved through personalising African writers. Individual columns have always proved a strong suit for the *Nation*, from 'Keeping Up With Jones' and Ng'weno's own 'With a Light Touch', through Joe Kadhi's 'Why?' pieces, to 'Whispers' by Wahome Mutahi, Brian Tetley's 'Mambo', Tom Mshindi's 'Barbs and Bouquets', 'The Week That Was' by Kwendo Opanga and 'The Cutting Edge' by Watchman. In 1964, the *Nation* carried commentaries by arguably the two most eminent writers in the country, Ng'weno himself (though his major at Harvard University was nuclear physics) and the soon-to-be-famous Ngugi wa Thiong'o. John Platter, a Kenya-born cattleman turned journalist, remembered the diminutive Ngugi 'hunched over his typewriter, secretive and very, very slow, being goaded by Joe Rodrigues about deadlines and accuracy'.

Curtis had a high opinion of Ng'weno, the Aga Khan even higher – they had been contemporaries at Harvard. So there was surprise and dismay when the first African editor resigned after barely a year in the job. 'He said he was depressed by the restrictions implicit in the government's attitude to newspapers and particularly in Achieng Oneko', Curtis reported. But in a 1979 interview with the German newspaper *Siddeutsche Zeitung*, Ng'weno said, 'It was the worst time of my life. Most of the editors were British and they thought this token Kenyan would ruin the paper. Many gave their notices the same day I arrived. I had many enemies. The problem was I would not and could not keep my mouth shut.' Having lost 20 pounds in weight, he left, aged 27. Ng'weno declined to be interviewed for this history, but when the author, who was Assistant Editor of the *Sunday Nation* at that time, suggested that no white journalists resigned and that they were indeed intrigued by the idea of an African editor, Ng'weno replied, 'Well, Gerry, you have your memories and I have mine!' Board minutes of the time contain no record of any other resignations and indeed Ng'weno was soon discussing becoming editor of the *Sunday Nation*. 'I am very happy indeed', wrote the Aga Khan on hearing this news. In the event, Ng'weno got an advance to write a book and pulled out, though he did contribute 'With a Light Touch'. In time, Ng'weno built his own media empire, which included a weekly newspaper, the *Nairobi Times*, subsequently sold to KANU, a ground-breaking children's paper, *Rainbow*, and the *Weekly Review*, a *Time*-style magazine of politics and economics, which earned the highest plaudits until it changed to open support for the KANU government and readers left in droves. It folded in 1999 and the title was later bought by the *Nation*. As the *Weekly Review* expired, Ng'weno opened his own TV station, *Stellavision*, though this later collapsed when its supplier went out of business. Ng'weno briefly entered high administration as chief of the Kenya Revenue Authority.

In seeking a new African editor, the ideal candidate would be someone close to the centre of power but with an independent stamp of mind, and Curtis believed he had found him in George Githii, Kenyatta's press secretary. A small, nattily dressed man who usually wore a spotted bow tie (and often a gun under his immaculate business suit), Githii was to prove a courageous, wayward, devious, sometimes vindictive, often brilliant editor, who had no qualms about using the newspaper as his personal weapon on the political battlefield. During two turbulent spells at the helm, Githii probably inflicted more agony on his mentors than all the other editors put together. Curtis was not to know this, however, when he reported, 'Very good news is that the President has agreed to release his Press secretary to take over from Ng'weno.' Thus the former trainee with both the *Standard* and the *Nation* was hired at £2,500 per annum (car allowance £15 per month) as the *Daily Nation's* fourth editor in six years. He promptly leapt into the fray.

Official corruption and misuse of public funds had already begun to gnaw at the national fabric, but they were rarely referred to in public. Githii broke the taboo. When he discovered that Alderman Charles Rubia, Mayor of Nairobi, planned to have the City Council buy him a luxury Rolls-Royce limousine for his official duties, Githii launched a virulent campaign, including page-one editorials that demanded to know why the mayor couldn't use his recently bought Humber Super Snipe, and, what's more, how come a certain £300-per-annum council clerk could be suddenly promoted to a £1,180-per-annum job? These were questions which excited ordinary Kenyans and the *Nation's* sales soared. Kenyatta banned the car.

With corruption by now inching its way onto the public agenda, the next item was altogether more serious. John Platter recalled in a note to the author:

*A civic-minded (or disgruntled) former colonial civil servant who was at that time attached to the Maize Marketing Board telephoned me one day, sounding very furtive. We arranged to meet at the Thorn Tree café outside the New Stanley hotel and he came with a heavy, thick folder which purported to prove that his chairman, Paul Ngei, was embezzling furiously. Ngei, a one-time detainee with Kenyatta, was a political heavyweight but he was a thorn in the side of the government [and in particular of Charles Njonjo]. Was this a set-up to get him or was he really purloining the country's granary? I mulled over the papers for a few days, made a few calls, then took the story but not the papers or my source, to Githii, who could hardly contain his excitement. George relayed the information to State House, so he told me, and said he had permission to go after Ngei. I wrote the story, George wrote a thundering leader, there was fury from the Ngei camp and Kenyatta ordered a Commission of Inquiry. We trooped over and solemnly gave our evidence and it began to look like an open and shut case of corruption [especially when Kenyatta suspended Ngei from the cabinet].*

But in a way that Kenyans were to become familiar with, that is where it ended. Elections were coming and the value to KANU of Ngei and his Wakamba support was critical. The Commission was quietly forgotten. In one sense, Platter believes, this was fair: 'Corruption was already rife, even in the higher quarters, and to single out Ngei would have been subjective targeting for political ends.' Platter's footnote: 'Soon after that, I encountered Njonjo and Ngei together at the sauna at the Norfolk Hotel. We laughed about it all as we sweated out the night before.'

In retrospect, this early failure to act against corruption was a milestone on Kenya's journey into venality at an official level. The difficulties of law enforcement and the inequalities between the races in colonial times had predisposed Kenyan society to securing advantage by favour and, as far back as 1907, Lord Delamere wrote, 'Time after time I have heard a native say they have been stopped by an Indian policeman and when I asked them how they got away, they always said, "Oh, I gave him something".'[5] The phrase came to resonate in the modern era when *kitu kidogo* (something small) became synonymous with a bribe. In a landmark Nyeri speech in 1952, Kenyatta said, 'We despise bribery and corruption, those two words that the European repeatedly refers to. Bribery and corruption are prevalent in this country, but I am not surprised. As long as people are held down, corruption is sure to rise and the only answer to this is a policy of equality.' Unhappily, Kenyatta did not seem to despise bribery and corruption enough, nor did it disappear with the achievement of at least political equality. By ignoring the opportunity in Ngei's case to demonstrate that even the most powerful of men are subject to the common law, Kenyatta paved the way to a shark-like feeding frenzy among men of power which eventually became endemic at all levels of society.

Malcolm MacDonald, Kenya's last Governor, first and last Governor-General, then first High Commissioner for Britain in Nairobi, was a fervent admirer of Kenyatta, but nine years after independence he wrote:

> *One of Kenyatta's most serious errors is his tacit assent to the acquisitiveness of some of his ministers and civil servants. Soon after attaining power, they began to buy (sometimes with money gained by dubious means) large houses, farms, motor cars and other possessions. This development not only tainted his administration with a reputation for corruption, but also produced a wide economic division between governors and governed, haves and have-nots ... it would have been more prudent as well as moral if Kenyatta had enforced on*

*his colleagues and subordinates a stricter code of conduct, preventing*
*them from becoming such a conspicuously privileged class.*[6]

That men and women close to Kenyatta enriched themselves handsomely
during his 15-year reign is not in doubt. Kenyatta's favourite charity was the
Gatundu Self-Help Hospital in his own backyard. During the 1960s and
1970s, visitors of consequence, particularly businessmen, were expected to
beat a path to State House and hand over the obligatory cheque for the
Gatundu hospital. Hundreds of fund-raisers were staged on its behalf. A
common joke was that it was a 'self-help' project, because the Kenyatta
courtiers helped themselves to the proceeds. Summing up the era was this
much-repeated story: During an official tour upcountry, Kenyatta spotted a
farm he fancied and instructed an aide to acquire it for him. Timidly, the
man said that was impossible. Impossible! Was he not the President! Indeed,
yes, but Mama Ngina (his wife) already had it.

Certainly, it was in the post-Kenyatta years that corruption became sys-
tematised, with an exponential increase in land-grabbing and the amassing of
vast personal wealth by politicians. But it can be argued that the conditions
for the spread of corruption through a once-pristine civil service, signalling
a national free-for-all, were set, with the best of intentions by the Ndegwa

*Problems dogging Kenya through most of its modern history.*

Commission in the Kenyatta era. Duncan Ndegwa, head of the Civil Service and for many years Governor of the Central Bank, chaired a year-long inquiry into Public Service Structure and Remuneration in 1971. It concluded that to maintain civil servants' living standards and motivation at a time when many bright Kenyans were going into the better-paid private sector, they should be permitted to engage in business, provided their business was not similar to their work responsibilities – thus an official in the housing department should not be involved with a house-building company. This precaution was widely ignored; personal business soon took precedence over public duty and the 'coat on the chair' made its appearance as a signal to colleagues: the bureaucrat would hang his coat over the back of his office chair and go off to attend to his private business. Said anti-corruption activist John Githongo in an interview:

> The Ndegwa Commission legitimised something that had already started to happen and which led ministers and government people to use all manner of means to earn some money. For instance, civil servants arranged for the government to buy goods from their own companies. What it did was change the entire culture of Kenya so that these things were no longer wrong. It coincided with pressures on Asians who had decided to stay after independence. They had to pay off government godfathers for trading licences and work permits. All this turned civil servants into criminals ethically but people stopped asking them, 'Where are you getting your money?'

What helped to entrench corruption was Nairobi's business expansion and the fact that many Kenyans, including ministers and senior civil servants, were offered directorships by companies under pressure from Africanisation. This new nexus legalised the dubious relationships which had already started to develop, and Kenya assumed the nature of an aggressively capitalist society. President Nyerere described Kenya as a dog-eat-dog society. The first huge tender fraud involved the £25 million Jomo Kenyatta International Airport in 1978 that expanded and largely replaced the Embakasi facility, which had been built by Mau Mau detainees. A high civil servant made so much money out of kickbacks that he was able to retire early in comfort. The money-earning techniques employed on the airport construction pointed the way to the massive and systematic corruption of later years. Karl Ziegler, who was a banker in Kenya between 1969 and 1980, said in an interview:

*The Mister Ten Percents became Mister Twenty Percents. It was more than bribery, it was extortion, protection money. If negotiations on a project were not going well, somebody very high in government would pick up the phone and say, 'The head of state thinks that your operation is very attractive and if you want to go on making the money you are making, then you look after KANU', or whatever organisation might be named.*

A Western diplomat who served in Kenya in the 1970s and then later in the 1980s said:

*Whatever corruption there was in the earlier 70s did not have a distorting effect on the economy, it didn't mean that bad projects or uneconomic projects were undertaken. By the time I went back in the 1980s, that was undoubtedly true. Projects were built which had no economic rationale, simply because it was in the interests of a particular individual that they should be built when they were built and that their companies should get the benefit of the investment. In the 1980s, corruption was a major topic for diplomats and presented problems for any of us who were dealing with the commercial side.*

Githii's first serious clash with the government came when he opposed the Preservation of Public Security Bill of 1966, which provided for detention without trial and other special measures under emergency powers granted to the President to combat threats to national security. Attorney-General Njonjo argued that the measures were temporary and subject to Parliament; they were needed to deal with external aggressors, arms smugglers, rumour-mongers and 'people who meet in secret against whom no evidence can be found'. Only one member of the House of Representatives, G.J. Mbogo (Embu North), voted against the Bill, describing it as 'very dangerous, South African-style legislation', but a former KANU official, the gadfly Martin Shikuku, objected that there was no limit to the period of detention. 'Does the Attorney-General intend to detain people until they die?' he asked. Several members objected that the legislation would require yet another amendment to the new constitution, which was beginning to look patchy.

Githii's editorials went for the jugular. The Bill, he said, 'provides for preventive detention, restriction and the compulsory movement of people; it seems to legalise censorship of ideas and information; it has provisions for the control of associations and societies. This is an issue of grave national importance [which] affects not only the liberty of this generation but also that of posterity.' Then, in a reference which infuriated Njonjo, he said, 'For these reasons, this newspaper does not flatter Mr Kenyatta or the government or the country by asserting that all these proposed powers are called for. An administration should not be allowed to have absolute power, there must be checks and balances.' As to promises that the powers would not be abused, Githii noted perceptively, 'We may accept Mr Kenyatta's assurances, but we should not presuppose the benevolence of those in power in, say, 30 years' time.'

Responding in Parliament, Mboya said, 'I respect the *Daily Nation* and I respect the editor. But on this occasion I disagree and disagree wholeheartedly. Reading the *Nation*, I got the impression that all the laws of Kenya were going to be suspended. Have we got to be told like a pack of schoolboys so we obey the wishes of the *Nation*?' (In fact, Githii, who received Curtis' strong support for his stand, had warned Mboya he was going to write the editorial and offered him space to reply.) Njonjo described Githii's reference to not flattering Kenyatta as 'the height of conceit' and warned, 'If newspapers want to continue publishing in this country, it behoves them to be careful … this Bill is not a Preventive Detention Act, as the *Nation* would like to think. Kenya is not abandoning the rule of law, this is where the *Nation* has got it wrong. We used to complain that Europeans managing this newspaper were irresponsible. The editor of this newspaper today is an African.'

Public condemnation apart, Githii was also subjected to private pressure. After his first editorial he was summoned to State House and a meeting with Kenyatta and Njonjo. Kenyatta listened attentively to his arguments and simply warned him not to go 'too far'. When he wrote a second editorial, Githii was telephoned by Police Commissioner Bernard Hinga, an old friend from his schooldays, who suggested that Githii had made his point and he would be wise not to carry the campaign any further.

Although the government took no action against Githii, a few months later, the *Nation*'s foreign editor, John Dumoga, a feisty, diminutive Ghanaian, was given 24 hours to leave the country. Privately, Njonjo told Curtis that Dumoga had been criticising the government openly and the President would not tolerate that sort of thing. Perhaps more to the point, Dumoga was a close friend of Githii and a known opponent of the Public Security Bill – he had been a victim of similar legislation under Kwame Nkrumah – and his deportation was seen in Nation House as an unsubtle warning to the Editor-in-Chief. Privately, Curtis wrote, 'Lively independent journalism is becoming harder and harder to achieve. Political control or influence over the press is becoming more marked and the shadow of the Preventive Detention Act looms large over everyone.' Hindsight was to prove Githii's fears wholly justified. By the time Kenyatta died in 1978, at least 26 people were being held in preventive detention, and, though they were freed by President Moi, detention without trial came back into regular use under Moi himself. When Githii protested again, this time in an editorial in the *Standard*, he was fired the same day, and left journalism and Kenya, too.

Whatever the protestations of Njonjo, it was clear that internal developments were the *raison d'être* of the Bill rather than any threat of external aggression. A KANU conference at Limuru had abolished the post of party vice-president held by Odinga which made him vice-president of Kenya, too. Eight vice-presidents representing the provinces were installed instead but Odinga was not nominated, and, without a post of any sort, he resigned and formed an opposition party, the Kenya People's Union. Joseph Murumbi succeeded him in the government but resigned a few months later, and Moi became the new national Vice-President. The Limuru changes effectively removed Odinga from the race for the presidency, a result which those close to Kenyatta had long sought. Odinga was joined in the KPU by radicals such as Bildad Kaggia, Achieng Oneko and Tom Okello Odongo, and by trade unionists including Dennis Akumu and O.O. Mak'Anyengo. They promised to pursue 'truly socialist policies to benefit the people'. Mboya swiftly crafted legislation providing that National Assembly members who crossed the floor must seek the voters' mandate anew under their fresh colours, and with 30 seats thus made vacant, a 'little general election' was called. As the campaign got underway, Kenyatta pointedly declared, 'I have today given my assent to the Public Security Act and will now deal very firmly with all trouble-makers.' When polling day came, the KPU was crushed by KANU and only Odinga and seven of his colleagues were returned. Kaggia and Oneko were among the vanquished. It was not long before KPU adherents began filling the detention cells under the new legislation.

All this excitement did nothing to hurt newspaper sales. The main focus of the circulation department was the *Daily Nation*. For its first five years, the paper hovered between 15,000 and 18,000 sales per day as it sought to overcome anti-tabloid prejudice, but in 1966, a year of major news events, it broke through to 24,263. This was partly due to a resumption of the Coast edition when the Standard's *Mombasa Times* folded. The *Sunday Nation* by then was already past 37,000 and the daily and weekly *Taifas* were selling 51,000. Staff were told that the company's priority was to break even financially in 1968 and push the daily paper past the *Standard's* maximum sales mark of around 34,000.

These tasks took on formidable proportions in May 1967 when the African Investment Trust Ltd, a London-registered subsidiary of Roland (Tiny) Rowland's huge conglomerate Lonrho, bought Consolidated Holdings Ltd, owner of the *East African Standard*, the *Tanzania Standard* and the *Uganda Argus*, for a reported £1 million. Kenyatta originally was unhappy about the deal because Lonrho's sources of wealth were based in white-ruled Rhodesia, and he telephoned the *Standard's* Charles Thetford. However, Kenyatta was persuaded that the investment Lonrho would bring to Kenya outweighed the political objections. Within two years, Lonrho had bought Motor Mart, becoming Kenya's largest foreign investor, then expanded into tourism and hotels, including the Norfolk Hotel and the Mount Kenya Safari Club, food processing (Farmers' Choice), real estate, ranching and plantations. Curtis noted, 'I am not entirely happy about the prospects as far as we are concerned. Lonrho is so enormously wealthy they will be far less reluctant than the present set-up has been to engage in extensive re-equipping, re-staffing etc.' Eric Marsden gave this view from inside the company:

> Lonrho made a killing financially and they gained great political influence. They got prime property in the heart of Nairobi, a great coup. But the first thing they did was to close down the office in Standard Street and kick us all out to the Industrial Area. The talk about Lonrho was that Tiny Rowland said to Kenyatta, 'The paper is yours to do what you like with, just say the word.' I believe that's true.

Udi Gecaga would later become Lonrho's first African director and, as Chairman of Lonrho East Africa and a relative of Kenyatta, he would facilitate Rowland's access to the head of state. When Kenyatta died, Rowland swiftly dropped Gecaga.

Two months after the sale, Curtis referred to 'a good, old-fashioned distribution war'. He wrote, 'There are piles of *Standards* wherever you go and they must be accepting phenomenal returns. Their front page has been given a typographical overhaul and whenever we put up a poster, they put up six. They are also subscribing to Agence France Presse.' Three months later: 'The *Standard* are spending wildly on distribution and new routes.' What the *Standard* did not have, however, was a Paddy Kearney.

This Irish former assistant police commissioner for the Rift Valley Province became the *Nation's* circulation manager in February 1966. He spoke fluent Kiswahili, and after 18 years with the police knew virtually every inch of Kenya and many of its movers and shakers, including Daniel arap Moi. Kearney recalled, 'Moi was a farmer in Nandi when I first knew him, then he became an MP and we sat on many committees together in Nakuru.' Kearney spent most of his time on the road with the van drivers, kicking at agents' doors at two in the morning to collect their payments. 'The drivers knew the importance of getting there first', he recalled in an interview. 'You closed your eyes when you left Nairobi and opened them when you reached your destination because if you opened them through the journey, you would be white-haired before your time. They took chances and regrettably some of them died.' The fearsome Mombasa run was contracted to the Light Transport Company owned by two volatile Italians, the Verulini brothers. Frequently the Athi River road towards the Coast was submerged under floodwater. 'When that happened, Giorgio would take the truck onto the railway line and drive along the rails and across the bridges and over the floods, bump, bump, bump, until he found the road was open again', Kearney recalled.

'The *Standard* went all out to break us', he said. 'They wouldn't share transport and they told distributors, "If you take the *Nation*, you won't get the Standard".' Because the *Standard* concentrated on the cities, Kearney targeted small towns and upcountry villages:

> *That was where we broke them, by opening up new rural areas and finding our own distributors. The local distributors were usually Africans and often we looked for disabled people. We took great chances on them but they were brilliant. They employed* totos, *wanting one cent or two cents a paper, and those kids went to all the shopkeepers who were only too pleased to get the* Nation *on their doorstep. They took hundreds of papers to tiny villages and it cost us relatively nothing. There was one seller on Ngong Road, Kamau. We gave him, say, 600 papers and he had 10 or 12* totos *delivering them to individual houses, about 400 of the 600. We went to places like Eldama Ravine, Molo, Embu, Meru, Nyeri, Karatina, Thika. We put vendors near bus stops. We were building a mass readership. The* Standard *never seemed to realise that Europeans were a declining readership.*

Kearney co-operated enthusiastically with fellow-Irishman and marketing manager Gerry Wilkinson on competitions ('A thousand prizes to be won'), which were new in Kenya and which the *Standard* generally disdained.

Before a *Nation*-sponsored race meeting at Ngong, the two men spent a day plastering the course with posters boasting: 'Nation, everywhere, everyday'. That Ngong racecourse was one of the last preserves of the old-timers, readers of the *Standard* to a man, was not lost on the two bill-posters. But Wilkinson wanted to raise the *Nation* profile beyond 'Spot the ball' and simple competitions and, under the auspices of the Nairobi Rotary Club, started the Annual Business Game, pitting teams of upcoming executives from blue-chip companies against each other. There followed the Annual Advertising Awards, which pushed the *Standard* further into the shadows.

Two money-spinning innovations were National Day supplements and bereavement notices. Kearney recalled:

> *The missionary priests and nuns were anti-*Nation *because it was a tabloid and occasionally mentioned sex. We were afraid we were not getting to the leavers from their schools, so we started National Day supplements. Not only did they produce good advertising but we persuaded the embassies to buy copies, sometimes as many as 10,000, for distribution to schools, thus making young people aware of the* Nation.

The *Standard* was still far ahead in classified advertising, but Kearney and Wilkinson saw a chance to fight back by printing not just the notification of a death but a photograph of the deceased, too. 'I might have picked up that idea from my local paper in Ireland or from some hodgepodge of a paper in East Africa but certainly I got that from the people I talked to in my job', Kearney said. 'I put it to the editor and it became very successful. That is where the *Nation* was good, with new products and new ways of thinking.' After a slow start, the death notice with photograph caught on with Kenyans who wanted to inform distant relatives of funeral arrangements. A few years later, the paper was carrying as many as five pages of such notices daily.

There is no doubt Kearney's tenure (1966–75) helped critically to transform the *Nation* from a struggling also-ran to unchallenged leader of the East African market. From 24,263 in 1966, the daily hit 28,063 in the first six months of 1967 and 30,121 in the last six months. In 1968, sales reached 33,903 and the *Standard* was finally overhauled the following year, when Kearney informed the Aga Khan by Telex that audited sales in the first half of 1969 (34,954) exceeded those of the *Standard* by 237 copies. 'That Telex I framed and it is still in my office', the Aga Khan told Kearney later. A 1969 *uhuru* anniversary supplement in *The Times* of London carried an advertisement for 'the largest selling daily newspaper in East Africa – Kenya's *Daily Nation*', a paper *The Times* once routinely snubbed. The advertisement gave average net sales since June of that year as 47,000 copies. In a letter to Kearney, the Aga Khan described the breakthrough as 'the beginning of an ascendancy which I hope now is firmly established', adding, 'I have heard from many sources how this is due to your personal enthusiasm.'

Gerry Wilkinson, who joined the group in 1971, aged 27, was the *Nation's* first marketing manager, a position that was something of a mystery to senior management. But then it had been as much a mystery to Wilkinson's previous employers at the *Irish Independent* in Dublin, where he was also the first to occupy this new-fangled role. As a result, the young marketer and former university lecturer was able to bring to Nairobi invaluable lessons learned in Ireland, where he initiated nationwide in-depth research into attitudes to the print media, learning why people preferred one paper to another, what they wanted to see and what angered them about papers – common practices today, but eye-opening in the Africa of the 1970s. Wilkinson's successes brought him a seat on the board and promotion to MD of the newspaper company in 1975. Kearney left Kenya reluctantly in October 1975, having failed to secure renewal of his work permit. But the ascendancy did continue, as the Aga Khan had hoped, and the newspaper completed its first decade in 1971 with a circulation of 57,972. Critical mass had been achieved and surpassed. The *Standard* meanwhile was stuck and remained so for many years. Old hand Nick Russell recalled, 'When I came to the *Standard* in 1963 as a sub-editor, it was selling 30,000 copies. When I came back as managing director in 1977, it was still selling 30,000 copies.'

A principal argument in the Kienbaum Report was that no matter how much reorganisation or cost-cutting was undertaken, only healthy and vigorous newspapers with a predominantly African readership would assure the future of the company. The truth of this became apparent as the *Daily Nation* finally climbed out of the doldrums. The company's loss in the financial year to 31 March 1961 had been £200,000, and as recently as 1964 it was £119,805. But as the cutbacks began to work in tandem with increasing circulation and healthier advertising, the losses dropped dramatically, to £69,651 in 1966 and £26,651 in 1967. Finally, in April 1968, Chief Accountant Reilly told the Board of Directors the company would show a profit of between £1,300 and £1,400 for the financial year to 31 March. The minutes of that meeting reported merely that 'Mr Curtis noted this was the first time the company would show a profit and congratulated all concerned.' It is not difficult, however, to imagine the joy and relief this report must have brought to the *Nation* pioneers, pre-eminently Curtis himself, after seven back-breaking years. With the circulation breakthrough the following year, the Holy Grail of passing the *Standard* and breaking even was achieved.

Githii's first spell as Editor-in-Chief came to an end in July 1968, when he resigned to pursue a degree course at Oxford University. During his three-year tenure, he had demonstrated a shrewd insight into what concerned the average Kenyan, and showed courage and foresight in his battle against the public security legislation. But his own political involvements were becoming a matter of concern at Nation House. When Njonjo produced a report from the security organs claiming Githii was attempting 'to renew old friendships' with Odinga, the editor angrily declared, 'There is no such friendship.' He accused Njonjo of waging a vendetta against him. He exploded again when Curtis asked him not to print any more letters on a feud he was having with Dr Kiano. 'Githii is extremely touchy about any management interference with his editorial prerogatives', Curtis noted. Githii was also agitating for extra editorial staff, arguing rightly that his department had suffered worst under the Kienbaum cutbacks. Nevertheless, the chief shareholder expressed his regret when he accepted the resignation and wished him well at Balliol College. Githii was succeeded by the steady and popular Boaz Omori, chief editor of the *Taifa* papers, of whom Curtis said, 'He combines qualities of gentleness and patience with considerable inner strength and a strictly professional approach to his job.'

Omori needed all his professionalism to handle a dispute that was making headlines every day, not only in Kenya, but in Britain, too. In pursuit of its Kenyanisation programme, the government passed legislation requiring Asian non-citizens to obtain new work permits and restricting the issue of trading licences to only a few towns. Kenya had an Asian population of around 190,000, a great many of them merchants, out of a total of 10 million. Of that 190,000, some 60,000 had automatically become Kenyan citizens on independence because of their birth, and a further 10,000 had chosen to acquire citizenship in the two years allowed under the Independence Act. The other 120,000 remained British citizens, as they were under colonialism. Technically the Kenyanisation programme was similar to that of most governments worldwide which favoured their own nationals in employment policies. But there was undoubtedly racist pressure from some African leaders. Most of the 120,000 largely middle-class Asians did not want to leave, but departures rose with the acceleration of Kenyanisation fuelled by inflammatory speeches by some British politicians. When

Britain's Labour government announced it would legislate to withdraw the automatic rights of entry to British citizens, panic set in. Fearing statelessness, Asians began emigrating at the rate of 750 per day and there were scenes of mass hysteria at Jomo Kenyatta airport. Sometimes, if those who were seeing off their friends could find a seat on the plane, they, too, embarked, leaving their cars in the parking lots. Others, unable to fly direct, went by longer routes and some flew via Moscow. In the two weeks before the debate on the Bill even began in London, 10,000 Asians rushed headlong out of Kenya.

That Britain's Race Relations Bill was racially inspired was indisputable. In what was to be a much-quoted speech, the Conservative Party MP and classical scholar Enoch Powell said Britons were being made strangers in their own country. 'I am filled with foreboding', he said. 'Like the Romans, I seem to see the River Tiber foaming with much blood.' Josephat Karanja, Kenya's High Commissioner in London, observed, 'If the people had been white, there would be no problem in Britain.' David Steel, leader of the Liberal Party, who spent his boyhood in Nairobi, wrote later, 'It was a most discreditable episode in our parliamentary history, a major concession to racism and a blot on the reputation of the Labour Party.'[7] Ironically, when the panic subsided, Britain seemed to lose its glitter as the El Dorado for Asians. The Bill provided for 15,000 vouchers to be made available per year for heads of households, but, in the first ten months after passage of the legislation, only 1,200 were taken up. Many emigrants went to Canada instead. Kenyatta said his government did not intend to force the pace of Kenyanisation, and, as time passed, Asians found that Kenya was not enforcing its work permit and trading licence legislation with any particular zeal.

Elsewhere, though, KANU rule had become so authoritarian that *The Times* of London could write of 'a suspicious government, some of whose members are inclined to regard an independent Press, like an independent judiciary, as a colonial relic'. It added, 'Since well before independence, newspapers have been periodically warned to watch their step and the editors of both the *Standard* and the *Nation* have presumably by now learnt just how far they can go.' This was a lesson that Githii refused to learn. Omori was more cautious. Allen Armstrong, a new chief sub-editor, recalled a quiet Sunday in October 1969 when staff reporter David Njagi, a former upcountry stringer and an unassuming fellow, dropped a story onto his desk without comment. It said that members of the KPU, including Odinga, were being rounded up in Kisumu and the party was being banned. 'I hurried round to Boaz, very excited', Armstrong recalled. 'As always, he was unflappable and said he needed to check it out and "take advice" whether we would run with it – advice from whom, I don't know.' In the event, the story ran big in a special edition which carefully noted that 'no word of confirmation was available from the Nyanza Police'.

The KPU roundup was just one event in the *annus horribilis* 1969, which also saw allegations of renewed Mau Mau oathing, the unprecedented stoning of the President's motorcade, new moves against the media and, catastrophically, the assassination of Tom Mboya. 'It seemed like civil war at the time', Eric Marsden recalled. As ever, much of the trouble surrounded the presidential succession. Unknown to the public, Kenyatta had suffered either a heart attack or a thrombosis in 1966 and by late 1967 factions were already forming, notably the Gatundu Kikuyu group on one side and Mboya with Luo and some multi-ethnic support on the other. Odinga was out of contention by now, but he seemed like a stone in Kenyatta's shoe. In early 1968, the President denounced the KPU as *kipu*, Kiswahili for 'chameleon', and said, 'Trample it underfoot, the time for mercy is over.' Bildad Kaggia, the KPU's VP, was sentenced to 12 months' imprisonment for holding a meeting without a permit (halved on appeal) and Odinga's passport was impounded. Some KPU offices were attacked and 1,800 KPU candidates for local elections were rejected on grounds they failed to prepare their papers properly. A formal move to kill off the KPU seemed imminent, but first came Mboya's murder.

That his life was in danger was knowledge the young politician had lived with for years. As early as August 1962, Curtis reported in a private letter, 'We are getting innumerable reports that Mboya has been threatened with physical violence, and also his wife.' In 1965, Governor General MacDonald said he had received intelligence reports from Britain and from the Kenya Special Branch that Mboya was under threat because he was 'getting all the headlines'. MacDonald told Mboya, 'Your life is in danger unless you calm down.' Mboya, though still in his 30s, had pursued a busy and combative political career which, by the late 1960s, had placed him in the antechamber to the presidency. He was the prime obstacle in the path of the Gatundu pretenders.

At midday on Saturday 5 July, Mboya was shot twice, in the shoulder and the heart, as he left a chemist's shop in Government Road, Nairobi. Allen Armstrong and reporter Peter Hinchcliffe ran to the scene from Nation House, only yards away, but their photographer was too far behind. Mohammed Amin, then a little-known freelance, was already shooting television and still pictures as a doctor tried mouth-to-mouth resuscitation. The

*Daily Nation* rushed out a special afternoon edition, 'Tom Mboya Shot Dead', and the next day the *Sunday Nation* carried the headline, 'Kenya Weeps', with one of Amin's photographs, a close-up of Mboya on a stretcher with a doctor's stethoscope to his chest. In stunned disbelief, the newsroom got on with the job. Kearney recalled, 'Stan Denman came down to handle the press run. The presses never stopped for 36 hours. I believe it was the first time we printed more than 100,000 copies.'

In the murk that has habitually surrounded Kenya's political assassinations, crucial questions remain unanswered. A young Kikuyu, Isaac Njenga Njoroge, was arrested and sentenced to death for Mboya's murder, but accounts differ as to whether he was ever hanged (Kenya has never announced executions), and one report spoke of his being seen years later in Ethiopia. Nor was it ever clarified to whom Njoroge was referring when he reportedly said, 'Why don't you ask the Big Man?' Njoroge, said to have been trained in Bulgaria, may indeed have pulled the trigger, but the instigators of the crime were never brought to justice. And in a mirror image of other suspicious deaths, the expatriate policeman who led the Mboya investigations died in a car crash. Two outspoken politicians had already died that way, Ronald Ngala and Clement Argwings-Kodhek, and others were to do so in the future.

Turmoil followed Mboya's murder, with grief-stricken Luos loudly charging Kikuyu involvement. Then came reports of a wave of enforced Mau Mau-type oathing. Alan Chester was running the *Standard's* syndication service, which provided news coverage of Kenya for foreign clients, mainly British newspapers. The Minister of Education, a Kamba, called a news conference, and accused the police of rounding up children from schools around his Machakos area and forcing them into the forests to take blood oaths. He also said he had received a letter saying oathing was taking place at the London School of Economics (LSE). Chester duly reported this to Fleet Street and the story was widely used by the British nationals. The *Standard* and the *Nation* both published the minister's comments without the LSE angle. Marsden was acting editor of the *Standard* because Kenneth Bolton was on leave, and he remembered treating the story carefully:

> *It was the day of the Kenya Agricultural Show and I led the paper with Kenyatta's comments and a big picture of him, and on the other side of the front page we had a foreign story and at the bottom of the page the minister's story about oathing. Next day, I got a letter from Charlie Thetford congratulating me on a wonderful paper, but then I*

*had a call from Njonjo who said, 'We didn't like the story on the front page today.' I pointed out that it was given at a public news conference by a minister of his government and he said, 'The man's a fool.' When I said, 'With all respect, he's in your government', he just said, 'When is Ken coming back?' In other words, things would be okay with Bolton in charge.*

That night Marsden went for a drink after work and a reporter rushed into the pub and said Alan Chester was being arrested. Chester recalled, 'I was in the office when two Special Branch guys came in, an African and an Asian, and served me with a deportation order. They were very polite and the order was actually signed, "Your obedient servant".' When Marsden got to his suburban Karen home, he, too, was politely told that he was an illegal immigrant and was taken straight to the airport. There he found Alan Chester and the *Nation's* news editor, Mike Chester. Nobody ever discovered why Mike Chester was expelled since he had no involvement in the story. There may have been a mix-up over the name of Chester or, some thought, he was simply the most visible senior white on the *Nation*. Marsden said:

> *What knowledgeable people were saying at the time was that they deported me as a warning because the* Standard *was veering from the line of support for the Kikuyu clique. Our reporters used to accuse Bolton and sometimes me of playing down stories so as not to upset the Kikuyu. It was not true as far as I was concerned but I suppose we all unconsciously acted with a view to making life as little uncomfortable as possible.*

The police wanted to handcuff the trio at the airport, but Alec Pearson, a veteran Kenya policeman and the head of Kenyatta's security detail, said no, and they were marched onto an East African Airways plane at 11 pm. The pilot invited them into First Class and offered them drinks.

A massive Press corps met the deportees at Heathrow airport in London and debates took place in the House of Commons. But the three found no assistance at the official level. Marsden was the only one who wanted to return to Kenya, but when he went to the office of *Standard* owners Lonrho, he was told, 'The only advice we can give you, young man, is to write a letter of apology to President Kenyatta.' Alan Chester asked the Foreign Office for help in getting his savings out of Kenya and was told that was impossible, this was a matter of international relations and the British government was giving loans to Kenya. Chester suggested they deduct his £2,000 from their next loan.

Marsden did return to Nairobi but it was a mistake:

*While I was away, my wife, Jackie, was terrorised. Somebody cut our pet cat's throat and hung it on the verandah. A few days later, the body of a naked African appeared in our garden and somebody called the police and said my wife had killed him. Our second child was a boarder at Nairobi Primary School and the head mistress sent my wife a letter saying. 'Will you come and pick up your son? We cannot have the son of a traitor in our school.' When I returned to Kenya, they started on me – death threats, attempts to plant phoney stories. A policeman telephoned and said my wife's car had been in an accident and an African was killed and they wanted to see her. It was all lies, her car had been parked all day at Unesco where she worked. But I think it had a big effect on Jackie, because she died of cancer a few years later, a young woman.*

Marsden believed the harassment probably came from low-level ex-Mau Mau thugs in the pay of Intelligence, and the terrorism was particularly vindictive because 'they did not like the idea of somebody who was thrown out being allowed to return – I was the first one'. After 13 years in Kenya, Marsden came to the end of a five-year contract in 1970. 'I said to my wife, "I think the love affair with Africa is over". She said, "I suppose so". And she really did love Africa.' They left and Marsden became an outstanding foreign correspondent for the London *Sunday Times* in Israel and South Africa.

The deportations had a chilling effect on the Nairobi Press establishment and four *Nation* expatriates resigned or chose not to renew their contracts. Marsden said, 'My expulsion convinced the *Standard's* other assistant editor, Michael Rowe, and his wife, Nancy, that there was no future for them in Kenya and they left in 1970.' Journalist and PR man Tony Lavers said, 'This episode made me decide to leave the country in which I had lived since early childhood and in 1969 I said goodbye to our old home in Karen, our friends and our servants, who were also friends, and emigrated to Australia.' In a contemporary memo, Curtis said, 'I am in no doubt that a nucleus of trained journalists will be essential for several years to come (but) there is a feeling that the climate is becoming and will grow increasingly more repressive.'

The effect of Mboya's murder, which his fellow Luos firmly believed was a Kikuyu-orchestrated plot to keep him from the presidency, was to unite that hitherto-divided community massively behind Odinga. Whether to test the waters or read the riot act, Kenyatta incautiously travelled to Kisumu in the heart of Luo territory on 25 October to open a hospital. Odinga, who was officially Leader of the Opposition in Parliament, greeted the President coolly, and the *Daily Nation* carried a photograph of Kenyatta sitting grim-faced on the VIP dais next to a worried-looking Moi. When Kenyatta inspected the guard of honour, gatecrashing Luos started shouting anti-government slogans and hurling stones at the presidential escort car. Chairs were thrown by demonstrators and security guards battled back with drawn guns. KANU Youth Wingers pitched into the fray. Briefly, order of a sort was restored and bodyguards hustled Kenyatta to his limousine, but the crowds showered the car with missiles as it drove away and the presidential escort opened fire with live ammunition. An official statement said five people were killed, but *Nation* reporter Cyprian Fernandes sneaked into the newly-built Russian hospital, donned doctor's whites and toured the mortuary. He counted 17 dead. Among them was the baby son of Abdul Dahya, the *Nation's* Kisumu distributor, gunned down while playing in his garden by retreating security men shooting wildly all round them.

The police swooped at dawn next day. Odinga and his KPU deputy, J.M. Nthula, were placed under house arrest and the other six KPU MPs were taken into preventive detention, as was Achieng Oneko, the party's publicity secretary. Four days later, the government announced that the KPU was proscribed for 'seeking active assistance to overthrow the lawful and constitutional government of the Republic of Kenya'. Like most of the new nations in Africa, Kenya was again a one-party state, and when a general election was held in December, only KANU candidates were available to the voters. The electorate expressed its feelings by rejecting two-thirds of the sitting MPs.

## *Notes*

1.   *The Power of News: The History of Reuters* by Donald Read, Oxford University Press, Oxford, 1992.
2.   *Looking for Trouble* by Richard Beeston, Brassey's, London, 1997.
3.   Bierman later became a BBC television correspondent, a magazine writer and a biographer of, among others, Raoul Wallenberg and Henry Morton Stanley.

4.  It was not the first time a suggestion was mooted to manipulate the contents of the newspapers in favour of commercial objectives. At an earlier board meeting, a non-executive director suggested that the *Nation* should target non-advertisers by giving favourable publicity to their competitors.
5.  *White Man's Country* by Elspeth Huxley.
6.  *Titans & Others* by Malcolm MacDonald.
7.  *Against Goliath* by David Steel, Wiedenfeld & Nicholson Ltd, London, 1989.

# CHAPTER 5

# A Disastrous Error

*A newspaper's primary office is the gathering of news. At the peril of its soul, it must see that the supply is not tainted. Comment is free but facts are sacred.*
C.P. Scott, Editor, *Manchester Guardian*, 1926

A dispatch published by the *Los Angeles Times* in August 1976 from its Nairobi correspondent Dial Torgerson read as follows:

*A copy of Nairobi's breezy tabloid, the* Daily Nation, *which gives the world news highlights from the news agencies and describes the Kenya capital exactly as it is, beset with crime, bright with cinema, bubbling with sex and outrageously capitalistic, is passed from hand to hand until it rots. Papers like the* Daily Nation *infuriate the information ministers of countries without Kenya's free Press.*

As the proprietor's aide in Evelyn Waugh's *Scoop* might have observed, 'Up to a point, Lord Copper.' Certainly, the *Nation* of that era infuriated Kenya's information ministers, but it frequently had much the same effect on its ownership. Only three months earlier, Minister of Information and Broadcasting D.M. Mutinda had protested formally that, during an international UN conference in Nairobi, the *Nation* pictured Kenya in a bad light by drawing attention to an epidemic of venereal disease, to corrupt policemen, starvation and social deprivation, while criticising some of the conference delegates. 'I suggest that in future, the Press … portray Kenya's good image', Mutinda said. 'Any deviation from this can only produce negative results.' Unmoved by this evident threat, George Githii, back at Nation House as Editor-in-Chief, sent an icy reply, pointing out that the letter should have been addressed to him, not to the managing editor, and stating dismissively that 'without prejudice, the contents of your letter have been noted'. Another Githii blow for media independence! Unhappily, this was also a period when the *Nation* was being accused of partiality in its news selection and bias, this time in favour of the government, in its editorial comment. It was beset by charges of inaccuracy – one reporter filed a story about proceedings in Parliament without going there – and a notice on the newsroom wall pleaded, 'Aim for accuracy. Check your facts. Then check again.' Githii was by now a figure of public controversy and had recently been burned in effigy.

Yet the decade started triumphantly. After going into profit in 1968 and overhauling the *Standard* in 1969, the *Nation* celebrated its tenth anniversary in 1970. By then it could claim, if not to have joined the establishment, at least to have gained acceptance by the rich and famous. When EAN sponsored a race meeting for the Jockey Club of Kenya, some 75 guests came to luncheon at the Ngong course. They included settler stalwarts Lord and Lady Delamere, Sir Charles and Lady Markham, Sir Ferdinand and Lady Cavendish-Bentinck and Sir Derek and Lady Erskine, along with the *Nation's* directors and senior executives and their wives. One African couple not connected to the paper were Mr and Mrs Mwai Kibaki. George Mbugguss, photographed chatting to his wife, wore an immaculate white suit with spotted tie, matching breast-pocket handkerchief and a dark trilby hat identical to one worn by director B.M. Gecaga. The menu offered melon and Parma (misspelled as 'Palma') ham, braised duck and orange, a Kenyan cold buffet and assorted desserts, cheeses and coffees. The 42-page programme for the meeting sold at two shillings. It was printed by Kenya Litho.

Beyond the social scene, the Aga Khan was looking to the future and gave instructions that a five-year development programme be drawn up providing for further expansion and Kenyanisation. Sales figures carried in a celebratory tenth-anniversary supplement showed the rise of the papers: *Sunday Nation* up from 27,169 in 1960 to 46,425 in 1970; *Daily Nation* up from 15,140 in 1960/61 to 46,496 in 1970; *Taifa* weekly over the same period up from 51,465 to 62,477. The Aga Khan declared, 'It is my hope that in the years ahead the group will continue to progress and contribute to the growth of well-being in East Africa and that the newspapers will be regarded as among the finest in any continent.' Certainly, the second decade got off to a sensational start.

During 1970, the *Nation's* staff man in Kampala, Paul Waibale, warned Nairobi that a military coup was in the making in Uganda. He was worried about his security in the event of a military takeover and it was agreed that if and when it happened, he should tip off Nation House with a short coded message, then get out of the office to safety. Allen Armstrong said, 'We suggested he send two words, "Guy Fawkes", after the man who tried to blow up the English Parliament, then we would chase the story in Nairobi by telephone and diplomatic contacts. Not knowing when the army would move, we were all given a diplomat to call in Kampala and I drew a European ambassador.' Armstrong was chief-subbing on the daily on 25 January 1971 when the teleprinter chattered briefly: 'I went into the Telex room and there it was, "Guy Fawkes".' The sub-editors dived for the phones and Armstrong got through to his diplomat in Kampala:

'Mr Ambassador, would you say that a military takeover is under way?'

Reply: 'I think you could say that.'

'How can you be certain?'

A short pause: 'Well, there's a tank in my front garden.'

The subs quickly got a splash story together introducing the wider world to Idi Amin and a 'Takeover in Uganda' special hit the streets. Just then, MD Frank Pattrick puffed excitedly up the back stairs. He had heard a bulletin on the BBC and drove from his Kitisuru home with a jacket over his pyjama top, eager to join the fray. 'I had a lot of respect for him after that" Armstrong said.

There was a fine follow-up. Idi Amin had made his move when President Milton Obote was in Singapore for a Commonwealth heads-of-government conference, which was being covered by chief reporter Cyprian Fernandes. When Obote decided to fly back immediately to East Africa, Fernandes set off in pursuit of his motorcade. Somewhere along the way, a taxi ran over his foot, but he made it to the airport and hobbled onto the same East African Airways plane. From his seat at the back, Fernandes sent four notes to Obote asking for an interview, but the hostess reported, 'He just looked at them blankly.' The *Nation* man put together a vivid first-person account of Obote's 13-hour flight back to Nairobi and how he returned from the cockpit blinded with tears after the captain's radio confirmed his overthrow. Back in the newsroom, Fernandes quaffed a medicinal brandy supplied by Pattrick, wrote his story, then went to hospital for treatment to his injured foot.

None of the Nairobi journalists had heard of Amin, the coup leader. They were not to know that his photograph had appeared on the front page of the *Daily Nation* back on 18 October 1962, when a Kenya magistrate gave his inquest verdict on the deaths of four Turkana tribesmen. The four had been captured by a Uganda platoon of the King's African Rifles in a joint operation with Kenya forces in the Northern Frontier Province. The aim was to disarm Turkanas who had been raiding into Uganda, Somalia and Ethiopia. Witnesses said the prisoners were kept in the open for periods of up to 30 days, periodically being forced to lie on their backs and stare at the sun; water was rationed and soldiers beat them with clubs, sticks, spears and rifle butts. The commander of their captors, 7th platoon, 4th battalion, KAR, was Lieutenant Idi Amin. The *Nation* described him as a six-foot-three former army heavyweight boxing champion and said he had just been promoted to temporary captain, the first African in East Africa to reach such a rank. In a spine-chilling observation, the newspaper added, 'Amin is considered one of Uganda's most promising officers and has been tipped for high rank in the future.' The magistrate concluded, 'I am of the opinion that an offence has been committed by some person or persons among the members of 7th platoon.' He sent a copy of his judgment to the Kenya Police Commissioner, Richard Catling. It is interesting to speculate on Uganda's future had action been taken against Amin. But Uganda had become independent only one week earlier and the Kenya colonial authorities decided it would not be politic to arrest a soldier of its sovereign neighbour's army. Nothing further was heard of the affair.

Much, however, was heard of Amin after he unseated Obote. For a while, he was treated as a buffoon by the Western media, often referred to as Big Daddy, as he delivered a stream of outrageous and highly quotable observations. His personal doctor, John Kibukamusoke, said later the Ugandan leader suffered from *hypomanic paranoia*, a state of mind in which a rapid succession of varying ideas receives oral expression. Deciding that Kampala's Grand Hotel sounded 'too British', he renamed it the Imperial. As head of the Uganda Defence Council, he ordered the Council to award him a CBE, Conqueror of the British Empire, upgraded his rank to Field Marshal and pronounced himself King of Scotland. Though barely literate, Amin declared himself a Doctor of Philosophy and Chancellor of Makerere University, an institution regarded by many scholars as the Harvard of Africa. He raced around Kampala in a red sports car and announced, 'My speed is very fast. Some ministers had to drop out of my government because they could not keep up.' He sacked his foreign minister and publicly accused her of having sexual intercourse in a toilet at Orly Airport in Paris, giving rise to the euphemism 'Uganda relations', gleefully applied by Britain's *Private Eye* magazine to anyone thereafter found in a compromising situation.

The British government's original enthusiasm for Amin cooled as their protege ordered a group of Britons in Kampala to carry him shoulder-high in a throne-like chair. He called reporters to witness training for Uganda's space programme, which consisted of soldiers rolling downhill in barrels. He frequently plunged into swimming pools and raced against his officers. He always won. But the laughter soon died. Amin had no popular power base, and sustained his rule by lavishing resources on the armed forces and ruthlessly eliminating perceived opponents. Ugandans died at the rate of 100 to 150 a day at times and thousands fled into exile, many of them to Kenya. By the end of his blood-stained rule in 1979, an estimated 300,000 Ugandans had been murdered, many only because they had money, education or influence, others random victims of Amin's torture and terror squad, the State Research Bureau. The victims included a chief justice, an Anglican archbishop and at least two cabinet ministers.

The single act that brought Amin's tyranny to the notice of the outside world was one of the earliest examples of ethnic cleansing in modern Africa – his brutal expulsion of Uganda's 80,000-strong Asian community in 1972. These were mostly Ugandan-born families whose ancestors arrived when the country was still a British possession. Many owned businesses, including huge enterprises that formed the backbone of the national economy. At first, only non-citizen Asians were expelled, and some who had taken Ugandan nationality criticised their fellows for lack of commitment. But the decree was later extended to all Asians and those who were citizens had their passports snatched away. The deportation covered Asians of all faiths, including Muslims, though Idi Amin himself was a Muslim, and Ugandan soldiers engaged openly in theft and violence against the beleaguered community. Amin expropriated businesses and property, and handed them over to his supporters and cronies as the heart of the country's trade sector hastened to board planes for Britain (30,000), Canada, Kenya, the sub-continent, America and elsewhere. Uganda's self-proclaimed President for Life described his action as an 'economic war' to free Uganda from foreign domination.[1] It gained him much popular support from poor Africans, but the exodus effectively killed the national economy. Inflation rose to 1,000 per cent, roads returned to cart tracks, tourists stopped coming and soldiers machine-gunned wild animals in the parks for meat.

In 1973, a government decree banned newspapers outright and many Ugandan journalists and broadcasters were jailed or killed. *Nation* managers made occasional sorties into Uganda to assess the situation, taking elaborate precautions. Paddy Kearney recalled travelling to Kampala with Gerry Wilkinson. He said, 'Our arrangement was that if we went into any official offices, one would go in and the other stay out, so if anyone was arrested, the other would try to sort it out. In the hotels, we would book our names under one room but actually take two rooms and sleep in the second one. If anyone came for us, we'd be out the window.'

Githii was welcomed back to the *Nation* in December 1972 after the sudden and untimely death of Editor-in-Chief Boaz Omori. Though Omori had been a steady hand on the tiller, Africanisation bequeathed him growing numbers of educated but inexperienced and sometimes politicised staffers. Stan Denman complained about the 'instability' of graduate recruits. An ugly form of self-assertion was taking the place of *uhuru* euphoria in some areas of society, and the Indian poet, Dom Moraes, wrote of a visit to Nairobi, 'The airport was full of brusque black officials. They seemed aggressive and eager to be offended. A Customs officer spent several minutes loudly telling a European woman that she must address him with respect, he wasn't her servant.'[2] Whether it was a sign of insecurity or grandiosity, the government ordered voluntary associations not to use the title 'president'. A directive said, 'The existence of the title of "president" amongst the posts of officers of societies can cause confusion with the title of His Excellency, the President of the Republic of Kenya. The government requires that the constitution of such associations be changed to make fresh provision for the title of such posts.'[3] When Kenyatta announced that Kiswahili would replace English as the official language, the *Daily Nation* supported him enthusiastically, declaring that 'irrelevant and anti-African ideas coming to us through foreign languages have done irreparable cultural and psychological damage in this continent'. A director drily pointed out that the paper seemed to be arguing for its own abolition. The *Standard* produced a page of Kiswahili and was bombarded by readers demanding it be dropped.

Another *Nation* editorial supported the principle of the Acquisition of Property Act in Tanzania, even though the disastrous effects of President Julius Nyerere's lurch to socialism were by then only too apparent. The Arusha Declaration of February 1967 called for an overhaul of the economic system based on self-reliance through a villagisation programme. Politically and socially, the policy proved hugely unpopular and in the end a complete failure. Peasants stubbornly resisted collectivisation of their farms while corrupt government servants enriched themselves at farmers' expense; efficient areas of the economy, mostly in the charge of Asians, were nationalised, starting a remorseless slide to ruin; Tanzania plunged further into debt, suffered a crisis in its balance of payments deficits and seriously damaged its relations with international donors. The assets of the Asian community were seized without compensation and, when the management of their schools was nationalised, the future of Asian education collapsed.

The upheaval was probably as damaging to Tanzania's Asians as Idi Amin's wholesale expulsions were for Uganda's Asians, only it went on longer. It was the mid-1980s before Tanzania realised socialism and self-reliance were little more than slogans, and agreed to implement International Monetary Fund (IMF) and World Bank economic reform packages. A business leader with interests throughout East Africa said, 'The Arusha Declaration was a national tragedy for all Tanzanians and resulted in close to a quarter century of economic despair while creating serious problems of official corruption.' The *Nation's* editorial espousal of Tanzania's nationalisation policy came at a time when the Kenya government was taking controlling interests in a series of large companies – 93 per cent of East African Power and Lighting, 60 per cent of National and Grindlays Bank (which became the Kenya Commercial Bank), 50 per cent of the Mombasa Oil Refinery. The paper's senior management feared a swing to the left in the editorial columns and a special meeting of EAN directors set up an Editorial Policy Committee while Omori was still at the helm. This was in effect a revival of the Editorial Board of the early 1960s which had sputtered on and off, mostly off, without editor-level enthusiasm to back it.

Consisting of Omori, Pattrick, Denman and Rodrigues, who by then was managing editor of the daily, the committee, it was decided, would be called together whenever an important news event took place. Although Curtis had relocated to the Aga Khan's office in Paris after ten years in Kenya, he remained chairman of the holding company, East African Printers and Publishers Ltd, and pronounced himself available by telephone. A directors' special meeting named Omori as principal leader writer, with Hilary Ng'weno to be called on as necessary and when available, and warned that 'ill-informed political tub-thumping' by columnists would not be tolerated. Editorial guidelines originated by Githii during his first tenure were revised by Omori and circulated to editorial staff. The six-page document said in part, 'We should continue to give unremitting support to the present Kenya government, criticising only in the public interest on specific excesses or injustices. The paper's fundamental political attitude is middle-of-the-road independent. Corruption, tribalism, racialism, religious and minority protection are areas where we have a watchdog role. But the basic rule is criticise not carp.' The guidelines banned identification of people by tribe or race, and warned against implied prejudice in the use of words and phrases such as blacks, whites, glorious revolution, bourgeois and Afro-Asian bloc. They concluded, 'All this boils down to is political moderation, common sense and caution. Don't risk it. Check it!'

The trouble was Githii did not believe in consultation. Less than a year after his return, Curtis noted, 'George has never accepted the idea of the Editorial Policy Committee.' A few months later, he referred to Githii's 'complete refusal to discuss any subject with senior management executives, he simply ignores them'. When Pattrick remonstrated with Githii on one occasion, the Editor-in-Chief barked, 'Are you God that you can look into my mind and do my job?' Then he walked out of his own office.

The business types meanwhile had another major project on hand: flotation. The Aga Khan had always intended that the group should go public once it achieved financial security and, as far back as 1961, Curtis told the International Press Institute (IPI) meeting in Geneva, 'In 10 years' time, shares will be available for local purchase by Africans.' The target was missed by just two years. The idealism underpinning the public issue was supported by the Aga Khan's financial advisers, who believed such a move would strengthen the papers' African identity and thus their competitive edge, and that African co-ownership would provide protection against nationalisation, then popular with many African governments. In March 1973, the various companies were renamed: the holding company, EAP&P Ltd, became Nation Printers and Publishers Ltd (NPP), EAN (Nation Series) Ltd became Nation Newspapers Ltd (NNL), and African Life Publications Ltd became Marketing and Publishing Ltd. The public offer was set for September to include these three companies, plus Kenya Litho Ltd (formerly Boyds, the printers) and its counterpart, Tanzania Litho Ltd. Tanganyika African Newspapers Ltd had already been sold and *Mwafrika* closed, and Uganda African Newspapers Ltd was not included because it was an associated and not a subsidiary company. The total payroll in newspapers, printing and packaging was over 800. The Aga Khan made available 40 per cent of his holding, 1.2 million shares at five shillings each, and this offer was more than twice over-subscribed among 3,200 different individuals and institutions. A further public issue in 1988 was almost three times oversubscribed, reducing the Aga Khan's shareholding to 45 per cent, while 10,000 individual Kenyans bought a stake in their own newspapers. The Aga Khan became principal rather than majority shareholder.

Foreign ownership of the media had always aggravated the political establishment, though the integrity of the newspapers was less an issue than the inability of the regime to control them. Attorney-General Njonjo attacked the *Standard* in Parliament for leading its front page with the demolition of shanties rather than a reduction in the price of maize. At the same session, Vice-President Moi warned newspapers to stop criticising foreign governments or face the consequences. Two days later, the *Nation* attacked Somalia for its 'antics' against Kenya. Sniping at the Aga Khan's involvement, despite his huge investments and the jobs thus created, became a regular weapon in the politicians' armoury, and as late as 1998 the KANU-owned *Kenya Times* characterised the *Nation* as 'the Kenya-based, Paris-owned Aga Khan media group'. Most often, the ownership issue was simply an excuse to attack the *Nation* when it embarrassed or offended the complainant. And Nairobi's *Management* magazine stated that 'those who scream to nationalise always fail to point out that in the day-to-day running and in their treatment of Kenya's affairs, both the *Nation* and the *Standard* are as Kenyan as a bag of posho'.

The Aga Khan took the attacks calmly and pressed on with his Kenyanisation programme, pushing for promising Africans to be promoted even at a pace likely to entail a lowering of professional standards. At an IPI meeting in Nairobi in 1981, he set out his thoughts as follows:

> *There is probably no infallible solution to the problem of media ownership. What matters is that the organisation, whoever owns it, develops sufficient resources and is committed to creating quality newspapers that are responsible, reliable and readable … the greater the number of companies that achieve financial independence and professional credibility, the greater the chances of building truly independent Press structures in the Third World.*

As the communications business became a global commodity, foreign ownership became less of an issue, and if at one point in Kenya the Aga Khan owned the *Nation*, Lonrho the *Standard* and Robert Maxwell a large part of the *Kenya Times*, so in England *Times* newspapers were bought by an Australian-turned-American, the *Telegraph* stable by a Canadian and the *Independent* group by an Irishman. In Australia in 1998 only two morning papers were owned by Australians, with the ex-Aussie Rupert Murdoch controlling 70 per cent of that nation's media. The Kenya situation was not to last anyway and Lonrho sold out to unnamed investors, widely believed to be Moi family members and friends, while Maxwell pulled out of the *Kenya Times*. On the *Nation's* part, two stock offers made it a Kenyan majority-owned and managed company, with transparent indigenous command and control.

The entity that went public in 1973 was in good shape. Circulation of the flagship daily rose from 57,609 in 1971 to 66,204 in 1972 to 71,656 in 1973, and, with full colour now available, advertising was buoyant. As early as 1971, the newspaper company was bringing in profits of £250,000 per annum, and, with a new awareness of promotional needs, £7,500 was set aside for sponsorships and public-awareness campaigns; 54 per cent of income was coming from advertising and 46 per cent from newspaper sales. The company wanted these figures reversed to guard against sudden dips in the national economy, though Kenya's tenth year of independence was one of its best, with export earnings from agriculture up, foreign investment streaming in and a balance of payments surplus of £96 million. Much of the *Nation* group administration moved into offices at nearby New Stanley House (14,000 square feet at 20 shillings per square foot) and a serious search for new headquarters was put in hand. In the month of the stock-market listing, the NPP board was told that forecast profit-before-tax for the year to March 1974 was £361,000 (the actual figure was £410,000) and that the Aga Khan's loans (totalling some £1.3 million) had been repaid in full.

The year of the flotation was also the tenth anniversary of Kenya's independence, marked by a public celebration in Nairobi made awkward by the presence of Idi Amin. In his book, *Fantastic Invasion*,[4] Patrick Marnham described how Amin arrived early, spent some time leaping with the Maasai dancers and then practised spear-throwing in a leopard-skin cap. 'The Aga Khan carefully picked his way before the crowd and selected a seat as far from the field marshal as he could manage', Marnham wrote. The reporter detected a lack of spontaneous joy from the sparse crowd, which he attributed in part to a warning that any shop in the city which failed to decorate its premises would be closed on sight.

The first formal storm warnings over Githii's editorship came in February 1974, little more than a year after he returned from Oxford, when two NPP directors, Mareka Gecaga and Dunstan Omari, expressed concern about 'recent controversial articles published by the editor-in-chief', and said a body of opinion was forming against the newspaper. Curtis defended Githii, saying he had raised journalistic standards markedly, but agreed he should consult with management and forewarn the MD of any controversial pieces. Frank Pattrick was more outspoken. He regarded Githii as unstable and unpredictable and noted that the Editorial Policy Committee was not functioning. Politically, Githii by this time seemed to have made his peace with Njonjo and was conducting a policy of support for KANU and the government, although this support was often rooted in factionalism and prosecuted with bitter aggression. His feuds with politicians Julius Kiano and Njoroge Mungai became legendary and an MP expressed concern about the power of the Press. Githii retorted, 'I have heard of governments taking over newspapers but I have never heard of newspapers taking over governments.'

In September 1974 a special meeting of the Nation Newspapers board was called to discuss coverage of a by-election campaign involving Githii's *bête noir*, Foreign Minister Mungai, and his opponent, Dr Johnstone Muthiora, in Dagoretti on the outskirts of Nairobi. Githii had thrown the entire weight of the paper against Mungai, who wrote to all the directors asking if they supported the company's editorial policy of neutrality. Pattrick said the *Nation* carried four photographs of Muthiora in one week and Denman said Githii appeared bent on making personal attacks on Mungai.[5] Githii responded combatively: he had nothing to apologise for, Mungai had refused to speak to *Nation* reporters, editorial policy was to write the truth, the wisdom of non-executive directors to champion the interests of one candidate stood to question, and any aggrieved party had the right of recourse to law. John McHaffie, chief sub-editor at the time, recalled:

> *One Sunday Muthiora had a tea party at his home and made certain statements and George ordered me to put it on the front page. I did so and Muthiora was called in by security and accused of holding an illegal meeting. That also went on the front page, of course, it was all lovely stuff for the campaign. The next Sunday the same thing happened and I put the story inside. When George came in, he said, 'What are you up to? Why is Muthiora not on the front page?' I said, 'George, do you want him to get into trouble again? Is that the whole idea behind this?'*

The Board was satisfied that Githii's campaign had compromised the newspaper's independence and a 'corrective editorial' was published. Githii later claimed it was slipped in when he was out of town. Mungai lost the election.

Githii's relations with some of his staff were as prickly as with senior management. Peter Mwaura, then a reporter but later to become editor-in-chief himself, protested to the Kenya Union of Journalists that when he wrote a story about a scandal at Kenyatta University College, Githii killed it. He also repeatedly ordered him to divulge to Special Branch the source of a confidential document on which the story was based. Mwaura refused. Staff at the time saw Githii as devious, politically involved, conspiratorial and paranoid about enemies real or imagined. He was brilliant, too. McHaffie said:

> *He is the only editor I ever saw who had books by philosophers, not on his shelves to impress, but on his desk. One by Kant or Hegel or*

*somebody, I asked him and he said he was re-reading it. He would pepper his editorials with classical tags. I told him once that Latin was not a common language in East Africa. He said, 'Well, it's an education.' This is the same man who stood up at an editorial conference and his gun fell to the floor from his shoulder holster, to the surprise of all around him.*

Probably not to the surprise of Chege Mbitiru, a senior editorial writer, who was called in by Githii and instructed to write a leader article against Njoroge Mungai: 'I said, "I'm not interested", and he leaned back and put his gun on the table and said, "Chege, I am in charge here". I carefully walked out of the door and went to a dance with my girlfriend, now wife, and danced all night. Then I got a plane to New York next morning and did not come back for a year.' One Githii victim did deliver a resounding raspberry, according to John Eames, who spent 13 years with the *Nation* group: 'George fired this flaky reporter, I've forgotten his name, and this guy summoned seven taxis and departed Nation House at the head of a motorcade.' It's a foregone conclusion that the bill was sent to the editor-in-chief.

Veteran *Nation* journalist Joe Kadhi recalled:

*George had close relations with the President, with Njonjo and with the big security guy, Ben Gethi. That was unhealthy. When he wrote an editorial critical of a group in KANU, they would turn out to be people the group that he belonged to didn't like, people Njonjo was fighting. Everybody knew Mungai was jostling for position in the presidential succession and they put Muthiora up against him. Githii ordered me to use a story about people walking away from a meeting of Mungai with a big headline, 'The people of Dagoretti boycott Njoroge Mungai'. Frank Pattrick came in and said he had received a call from the foreign minister suspecting we were using the story unfairly against him. So I was trying to reshape the story and make it fair – only a few people had walked away – when George came in and said, 'What I told you stands.' I was between the devil and the deep blue sea so three of us went to Githii's office and he picked up the phone and called State House and started to talk to Jomo in Kikuyu. Now I know Kikuyu and all he was doing was greeting the old man – 'I haven't heard from you for a long time' and so on, just chatting. But that scared Pattrick so much he walked out and Githii's story stood. Githii was the last really powerful editor the* Nation *had and he spoiled it for his successors by opening the way to unacceptable management interference.*

Kadhi's contemporary, George Mbugguss, the long-time editor of *Taifa Leo*, shared the same birth date and given name as Githii and both came from Kiambu, but they were not close. Githii's paranoia about his personal safety became evident when they had a rare lunch together. 'We looked at the menu and he asked me what I wanted', Mbugguss recalled. 'I said pork chops and he said he would have the same. When the waiter brought the food, George took my plate and gave me his. He had a suspicion someone was trying to poison him.' It was about this time that Githii had extra floodlights installed at his home.

Smarting from the blow to the company's reputation brought about by Githii's tendentious handling of the Dagoretti by-election, management revised the editor-in-chief's terms of reference, and these were discussed at an NNL board meeting in February 1975. Curtis, in the chair, said the revision had been occasioned by 'past events' and 'the wish of the board to streamline communication between the EIC and management'. Githii, himself a director, objected to the board discussing the document and said this was between himself and his superior. When he was outvoted, he went through the terms line by line, seeking clarifications, definitions and amendments. Demanding a precise interpretation of 'accuracy', he accepted 'factual correctness'; when Curtis said the definition of 'prominent figure' was 'what a reasonable man' would understand, Githii said he could not understand what was meant by 'a reasonable man'. He objected to the use of 'sensitive issues' and 'editorial campaign' as being dependent upon value judgment. And though he accepted the document on the assurance there would be no suppression of news, he warned that it would be unworkable. Curtis said that in that case, there was not much hope for it. The meeting dragged on for three hours and ten minutes.

Githii and Curtis were both unhappy about the outcome and at the Aga Khan's request Kenyatta called in both men a few days later. A record of the encounter has Kenyatta saying, 'This is a serious matter, I would like to hear more details.' Curtis said, 'The central problem is consultation, management's right to know what is going into the paper, the duty of an editor to consult and inform on major issues.' Githii said, 'The problem is I do not know who I am dealing with. I accept that an editor is answerable to the laws of sedition, libel and slander but after that he should be free to use his judgement.' Curtis said a three-hour, 'at times bitter', meeting had been held to discuss the editor-in-chief's terms of reference and it had ended with Githii pronouncing the document unworkable: 'The situation is like a man and wife who have disagreed and quarrelled so often that perhaps a separation is the only answer in the interests of the family.' Githii interjected, '*Mzee*, I want to make clear I did not refuse to accept the resolutions [terms of reference]. I am also prepared to withdraw my remark that this will never work.'

Kenyatta: 'Mr Githii, these resolutions represent what management need of you. What is the saying about the piper and the tune?'

Curtis: 'He who pays the piper calls the tune.'

Kenyatta: 'That is right, do you understand, Mr Githii?'[6]

Githii's position was now crystal clear, yet the greatest disaster in the *Nation's* history lay only a few days ahead. Wittingly or not, the editor-in-chief perpetrated an error that brought anger and contempt upon his newspapers and damaged their credibility for many years. Ironically, consultation was not an issue and Githii survived in his job, but hindsight suggests that his closeness to high circles in government laid him open to fatal misjudgement. The story concerned the murder of populist MP Josiah Mwangi Kariuki, which turned into Kenya's gravest political crisis since independence. J.M. Kariuki, a one-time Mau Mau detainee and a former assistant minister, had become an outspoken critic of Kenyatta's government and a champion of the poor. He once famously remarked, 'A small but powerful group, a greedy, self-seeking elite in the form of politicians, civil servants and businessmen, has steadily but very surely monopolised the fruits of independence to the exclusion of the majority of the people. We do not want a Kenya of ten millionaires and ten million beggars.'

These sentiments resonated among the growing poor. More than a decade after independence, Kenya's economy was doing well, but the wealth belonged to a narrow elite and there was massive and growing unemployment. Kenyatta ran the country from Gatundu with his Kikuyu advisers and the cabinet rarely met. Conceivably, Kariuki's stance as champion of the underdog was opening a path to power for a candidate outside the royal circle and the Gatundu heavies were worried. As early as April 1970, Boaz Omori wrote in a letter to Curtis, 'The internal power struggle goes on, with more cabinet ministers openly attacking JM, who seems undeterred, feeling confident he has the support of the common man.' Karl Ziegler, then a business deal-maker in Nairobi, knew Kariuki and warned him that his remark about millionaires and beggars was going too far. Kariuki replied, 'Ah, they're too afraid, they know I'm too powerful for them to challenge me or threaten me. They haven't got the courage.' That Kariuki had presidential ambitions is incontestable. Malcolm Payne, assistant editor of the *Standard*, met with him at Ngong racecourse on Sunday 2 March 1975. Payne recalled, 'We were leaning on the rails and JM said, "When I am President, you'll be my minister of information".' Later that day, Kariuki was lured from the Hilton Hotel in Nairobi.

The first that Kenyans knew of his disappearance was a *Daily Nation* special edition on Friday, 7 March 1975, 'JM Kariuki is missing', which quoted Justus ole Tipis in the Office of the President as saying, 'All we know is that his wife informed the police that her husband has been missing since 2 March.' This sensational news was received with foreboding by Kenyans who remembered the murder of another contender for the presidency, Tom Mboya, just six years earlier. Then came the first of two catastrophic *Nation* blunders. Chief sub-editor McHaffie recalled, 'Githii and Michael Kabugua, the news editor, came out of George's office and said, "We've found out where he is. We've had reliable information, he's in Zambia, in the Intercontinental".' Saturday's issue splashed the headline 'JM "in Zambia"' over a story bearing the joint byline of Githii and Kabugua. It said the Intercontinental Hotel in Lusaka confirmed Kariuki had stayed in the hotel and later checked out. Rumours in Nairobi that he was missing were there-fore unfounded and damaging, it said. But four days later, Kariuki was known beyond doubt to be dead. That was where the *Nation* got it wrong again. While the *Standard* declared straight out that the missing man's body had been positively identified in the Nairobi City Mortuary, the *Nation* hedged. Its headline was, 'Kariuki dead, claims wife', and the story, bizarrely putting quote marks around the word 'dead', said no official confirmation was avail-able. Taken with the false Zambia report, it convinced the public that the *Nation* was trying to cover up the assassination of the people's champion.

McHaffie recalled:

> *There were demonstrations in the streets. Copies of the paper were shredded and burned, effigies of Githii were burned, students were chanting for Githii's head and some people felt nervous about being seen carrying the paper. It was embarrassing to work for the* Nation *for a while. The* Standard *got on their moral high horse and joined the bandwagon. It was a big body blow in terms of morale and circulation and reputation.*

Sub-editor Gavin Bennett said, 'There was a campaign, "Join the swing to the *Standard*", with fliers on the streets and walls and wrapped around electricity poles'. The *Nation* was deeply, spiritually felt to be the people's paper, but the 'JM lie', as it was called, changed all that. A page-one editorial by McHaffie tried to explain away the Zambia error, saying the *Nation* had no reason to doubt the information from the Lusaka hotel, but 'we now know that we were tragically wrong'.

An investigation of the murder by a Parliamentary Select Committee accused the police of a massive cover-up, pointed accusing fingers at senior figures in the administration and expressed suspicions about the *Nation's* role. It said Kariuki had been taken from the Hilton Hotel to the Ngong Hills and shot four or five times, once while he was kneeling. The report named 13 men as being 'directly or indirectly connected with those who murdered Mr Kariuki'. They included the Commandant of the paramilitary General Service Unit, Ben Gethi, with whom Kariuki was seen leaving the Hilton, and the Commissioner of Police, Bernard Hinga.[7]

A subsequent exclusive by the *Nation* disclosed that the body had been discovered by Maasai herdboys, who reported their findings to the Ngong police station. Not knowing that this was a corpse which was supposed to be eaten by hyenas, the police moved the body to the city mortuary. Questions have been asked about why the killers left the body and risked its discovery, why the body was moved and why Maasai cattle herders dared to enter a police station manned by Kikuyu officers when normally they would remain safely at a distance. Kenyans, especially in the rural areas before Christian burial rituals became common, frequently disposed of their dead by leaving them for wild animals. If for no other reason, it obviated the necessity for digging a grave in sun-baked ground. One Kenya journalist said, 'There is no doubt the body was supposed to be eaten by hyenas and given another 24 hours probably would have been. It was certainly unusual for the Maasai to go to a police station but the reason they gave was that the body was so well dressed and obviously a leader, they thought they might get some money.'[8] Unconfirmed reports at the time said there was a change of shifts at the police station, and the officer who took over was unaware of the 'situation' and thus sent Kariuki's body to the mortuary, where it was identified.

Githii appeared before the Select Committee and at an internal *Nation* inquiry. He said Kariuki's brother-in-law, Harun Muturi, had told him that the MP, who was a wealthy businessman, was expecting goods from Zambian Foreign Minister Vernon Mwaanga. Githii telephoned Mwaanga's home in Lusaka. The minister was out of the country and his wife said Kariuki was not staying there. She suggested he try the Intercontinental Hotel. Githii testified:

*I was connected to the receptionist who informed me that Mr Kariuki 'was not around'. On insistence, the attendant asked me to hold on and after a few minutes came back on the phone and said, 'Mr Kariuki is not around, he has checked out.' It was on the basis of that information that I wrote the story. At the time I sincerely believed he was alive and in Zambia. It would be foolish for any editor to write such a story under his name if he knew or thought it to be false.*

McHaffie, who had worked previously in Zambia, telephoned a reporter he knew in Ndola without result. There was no direct dialling in those days and attached to Githii's statement were switchboard records showing Githii's two calls and one by McHaffie. Whatever the truth, the fallout for the *Nation* was painful.

Pattrick noted in a letter to Paris, 'In a matter of 10 days, our competition appear to have achieved what they failed to do in the last 10 years – they are now the paper of the people. We are paying the penalty for becoming too closely involved with the regime. Public opinion is that George Githii was deliberately used to mislead the country.' An emergency meeting of the Nation Newspapers board concluded that Githii's reporting had been honest and the fudge on the identification was a responsible group decision. Whether Githii was justified in running his 'JM in Zambia' story on the fragile evidence of one inconclusive telephone call is debatable and Curtis described the decision as 'a serious misjudgement', though he believed there had been 'no deliberate attempt to mislead the public'. But MD Gerry Wilkinson clearly felt public suspicion about the *Nation's* integrity was being fuelled by Githii's continuing to soft-pedal contentious news. He pointed out that while the *Standard* front-paged stories that might vex the government, such as a threatened general strike, reports of oathing, court cases, Kariuki follow-ups and labour disputes, Githii relegated them to the inside pages.

Statements by Curtis at board meetings on consecutive days reflected the problems of a newspaper trying to maintain its independence in a repressive political climate. On 4 June, he drew the attention of NPP directors to the question of survival. Political pressures on the Press were bound to increase, he said, and it was better to have a live newspaper than a dead one; freedom of the Press could never be absolute and there were substantial grey areas where an editor could only use his best judgment. When a discussion took place on editorial policy at the NNL board meeting the following day, Githii stated that since Kenya had become independent the *Nation* had supported the government, so had this policy changed? Curtis responded that support for the government was not necessarily an unchangeable policy and there must never be a position where the paper could not constructively criticise the government – the editor-in-chief had often done so himself, to considerable effect. It would be fatal, Curtis argued, if the *Nation* became a rubber stamp for government actions. Finding the balance between these positions preoccupied editors throughout the *Nation's* history.

Although profit before tax for the year to 31 March 1975 crossed the half-million-sterling mark for the first time, at £501,746, what worried managers was the effect of the Kariuki affair on circulation. The *Standard's* sales leaped from 25,854 in February to 48,617 in March, the murder month, dropping to 41,391 in April and 35,827 in May, then up again to 40,997 in June, when the Select Committee's report was released. The effect was to give the paper a 30 per cent increase in ABC figures for the six-month period, January to June, its best ever performance. Much of the increase clearly came from disenchanted ex-readers of the *Nation*, whose March/April/May sales were the lowest for 12 years. What the *Nation* still enjoyed, however, was a greater overall sales figure, and, although the six-month average of 68,271 was 2,209 down on January–June of 1974, it remained significantly higher than the *Standard's* and the board concluded that 'our initial fears as to the effect of the Kariuki affair seem to have been exaggerated'. Thus the company survived the worst financial effects of its editorial misjudgements. What hurt more was the perception of the *Nation* as a sensationalist and tendentious newspaper. The *Standard* was not slow to cash in.

In 1973, Lonrho decreed a change of name from the cumbersome *East African Standard* to simply the *Standard*, and in 1977, its 75th anniversary year, the big, billowing broadsheet finally went tabloid. Nick Russell, a former *Standard* sub-editor and editorial trainer, was brought back to mastermind the change and he spent a month on the road investigating the two rivals' strengths and weaknesses. 'One thing I discovered was that a great advantage of the *Nation* was Paddy Kearney. Wherever you went, he was there. If one of the drivers was asleep in his van at two in the morning in the middle of nowhere, there would be a knock on his window and there would be Paddy Kearney.' Russell said he also discovered that 'if the *Nation* printed a scandal story, people read the *Standard* to see if it was true'. With the Kariuki affair still vivid in the public mind, Russell coined a slogan for the new tabloid: 'The paper you can trust'. Though Kearney earlier had bill-poster fun with the competition ('*The Nation*, a higher *Standard*'), Russell's slogan in the Kariuki context hit hard. Indeed, the Kariuki fallout was still being felt as late as 1978 when Wilkinson contracted Research Bureau Ltd to test public perceptions of the two dailies. Three focus groups were set up: executive and managerial, clerical and manual, and women. All three groups considered the *Nation* to lack reliability, to work under 'control' and to praise the establishment too much, while the *Standard* was considered honest, less sensational and less afraid of sensitive issues. These were devastating results and Wilkinson commented in an internal memo, 'There is no doubt all this is related to the Kariuki affair. While we all accepted there was still some suspicion harking back to 1975, I don't think any of us realised how deep this ran and how widespread it is even today.'

Important changes at the top of the *Nation* structure took place in 1976 and 1977 and Githii had his final row. After nearly 20 years with various *Nation* companies, Frank Pattrick retired as Group MD, a position he had assumed when Curtis went to Paris. He was succeeded by Stan Denman, while Gerry Wilkinson moved from his marketing slot to take Denman's job as MD of Nation Newspapers. Albert A.A. Ekirapa ('Triple A' as he became known to his staff) had joined the group in 1974, and was made chairman of Kenya Litho and a director of Nation Newspapers. A few months later, Curtis stepped down as group chairman, while remaining on the boards of Nation Newspapers and NPP, and Ekirapa succeeded him at the pinnacle of the organisation, thus Kenyanising decision-making at the top. Stan Njagi, general manager of NNL, became a director of the newspaper company.

Over four years, the *Nation's* bosses crossed swords with Githii on a long list of issues, but when he waded aggressively into the delicate arena of Islamic sensitivities, he breached a no-comment-on-religion rule that had been carved in stone since the earliest days and there was no way back. The *Daily Nation* of 4 May 1977 carried the following item:

> *The board of Nation Newspapers Ltd met yesterday and considered the resignation of Editor-in-Chief George Githii. Mr Githii's resignation was accepted with regret, the board said, noting that the issue had arisen from matters of principle held by both sides. Mr J. Rodrigues has been appointed acting group Editor-in-Chief while retaining his responsibilities as managing editor of the* Daily Nation.

The statement gave no hint of the furore that had taken place involving the Aga Khan, Githii, the Nairobi management and the company's directors. On 13 March 1977, Githii had published an editorial alleging divisions within the Shia Bohra community. Aware that the editor had no specific knowledge of the Muslim dialectic and puzzled by his motives for raising the issue, the Aga Khan sent a corrective article. Githii, however, refused to use it as an editorial, arguing that the views were those of the proprietor but not the newspaper. The NNL board suggested the piece be published as a feature article (which eventually it was, with a Special Correspondent byline), but by then Githii had sent a letter of resignation to chairman Ekirapa. When the *Nation* did not publish this immediately, Githii went to VOK, which happily broadcast the item on its 9 pm General Service newscast of 29 April.

Githii's resignation letter charged that the chief shareholder had compromised the newspaper's editorial integrity, and in an article for Ng'weno's *Weekly Review* he called on the Aga Khan to surrender his shares and for Kenyans to assume control of the *Nation* group. An editorial in the *Nation* said the Bohra item contained errors of fact which could not go uncorrected. It added that 'the Aga Khan has made it a cardinal rule never to direct the editorial policies of this newspaper, which are the day-to-day responsibility of a Kenyan editor answerable to the local board … the editorial policy has always been and will always be determined by Kenyans in Kenya'. Privately, *Nation* executives were angered by Githii's claim of frequent interference since he knew that the Aga Khan had only once before intervened directly, over Githii's own anti-Mungai campaign; they also considered he had breached his own Terms of Reference, which forbade taking sides on religious issues.

Rodrigues, the acting editor-in-chief, was a consummate newsman, widely admired by his staff and with a long record of loyalty to the company. But though he was a Kenyan, he was not an African and senior management felt an African should occupy the top editorial position. Filling senior editorial slots on a newspaper is always a headache because candidates are required to embody a range of diverse qualities: to be tough yet flexible, strict yet understanding, critical but not crushing. An editor should also be a fine writer, knowledgeable about production processes and politically adept, with excellent contacts.

At one head-hunting meeting at the Aga Khan's Aiglemont offices, an executive director remarked drily, 'What we seem to be looking for here is a combination of Mother Teresa and Muammar Gaddafi.' Names considered as Githii's successor, in addition to Rodrigues, included: ex-editor Hilary Ng'weno; novelist and former *Nation* columnist Ngugi wa Thiong'o; Jared Kangwana of VOK; Odhiambo Okite, who edited a feisty Christian newspaper, *Target*; Henry Gathigira, editor of the *Standard*, who had also been with the *Nation*; *Taifa Leo* editor George Mbugguss; and jack of all trades Joe Kadhi. A confidential memo ruled out Ngugi as 'an intellectual political ingenue ... difficult and dangerous'. (Ngugi had just published a novel, *Petals of Blood*, which strongly criticised post-*uhuru* society.) The same memo described Ng'weno as 'a cultivated radical', but it was clear the old favourite had the inside track. An approach was made but Ng'weno was busy preparing for the launch of a weekly paper, the *Nairobi Times*, and there was lingering ill-feeling over the failure of the *Nation* group to take an interest in Ng'weno's publishing company, Stellascope. Ng'weno refused the offer and, after nine months as acting EIC, Rodrigues was confirmed in the position. It was hardly a resounding affirmation, and though Curtis described him as 'perhaps the best journalist in the country', he said management was considering recruiting three Africans for training with a view to one of them taking over once he was ready. Rodrigues would then become Editorial Director, with a seat on the board.

The public anger over Kariuki's murder shocked the ruling clique. Four days of violence followed news of the assassination. Taped songs in praise of Kariuki were heard from vendors' street stalls and a stream of anonymous anti-government leaflets appeared. Denman recalled, 'Letters started pouring into the paper saying "Kill Kenyatta". The CID came round and were picking them up with tweezers and putting them in plastic bags.'

The regime decided on a hard-line response. When three ministers voted against the government in a debate on the Select Committee's investigation, Kenyatta promptly sacked them. A KANU meeting ruled that any MP deviating from the party line henceforth would be expelled and thus lose his parliamentary seat. KANU also pushed through a constitutional amendment empowering the President to pardon MPs for electoral offences, the immediate beneficiary being Paul Ngei, who had been found guilty of such offences in 1974. During a parliamentary debate in October, maverick MP Martin Shikuku described KANU as dead, and, when Deputy Speaker John Marie Seroney declined a request for substantiation on grounds that 'there is no need to substantiate the obvious', the two were arrested illegally within the precincts of parliament and detained. The *Standard's* Malcolm Payne, friend of Kariuki, said several of his reporters were picked up and questioned after they reported Kariuki's death. 'It was a dangerous time', he recalled. Two months later, Payne wrote an editorial questioning the benefit of government rallies. A front-page apology appeared next day, but he was told to leave the country within three months. Kenyatta delivered a series of hard-hitting warnings to dissidents and, in his supporting VP role, Moi said, 'The son who is jealous and ambitious to sit on his father's throne dies young and leaves his father still kicking hard.' By the end of the year,

Kenyatta had re-established his authority, but the Kariuki killing had damaged his prestige beyond hope of repair.

It may have come as a relief to the embattled Nairobi government that 1976 and 1977 were dominated by external events: the Israeli commando rescue of hostages at Entebbe Airport in Uganda, border problems between Kenya and Tanzania, and the collapse of the East African Community – the end of a dream for generations of administrators. In 1978, Idi Amin invaded Tanzania's Kagera Salient, and the Tanzanian Army, with the support of armed Ugandan rebels, counter-attacked, forcing Amin to flee to Libya, then in 1979 to Saudi Arabia, where he ended his days. Nyerere used his dominant position to reimpose Milton Obote, but his rule proved quite as murderous as Amin's until he in turn was overthrown in 1985 by Yoweri Museveni. Since independence in 1962, Uganda had changed government via two military coups, an invasion, two palace coups, a disputed election in 1980 and a guerrilla war. Moves to reconstitute the tripartite relationship had to wait for Museveni to restore stability to Uganda.

Kenya readers over the years became accustomed to the two major national newspapers carrying roughly the same news menu on their front pages, indeed sometimes the same headline.[9] But not on the morning of Monday 27 September 1976. The *Standard* ran a page-one splash, 'Nakuru Rally hears demand: Change the Constitution'. The *Nation* had nothing on this event. The *Standard* story by Zack M'mugambi said:

> *A demand that the Kenya constitution should be amended 'so that no future vice-president may assume the presidency automatically in the event of a reigning President retiring, becoming physically or mentally incapacitated or in the case of his death' was made at a KANU public rally here today. Calling it his own personal idea, the MP for Nakuru North, Mr Kihika Kimani, told the rally that the obtaining clause in the constitution was 'all wrong and should be amended and updated'.*

The story quoted three cabinet ministers as supporting the demand along with former Foreign Minister Njoroge Mungai, nominated MP Njenga Karume and 20 other parliamentarians. The Minister for Lands and Settlement, Jackson Angaine, urged Kihika to table a motion in parliament seeking a constitutional amendment. A week later at a Limuru fund-raising, Kihika again urged a change to the succession procedure, which provided a 90-day grace period for a VP to succeed. Kihika argued that the system might 'cause chaos in the country [and] allow an unscrupulous person every opportunity during his 90-day tenure of office to eliminate his political rivals'. The same ministers and MPs were on hand to provide vocal support, the *Standard* again gave the story headline treatment and the *Nation* gave it six paragraphs on an inside page.

Kenyans were quick to grasp that a group of powerful leaders associated with GEMA were trying to get VP Moi out of the way so that one of them could succeed to the presidency, and that they had enlisted the *Standard* in their cause. In their book, *The Kenyatta Succession*,[10] Joseph Karimi and Philip Ochieng say Mungai told them at the Nakuru meeting to expect 'a bombshell' in the *Standard* next day. Githii, an ally of Njonjo who was close to Moi, did not like the idea, not least because his long-time enemy Mungai was being whispered about as the GEMA candidate for president. In particular, he disliked the *Standard's* pious assertions that the Change the Constitution group was acting not for personal advantage but for the good of society. A *Nation* editorial asked, 'Why do some of these people want to remove Mr Moi? Is it because he is not a Kikuyu or Luo or Kamba? Is it because some of them have openly expressed the wish to be number two in this land?' Changing the constitution to facilitate a grab for power by a self-interested clique was not something Githii intended to support.

With the presidential system inviolate, the obstacle was the constitution. This document stated, 'If the office of President becomes vacant by reason of the death or resignation of the President … an election of a president shall be held within the period of ninety days immediately following the occurrence of that vacancy … while the office of president is vacant as aforesaid, the functions of that office shall be exercised by the Vice-President.' The 90-day hiatus was clearly time enough for any competent politician to consolidate his position and pave the way to his own accession, and it was this clause that the GEMA pretenders were targeting. By the mid-1970s, with an ageing Kenyatta increasingly remote and periodically ill, time was of the essence, and the Change the Constitution campaign was launched. Mungai, the presidential hopeful, was a nephew of Kenyatta and his personal physician; GEMA was led by a rich Kiambu tycoon, Njenga Karume; Kihika was the front man; support came from veteran politicians Angaine, Ngei and James Gichuru, and from John Konchella, George Anyona and Grace Onyango outside of the Gatundu circle. Oginga Odinga had his doubts about the succession clause but never joined the group. Opposing them were VP Moi, Njonjo, the powerful attorney-general, and Mwai Kibaki, Kikuyu leader from Nyeri who was Kenyatta's minister of finance.

Njonjo was Kenya's mover and shaker. An Anglophile from his days studying law in London, he dressed immaculately in three-piece Savile Row-tailored pin-stripe suits, with a watch chain looped across his waistcoat and a red rose or carnation in his buttonhole. The son of a chief who had been a loyalist during Mau Mau and married to a Scotswoman, Njonjo lived in Kabete and was sometimes known as the Duke of Kabeteshire. He was an urbane, right-wing elitist and sharp-tongued opponent of socialists, radicals, President Nyerere and East African federation. Njonjo was usually in his Attorney-General's chambers by 7 am, sometimes having seen Kenyatta at Gatundu at 6 am and read the newspapers to him. He was abstemious in his habits, rarely taking more than a glass of wine with dinner. Punctuality was a fetish and he would refuse to see people if they were late for an appointment, an alien concept to many Africans and Asians.

*Newsweek* bureau chief Ray Wilkinson remembers an uncomfortable meeting with Njonjo during Moi's presidency. He said:

> *Kay Graham, publisher of the* Washington Post *and* Newsweek *and one of the most powerful women in America, was making a visit to Africa. We asked to see Moi and he refused. There was a function and the Aga Khan was there and Moi asked him about 'this Mrs Graham'. The Aga Khan explained who she was but he still refused. We were also seeing Mwai Kibaki and the foreign minister, Robert Ouko, but Njonjo was scheduled first. Unfortunately, Mrs Graham arrived from South Africa an hour late because somebody forgot to factor in the time difference. When we met Njonjo he was in his usual pin-stripe and carnation. An American editor in the party asked a stupid question and Njonjo looked at us and said, 'Obviously, he [Wilkinson] hasn't briefed you very well on Kenya. I'm a very busy man, perhaps we could meet later. I have to go to Parliament.' I think he was upset because we were late and then got a silly question. So within half an hour of arriving in Kenya, this important woman was dismissed by an officer of state. Of course, there was no follow-up meeting.[11]*

If he could be brusque, even with important foreigners, Njonjo was loyal to and protective of his staff. Former High Court judge Frank Shields, who worked in the Attorney-General's chambers for 12 years, said in an interview, 'He was a very nice guy in many ways, very kind. A few of the girls in his office had matrimonial problems and he went to infinite trouble to get them government flats, that sort of thing. If a young state counsel wanted to buy a second-hand car, Njonjo would see that he got it at the cheapest price. He did a lot of things for his staff.' He was also strict about dress:

> *The women were not allowed to wear trousers. If Njonjo saw a girl in trousers, he used to ask, 'Are you on leave?' He was more British than the British, but there was a lot of Kikuyu in him and he sometimes talked in Kikuyu to his second-in-command and we were not part of it. I don't know if he knew a lot of law but he was able to manage things awfully well and the AG's office was very properly run in those days. It was a privilege for the female members of the staff if they could have one Saturday off a month. That was before Moi abolished Saturday working.*

With Kenyatta mostly distant in Gatundu, Njonjo effectively ran the government from Nairobi, appointing his own men to positions of influence and masterminding legislation such as the Preservation of Public Security Act to strengthen the position of his boss, and thus himself.

This was the man, metaphorically donning his lawyer's wig and gown, who delivered the coup de grâce to the Change the Constitution movement on 6 October. Njonjo made the following announcement:

> *In view of the recent sudden wave of statements at public meetings about the alleged need for amendment to our constitution, I would like to bring to the attention of those few who are being used to advocate the amendment, that it is a criminal offence for any person to encompass, imagine, devise or intend the death or the deposition of the President. Furthermore, it is also an offence to express, utter or declare such compassings, imaginings, devices or intentions by publishing them in print or writing. The mandatory sentence for any such offence by a citizen is death, and any person who aids in such offence by being an accessory after the fact of it, is liable to imprisonment for life. Anyone who raises such matters at public meetings or who publishes such matters does so at his peril.*

The boldness of the intervention was breathtaking, but characteristic of a man entirely confident of his political power. Whether Njonjo could have successfully prosecuted any accused offender is a matter of some doubt. Shields recalled:

*Charles came down from his office to the parliamentary secretary and myself and the draughtsmen in the office with a piece of paper and said, 'What do you think of this?' And we told him we thought it was a great nonsense to imagine the death of a president being the offence of treason. There is a statement in the Treason Act about imagining the death of a king or sovereign but what exactly that means I do not think has ever been defined. Charles responded, 'I'll try it anyway', and he did and it was successful. Everyone got very frightened and it effectively chopped off the debate.*

Githii welcomed Njonjo's statement in an editorial, declaring that those going round the country denouncing the VP were 'on the borderline of treason'. Elsewhere in Nation House, the announcement caused rather more disquiet. In common with newspapers everywhere, the *Nation* planned for future developments, and clearly one of these was the inevitable death of Jomo Kenyatta. Fearing chaos at such a time, a front-page article and an editorial had been written (typeset in Britain) calling for respect for the sanctity of the constitution during the transition. This was not only imagining the death of the President but publishing such an imagining, the penalty being execution! The paste-ups were hurriedly hidden behind a bookcase in Gerry Wilkinson's office. When Kenyatta died, Wilkinson was away on holiday, but he had told production manager Vin Durnan about the paste-ups and they were pulled out on the day and duly published.

It was some time before the *Standard* got Njonjo's message. A sharply-worded, page-one editorial, 'The big bluff', suggested the Attorney-General was acting in a personal capacity and not speaking for the government. The MPs and ministers themselves rejected Njonjo's implications of disloyalty and claimed majority support for their stand. Paul Ngei led a delegation to meet with Kenyatta and declared, 'We shall pursue this matter relentlessly to achieve what is right for our people.' It was only after Kenyatta called a cabinet meeting at Nakuru and told his ministers, including Ngei and Gichuru, that Njonjo's statement was final and a joint cabinet statement was issued to that effect that the movement fell silent. The *Standard* hurriedly backtracked, rounded on publications abroad and opportunists at home for distorting the arguments, and described as a 'government statement' the Njonjo warning it had earlier disparaged as his personal opinion. Njonjo did not forget and when the newspaper praised him in 1978, with Moi now President, for defending the constitution in 1976, he derided its hypocrisy in scathing terms. It is interesting to speculate on the weight of opinion that could have been brought against Njonjo in that crucial year had the Aga Khan not resisted the Muigai/Gecaga attempt to take control of the *Nation* group.

The fun event for the competitive-minded was the *Standard's* 1977 transformation into a tabloid. Editors wryly recalled the late Ken Bolton's fulminations about the tabloid format in an article which concluded that the only selling point was its 'easy secretion', presumably meaning it could be tucked into a pocket or handbag. But the *Standard* had moved on from the days when 11 European sub-editors produced a single edition and were in the Sportsman's Bar by 7.30 pm. The Easter 1977 promotional campaign, which *Nation* spies heard was budgeted at some £20,000, featured a hen sitting on an ever-growing egg with promises of surprises on 6 April. A not-too-subtle accompanying line said, 'Setting a new standard for the nation'. The *Nation* responded with a huge rooster, foot poised on the *Standard's* egg, above the caption, 'Beware of imitations'. The *Standard* gave all its vendors bright company jackets and caps. When the new tabloid proclaimed itself 'The paper you can trust', the riposte was 'Nation: All you need'. On the day of its rebirth, the *Standard* produced an 80-page paper and the *Nation* went up against it with a five-column, full-colour Safari Rally picture of local hero Joginder Singh. The *Standard* suffered printing and collating difficulties and did not get onto the streets until 8 am. The *Nation* sold out its 98,000 print order by 10.30 am. Against an ABC figure of 30,500 for July–December of 1976, a significant boost was expected with the new product, and the *Standard's* April sale did indeed rise markedly, to 41,000. Still, the *Nation*, at 79,000, was regularly outselling the competition by nearly two to one and staff had to be warned against complacency. A 100,000 target figure was set for June. In the event this was reached by the *Sunday Nation* a year later, and by the daily in 1981.

The *Standard's* editorial advances were not ignored at Nation House, where page design generally changed according to the whims of the sub-editors. In 1978, Gerry Wilkinson asked Allen Armstrong, formerly chief sub-editor, then in charge of training and editorial development, to bring some coherence to the newspapers' pages. Armstrong switched to a six-column format, giving design sub-editors greater flexibility and boosting classified advertisement revenue by extending the line depth. The 'sock-it-to-em' *sans serif* Futura and Gill typefaces were replaced by the more elegant Century and Schoolbook. 'Picture power' did not exist (too many 'firing squad' line-ups and official handouts from State House), so Armstrong sought a photo–text balance with pictures predominant when they were good enough. After the redesign appeared to great fanfare, an article in the British media journal, *UK Press Gazette*, described the *Nation* as 'an offset litho sheet which for clarity, colour and crispness surpasses many of our own [British] offset publications'. It was, the magazine said, 'an eye-opening tabloid'. Unhappily, over subsequent years standards dropped, and Armstrong, who had left by then, commented sadly, 'The *Nation* seemed to enter a phase blighted by careless cut-and-paste work, allied with shoddy printing and poor-quality newsprint. The result was often appalling, with paragraphs chopped and pasted at odd angles and the black ridges of excess cow gum showing up on the printed page.' Full-page, computerised makeup and a blitz on quality later got things back on an even keel, but the technical failures did little to support the company's claim to primacy at that time.

On New Year's Day, 1978, the *Daily Nation* carried a page-one picture of Kenyatta, in sandals, sports shirt and slacks, dancing sedately with Mama Ngina at a party the night before in State House, Mombasa. Eight months later, on 21 August, photos showed him cheering with a large group of athletes. Two days after that, inside a thick black border, the newspaper front-paged 'Kenya mourns, Mzee is dead, Moi is sworn in'. The long-prepared hidden editorial urged, 'Let us all tread the path of constitutionality that he set for us.' It went on, 'The mantle of office has fallen on the able shoulders of the man who for many years has made his own enormous contribution, in his capacity as Vice-President, to the official work of this country, Mr Daniel arap Moi. While the constitutional processes are at work, let us all give Mr Moi and the government all the help they need in their onerous duties.'

The transition, particularly the handling of the funeral, proved to be among the *Nation's* finest hours. Chief sub-editor McHaffie recalled:

> We all knew we were dealing with history. I got a call at home when the old man died and everybody rushed in and produced a special edition, then every day of the week was a challenge to get out the best paper. When the body was taken from State House to Gatundu, somebody shouted, 'Kenyatta is coming' and we all went out and stood in Government Road and there were motor-cycle outriders and just his coffin with his C-in-C's hat on top of the flag. It was a very emotional moment and the hairs stood up on the back of my neck. There was total silence. Even in death, there was an incredible feeling about this man. Then we all went back upstairs and got on with the job.

The issue that reported Kenyatta's funeral became a collector's item. McHaffie said:

> *There was a week between the death and burial and all that week I*
> *was thinking about how we should present the funeral. I decided we*
> *should do a colour wraparound which would stand alone as a front*
> *page but would also fold out, showing front and back as one big*
> *composition. I instructed the photographer Duncan Willetts, who had*
> *done some great lying-in-state pictures for us, to give me a horizontal.*
> *I actually had it designed a couple of days before the event.*

On 1 September 1978, *Nation* readers were presented with a view of soldiers in scarlet tunics marching alongside the gun carriage that bore Kenyatta's coffin, covered by the green, red and black national flag. Above was the single word, 'Farewell'. When the paper was opened out, the photograph doubled in size and the full headline read 'The final farewell'. The colour was brilliant and the impact stunning. McHaffie said, 'Colour was still a bit of a rarity in those days and we sent the photographs to an outside laboratory to do the separations and there were delays. The paper came out late because of the colour but there was such a demand for it, we were reprinting up to midday.'

Kenyatta, 86, died in his sleep at State House, Mombasa at 3.30 am on 22 August 1978. An emergency cabinet meeting was called at State House, Nairobi, at 3 pm, and Moi was sworn in by Chief Justice Sir James Wicks 'to exercise the functions of the office of the President'. Among those who watched the ceremony were Change the Constitution protagonists Ngei, Gichuru and Angaine. Njonjo told reporters Kenya's new president would be elected 'strictly according to the constitution'. And so he was. Moi was unanimously declared President of the ruling party, KANU, at a special delegates conference on 6 October and was elected unopposed as President of Kenya four days later. 'Moi's the One', the *Nation* bannered. What the *Nation* and the nation did not know was how nearly he was not the one.

Shortly after the changeover, Njonjo told an incredulous parliament that a private army, known as the *Ngoroko* after a bunch of ferocious cattle thieves, had been formed at Nakuru to assassinate key national leaders on the day of Kenyatta's death. *The Kenyatta Succession* quoted government sources as saying there were 15 names on the primary list but 300 in all, including the alpha victims' deputies, families and friends. The prime targets, according to these sources, included Moi, Kibaki, Njonjo, General Service Unit (GSU) chief Ben Gethi, Director of Intelligence James Kanyotu, the auditor general, the head of the civil service and a number of permanent secretaries. A second list named the army commander and George Githii among others. Ochieng's and Karimi's sources set out the plan as follows: When the *Mzee* died, the 15 principal targets would be called to State House at Nakuru on the pretext that he was critically ill; the three most wanted, Moi, Kibaki and Njonjo, would be conducted to the room containing Kenyatta's body and there shot dead by *Ngoroko* men with silencers on their weapons; their bodies would be removed and the remaining 12 would be dealt with likewise; the *Ngoroko* would then fire bullets into Kenyatta's body and an announcement would be made that the 15 were killed by presidential guards who caught them in the act of murdering Kenyatta. A curfew would be declared in which the hundreds of other targeted leaders would be killed across the country and then a provisional government would be announced. A list made available to the two authors showed that the massacre organisers would take the positions of President, VP, executive prime minister and six key ministries.[12]

When the old man died, his heart having finally given out, Njonjo was out of the country but due back that day, and Kibaki, who was in Mombasa, was hastily informed. Moi was urged to leave his home on the Tugen escarpment and drive immediately to Nairobi while it was still dark to avoid *Ngoroko* road blocks. Several accounts say Moi did go through such a road block near Nakuru, but he had no accompanying escort car and was not recognised. Njonjo, in his revelatory statement, said *Ngoroko* members would be identified and brought to book, but no trials were ever held, and their alleged commander, Assistant Police Commissioner for the Rift Valley, Ephantus Mungai, was allowed to go free when he returned to Nairobi after fleeing abroad. Njonjo said this was in the public interest and Moi summarily declared that it was time to end the *Ngoroko* debate.[13]

At the time of Moi's accession, Kenya was acknowledged as one of the few stable nations in Africa. When 32 heads of state and government signed the Organisation of African Unity founding charter on 23 May 1963, a British newspaper noted, 'Africa is an insecure continent suffering from a series of political bushfires and seems incapable of operating its own fire brigades.' By the time Kenyatta died, only eight of the 32 OAU signatories remained in office. Three had died of natural causes, 20 were overthrown or killed in coups and one (Milton Margai of Sierra Leone) left office voluntarily after losing an election.

Moi's presidency got off to a good start. He was 54, a husband and a father (though he had broken with his wife after a fracas during a New Year's Eve party hosted by Kenyatta); he was a farmer with business interests, long experienced in politics, an avowed Christian, and a non-smoking, non-drinking Chief Scout of Kenya. He announced his policy of *Nyayo* – to fol-low in the footsteps of Kenyatta – and he adopted the slogan, 'Peace, love and unity'. As he was to do throughout his presidency, Moi made strenuous tours to every part of the country and was warmly received by Kenyans grateful to be spared the violence that accompanied leadership changes in so many other African nations. As a Kalenjin, Moi was clearly not part of the widely feared and by then despised Kikuyu elite that had gathered around Kenyatta, but he reached out to ordinary Kikuyus as well as to the resentful Luo com-munity. He appointed the experienced Mwai Kibaki, a Kikuyu untainted by Gatundu links, as Vice-President, and fired those permanent secretaries, ambassadors and senior policemen whose loyalty he doubted. Githii's old nemesis, Police Commissioner Bernard Hinga, who came under fire after the *Ngoroko* revelations, retired.

The new President swiftly earned popularity by denouncing corruption and land-grabbing, and introducing a series of populist measures such as

*A later view of Moi's* Nyayo *policy of following in the footsteps of Kenyatta, when the footprints came to seem like potholes.*

the provision of free milk in schools, abolition of school fees for younger children and the building of roads in pastoral areas. Above all, on 12 December, the 15th anniversary of independence, he released all 26 political detainees. They included MPs Shikuku and Seroney, who had angered KANU stalwarts with their jibe at the party, and Ngugi wa Thiong'o, former *Nation* commentator and later Professor of Literature, novelist and dissident, who had spent 12 months in the cells. 'I haven't read a newspaper for more than a year', he told a reporter upon walking free. 'How is the *Nation*?' Crowds at Uhuru Park greeted Moi's announcement of the releases with cries of '*Moi juu*' (Up with Moi) and students cheered him in the streets.

## *Notes*

1. Amin claimed he had been told in a dream that it was his destiny to rid Uganda of Asians, but a story has persisted that he was angered by the refusal of a widow in the wealthy Madvhani family to marry him.
2. *A Matter of People* by Dom Moraes, Andrew Deutsch, London, 1974.
3. This was a problem President Nyerere had addressed in Tanzania ten years earlier. When guests at an Arusha hotel failed to stand as the visiting President Sekou Toure passed through the lounge, the Regional Commissioner ordered the hotel closed. Nyerere reversed the decision and called on politicians and civil servants to 'help in stamping out the disease of pomposity'.
4. *Fantastic Invasion: Dispatches from Contemporary Africa* by Patrick Marnham, Jonathan Cape, London, 1980.
5. In an interview for this book, Denman said at one point he warned Githii against publishing an anti-Mungai tract: 'I said I would drop a spanner in the press if he went ahead – and I knew exactly where to drop it. George telephoned the Mzee.'
6. The meeting solved the immediate problem, but stirred unease among senior editors that the head of state had been involved in the *Nation's* internal affairs. They felt this sat ill with the newspaper's assertions of independence. The opposite view was that Kenyatta's relationship to the editor was close – Githii had been his press secretary – and it was essential to understand his position. In the event, Kenyatta made it clear that he had misgivings about Githii and was not prepared to intervene for him.
7. Two pages were said to have been removed from the parliamentary report at the last moment and there was widespread speculation that they contained references to Githii's role.
8. Among many unsubstantiated rumours, one said Kariuki's face was doused with acid and this repelled the hyenas.

9. John McHaffie recalled putting the *Nation* to bed one night, then going to Robbie Armstrong's Starlight bar and chatting with Clive Durham, his opposite number on the *Standard*. Bjorn Waldegard had won the Safari Rally that day and both chief subs had written the same headline, 'A star is Bjorn'.

10. *The Kenyatta Succession* by Joseph Karimi and Philip Ochieng, Transafrica Book Distributors, Nairobi, 1980.

11. The remainder of Mrs Graham's trip did not go much better. Ray Wilkinson said, 'We went to see the minister of information, some nobody as they always are in Kenya. Local reporters and photographers were milling around and the minister sat us on a horseshoe-shaped seat with him opposite and then he lectured Mrs Graham about how the Western Press had a lot to learn from the African Press. Kay Graham sat there with a fixed smile, the Smile of Death.'

12. This account leaves several questions hanging; primarily, what did the plotters intend to do about the army, which had a record of constitutional propriety, and why was the conspiracy predicated upon Kenyatta dying in Nakuru when in recent years he had shown a strong preference for Mombasa?

13. Kihika Kimani, the front man in the Change the Constitution group, told the Akiwumi Commission on tribal conflict in 1999 that the political climate changed radically after Kenyatta's death. 'It was very hot for me', he said. 'I found it very rough when President Moi took over.'

# 1982 Coup Attempt

*The greatest threat to freedom is the absence of criticism.*

Wole Soyinka, winner of the 1986 Nobel Prize
for Literature

The *Weekly Sun* of Zimbabwe once declared that 'a newspaper has the inalienable right to present a piece attractively or in a dull manner', and promptly demonstrated where it stood with the headline 'The importance of vitamin E to chickens'.

*Nation* reporters and sub-editors have traditionally taken the opposite tack, boldly assaulting the English obstacle course with a reckless and inventive zeal that owes less to grammatical competence than to auditory perception and referential phobia. For years, the great unread books in the *Nation* newsroom were those volumes at every journalist's elbow, the house stylebook and the English dictionary. 'Sammy Soundalike' was the name that training editor John Lawrence invented for the perpetrator of those errors which have recurred with mind-numbing regularity, words that Kenyan journalists spell as they pronounce them. Thus snickers for sneakers, crashed for crushed, barried for buried (but oddly buffled for baffled), curve for carve, buggle for burgle (and buglary or even buggery for burglary), fanfair for funfair, rapture for rupture, going after the small fly (instead of the big fish) and breeding from the nose. Not to forget the Kenyan version of dilly dallying: dilly darling. All these have graced the columns of the papers. Then there are the cliches from which no self-respecting Kenyan journalist would ever be separated: sweet-talking conmen, a section of the Press (meaning the other guys, not us), scribes for journalists and gun-totting police who swing into action, leave no stone unturned, beef up security and vow to bring culprits to book. VIPs jet into Nairobi and MPs shoot up to ask questions in the august [sometimes August] House. Tortured grammar, dodgy spelling and mistaken idioms produce heart-rendering for rending, whooping for whopping, renumeration for remuneration, over-speeding, over-bleeding, in hot soup, a thorn in the neck, avail for make available, advocate for instead of advocate, fled for his dear life, mid-last week, the past one month, shed off for shed, a bush for the bush, pick for pick up, flock the church, swarm the building, admitted at hospital, machineries, deadwoods, underwears, far more better and severally for several times. A photo caption for a service involving a mitred archbishop referred to 'Maurice Cardinal Otunga (in priestly hat)'.

Kenyan sub-editors use words that are rare in the real world: kudos, sleuths, lauds, rails at, revellers, hail, festive merrymakers and a headline favourite, tips (for suggests or advises, as in 'Nation MD tips on why firms collapse'). Cliches repeated endlessly from the world of politics include: money has been poured to finish me, when funds become available, a few disgruntled elements, enemies of development, and many more. That some of the journalists' malapropisms confer added value to the breakfast read is incontestable. To learn that someone was crashed in an accident or strangled to death is to receive an image of violence which correct usage is too pallid to convey.

Perversely, Kenyans generally tend to prim understatement. In their let-ters to the editor, readers frequently describe instances of quite outrageous misconduct, then conclude mildly that 'this behaviour leaves much to be desired'. A *Nation* reporter described a scene where nine bandits with AK-47 automatic rifles emerged from cover and surrounded a tourist bus. Next sentence, '*Sensing danger*, the driver accelerated'. From a film review in the *Daily Nation's* Saturday magazine: 'She has a holiday romance but things go awry when he tries to kill her.' The position of the time element may have had something to do with this story: 'A woman who was shot three times with a pistol yesterday said she feared her life was in danger.' And punctua-tion problems resulted in the following in a 1999 story: 'At Tsavo, Bishop Chapman said they crossed the forest which is inhabited by lions trembling in fear.' Straight misreporting has always played a part. Judge Shields was disappointed that his neat reference to a case being 'like *Hamlet* without the Prince of Denmark' was rendered 'like *Hamlet* without the province of Denmark'. Columnist Wahome Mutahi recalled a young reporter writing that two cars had collided 'buttock to buttock'. Nuance has always proved a danger area, including what is slang (clobber, scam and ripoff) versus what is correct (beat, scandal, theft). As late as 1999, the *Daily Nation* used the word 'crap' in a story and headline, both writer and sub-editor apparently unaware that this was not a word used in polite society. Worse is the application of inappropriate adjectives: randy rapist, sexy granddad, amorous defiler. Some journalists have made words up (abhorrable) and a leader writer produced one nobody had ever heard of, irrefragably. It means indisputably. Also the tediously pedantic anti-riot police. Sometimes writers clearly have not understood the meaning of an English word, as in 'Lamenting the untimely death of Mrs Kariuki' under the headline, 'Woman dies at 102'.

The *Nation's* headline writers have contributed more than their share to brightening the reader's day: 'Moi's pledge to cane farmers', 'Salvage Lord Egerton's organ', 'Bishop alleges fowl play', 'Gumo's body will make history' (Nairobi City Commission, the body in question, clearly would not fit). Which is not to say that the competition has been any better, as this *Kenya Times* headline indicates: 'African should privatise parts, urges Ntimama'. If introducing an error into a correction is an editor's first nightmare, his second is to see a perfectly good headline changed for the worse. Executive editor Sean Egan remembers spotting 'Women press corp barred' on proof. He changed it to 'Women press corps barred', adding the necessary *s* to 'corp'. It appeared in the paper as 'Women press corps barried'. A first-edition headline, 'Why 8–4–4 is a burden to students' was 'corrected' in the final edition to 'Why 8–4–4 is a barden on students', and 'Poll debacle leaves Swedes with hangover' became 'Poll debacle leaves Swedes hangovered'. A headline that probably provided as much amusement as any, while being perfectly correct, was 'MP forced me to take bribe', while the cleverest in later years, with a spin on bribery and developmental journalism, appeared not in the *Nation* but in a journalists' magazine, *Media Focus*. It read, 'Envelopmental journalism'.[1]

An exasperated Lawrence complained in 1990 that the *Nation* newsroom had access to his weekly bulletin, *Let's Get It Right*, and to the company stylebook, both inherited from a predecessor, Bob Hitchcock, and updated by Pamela d'Angelo to his own electronic style guide in the database, and to the English dictionary plus all the reference books in the library. Yet he found a story which, after editing, contained 23 errors. Lawrence recalled a memo from Ekirapa to George Mbugguss, saying, 'John Lawrence seems to be drawing attention over and over again to the same mistakes that Bob Hitchcock referred to.' In a note to the author, Lawrence said, 'I started *The Plus and Minus Book*, a compendium of the day's hits and misses, praise where it was due and a kick in the pants when somebody got it wrong. What appalled me was the number of mistakes that recurred day after day.'

That said, sympathy must be extended to sub-editors who had to grapple with sometimes incomprehensible copy. The following telephoned story was once placed in the sub-editors' basket:

> *The tragedy struck the home of a Hero businessman Opiyo Champion yesterday when his two wives were en-electroniced by lunch and died on the spot. The wives Veronica and Jeneifer had just completed their lunch and were arresting at their home before they mat their tradegic fate. It was said that the incident started when Veronic was chewing sugar and when she went to throw the remains on the cane in the coumpand space through fenced wire was wehen she struck tumuor. Then came her short lived sprean for help. Jenefer, with limited knowledge of electric dogmas went to her rescue and as she grabbed her co-wife she found herself also in dragness. The berieved husband also went for their ordeal with a sharp piece of wood separated them when they were already tied despite milited effort. Mr Oreso Odoney medical officer in charge of Ahero dispensary to resuctate the victims it was all in vain.*

It might be felt that the copy-taker in Nation House who took the story over the telephone should bear more blame than the hapless correspondent in Ahero, but that made the sub-editor's job no easier.

In a society where 'sausage and chips' appears on menus as 'sosange and sips' (with 'tomato sos'), where some vernacular tongues do not differentiate between *r*'s and *l*'s, where teachers, as well as mothers and fathers, mispronounce English words in the same uniquely African way, and where the great majority of journalists are writing in their third language, it is understandable that Kenya's newspapers did not reach the standard of English found in the Fleet Street qualities. Old-timers may also remember Jack Beverley of the *Sunday Nation* getting into hot water for writing of 'expatriots' when he meant 'expatriates'. But English-language newspapers in other former colonial territories, such as the *Trinidad Guardian*, *The Times of India*, *The Sowetan* in South Africa, the *Straits Times* of Singapore and the *South China Morning Post*, achieved markedly higher linguistic standards (and the latter two became at one point the world's most profitable newspapers on turnover). What dismayed *Nation* managers was the ill-concealed hostility that greeted many of their efforts to provide training opportunities and the lukewarm support for training editors from some senior editorial people. Lawrence, an Australian, said, 'I remember complaining to George Mbugguss one day and he responded quietly by asking, "How long has Australia been a nation?" "Two hundred years", I replied. "Well, Kenya has been a nation for only 29 years". I guess he was saying Rome wasn't built in a day, but I felt this attitude was a bit of a cop-out. I felt he could have reinforced my efforts more stringently.'

Training was a serious commitment of Nation Newspapers from the very beginning. 'We must write ourselves out of our jobs in 10 years', Curtis had famously said, and as early as 1962 he asked the IPI for someone to run a three-month training course for African sub-editors. By June 1963, *Nation* journalists were attending IPI classes. The Switzerland-based IPI, with ground-breaking work done by Charles Hayes on loan from EAN, ran training establishments in Nairobi and, for a time, in Lagos, Nigeria. Specialist trainer Frank Barton managed the Nairobi centre, which later became the School of Journalism at the University of Nairobi. He recalled in an interview:

> *I got to Kenya in 1963 and we trained a helluva lot of* Nation *people, four or five on every course. Our job was to put black faces behind desks. I remember Michael Curtis saying, 'We want to get as many Africans in as early as possible, how long will that take?' I said, 'You're talking five or ten years if you start now', and they started right away. There were very few black journalists at the time and you had to hand it to Michael, it must have been hell in the early days.*

Academic ability apart, there were cultural factors which made the aggressive art of reporting problematic for polite young men brought up in a tradition of respect for older people and for persons of stature. Barton recalled organising mock press conferences at his training workshops in which he or another instructor would act the part of a VIP to test the interviewing skills of his students. One such occasion posited the arrival in Kenya by some error in flight scheduling of Ian Smith, then Prime Minister of Rhodesia and a reviled outcast in black Africa. Barton, playing the role of Smith, called for the first question. 'Mr Smith', the student said, 'did you have a nice flight?'

As well as sending staffers to IPI courses, the *Nation* brought in the first in a long line of training editors in 1969. When some of the early ones did not work out, the portfolio was handed at different times to experienced journalists. But a board minute from 1976 records that George Odiko, general secretary of the Kenya Union of Journalists (KUJ), 'failed to co-operate [with an in-house training course] and agitated members to frustrate the scheme'. Denman quoted Odiko as saying the KUJ did not want a new training editor at Nation House; in fact, they were not interested in training at all. The union was also demanding it should receive and administer aid being provided to the School of Journalism by the Swedish government. Gerry Wilkinson complained that the KUJ had 'absolutely no vision for the development of its members'. Barton noted, 'In-service training has never been popular among African journalists, probably because they resent being shown how to do it at their own desks. And often, it must be said, the white training officer is of dubious quality.' Not so the dedicated Bob Hitchcock, *Nation* training editor 1982–5, but he had a baptism of fire anyway, as he recalled:

> *I walked into that office and there was a deadly hush. They didn't want me there. There was a KUJ protest and I really had to assume it was racial, they didn't want a white training editor. The first two weeks were impossible because nobody would co-operate but I won over George Mbugguss and Peter Kareithi, the news editor, who was a forceful character. But it took almost a year to convince the journalists that I wasn't some kind of managerial stooge. They were referring to me as 'that man from Paris'. Still, I ran my first seminar at Naivasha within three months and after the first year, things went very well and I had no more problems.*

Hitchcock added:

> *What I realised later was that the staff had a lot to be unhappy about, working under bad conditions and some of them doing very long hours and never a thank you. An important point is that the newsroom was not forewarned of my appointment, they suddenly found this funny, skinny man sitting among them wearing a cravat. They were mishandled, I felt. Once you convinced them training was to their advantage, they were keen to learn.*

Hitchcock represented a disappearing breed of newspapermen who learned their craft by doing it. In Nairobi, as elsewhere in the industry, recruits were increasingly required to have a high academic background to cope with an increasingly complex news agenda; the practicalities they could learn on the job. The graduate recruits did not always see this latter requirement as important. At a company review meeting chaired by the Aga Khan, Denman reported that university recruits to the editorial staff 'tend to be politically unstable and reluctant to undertake routine reporting and writing'. McHaffie, the *Nation's* last white chief sub-editor, agreed: 'They disliked the practical exercises I set for them and considered because they had degrees, they were already bona fide journalists.' The Aga Khan's response was to suggest the company explore the postgraduate level for more stable candidates. But even some of those graduates who also completed a School of Journalism course proved a disappointment; primarily, the company believed, because of dipping standards at the university.

Over the years, the *Nation* broadened its training schemes from in-house and IPI/School of Journalism courses to include postgraduate study at the University of Wales in Cardiff, where several senior editors completed year-long MA courses; attachments to universities in Europe and the USA; and lengthy exchange visits with journalistic and management counterparts at the *St Petersburg Times* in Florida, under a twinning arrangement originated by the Aga Khan in 1981. Over the years, standards, though far from perfect, improved immeasurably from the sloppy-cum-arrogant days when the union impeded training initiatives. Veteran training editor Frank Whalley said in an interview in 2005, 'There are still people here with delusions of adequacy though that is largely due to lack of exposure to high-level competition, and I do get annoyed by repeated errors. But generally I have found staffers enthusiastic about training and genuinely willing to learn and no union problems.'

If the *Nation's* second decade was peppered with editorial problems, marketing and promotion came into their own. With Gerry Wilkinson's arrival, greater emphasis was placed on image-building and more sophisticated methodology was employed to cultivate commercial credibility, as well as run damage limitation for the Kariuki affair. One day in Dublin, an Irishman working in advertising for the *Daily Telegraph* in London, Aidan Flannery, came to lunch with Gerry Wilkinson at the *Irish Independent*. Very soon afterwards, he joined the *Nation*, where he spent eight years in charge of advertising then marketing. In marketing terms, Flannery considered the *Standard's* belated decision to go tabloid helped the *Nation*: 'It was a psychological boost to us because it meant they had joined us now, not just joined, but followed. A lot of their A-class readers, the snob element, couldn't bear it, but now there were only two tabloids and it opened up their classified ads market, too.' As for the Kariuki fiasco, 'there was a lot of gnashing of teeth in Nation House', Flannery recalled. 'It did not affect advertising but it certainly hit our circulation, so what I did was use the last year's reader-ship survey and I talked readership, readership, readership, not circulation. Which is not to say that people didn't notice we stopped publishing the ABC sales figures for a while. The negative effect lasted for about a year and then we started recovering.'

To promote at the lower end of the market, Flannery and Wilkinson would set up a football match for a poor school, bring a sponsor with 20 coolers for soft drinks and front-page the event in *Taifa Leo*. For the upper end, they started *Nation* golf tournaments, promising a Toyota automobile for a hole-in-one (insurance cost £600 but the car was never won), and Wilkinson's Nation Business Game, using printouts by computer, just then becoming the accepted office tool. Sponsored competitions would bring in as many as 600,000 replies (in later years well over a million). The company started the Nation Advertising Awards, later taken over by the Marketing Society of Kenya. All this was a far cry from Spot The Ball, with a prize of 200 shillings and a Sanyo radio.

If the *Standard* had been lackadaisical for many years about the challenge of the *Nation*, that changed in 1980. Unsurprisingly, the driving force was George Githii. After his angry departure from Nation House, the company's stormy petrel stood for Parliament in the November 1979 general election against, naturally, his old enemy Dr Njoroge Mungai. Githii's stated con-tempt for the *Nation* did not prevent him from soliciting the newspaper's support for his campaign, typical chutzpah, which met with a stony response. In the event he lost, and was appointed chairman of the *Standard* group in March 1980 and later editor-in-chief. His combativeness was in no way reduced, and when Mwai Kibaki remarked that there was nothing spe-cial about being chairman of the *Standard*, Githii retorted that there was nothing special about being Vice-President. Soon after his arrival, Githii wrote a personal letter on *Standard* notepaper to the Aga Khan assuring him he bore no bitterness or ill-will, and signing off 'warm personal regards'. This must have amazed the *Nation's* directors and managers who at that very time were discussing a 'declaration of war' by the *Standard* and its 'determination to kill off the *Nation*.' Primarily, this focussed on approaches to top editorial people in contravention of a gentleman's agreement not to poach each other's staff. Kul Bushan, Justin Macharia and James Kimondo jumped ship after receiving what a board minute described as 'very high salaries and ben-efits they could not refuse'. Another newsroom executive listed the terms he was offered: salary £6,000 per year, tax-free dinner allowance £1,800, petrol allowance £600, rent-free house, light, water, telephone, provident fund, medical care and guaranteed promotion to chief sub-editor when the position became vacant. Since the *Nation's* top editorial salary at the time was £8,000 – for the editor-in-chief – such offers were hard to resist. At least seven *Nation* journalists were targeted and the same board minute stated, 'These are extremely serious developments. Lonrho executives in Nairobi are very concerned about these developments, which do not make commercial sense for the *Standard*, but they are apparently powerless to prevent them.'

A *Standard* editorial accused the *Nation* of conspiring with Milton Obote to regain the presidency of Uganda and Ekirapa said there had been attempts to interfere with *Nation* transport. Several airlines removed their advertising from the *Nation* when the *Standard* offered discounted rates or 100 per cent barter deals. More seriously, the *Nation* lost the government advertising tender to the *Standard* at a cost of £160,000 for reasons which a board paper described as 'political rather than commercial'. The *Standard* had by then finally launched a Sunday paper, described by one *Nation* executive, wistfully or critically, as 'racier and livelier' than the *Sunday Nation*, though after a year in the market it was selling just 38,000 against the *Sunday Nation's* 104,000. The principal victim of the new paper was Ng'weno's *Nairobi Times*, which stopped circulating outside of Nairobi. During one of many tense board meetings to discuss the *Standard's* offensive, Curtis, who bore the scars of many encounters with Githii, perceptively remarked that it was possible he would soon fall out with the *Standard* management. And so it proved. Githii precipitated a crisis which cost him his job and forced his paper into a posture of cringing subservience to the government.

When Moi promised at the time of his accession to follow in the footsteps of Kenyatta, most Kenyans overlooked the *mzee's* intolerance of opposition, a path which Moi followed with enthusiasm. Indeed, while Kenyatta tolerated a degree of free expression in Parliament, his successor considered criticism by MPs as tantamount to treason and issued stern public warnings against 'traitors' and 'dissidents'. He banned tribal societies including GEMA, the Luo Union and the Kamba Union, closed the University of Nairobi repeatedly and used the security apparatus against demonstrators. Beset with economic difficulties, not least a shortage of maize meal caused by corruption in the marketing board, Moi's response was to become ever more authoritarian. In mid-1982, three-and-a-half years after releasing Kenyatta's detainees, he began putting his own opponents behind bars without benefit of trial: first, Stephen Murithi, a former deputy director of intelligence, who challenged a transfer out of the police; followed by Murithi's lawyer, John Khaminwa, and then six academics allegedly teaching subversion. Also picked up, on the day he planned to launch the Kenya Socialist Alliance, was George Anyona, an MP who openly opposed new legislation to make Kenya a *de jure* one-party state. The next day this constitutional amendment was read into law in one hour 45 minutes by Njonjo while a cowed National Assembly sat in silence. By then an elected MP and the Minister for Constitutional Affairs, Njonjo took the opportunity to declare that preventive detention was entirely constitutional and not subject to dispute in any court of law.

An Africa Watch human rights report on this period observed, 'Although the [one-party state] amendment arguably only sanctified what already existed in practice, it radically challenged Kenyan politics in "legitimising" the ban on all opposition parties. It effectively licensed the persecution of opposition groups by criminalising them and creating an underground context.'[2] The *Nation* was unhappy. It had argued against one-party rule for years and now, defeated, called on the politicians to explain what advantages would accrue from it. 'It is our hope that the one-party state will still have room for multiplicity of opinions on matters of public interest and that the freedom entrenched in the constitution will continue to guide the party', an editorial forlornly said.

Githii's abrupt separation from the *Standard* came after he wrote a bold editorial for the 20 July 1982 issue which declared, 'In the last six months, this country has been increasingly gripped with fear, the fear of detention of individuals without trial.' He referred to university lecturers resigning in a state of trepidation, and to the government banning plays, telling editors what they could publish and intimidating lawyers. He called on the national leadership to release detainees or put them on trial, and to repeal the legislation providing for detention without trial. 'The Preservation of Public Security Act that enables the state to deny people their basic human rights should be removed from our constitution', he declared. In the prevailing climate, Githii must surely have known this would be his last editorial, though he could hardly have envisaged the craven reaction of his employers. The *Standard* rushed a special issue onto the streets carrying an abject apology in the form of a page-one lead story. Under the headline 'Standard Editor-in-Chief Dismissed', it said:

> *The shareholders, directors and management of the* Standard *unreservedly apologise to the government of Kenya for the provocative editorial which appeared in yesterday's issue of this newspaper. The views expressed therein are considered by our shareholders, directors*

*and management to be contentious and do not reflect this newspaper's long-established policy of support for the government of Kenya. At a special meeting of the Board of Directors of The Standard Limited this morning, it was unanimously resolved that the Editor-in-Chief, Mr George Githii, should be immediately dismissed from his post.*

Githii was told to be out of the office with his belongings by 1 pm.

If the *Standard's* hasty grovel was aimed at pre-empting a closure order, it succeeded, although when an emergency debate took place in Parliament, several MPs called for just such a shutdown, and Paul Ngei urged the directors and management to 'come out now and clear themselves'. Others demanded Githii be locked up under the very legislation he had denounced, and this was the headline that the *Standard* chose for its report on the debate, 'Detain Githii, say MPs'. The maligned editor's old friend, Njonjo, made clear his view of the media role in Kenyan society: 'For a newspaper or editor to challenge a law provided for by this House is a diabolical act.' In this atmosphere of bilious outrage, several MPs obsequiously signalled their personal loyalty to the head of state, including VP Mwai Kibaki, who said the editorial 'sought deliberately to challenge the executive, which is embodied in the President in whom 17 million Kenyans have total faith, confidence and commitment'. Roared the only white cabinet member, Philip Leakey, 'What is this newspaper that challenges the President of this country!' But Foreign Minister Robert Ouko noted shrewdly that 'the champions of the politics of elimination are the people who shout loudest about being the supporters of Nyayo', with its rallying call of peace, love and unity.

For many years, Kenya's two national newspapers demonstrated a mean-spirited reluctance to defend each other when unjustly accused, even though silence strengthened the hand of their joint persecutor. If Githii hoped for support from the newspaper which carried his original ringing condemnations of preventive detention, he was disappointed. The *Nation's* editorial board met to discuss the matter and concluded that the issue was so sensitive that any comment would be 'extremely dangerous'. Ng'weno's *Nairobi Times* also remained silent, and his *Weekly Review* quoted other Githii editorials to argue that he was a sudden convert to the cause of human rights.

If there had been an element of *schadenfreude* in the *Nation's* decision to remain mute about Githii, it would have been understandable considering the glee with which the *Standard* greeted the *Nation's* Kariuki fiasco and the war Githii waged to denude his old employer of editorial talent. However, memories of executives from that time argue otherwise. Said one, 'We knew

that without the *Standard* we would be totally exposed. A lot of Kanu people wanted to get rid of the two papers and start a party paper. Things were
getting blacker, we were having a very rough ride ourselves and anything we
said would have heaped more trouble on us.' As for Githii, it was the end of
his career in Kenyan journalism. He told the *Nation* he was not bitter and
would look for another job. The story described him as 'a legendary figure,
colourful, controversial [who] went out with a bang, not a whimper'.
Appropriately, perhaps, for a person with his explosive record, Githii joined
the International Atomic Energy Agency in Vienna. Later, he became a
preacher in Canada. Githii declined to be interviewed for this book, saying
the Bible prohibited him from considering events of the past.[3]

If Moi's coming proved to be a false dawn in political terms, so it was for
the media. Self-censorship was already an accomplished skill of the Kenyan
journalist. Gavin Bennett, sub-editor in 1975–8, explained, 'You had to
understand what would cause a fuss and what wouldn't. You could take a
calculated risk if you felt something really important needed to be said.
Everyone from the lowest reporter had to know what was acceptable.' The
tricky question was, How far could you go? Soon after Kenyatta's death, Joe
Rodrigues was able to report, 'President Moi's accession has led to a less
restrictive atmosphere as it affects the performance of politicians, public and
the Press.' But by mid-1980, he was writing of fruitless talks with the administration:

> I and other Nairobi editors were invited to separate meetings with the
> Minister of State in the Office of the President, Mr G.G. Kariuki, who
> conveyed a request from the government that the media should not
> flog dead horses in the shape of scandals perpetrated under the former
> regime. He also said President Moi felt he had been remiss for not
> keeping close contact with editors and would rectify this. Kariuki said
> Moi would invite the editors to lunch, but so far it hasn't happened. It
> has remained very much the mixture as before – we have to make our
> own checks, contacts and confirmations.

And a few months after that: 'We have had our lunch with President Moi and
there was an exchange of views at which it was hinted, not by the head of
state, that the police might be used against over-enterprising journalists.'

When the storm finally broke over the heads of editors, it came after
repeated affirmations of media freedom at the 1981 general assembly in
Nairobi of the IPI. 'We in Kenya steadfastly uphold the freedom of the Press',

Moi told the delegates, and Information Minister Peter Aloo Oringo said the Press should be seen not as an enemy but as an ally in the fight against under-development. It was at this gathering that the Aga Khan moved to defuse the hostility then building between the West and the developing world over controversial proposals by Unesco for a new world information order. The industrialised countries strongly opposed a proposal to license journalists, arguing this was a step towards government control, while the developing nations protested against the imbalance in the flow of news and superficial, sensationalist and condescending reporting of their affairs. What the Aga Khan suggested was an alternative to the new order. 'We have all heard of twin cities', he said. 'Why not twin newspaper companies and news organisations between the industrial world and the developing world? These could provide mutually beneficial exchanges of managerial, technological and editorial experience and news.' The suggestion was widely welcomed by delegates. (It also attracted extravagant praise from the KUJ, especially the part which referred to making journalism attractive by giving adequate remuneration to its practitioners. The union promptly handed in a memorandum demanding an immediate review of its members' wages.) The Aga Khan's idea was swiftly implemented by the *Nation*, which set up a twinning arrangement with the *St Petersburg Times* of Florida, a relationship which saw many *Nation* managers cross the Atlantic in ensuing years.

Hardly had the self-congratulatory applause at the IPI meeting died down than the government unleashed two vitriolic attacks against the *Nation* and arrested six of its journalists. In early April, the political firebrand from Nyanza, Oginga Odinga, declared, 'I clashed with President Kenyatta because he wanted to grab land and he wanted me to do the same but I refused. That is why today I am working with President Moi, because he serves *wananchi* [the people] not himself.' Being linked to Odinga did not please the head of state, who responded that anyone who abused Kenyatta was not likely to appreciate the Nyayo government, 'leave alone fit in it'. KANU apparatchiks took the hint and refused clearance for Odinga to fight a forthcoming by-election for the Bondo parliamentary seat, which he certainly would have won. An editorial by Rodrigues said the decision was 'unconstitutional, undemocratic and not conducive to the national compromise to which President Moi has been exhorting Kenyans'. The editorial said Odinga should be allowed to stand in the interests of national unity. It was headed, 'A time for magnanimity'.

A choleric government statement accused the *Nation* of trying to assume the role of an opposition party, of adopting a rebellious attitude, and of selecting news on a sectarian and tribally motivated basis. It warned that the Press 'must at all times avoid inciting the public over decisions that are national and collective'. Statements poured in from KANU branches countrywide echoing their masters' sentiments, and Rodrigues was arrested and interrogated. The *Nation* might have argued that a moderately worded statement of opinion on an issue of national importance was part of that Press freedom the President had boasted of at the IPI assembly; instead, two days later, it published an 'assurance' that the newspaper fully supported KANU, the government and the President, whatever unfortunate impression the Bondo editorial may have given. The world 'apology' was not used.

The second crisis struck as Rodrigues was about to leave home on the morning of Friday 22 May 1981. The telephone rang; the caller was the head of state. He was angry about the use of the word 'anonymous' in a *Nation* story about a national strike by doctors. The relevant sentence said, 'On Wednesday, the Kenya News Agency released an anonymous statement said to have been released by KANU, condemning the strike and calling on the government to deal with the strikers.' The wording seemed to throw doubt on whether this was a genuine KANU statement, but that was not what had offended Moi. A KNA statement quoted him as saying, 'KANU is the ruling party. It is the government and therefore my voice. How can the publishers of the *Nation* imagine the views of the party are anonymous? They also want to say Moi is anonymous.' Later that day, during a visit to a factory, Moi said, 'I have full powers to ban this paper. I think such publications have grown horns because of our democratic nature. They have become irresponsible and outright rebellious.'

The word 'anonymous' had been inserted into the story by the chief subeditor, Philip Ochieng, whose English was impeccable. The statement bore no indication which KANU official or officials had issued it, and this was what Ochieng was trying to point out. In the conspiratorial world of Kenya politics, his semantic intervention was given a sinister connotation. At about 4 pm that same day, an Assistant Police Commissioner, Joginder Singh Sokhi, appeared in Nation House and arrested Joe Kadhi, the *Daily Nation's* managing editor, and the acting news editor, John Esibi. Picked up soon after were Rodrigues, Ochieng and two reporters, Gideon Mulaki and Pius Nyamora.

Many Kenyan journalists have seen the inside of a police cell in the pursuit of their duties Ochieng three times at this point, Rodrigues ditto. Kadhi recalled:

*We were sitting there together in that cell, a cell of* Nation *people, with a concrete floor, very cold and we were left to sleep there. It was a terrible thing for me because that was Langata police station and I lived in Langata, not far from the police station, and I knew my kids were only yards away. We didn't know what was going on. We were taken to CID headquarters across town and made to write statements. At one point, I was being interviewed by Sokhi and I could hear our company lawyer outside, Reg Sampson, asking if we were there and a voice saying, 'We don't know about any Joe Kadhi.' I couldn't shout because this man Sokhi, as he was interviewing me, he was polishing his gun, not pointing it at me but polishing it and blowing on it. That was a form of mental torture when I couldn't shout, 'Reg, I'm here.'*

The KUJ appealed to the government to release the six. The *Standard* front-paged news of the arrests but did not make a similar appeal. G.G. Kariuki, who had set up the editors' lunch with Moi, accused the *Nation* of 'deliberately ridiculing the government' and warned that no professionals were above the law. 'It is only President Moi who is above the law', he declared, to the surprise of constitutional experts. The minister of tourism, Elijah Mwangale, called for journalists to be licensed.

Rodrigues was released after 24 hours, the other five after three days. Sedition charges were laid but never proceeded with. 'When we got back to the office, everybody was waiting for us', Kadhi said. 'I never saw greater solidarity than at that time. Rather than scare the staff as was intended, it boosted their morale.' The arrests were widely covered in the international media, muddying the government's carefully cultivated 'island of tranquillity' image for Kenya, and an in-house *Nation* memo said, 'In many ways, this action against the newspaper appears to have earned us more friends among the readers.' The next day's *Nation* pointedly front-paged a photograph of the released detainees surrounded by a sea of smiling colleagues. But the page also carried a story headed, 'Apology to President Moi and KANU'. It said, 'We now recognise that our use of the word anonymous was due to human error and uncalled for. There was absolutely no intention on our part to call into question the KANU statement or to doubt its authenticity or to question the position of His Excellency the President as president of the ruling party.' Unreserved apologies then followed to the head of state and to KANU officials and members. Why did the government react so violently to what was fundamentally an innocuous editorial interpolation? Amnesty International's conclusion is worth consideration: that the arrests were a delayed reprisal for

Rodrigues' Bondo editorial, surely a weightier matter than the attribution of a mundane party statement.

Maintaining some kind of independence while keeping newspapers out of trouble with a quickly offended leadership was a mind-numbing task. Flattery was one reliable tactic. In March 1981, the *Standard* put Moi's picture on the front page 18 times – and that was only on weekdays in a month when he left the country to visit Nigeria. By the same token, back in February 1975, the *Nation* put Kenyatta on the front page 22 times. McHaffie recalled:

> *Jomo was not averse to phoning up the editor. He called Joe Rodrigues one day and the following conversation ensued:*
> *'Who is the President of this country?'*
> *'Why, you are, Your Excellency.'*
> *'Then why is this fellow always in my picture?'*
> *This fellow was his aide-de-camp, whose job was to stand right behind the President at official functions. Kenyatta had apparently taken an aversion to this man always towering above him. It would have been easier for Kenyatta to order him out of the way, but we decided we better remove this ADC and we started to airbrush him out of Kenyatta's pictures. There was a famous case where we painted out the top but not the lower part and the picture appeared with a mysterious pair of legs.*

McHaffie said, 'Jomo went on the front page every day, though I cannot remember any specific instruction. That was an indictment of us. We did it to ourselves because it was safer.'

In the troubled early 1980s, most journalists thought Rodrigues' were the safest hands in the business. He had joined the *Nation* in 1960 as a sub-editor, becoming assistant editor (news) in 1964 and managing editor of the daily in 1969. He served under Bierman, Rees, Ng'weno, Omori and Githii. He had an acute political sense and a wide range of contacts, and he was a superb newspaper technician. But the long delay in his confirmation as editor-in-chief after Githii's final exit probably told him that he was not number one on everybody's list. Further signals came after a terrorist bomb destroyed the Norfolk hotel in Nairobi on 1 January 1981, killing 15 people and injuring 85 others. It was widely assumed that the attack was the work of Palestinian terrorists in reprisal for Kenya's assistance to Israel in the Uganda hostage drama; also the Block family who owned the hotel were

Jewish. Joe Kadhi wrote one of his 'Why?' columns, denouncing the Libyan-funded Nairobi newspaper *Voice of Africa* for claiming that the bomb was planted by Israel; he also attacked the Palestine Liberation Organisation for describing Kenya as 'a police station for US interventionism'. These comments were fair and in line with government policy, as Rodrigues pointed out in a letter to the board, stating, 'This country is moving closer to Israel in the intelligence and security fields and away from the Arab world. The promise of cheaper oil has not materialised and the machinations of the *Voice of Africa* and its Libyan backers, particularly vis-à-vis the Norfolk bomb and its aftermath, have combined to harden the government's attitude.' Certainly the *Nation's* position chimed with the prevailing political winds, but the Kadhi column was felt in some circles to have given a negative impression of Arabs generally and a barrage of complaints was directed to the Aga Khan. Since the editor-in-chief was responsible for all columns and commentaries, he came under fire for letting this one through.[4]

A 3 February NNL board meeting gave its support to the editor-in-chief and referred to 'assurances that employees would be protected from action arising as a result of complaints directed to the principal shareholder'. It was not then, but after the 18 April Bondo editorial and Rodrigues' arrest and interrogation that the axe fell.

His wife, Cyrilla, recalled in a letter, 'Joe was sent for by Sir Eboo Pirbhai (veteran leader of the Ismaili community in Kenya) and told that the message from Paris was that he had to resign in the interests of his own security.' Mrs Rodrigues said, 'Like everybody else, we suspected that Njonjo had a large hand in the whole saga.' Rodrigues himself, in a letter to Harold Evans, then editor of the London *Sunday Times*, said he had been told a decision was taken to revert to an African editor-in-chief and that he was in grave personal danger. Personally, he believed the Arab issue was responsible. A BBC *Focus on Africa* commentary by Tim Llewellyn said there had been a concerted Arab and Muslim campaign for the Aga Khan to get rid of Joe Kadhi, and that Rodrigues 'took the brunt of that pressure'. There can be no doubt that the Arab issue was a factor in Rodrigues' departure, but a greater one was government unhappiness over his more independent stance after years of unquestioning support from Githii.

Official unhappiness with the *Nation* was demonstrated when Njonjo publicly blasted the paper for 'sensational reporting' of a case in which his cousin Alfred Muthemba was accused of treason, and an internal report said, 'He [Njonjo] remains convinced he has enemies in the *Nation*.' Rodrigues was out of the country when the case was reported and

Muthemba was later acquitted. But the signals from the powers-that-be were unmistakeable and a decision was taken to seek a new editor-in-chief. A senior director referred to Rodrigues' 'effective collapse over the last six months and his failure to perform any of the tasks allotted to him'. Once 'the best journalist in Kenya', he was now described as simply 'a very competent production man'. But the company was well aware that Rodrigues was extremely popular for his stand on Odinga's rights and his removal could be seen by the public as bowing to government pressure. Moreover, for 20 years he had performed exceptionally well. A plan was devised to give him the title of Editorial Director but find him employment outside of Kenya as Deputy Director of the IPI, so that his departure would be seen as promotion to a world body. Neither position materialised. Rodrigues described the job he was finally offered by IPI, on a three-year-contract, as 'being a general dogs-body and editing the *IPI Report*'. An offer to join *The Statesman* in India would have meant his taking Indian nationality. He stayed in Kenya and bought into freelance journalist Henry Reuter's stable of magazines.

Rodrigues' departure from the *Nation* in August 1981 was painful and embarrassing. Though he got the traditional mock front page ('Goodbye Mr Chits'), a senior executive described the official farewell dinner as 'more like a funeral wake'. In the course of it, he was besieged by union officials who wanted to know if more sackings were planned. At a private party paid for by the staff to which no managers were invited, Rodrigues said he had neither resigned nor retired, he had been sacked. Joe Kadhi remembered, 'We all felt vulnerable and insecure. It was then that I started taking correspondence courses to get a degree.' John Platter, who had been hired by Rodrigues when he walked in off the street in the very early days, said, 'Joe was subtle, talented, dependable, devout and generous. Ultimately, he was the victim of the roughhouse politics of Africa which he understood better than most and enjoyed, but also disdained.'

That Rodrigues was admired by his colleagues is indisputable. Of the many journalists interviewed for this book, only two were less than fulsome in his cause. 'Morale was high under him', Kadhi recalled. 'Everybody aspired to become a Joe Rodrigues, a man who could pump out an editorial in half-an-hour, who could edit a mountain of copy immaculately, who could brief and debrief reporters and who never violated ethics.' McHaffie said, 'He was an amazing journeyman and I mean that in the best way. He could turn his hand to anything, create an editorial then sit down and dissect an entire Budget speech. He had an astonishing professionalism.' Sub-editor Colin MacBeth: 'He was a true editor, he knew what newspapers were all about, a newsman down to his toes. He was hands-on and knew everything that was going on.' Chege Mbitiru:

> *For a time under Joe I was a roving foreign editor. At the start of the*
> *year we would sit down and list the stories I would cover. He was very*
> *keen on this and our sustained foreign coverage gave the paper status*
> *and gravitas. He knew everything about his staff. One guy started*
> *building a house and he ran out of money and needed*
> *KSH 3,000 and the company refused a loan. Joe was so angry about*
> *this, he gave him the 3,000 out of his pocket.*

Joseph Odindo: 'He was very professional and could take decisions very quickly. He remembered things and he once threw back at me a remark I had made three years earlier. His departure was a disaster for the *Nation*, an inglorious episode, and it was only when Wangethi Mwangi came in years later that the paper started recovering.' Ray Wilkinson, a long-time reporter on Africa for United Press International (UPI) and *Newsweek*, said the Nairobi-based foreign correspondents were so angered they considered signing a joint letter of protest: 'Joe was sacrificed to high financial politics and I lost any respect for the *Nation* after that because if you sacrifice your own, how are you going to turn round and say, "We are a crusading newspaper that stands for the truth"?'

Mrs Rodrigues said her husband received a £7,000 payoff and no pension: 'He was treated shabbily after working for 21 years, seven days a week, 14 or 15 hours a day. He was even barred from the office afterwards when he went in to file for the *Daily Telegraph*. It was not so much anger we felt as deep hurt.' Rodrigues died of a heart attack in his doctor's office six years later. He was 56.

Rodrigues was succeeded by Peter Mwaura, Director of the University of Nairobi School of Journalism, whose three greatest assets were listed in a recruitment briefing paper as: (1) he was a Kenyan African; (2) he had an illustrious academic record and a clear intelligence; (3) he was a strong character, though not in an extrovert sense. The first two qualities were indisputable, but most of his staff came to question the third. Further, though he had done good work for the *Nation* as a reporter under Githii, he had never edited a newspaper. Another important change had just taken place: Stan Denman, MD of NPP, retired after 23 years and was replaced by Dugal Nisbet-Smith, formerly MD of Times Newspapers in London, who arrived with a bang. He recalled:

*The first night I was there I went into the composing room and I read a story in paste-up. To my horror, it described allegations against a bank manager, who was an Indian, which said he had sexually tormented his African female staff, had propositioned them and when they refused, stubbed out cigarettes in the palms of their hands. It quoted a union leader but there was no rebuttal from the manager. It was libellous in the extreme and I pulled it. There was no way I was going to sit round in charge of this newspaper and have stories like that appearing. That was my first collision with Kenya journalism, to give it a dignified title.*

To say that Nisbet-Smith was unimpressed by the *Nation's* editorial standards is a serious understatement. He said in an interview for this book, 'I had never seen a newspaper so crass, so awful, so brutally, badly written, full of inaccuracies, prejudices, bile and typographical mayhem and sometimes so ungrammatical that it was almost too dense to read. It was a helluva shock.' Nisbet-Smith said the *Nation* had more than 100 libel cases pending, while the London *Sunday Times* would never have more than about 40 at any one time

*I acquired a strong suspicion that a lot of the journalists had patrons, both political and tribal, if you can separate the two. Certain politicians were aware of what was going on inside Nation House all the time. A lot of the stories had spin, real spin. I felt unsafe, that there were very few people you could trust to write in an independent and professional way. I felt as though we were being dragged over the cliff. Editorial became my first responsibility. The company as a whole was doing well, the paper was the prime concern.*

Nisbet-Smith had been both a journalist and a manager – reporting in his native New Zealand, five years' reporting and feature-writing for the London *Daily Express*, seven years' editing and training in Barbados, a brief stint in West Africa, then MD positions with the *Mirror* group in Britain before *The Times*. He said he was specifically entrusted with an editorial role: 'I went to Kenya after many meetings with the Aga Khan about what he saw as his vision of newspaper publishing in Third World countries and I agreed with everything he said. His views were superb and I went imbued with his ideals of editorial excellence and neutrality in coverage.'

The first move of the new MD was to hire Willie Robertson, deputy city editor of the *Times*, who improved layout and presentation, but relations with Mwaura deteriorated and Nisbet-Smith concluded more radical action was needed:

> *I think Peter started off with high ideals but the circumstances pulled him down. We had meetings, Ekirapa, the general manager Njagi, Mwaura, Robertson and myself, and they were ferocious. I used to mark the paper in the mornings and sometimes you couldn't see the original type for the markings. I would have these delivered to Peter in the hope that he would show them to the subs and I discovered that he was throwing them in the bin.*

When the *Nation* was in trouble on one occasion, Mwaura pointed out that it was him who would go to jail; the expatriates would simply be deported. Nisbet-Smith commented acidly, 'He gives the impression that the price of the first supposition is worth the pleasure of the second.'

Nisbet-Smith's proposed solution was to remove Mwaura from day-to-day editorial responsibilities, leaving him with the title Editor-in-Chief, whilst making Roberston executive editor; three additional expatriates would be brought in on three-year contracts as day editor/trainer, night editor and production editor; the St Petersburg twinning scheme would also be implemented, though Nisbet-Smith described it as having 'limited value'. The proposal ran into serious trouble when it was presented to the NPP board. Ekirapa said the company had long boasted of being the first newspaper to Africanise its editorial management and the Nisbet-Smith plan would put the clock back nearly 20 years; Mwaura would almost certainly resign along with senior journalists and non-journalists, possibly sparking off a major industrial confrontation. After long debate, action was deferred.

Instead the board discussed an editorial policy document which was adopted by shareholders at the 1982 AGM. A 32-point list of editorial objectives was circulated to senior staff. A preamble to the policy statement in the chairman's AGM report expressed concern at suggestions that freedom of speech should be controlled and at the arrests of the Nation Six. The editorial policy said the newspapers would loyally support the President, the government and the constitution, but would not shrink from objective criticism where it was well founded. The editorial objectives warned journalists that if criticism of the government was necessary, 'this will be both objective and responsible'. Editorial aims ranged from training, through the need for systems to eliminate error to a directive that hard news should take preference over political trivia and other establishment coverage. The two documents were clearly aimed in the first place to secure public goodwill in the face of government pressure and in the second to alert staff to the dangers of falling standards – of much relevance in view of Nisbet-Smith's radical proposals.

The new chief's abrasive style and the pungent nature of his criticisms offended many African staffers, who accused him of racism. Some suspected he was briefed to shore up relations with Njonjo, though Nisbet-Smith said he was no friend of Njonjo:

> *Njonjo tried to adopt me when I first arrived. I found myself being invited to receptions and dinner parties and when I got there, Njonjo would be among the first to greet me and after a short while, realising Njonjo's dominant role in politics, I cried off. With Njonjo, if you weren't for him you were against him and I had the feeling after that that he disapproved of me. Our contacts were then nil.*

Nisbet-Smith felt uncomfortable in Kenya from the beginning of his tour:

> *When I went for my work permit, I was taken to the office of the Chief Immigration Officer, a fat, sweating man with a purple pinstriped suit and a vomitorious tie. He was sitting behind his desk in a very hot office with his closed-circuit television set on the desk turned towards me so that I could see the prisoner in the cell below. He was an African, just sitting there disconsolately. He hardly ever moved but he was on the screen all the time and I was meant to see him. Before I was given my permit, I was treated to a very threatening lecture.*

Nisbet-Smith also saw President Moi: 'Soon after I arrived, I was summoned to State House at 7.30 in the morning, with Njonjo and Eboo Pirbhai there, and I was lectured, as I had been by the immigration officer, for about an hour by this terrifying man, sitting on a raised dais like a throne.' There was a tricky moment when Moi asked why he had the same name as Njonjo's wife, a Scot named Elisabeth Nisbet. 'We're from the same tribe', Nisbet-Smith replied, laughing, then froze when he remembered 'tribe' was no longer politically correct in Kenya. But Moi roared with laughter, where-upon everyone else laughed, too.

In financial terms, the *Nation* group was booming, despite a 15 per cent devaluation of the Kenya shilling which increased the cost of materials by £800,000 per annum. Nisbet-Smith reported that group profit to 31 May 1982 stood at £530,000, advertising was buoyant and sales of both the *Daily* and *Sunday Nation* were comfortably over 100,000 against 53,000 for the *Standard*, and an estimated 6,500 for the *Nairobi Times*. These results had been achieved by a drive for profit maximisation which did not sit well with all executives. Denman recalled, 'Running the paper in the 1970s was like going through a minefield. We went through a period when profit was the only thing. We were highly profitable but they pressed and pressed for more and it held back development.' When a £100-a-day consultant was hired in 1980 to assess the company's operations, Denman added his own scathing comments to his report.

'Change and development are normally associated with capital expenditure', he wrote. 'At Nation Newspapers Limited this is done as a norm by crisis and out of sheer necessity.' He said that when sales growth began to outstrip printing capacity, modifications were proposed to the ailing press, but after two years no firm decision had been taken and finally a massive breakdown lost the company an entire day's issue at a cost of £100,000. Investment was needed in people, too, he argued, but in quality not volume: 'Management's answer to inefficiency is to employ more people but not to rock the boat by getting rid of the present incumbent. Ten years ago, with 100 fewer people, productivity was greater than it is today.' He criticised working conditions at Nation House, where one toilet was available for 90 people, and said if a new headquarters building had been secured, technical development could have been properly planned. Although there had been references to the use of computers in the *Nation's* earliest days, and although this technology had been put to use in the accounts department, no firm steps were taken to computerise editorial or advertising. At a July 1980 meeting at Aiglemont, Rodrigues pointed out that newspapers such as the *St Petersburg Times* were entirely computerised while the *Nation* faced consistent problems through failing and old-fashioned equipment. Technically, he said, the *Nation* was no longer an advanced newspaper, even by the standards of developing countries. Denman concluded, 'This maxim of maximum profit has seeped through to all of us and it has taken an outsider [the consultant] to see the appalling conditions people work under. Do these conditions and lack of refinement add up to the very healthy profit NNL has enjoyed for a number of years?' It is difficult to assess what effect these arguments had on long-term company philosophy except to note that in later years massive capital expenditure was ploughed into computerisation, additional products, relocation of operations, and a new press and printing hall.

On 2 August 1982, the *Nation* failed to appear for only the third time in 22 years. A strike and a press breakdown were the causes of the first two failures, an attempted coup d'etat was the reason for the third. In hindsight, the rebellion should not have been the shock it was, given the mounting economic pressures of the time and the resentment caused by Moi's authoritarian rule. A cash crisis early in the year caused delays in paying army and civil service salaries. Living standards dropped as inflation soared and there were few jobs for school leavers. The government clamped down on criticism. Odinga was expelled from KANU after calling for a second political party and his passport was impounded. The first political detentions under Moi's rule took place, the one-party state became official, Githii wrote his famous editorial in the *Standard* and, as pressure was increased on the universities, a cultural crackdown took place, too. A musical play by Ngugi wa Thiong'o was banned, and the Kamirithiu Community and Cultural Centre was deregistered and later destroyed by fire.

When he heard shooting and explosions on the morning of Sunday 1 August, Wangethi Mwangi, the *Nation's* editorial-chief-to-be but then a young sub-editor, telephoned the newsroom and was advised by a colleague, Bernard Nderitu, to stay where he was in Buru Buru: 'Then people began running into the estates with stories about shooting and looting and killing and that the army had taken over. The radio was blaring martial music and at one point there was an announcement that the military had taken over.' Seizures of power by the armed forces had become common in independent black Africa, but after nearly two decades of civilian rule, Kenyans had come to believe their country would prove an exception. The following day, Mwangi and a fellow sub-editor walked to the Bunyala roundabout near Nyayo Stadium in central Nairobi and started seeing soldiers with guns: 'They were pulling people out of their vehicles and making them walk with their hands high clutching their IDs all the way into town and that's what we did. At every corner, the army wanted to see your ID.' But at least these were government soldiers, not rebels. The coup attempt had already been defeated. Mwangi recalled:

> There was a dusk-to-dawn curfew which meant we had to be out of town by 6 pm and that meant we had to finish the paper by 3 o' clock. That's what we did. The paper was a patchwork affair with very little editing and a lot of it did not make sense. Still, it was a brave effort. We couldn't do a paper the day of the coup but after that we got a

*paper out every day without about half the staff. Many couldn't get in and some were so scared they didn't even try. The real heroes were our paper sellers, out on the streets among all those guns.*

The front page of the 'coup' issue of 3 August splashed the headline '1,000 KAF men held', carried a file picture of Moi, a story about the curfew and an editorial entitled, 'The tragic folly of a coup'. This declared, 'An elected government, no matter how corrupt or bad, in most cases is preferable to a military junta … the open rebellion by the Kenya Air Force will leave a permanent scar in the political life of this nation and things will never be the same again. But we should be grateful that we are not under military rule. The foretaste has been most traumatic.' Among the unproofed stories was one about the closure of the 'Ukniversity of Nairobi', which said in part, 't e Government said t at this had been necessitated by the unwarranted participation of the students in widesiread looting' (Mwangi was not joking about stories that made no sense). The strongest elements of the first few issues were dramatic photographs of bullet-riddled victims, looted shops, armed soldiers and citizens holding up their IDs, alongside eyewitness accounts from people who had been caught up in the fighting.

Nisbet-Smith was on holiday with his family in Mombasa: 'I called the office in Nairobi and frightened voices said all hell had broken loose and I could hear gunfire in the background. I packed the family in the car and drove to Nairobi. We passed through 12 military checkpoints with drunken or drugged soldiers armed with Kalashnikovs. I suppose we should have stayed at the Coast.' It was time to leave Kenya anyway:

> *I wouldn't say the country got worse during the time I was there, I just understood it better and I got to the point where I thought Kenya was no place for me to be. I was told my telephone was tapped and I was being watched, that there were government pressures on me and they wanted me out. This didn't surprise me at all though I don't know who I offended. Ochieng said in a book that I was deported. I was not deported. I left in September because the company believed, and I agreed, it was not feasible to continue.*

Shortly afterwards, without giving notice, Robertson, the editorial adviser, travelled to the airport, parked his car, climbed aboard an airplane to London and left for good. He was not the first or the last expatriate to depart in such a fashion.

The coup attempt was launched by the 2,800-strong Kenya Air Force (KAF), which was the smallest of the armed forces, politically aware and the best educated. A broadcast by the Kenya People's Redemption Council accused Moi's government of corruption and being a 'gang of local tyrants' who had 'made life intolerable in our society'. The official death roll was put at 160, but figures from churches and independent sources ranged up to 2,000. Many of the dead were looters who raided Asian-owned shops after the rebels claimed that the government had been overthrown – one woman who stopped long enough to try on a stolen pair of shoes was shot dead in the act. Other victims were students who demonstrated jubilantly in favour of the coup. One Kenyan reported that the only shops not looted on Ngara Road were the bookstores and the African Boot and Shoe Co., though this was actually owned by an Asian. Eye-witnesses saw civilians shot because they were wearing blue shirts, the same colour as Air Force uniforms. Army troops were accused of brutality, rape and looting in the slums of Mathare, Kibera and Kawangare, and in poorer Asian areas. Soldiers went from house to house demanding to see the sale receipt for the household television set; when the owner could not produce one, the military would declare it looted and loot it for themselves.

In a harsh crackdown, Moi disbanded the Air Force and 1,000 men were court-martialled, receiving sentences of up to 25 years. The alleged coup leaders, a Luo sergeant and private, Hezekiah Ochuka and Pancras Oteyo Okumu, fled to Tanzania, but were extradited and executed along with ten others at Kamiti Prison on 9 and 10 July 1985. The KAF Commander was sentenced to four years. Hundreds of people were brought to court accused of 'rejoicing' during the coup attempt. The University of Nairobi was closed and 71 students were charged with participation in rebellion. Ten of them received sentences of between three and ten years, and the remaining 61 were freed after a year in custody. Titus Adungosi, leader of the Students Union, was jailed for ten years for sedition, and Professor Maina wa Kinyatti, an historian of the Mau Mau era, got six years for possessing seditious publications. Oginga Odinga was restricted to Kisumu; his son Raila was charged with treason, placed under house arrest for seven months, then detained without trial for six years. Otieno Mak'Onyango, assistant editor of the Standard, was accused of misprision of treason. Ben Gethi, by then commissioner of police, was sacked and spent several months under house arrest. After the coup attempt, police for the first time began carrying guns as they patrolled city streets. In his 2006 book, Raila Odinga: An Enigma in Kenyan Politics, the Nigerian scholar Dr Babafemi A. Badejo claimed that

Raila 'facilitated' the coup attempt by securing a command post for the plotters. In interviews for the book, Raila neither denied nor confirmed involvement. Charles Njonjo denied claims in the book of his participation. He told the Sunday Nation, 'I never planned one and I had no intention of ever doing so.' Laughing, he added, 'You know me, had I planned one, it would have succeeded.'

It has been stated that in some other African countries the plotters would have been strung up in a public square or shot before spectators in a sports stadium, and it is true the Kenyan authorities invested their retribution with the forms of legalism. But the trials set the pattern for future crackdowns on opposition groups and dissidence in all forms, including the shadowy Mwakenya and FERA organisations, whose reality, except in the minds of Special Branch, came to be seriously questioned.

## Notes

1.  One senior African editor confessed wistfully that his all-time favourite headline came from a British tabloid's account of the Church of England synod which rejected an appeal to ordain women priests: 'Bishops say no to vicars in knickers'. He was wise enough to know the *Nation* would never wear it.
2.  *Kenya: Taking Liberties*, Africa Watch, London, 1991.
3.  George Githii wrote to the author from Ottawa on 14 July 1998 as follows: 'I was not a Christian during the days that I was editing the *Nation*. However, I am one now, having become a partaker of Salvation through the grace that is Christ Jesus, who has redeemed me from the power of darkness and has translated me into his everlasting Kingdom. As such, the Lord has dealt with my past to eternity and I have of course forgiven and forgotten all things that were done to me during those days, just as I have been forgiven all my sins. Therefore my spiritual persuasion precludes the remembering and considering of former things, for the Lord has said to me, according to Isaiah 43:18, "Remember ye not the former things, neither consider things of old". And I hope that you will find some other way of assessing the events of my editorship other than by interviews with me. Please inform Gerry [Wilkinson] that this decision is in no way a reflection of my relationship with him for he knows that I have always held him and his wife in the highest esteem, but rather that my time is wholly given to spiritual matters concerning the imminent return of Christ. Likewise, please ask him to convey my greetings and highest consideration to the Aga Khan.'
4.  The Arab-Israeli question had always been a sensitive one for the *Nation*, particularly under Githii, whose sympathies appeared to lie with Israel.

# Banned from Parliament

*Liberty is precious, so precious that it must be rationed.*
V.I. Lenin (1870–1924)

When Peter Mwaura took over from Rodrigues in August 1981, he published a personal letter to readers in which he said, 'A lot of nonsense has been written and said about the change of guard at Nation House. I would like to put the record right. I am here because I am. The only new thing at Nation House is me. The *Nation* group of newspapers remains the same newspapers you've always trusted and depended upon.' He reminded Kenyans that the *Nation* and *Taifa* stood alone in supporting KANU in the first general election, and 'our loyalty to this nation is beyond question'. He promised continued independence and objectivity and declared, 'We will not be a party to any political groupings or factions. We have no masters to serve except our readers.'

Joseph Odindo, a sub-editor at the time, said:

> *His idealism was welcome. He felt newspapers should reflect African values and there were a lot of us who said, Yes, just what we want. Mwaura was very particular about references in wire-service copy such as 'this impoverished East African country'. If you let that through, he would always write you a note. Also things like 'regime' for 'government', the sort of thing you heard in lecture halls. He was also very strong on the use of local commentaries on page six where we usually carried foreign features and he encouraged good staff writers like Philip Ochieng and Mbatau wa Ngai to submit pieces for that column.*

By January 1983, in a review of his tenure, Mwaura was able to point to the following plus points: Editorial Policy and Objectives adopted; twinning programme underway; bureaus opened in Nakuru and Nyeri; visits from schools to Nation House increased; libel cases down to 29; more local features; continued production during the coup curfew period; special daytime editions for a cabinet reshuffle and the death of Mbiyu Koinange; addition of Agence France Presse international news wire; coverage by *Nation* staffers extended to Organisation of National Unity (OAU) meetings, the President's foreign travels and international sports events; the highly popular Bogi Benda comic strip introduced; and a Kenyan recruited to do editorial cartoons. Sales were up to 111,000 for the daily, 115,000 for the Sunday and 55,000 for *Taifa Leo*. The profit line was a handsome £670,783. But Mwaura added, 'The newspapers continued to attract criticism centred on our coverage of stories of a political nature and sometimes we were incriminated, sometimes justifiably, for inaccurate reporting.'

That poor professional performance might have something to do with wages and conditions should have become clear to management when Mwaura called an open meeting to let staffers ventilate their grievances. These were many: wages were uncompetitive and there was no pension scheme; management looked for loopholes to deny medical claims; too many signatures were needed for expense claims; drivers' overnight allowance was so small that reporters had to lend them money for food; merit increases were rare and in one case withdrawn without explanation; little upward mobility (once a reporter always a reporter); *Taifa* staffers were treated as second-class citizens; cars were sent to fetch reporters for urgent jobs, but not provided to take them home after dark; tea cups were filthy and so was the toilet. The three managing editors were asked to comment. Kadhi (*Daily Nation*): 'This was a useful meeting and we should have more of them so that we can talk freely and make our feelings known.' Mbitiru (*Sunday Nation*): 'I have heard all this before and if I could have done something about it I would have done.' Mbugguss (*Taifa Leo*): 'It's time for lunch.' Mwaura said he would convey the staffers' feelings to management, although many of the issues fell within the competence of the KUJ.

By May 1983, the *Nation* was the target of frequent complaints from the business sector, a number of individuals and the religious community. Stan Njagi, MD of the newspaper company, called an emergency meeting of senior editors and said there was a feeling the paper was going out creating enemies, while its relationship with the government was a 'political quicksand'. That all blame rested with the *Nation* was far from proven, however.

Mwaura had already addressed a long list of complaints in an internal memo. One clearly stemmed from an editorial error: when Moi described a certain Kesia as a political troublemaker, the reporter thought he had said 'Chesire', and Reuben Chesire of the Kenya Farmers' Association promptly sued. What other complaints revealed, however, was the government's extreme sensitivity to criticism and a readiness by self-interested business-men to apply commercial pressures. When the Minister for Local Government, Stanley Oloitiptip, boasted that he would 'spend millions' on the wedding of his son and then made use of Nairobi City Council services for the event, there were noisy protests in Parliament. But when the *Nation* reported later, quite accurately, that Oloitiptip was being sued by a contrac-tor, Mwaura said, 'That did not seem to please the government.' After the paper reported that the KAF commander at Embakasi was involved in the coup attempt, eight security men descended on the office and picked up the reporter. The officer was subsequently court-martialled and convicted. A number of stories about Odinga prompted the government to complain about 'all this fuss' over the Luo leader, and when an announcement of a visit by Moi to Siaya District was used as a back-page filler, the regime protested that it had been purposely downplayed.

The Bata Shoe Company withdrew its advertising because the *Nation* reported a strike at its Limuru factory; Kenya Canners cancelled a contract with Kenya Litho to print its labels after the *Nation* disclosed an agreement between Kenya Canners, the fruit giant Del Monte and the government that gave the company a monopoly of the pineapple market; Firestone East Africa Ltd stopped advertising for three months after the *Nation* reported on its difficulties in getting foreign exchange to buy raw materials and spare parts. Clearly it was open season on the *Nation* and Mwaura determined that the newspapers must not be seen as an easy touch. It was essential to fight back.

One battle concerned the Nakuru stringer Paul Muhoho, aged 19, who Mwaura was forced to withdraw from duty because of police intimidation. On 10 June 1982, the *Daily Nation* printed the following story from Muhoho:

> *A man who shouted at President Moi during a Kanu rally at the Afraha Stadium, Nakuru, last Sunday has been jailed for three months. Wilson Kipsoi arap Chumo shouted at President Moi saying he had increased the price of commodities and had not given out land. Nakuru senior resident magistrate Mr V.D. Shevde warned Chumo that his utterances were irresponsible and could have*

*subjected him to mob justice if security officers did not intervene
immediately. Chumo appeared in court charged that on June 6 in
Afraha Stadium he behaved with intent to provoke a breach of the
peace by shouting at President Moi. Chumo pleaded guilty. He said he
was a driver and earned only 450 shillings a month.*

After publication of this story, police questioned Muhoho about 'malicious and anti-development reporting' and 'tarnishing the good name of the President'.

Mwaura complained about the Nakuru police in a letter to Attorney-General Matthew Muli that also reported violent and intimidatory actions which he characterised as 'uncalled-for police harassment'. It was clear that the overwhelming dominance of the ruling party had obscured any faint memory of rights to free expression, that the role of the Press was officially perceived as necessarily supportive of the ruling party, and that the organs of state, including the police and the provincial administration, were employed to enforce this perception. The cause of freedom was not helped by the appearance of a KANU newspaper, the *Kenya Times*, formerly Ng'weno's *Nairobi Times*, and its Kiswahili sister *Kenya Leo*, whose editors lost no time in joining the *Nation*-bashing campaign. Mwaura received a vague promise to investigate the Nakuru affair.

In April and May of 1983, the *Nation* came under fire successively from President Moi, Attorney-General Muli, Commerce Minister John Okwanyo, Minister of State in the Office of the President Justus ole Tipis and various KANU camp followers. On many of the issues, the newspapers had a perfectly adequate defence, but one horrendous misjudgement rendered this largely nugatory. On 20 May, the *Daily Nation* led its front page with the story 'Tribal fight erupts in Mathare'. It said one person was killed and six others injured in a clash between Kikuyus and Luos in the vast Nairobi slum. The story did not use the word 'tribal', and the last paragraph quoted villagers as saying there had been a series of fights recently involving brewers of *chang'aa* liquor. Aware of the political sensitivity concerning tribalism (it was supposed no longer to exist in Kenya), senior editors wanted to use the word 'communal' in the headline, but this was not possible 'for technical reasons' (presumably, it would not fit). Convinced by a police officer and hospitalised victims that the fighting was tribal, the editors went with the T-word. Chief sub-editor Ali Hafidh was not persuaded of the choice, gave the editing job to his deputy and went home early, and Mbugguss refused to use the tribal angle in *Taifa Leo*. The *Sunday Nation's* Chege Mbitiru believed it was simply a fight over brewing rights. Okwanyo immediately called for the *Nation* to be banned, and Moi denounced the newspaper and its 'foreign masters' for blowing a story about drunkards out of proportion and 'trying to destabilise the country by creating tribal animosity'. Ekirapa hurriedly announced an internal inquiry.

For eight days between 3 and 18 June, five directors of Nation Newspapers Ltd – Ekirapa, Njagi, Professor Simeon Ominde, Curtis and the successor to Nisbet-Smith, Patrick Cooney – met in Nairobi and heard evidence regarding five controversial issues: the Mathare fight; harassment of the Nakuru correspondent; an editorial on Nyanjega Primary School; a story about civil service corruption; and reports of a Kitui land dispute. Numerous witnesses were called and the record ran to 50 foolscap pages. The investigating committee also met with government officials. The benchmark issue was the procedure to guard against editorial error: Had there been breaches of the editor-in-chief's terms of reference, of a 1982 editorial policy statement or of 32-point editorial guidelines which were put in place for just that purpose? In the Muhoho case, editors argued that the Nakuru police were angered by the reporter's coverage of a separate issue – land-buying companies – and that he had been harassed three separate times until he feared for his life. The primary school complaint concerned an editorial which criticised Provincial Commissioner David Musila for barring all media except the government news agency from a meeting called to discuss land issues involving the school. Corruption in the civil service had been mentioned by Muli, and both the *Nation* and *Standard* quoted him as saying it was a cancer. But the *Nation* alone reported that 'corruption in the Civil Service has reached an alarming proportion'. Muli denied using the phrase. Investigation of the Nzalae, Kitui District story focussed on a *Sunday Nation* headline, 'Ranchers and squatters in battle' (over trust land), and a complaint by Muli that the use of 'squatters' was incorrect.

Giving its decisions, the probe committee in the Nakuru case doubted the wisdom of hiring a schoolboy of 19, but formed a high opinion of Muhoho's ability and certainly did not think he had invented the idea that he was harassed. On the primary school, the committee said the provincial commissioner should expect to be criticised, but the manner of the editorial's composition was 'contrary to company practices'. The corruption dispute was one man's word against another's and, since the reporter could produce no notes, the committee concluded that the disputed sentence had gone beyond what Muli said. Reporting of the Nazalae story was accurate and balanced and there was some misunderstanding about the use of 'squatters'; thus criticism was confined to the strength and wording of the *Sunday Nation* headline. So far, so trivial. It was the Mathare story that brought an end to Mwaura's career with the *Nation*. The committee concluded that the reporters and photographers performed well, that news editor Peter Kareithi failed to obtain material facts from Mathare itself, relying entirely on hospital patients and police, and that managing editor Joe Kadhi failed to probe the full dimensions of the incident and justified the word 'tribal' by its use in a story of conflict the previous year. The key charge against the editor-in-chief was his failure to follow that clause in the editorial policy statement which said, 'Nation Newspapers will continue to stand for racial, ethnic, religious and communal harmony; they will aim to help readers of all races to see Kenyan, African and international events in perspective and to understand their inter-relationships.' The committee said Mwaura had failed to consult with the MD, allowed the ME to take the crucial decision on the use of 'tribal' in the headline, failed to ascertain the scale of the fighting and failed to consider whether the story could be held over for further investigation.

Eight days after the inquiry ended, the *Daily Nation* carried a front-page headline, 'Nation appoints group managing editor', over the smiling face of George Mbugguss. The story said the editorial department had been reorganised to provide for more effective decision-making and a new position of Group ME created, with Mbugguss, Managing Editor of *Taifa Leo* since 1968, appointed to the post. The last paragraph said, 'Mr Peter Mwaura has resigned from his position as Editor-in-Chief and will be leaving the employment of the company on 1 July 1983.' An internal document said that while there had been an improvement in the quality of news reporting and editorial writing under Mwaura, there were failures to follow editorial policies and procedures. Kadhi and Kareithi were cautioned. The new post would give the group ME the same full and effective powers as those of an editor-in-chief.

Mbugguss did not have long to wait for his first major challenge – the sensational naming of Charles Njonjo, Moi's right-hand man, as a traitor and a plotter. Moi had been deeply shaken by the Air Force's attempt to overthrow him, and his Minister for Constitutional Affairs had accumulated so vast a range of power that he was seen by many to be effectively running the country. In his characteristic allusive style, Moi set off the anti-Njonjo campaign then watched it run its course. He said foreign powers were grooming 'a certain person' to take over the presidency, making clear he did not mean his Vice-President, Mwai Kibaki. There was uproar.

'Leaders up in arms against traitor' cried the *Nation* as ministers hastened to pledge their loyalty and demand the identity of the traitor. Several days later, the paper gave page-one prominence to a mundane story about Njonjo returning from a foreign trip, slyly juxtaposing it with the lead story about the traitor. Few Kenyans missed the connection. An extraordinary *Nation* exclusive then took the drama a crucial step further. News editor Kareithi and stringer Waruguru Mwangi reported a service at the Presbyterian Church at Rungiri in Kikuyuland which Njonjo attended. Their account carried the blandest of introductions: 'The people of Kikuyu constituency yesterday offered special prayers for peace in the country.' But deep in the story there was dynamite. An elder of the church, Samuel Githegi, quoted a Kikuyu proverb, *ingithua ndongoria itikinyagira nyeki* (when the lead sheep limps, the others will not reach the grass). The Rev. Geoffrey M. Kaburugu referred to Daniel surviving in the lions' den with the sort of strength that guided the Kikuyu tribe. And Njonjo read from the Acts of the Apostles how the evangelists Paul and Silas were in prison, but when an earthquake occurred their chains fell off.

This sort of story bamboozled expatriates, but MPs in Parliament recognised the allusions and could talk of nothing else. The limping sheep could only be the President, said one, but who was Daniel? Cried Justus ole Tipis, 'We should be told who inflicted injury on the leader to make him limp.' Wasike Odombi: 'This implies that the leader of this nation is limping and that he would not take Kenyans to the grass.' Finally, after much prompting, Tourism Minister and fervent Moi admirer Elijah Mwangale declared, 'If you ask the people in this house and those outside who the traitor is, they would turn to Mr Charles Njonjo.' The accusation was followed by prolonged and delighted applause. In the course of his steady accumulation of power, Njonjo had alienated many inside Parliament, including mavericks such as Martin Shikuku, Koigi wa Wamwere and George Anyona, who, with several colleagues, he had dismissed contemptuously as 'the seven bearded sisters'. Outside of the National Assembly, he had infuriated radical lawyers and professors and Luos as a group. Though he had disarmed the Change the Constitution campaign and loyally piloted the constitutional process which brought Moi to power, there was a widespread feeling that Njonjo had come to see himself as the nation's puppet master. Journalists recalled Njonjo saying casually at cocktail parties, 'We must make Daniel understand this … [or] we will have to persuade the President that.' Many foreign businessmen and diplomats believed a line to Njonjo was more valuable than access to Moi himself.

At a later sitting, Njonjo told a crowded, excited Parliament that he regretted the political overtones at the church service, and that it was not Moi who was the limping sheep but he, Njonjo, because he had not initiated development projects in his constituency. This argument did not wash. MPs who felt they had been ignored, insulted or victimised by Njonjo saw the church meeting as a seditious, anti-Moi gathering which would have gone unmentioned but for the presence of the *Nation* reporters. George Mbugguss saw which way the wind was blowing. When Shikuku accused Njonjo of owning a farm in detested South Africa, the Associated Press' Nairobi correspondent Andrew Torschia discovered that this charge had been published in a South African satirical magazine, and was intended to be a joke lampooning Njonjo and a certain type of African leader who cultivated an image of Englishness. The *Sunday Nation* was keen to use the AP story and Mbitiru on a Saturday night tracked down Mbugguss, who was socialising with KANU man Joseph Kamotho. 'I called George out and explained to him what I had', Mbitiru recalled, 'but he said, "No, we can't publish it". I said, "Why?" He said, "Because the government want the man out".' Moi announced a judicial inquiry and Njonjo resigned from Parliament.

When the inquiry began, the *Nation* demonstrated the deft touch it frequently showed in reading the public pulse, whatever other problems it might be having. Mbugguss plunged for unprecedented verbatim coverage, devoting an average six-and-a-half pages a day to the hearings. Wangethi Mwangi recalled, 'The rationale was that people were deeply interested but they couldn't be there in person so we had to take the proceedings to them. The *Standard* and the *Kenya Times* realised very late that that was what the readers wanted but they could not match us because our reporters had picked up the skill very well and could put together quick and accurate reports.' Copy ran at about 8,000 words a day, or an average-size novel every ten days. Whatever problems this posed for general news coverage, the policy paid off handsomely in circulation terms, boosting sales from 130,000 to 154,000. At one point, the *Daily Nation* print order went over 200,000 for the first time, while *Taifa's* exceeded 80,000. The Aga Khan sent a cable to Ekirapa: 'Please convey to all staff how absolutely delighted I am … I congratulate most warmly the group managing editor and his staff, who have achieved a product whose objectivity, balance and fairness is appreciated by more and more of the Kenya public.'

After 109 days, the judicial inquiry came to an end and Njonjo was pronounced guilty of a wide range of charges, including plotting to overthrow the government in the 1982 attempted coup, but not of organising the prayer meeting or of arrogating to himself the duties and powers of the President. Some Kenyans were uneasy that the judiciary had been used to solve what was a political problem, but a *Nation* editorial stated, 'Many individuals in Kenya and East Africa have yearned for Mr Njonjo's blood. Had Mr Njonjo been a national of another country and been proclaimed "the traitor" there, the chances are that he would have been executed a long time ago.' This was undoubtedly true. Moi had cleverly engineered the bloodless removal of the 64-year-old *éminence grise* who had aided him signally in 1976 and 1978, then sought to manipulate him in office. On Jamhuri Day, 1984, Moi pardoned Njonjo 'in view of his previous faithful service'. The head of state said, 'He had all along endeavoured to serve the country faithfully until some time in 1980 when he started developing and entertaining misguided ambitions. However, considering his age and total life in public service, I have decided to pardon him on many of the confirmed allegations.' Njonjo did not spend a day in prison but politically he was finished.

Moi had by now secured his position following the KAF rebellion, but rumours of impending coups sustained a relentless hunt for enemies and scapegoats. Moi called elections in September 1983, a year early, 'to cleanse the system' and wipe out disloyalty in his administration. He was returned to power for another five years, along with Kibaki as VP, while 760 KANU candidates contested 153 available parliamentary seats, with up to 15 hopefuls vying for a single vacancy. The 48 per cent turnout was the lowest since independence and five full ministers were defeated, including two persistent *Nation* critics, G.G. Kariuki and Joseph Kamotho. A campaign was started to promote KANU as a mass political movement, and Moi indicated where Kenyans should stand with a famous speech in September 1984. He said:

> *I call on all ministers, assistant ministers and every other person to sing like parrots. During* Mzee *Kenyatta's period, I persistently sang the Kenyatta tune until people said, 'This fellow has nothing to say except to sing for Kenyatta.' I said I did not have ideas of my own, who was I to have my own ideas? I was in Kenyatta's shoes and therefore I had to sing whatever Kenyatta wanted. If I had sung another song, do you think Kenyatta would have left me alone? Therefore you ought to sing the song I sing. If I put a full stop, you should put a full stop. This is how the country will move forward. The day you become a big person, you will have the liberty to sing your own song and everybody will sing it.*

Being a Moi parrot meant being a KANU devotee. Recruitment for the party was carried out largely by the provincial administration and the police, and enforced by the thuggish KANU Youth Wing. Market women were prevented from selling their goods unless they produced party cards, and non-members were routinely booked for vagrancy or deprived of trading licences, education for their children and administration services. Moi decreed that all civil servants must be KANU members and said the government would hire no one who was not. The women's organisation *Mandeleo ya Wanawakare* and the Central Organisation of Trade Unions were affiliated to KANU, effectively giving the party control over women and workers. By 1985, KANU membership had soared from a few hundred thousand to more than 4 million in a population of 19 million.

Such a massive organisation clearly needed control and the KANU National Disciplinary Committee was established, swelling in power and arrogance until it virtually ruled Parliament. Its most feared weapon was expulsion from the party, which automatically cost an MP his seat and jeopardised the livelihoods of lesser lights. The committee began to summon MPs before it if they spoke in the National Assembly in a manner deemed contrary to KANU policy. Several independent-minded MPs were forced out and the remainder cowered in silence. Thus was the principle of Parliamentary supremacy undermined. Njonjo was expelled from KANU, as were six other former ministers, including heavyweights and former favourites G.G. Kariuki, Francis Lotodo, Clement Lumembe and Oloitiptip. Mbugguss said:

> The committee was getting absolutely ruthless and terrorising politicians. They summoned Elijah Mwangale, the man who fingered Njonjo in Parliament, who was by then foreign minister, and I splashed the story. I got a call from Moi. He said, 'What's this I hear you are doing a story on my foreign minister? I don't want that story in the Nation tomorrow. These people have no right to summon my foreign minister.' I said, 'Mr President, don't you think these are the people who should be disciplined, not Mwangale, for issuing such statements without your knowledge and you are president of the party?' He said, 'I'm going to discipline them.'

Mbugguss killed the story and Moi disbanded the committee on 10 September 1987 when he returned from a ten-day tour in Europe. The Soviet-style terror abated, but discipline continued to be meted out by

KANU branches, and politicians continued to be suspended or expelled until the legalisation of opposition parties several years later prompted a rethink of the attrition wreaked by KANU in its own ranks.

By the time its silver jubilee arrived in 1985, the *Nation* was on a steadier course. Mbugguss was perceived as a sound professional and political backstop, if no conceptualist, and a realistic appraisal took place of remuneration and editorial responsibility. A high-level meeting decided the group was uncompetitive when it came to senior executive salaries, and 'more creative solutions' must be sought. A visiting director reported that 'the management structure, for historical reasons, is too overbearing in relation to its influence on editorial'. He recommended the return of 'some authority and responsibility to the editorial department, hoping that while the risks will be minimised, this will motivate a more purposeful and creative approach to editorial management, planning and staffing'. This was a surprising suggestion from director level but it was shunted into cold storage, perhaps because memories of Githii were still fresh.

On the 25th anniversary day itself, 20 March, the *Daily Nation* produced a 24-page paper plus a handsome giveaway, a 102-page, A3-size year-by-year account of the *Nation* story. Executive editor Sean Egan, title notwithstanding, worked mainly with Mbugguss on special projects. He explained, 'I got a researcher, Hilary Wilkinson, to dig out the material and Steve Lawrence, who had been a sub with the *Nation*, to write it and I pulled it together.' The glossy foldout cover carried reproductions of 29 front pages, in colour and black and white. They included the first issue, '14 new arrests in Ghana'; the *uhuru* edition, 'Kenya free!'; the first assassination, 'Mboya shot dead'; McHaffie's celebrated design for Kenyatta's funeral, 'The final farewell'; 'Moi's the one' on his accession; '1,000 KAF men held' the day after the coup attempt; and 'Njonjo found guilty'. The jubilee newspaper led page one with a *Nation* scholarship programme to sponsor 86 students for four years at state secondary schools. The scheme was announced by the Aga Khan at a luncheon attended by UN Secretary-General Kurt Waldheim, at which Moi reaffirmed his government's 'firm and unshakeable' commitment to freedom of the Press. At the annual general meeting, chairman Ekirapa announced a record pre-tax profit of £1,011,700 – the first to pass the million pound mark – with a record print order in 1984 of 225,000 copies. (Actual sales in 1984 averaged 140,835 and in 1985 they were 139,978. Circulation went past 150,000 in the first six months of 1986.) The Kiswahili papers sometimes exceeded the total sales of all other newspapers in Kenya combined, the *Nation* excepted. Ekirapa mentioned in passing that of the 693 people employed by the group, only 13 were expatriates.

It was clear to shareholders that 'the newspaper that serves the nation' had, in football terms, entered the Premier League and company executives believed significant capital investment was needed to keep it there. Newspaper capacity was being restricted by the lumbering Goss Urbanite press, which imposed unrealistically early deadlines, and much other equipment was obsolete, inadequate and expensive to maintain. While Western newspapers were using computerised direct input, *Nation* reporters were still pounding typewriters chained to their desks. So, too, were all of Kenya's other journalists (without the chains perhaps), but the *Nation* was supposed to be the pioneer. Inspired by the sophisticated technology that visitors from all *Nation* departments had seen at the *St Petersburg Times*, the company invested in a front-end input system for editorial, classified advertising and some production functions. A second press line was acquired and also, finally, a plot on Kimathi Street in the centre of Nairobi for a purpose-built headquarters. Capital investment soared from just over £350,000 in 1984 to more than £22 million in 1987.

Although the coup attempt gave a severe jolt to Kenya's carefully nurtured 'island of tranquillity' image, the issue of human rights had never seriously or systematically intruded on the political scene. When Amnesty International protested against the arrests of Shikuku, Seroney and Anyona, Njonjo dismissed Amnesty as 'a busybody organisation of frustrated old women and young people'. Even in 1982, the post-rebellion crackdown was accepted by many Western watchdogs as a necessarily forceful action to restore order. However, 1986 saw a sudden sharp rise in preventive detentions, sedition trials and allegations of torture, and those numbers more than doubled in 1987. A survey by *Index on Censorship* revealed that human rights infringements in fact had been increasing steadily across an ever-widening catchment area. Since Ngugi wa Thiong'o was detained in 1978, action had been taken progressively against journalists, students, ex-students, businessmen, playwrights, teachers, college lecturers, civil servants, union officials, local churchmen, foreign missionaries, carpenters, printers and newspaper vendors. Publications had been banned for disrespect to the government and ridiculing the police, plays had been cancelled, theatres closed, colleges and universities shut down, films rejected, a library raided, television programmes interrupted, book serialisations stopped and radio workers dismissed. Lord Chalfont of Britain was declared a prohibited immigrant for making a television film which the government did not like,

Githii was refused an exit visa, Kenyan journalist Salim Lone was deported while working for the United Nations and visiting US Congressman Howard E. Wolpe was prevented by Special Branch from discussing human rights with local churchmen. *Kenya Times* reporter William Onyango was interrogated about his sources for an exposé of textile smuggling, and his name disappeared from a list of candidates for Journalist of the Year.

The courts were used against quite ordinary people expressing a sense of injustice. In February 1978, Peter Luna Maponge was jailed for three months at Kakamega for sending a letter to the police requesting the release of Shikuku, Seroney and Anyona. In 1988, truck-driver Peter Makau refused a lift to a man with car trouble because his company prohibited hitch-hikers. Unfortunately for Makau, the hitch-hiker was Provincial Commissioner Yusuf Hajji. Makau was swiftly located and sentenced to three months for 'unbecoming behaviour' towards a government official. The conviction was later overturned, but these cases demonstrated official readiness to use the judicial system for political repression, not to mention personal vengeance.

A major campaign against opponents of the regime was launched in 1986. It targeted an obscure organisation named Mwakenya (a Kiswahili acronym for *Muungano wa Wazalendo wa Kukomboa Kenya*, or Union of Patriots for the Liberation of Kenya) which Ngugi wa Thiong'o was alleged to lead from London. KANU leaders began to attack Mwakenya vehemently at public rallies and an MP condemned it in Parliament as 'a disgruntled group that intends to bring strife and instability into the country'. Moi warned, 'We know who they are. They cannot sleep easily because as soon as we pick one of them up, the others know it will soon be their turn.' Kenyans were already being picked up, almost all of them university students or lecturers. Charges ranged from failing to report the existence of Mwakenya and/or seditious publications to knowing the contents of such publications and/or destroying them. By describing any document critical of officialdom as seditious, the government effectively criminalised dissent. Student David Onyango Oloo was found with a half-completed essay questioning recent legislation and was jailed for six years. Between January and May, more than 100 people disappeared or were arrested, allegedly for links with Mwakenya. In March alone, 14 were arrested and 11 were jailed, and Kenyatta University was closed indefinitely.

Andrew Kuria reported almost all the Mwakenya cases for the *Nation*. He said in an interview:

> *The accused were brought in at odd times, often 4 pm or 5 pm after the regular court sittings had ended. Most were charged with*

*possessing seditious documents but they were always photocopies, never originals. The suspects never had lawyers and they always pleaded guilty. If they didn't admit, they would be brought back in two weeks and then they would admit. They almost always said they had been tortured. One came with a rotten leg and said he had been put in water for seven days. They would put electricity in the water. You could tell they had been beaten. The arrestees were mainly university lecturers, civil servants and newsmen. They were all tried in Nairobi by the Chief Magistrate (H.H. Buch, a holdover from colonial days and the man who had jailed the letter-writer from Kakamega) and the prosecutor was always Bernard Chunga, and they were always brought by Special Branch. They would usually get four or five years, rarely less than two.*

Talk at the time was that Special Branch planted the documents or sent them through the post and arrested the recipients when they went for their mail. Although Moi banned parliamentary debate on Mwakenya, the authorities were keen that people should know about the security arrests. 'Usually the police would tip us off about the court sittings', Kuria said.

Among those arrested were *Sunday Nation* columnist Wahome Mutahi, who was taken from Nation House, and his brother, Njuguna Mutahi of the Kenya News Agency. They got 15 months each after pleading guilty to failing to report the existence of an anti-government organisation and publishing a seditious publication. The brothers knew nothing of Mwakenya, but Wahome later wrote a novelised version of his experience which demonstrated why he, and everybody else, pleaded guilty. *Three Days on the Cross*[1] described his torture in vivid detail, being blindfolded, slapped, stripped naked, burned in the groin with cigarettes, blasted by a hosepipe at cannonball force and left to sit in the water until his flesh blanched. He said later, 'Everything in the book happened to me personally. I didn't make anything up.' Other tortures reported by victims of the Mwakenya terror, which mostly took place in the basement of a government building in the centre of Nairobi, included electric shocks, whippings, hot irons, gagging, sleep deprivation and confinement in a small, unlit cell.

The reason that arrestees always professed total ignorance of Mwakenya, at least until tortured, was that it probably did not exist, except as a creation of Special Branch. Wangethi Mwangi recalled, 'The Press did not have any independent confirmation of Mwakenya, everything we had came from the government, the literature, everything. Nobody willingly stated that they were Mwakenya.' Newsmen got no calls from Mwakenya, its local leadership was unknown, it issued no manifestos, no protests, no press releases. Ngugi wa Thiong'o was originally named as the organisation's leader, and Philip Ochieng remembers faxes arriving at the *Kenya Times* bearing Ngugi's name, claiming responsibility for train derailments in Kenya. Yet in 1987, Kenyan opposition groups abroad met in London and formed Umoja, the United Movement for Democracy in Kenya, under Ngugi's chairmanship. Why would he start another anti-government group if he already led Mwakenya? As for faxes, anybody can send them.

*Nation* journalist Mohammed Warsama believed the crackdown was provoked by students expressing glee at the prospects of Moi's departure during the coup attempt. He said in an interview:

> *Many of those who were picked up were at the university in 1982 and they were usually Kikuyus or Luos and perhaps involved in some community organisation. After the coup business, everybody at the University of Nairobi, and I was there at the time, had to report to his Chief once a week and then be interviewed by a guy from military intelligence and a policeman. The idea was to crack down so hard nobody would ever again think of doing something like the 82 coup.*

Did it work? John Githongo believes the campaign emasculated the universities: 'After the Mwakenya cases, the universities were finished as think-tanks for politics.' A simple theory is that the government invented Mwakenya to justify continued repression.

Whatever dubious advantages accrued internally from Mwakenya, the government's image became increasingly tarnished abroad. Moi cut short an official visit to the United States when congressmen and the State Department questioned Kenya's human rights record, and he cancelled planned state visits to Norway and Sweden after the Oslo government said it would raise the issue officially. Amnesty International published a 60-page report detailing the routine torture of political prisoners and Congressman Wolpe spoke of 'a startling level of fear' in Kenya. Some voices spoke up in Kenya, too. In a bold sermon, Anglican Bishop Alexander Muge of Eldoret said, 'People are the victims of threats, fear and tyranny. What is the point of protesting against injustices in South Africa when there are worse violations at home?' Oginga Odinga spoke of a gradual slide towards dictatorship and called for a return to multipartyism, and the Roman Catholic bishops protested that KANU was assuming a totalitarian role. In response to the official mantra that the churches should keep out of politics, Methodist Bishop Lawi Imathiu said, 'While we must respect politicians, they must know that the country is ours as much as it is theirs and we have every right to talk about our country and criticise any evil or shortcoming.' The government simply turned the screw.

Moi announced the abolition of secret voting for election nominations and, in response to Wolpe's criticisms, also ordered government officials to seek permission from the foreign ministry to visit embassies. By 131 votes to nil (38 abstentions), Parliament amended the constitution to allow the President to dismiss the attorney-general and the auditor-general without convening a tribunal. A later announcement gave the President the power to sack judges without an independent investigation and allowed the police to hold capital suspects for 14 days instead of 24 hours. Among many detainees was human rights lawyer Gibson Kamau Kuria, who was held for ten months and said he had been tortured. 'I was blindfolded and forced to do exercises when naked', he told *Washington Post* correspondent Blaine Harden. 'They were commenting adversely as to my private organs throughout my interrogation.' It was Harden's story, published while Moi was in Washington DC, and the furore it caused that persuaded the Kenyan president to avoid the Press, cancel a meeting with the UN Secretary-General and return home in a huff.

On 22 February 1988, KANU selected its candidates for the 21 March general election by requiring party members to queue behind a large photograph of their preferred candidate. About 43 per cent of the 4.5 million registered members participated. Moi, who had already been declared President for a third five-year term, and 11 other candidates were returned unopposed. This fact, and the rule which allowed any candidate who received more than 70 per cent of the party vote to enter Parliament unopposed, meant that only about two-thirds of the 188 parliamentary seats were contested by secret ballot on 21 March. The poll became known as the 'rigging election' and the result was the worst parliament in Kenya's history, a House purged of critics and the independent-minded, and packed with sycophants and yes-men.

One MP told the human rights organisation Africa Watch that he was 'rigged out' to make way for a candidate with powerfully placed relatives. 'They did everything possible to make my opponent's queue longer', he said. 'They used trucks to go and get people and they brought them food and drink. They even brought in children who had no ID. Once the queue gets that long, people get fearful anyway, so they went to that queue. It is very obvious which queue you should be in. You had to be very brave to stand in my queue.' Women said they were threatened with eviction from their village plots and beatings from their husbands if they failed to support Moi's candidates; men were told they could lose land and trading licences. When Charles Rubia, former Mayor of Nairobi and the sitting MP for Starehe, demanded a recount of figures which only put him in a run-off position, the revised total increased the vote for his rival to over 70 per cent, ensuring Rubia's defeat. Martin Shikuku lost his long-held seat when the Butere general election ballots became mysteriously mixed with those of Emuhaya constituency.

Although the *Nation* reported claims of rigging by defeated candidates, it backed off from targeting the many highly visible abuses, and a 23 March editorial commented blandly, 'On the whole, barring a few noisy upheavals during the campaign, the elections have been completed satisfactorily.' As to claims of cheating, the courts would deal with those, it said, and what was important now was to heal the wounds of acrimony. The editorial was headlined, 'Let's all get back to nation-building'. It was an extraordinarily supine and uncharacteristic response to a flagrant abuse of the democratic process. Where in the past the *Nation* had taken pole position in defence of *wananchi's* rights, now it was leaving the battle to lawyers and churchmen. Clearly the Mwakenya terror influenced this stance, transforming the issue of newspaper survival to one of personal survival. Mbugguss recalled those years as a time of 'threats from all over'. He said, 'Editors were being followed right, left and centre. You never felt safe. They instilled a fear that you might not get home safely and if you did, would you find your family in one piece?' Outsiders have no moral right to pass judgment on decisions taken by editors exposed to daily intimidation. Purely on the facts, however, it is arguable that the *Nation's* decision to turn a blind eye to the election rigging, allied to a subsequent failure to defend itself when attacked in Parliament, paved the way for serious government action against the group just one year later.

If the *Nation* was not ready to meet the government head-on, others were. Bishop Muge proposed that the churches hold a referendum on queue-voting, and another Anglican bishop, George Muiru Njuguna, urged the government to establish a committee of inquiry into the system. Constitutional lawyers questioned the validity of abolishing the secret ballot. For Moi, this sort of talk was as welcome as a wasp at a picnic, and six weeks after the election, he ordered the debate on queue-voting to come to an end. In a decree from State House, Nakuru, he declared that KANU would take its time and decide on the issue as, how and when it deemed fit.

That one man could decide what Kenyans were permitted to talk about was a reflection of how far the country had gone in creating a presidential cult. An aura of reverence surrounded the head of state and direct criticism of Moi became unimaginable. His portrait was printed on currency notes, and his photograph hung in government buildings, private offices, shops and schools. Every VOK news bulletin began, 'Today, His Excellency President Daniel arap Moi…', and, on most Monday mornings, newspapers showed the head of state singing hymns in church the day before. A massive pyramid-style monument of black ceramic tiles, slate and steel was constructed in Nairobi at the junction of Uhuru Highway and Kenyatta Avenue depicting Moi's fist, clutching his trademark *rungu* (baton), thrusting skywards out of Mount Kenya. Built at a cost of KSh18 million (£124,000) to mark ten years of the Nyayo era, it was dedicated by Moi himself amid great fanfare. The President's name was bestowed upon stadiums, streets, schools, hospitals and Mombasa airport. On children, too. An erstwhile Moi opponent in the Change the Constitution affair, Jackson Harvester Angaine, self-styled King of Meru, named his son Napoleon Bonaparte Wiseman Moi.

*The Kenya Anti-Corruption Commission, all bark and no bite.*

Although KANU's men of power got what they wanted by rigging the 1988 election, the fraud backfired on them in a way that would change the nation's future and bring about their own downfall. The election ousted a number of respected leaders, who, if not liberal in the Western sense, were sufficiently independent to recognise the threat posed by internal repression and growing corruption, a crumbling economy and a deteriorating international image. Rigged-out politicians such as Rubia and Kenneth Matiba were substantial, wealthy establishment figures, with extensive business interests and strong, if largely tribal, power bases. As an Africa Watch report stated, 'President Moi created an opposition group which ultimately found its political impact was greater outside of parliament than within, and which provided the most serious focus for discontent since the 1982 coup attempt.'

If the *Nation* had not publicly nailed its colours to the mast over queue-voting and the rigged election, it did not shy from carrying lengthy news reports on these and other issues which the government would have preferred to go unmentioned. For instance, when the Law Society of Kenya opposed the planned removal of security of tenure from judges, the *Daily Nation* splashed the story and published the full text of the lawyers' 22-paragraph statement. Just two days later, the government launched a carefully orchestrated attack on the newspaper in Parliament. The MP for Bomet, Kiprono Kones, asked what was the government's feeling about 'the attitude and coverage' of events by Nation Newspapers, particularly those of a sensitive nature, and would the newspapers be cautioned that such reporting could compromise the interests of the country? The Assistant Minister for National Guidance and Political Affairs, Professor Joseph Ouma, began by ritually reaffirming the government's support for freedom of expression, avoiding any mention of banned publications or imprisoned and tortured journalists. Lamentably, he noted, the *Nation* group had 'repeatedly handled sensitive issues with a decided and consistent bias in favour of interests divergent from and external to the national interest'. Examples were reports on a railway scrap metal scandal, unrest by dockworkers and statements by Bishop Muge: 'There is a perennial tendency by the group to promote the interests of persons, institutions and groups who have demonstrated negative interests and even consort with dissident elements.'

Through the fog of Ouma's bureaucratese, it was clear the newspaper was being warned off. While it did not respond publicly to Ouma's attack, neither did it desist from reporting issues that angered the leadership. In a society where the 'national interest' had come to mean the party/government interest, and where questioning of official policies became 'virulent dissi-

dence', *Nation* editors felt they could do no other. This stance led to the flagrant misuse of a rubber-stamp parliament against the newspaper in contravention not only of the constitution, but of the legislature's own procedures.

On Madaraka Day of 1989, the 1 June celebration of self-government, Moi
declared an amnesty for Kenya's political exiles, released four of the seven prisoners being held without trial, including Raila Odinga, and ordered an
increase in the minimum wage. A *Nation* editorial waxed lyrical, in a syntacti-
cally confused sort of way, at this display of compassion: 'The presidential olive
branch extended to remorseful Kenyan nationals living out an empty existence
as angry exiles abroad and the release from detention of four former inmates
shines brighter against the equally sunny spark of the salary raise also
announced by the President on the sombre occasion of the 26th anniversary of
Madaraka Day.' The tortured prose went on: 'The President's goodwill gesture
… is a powerful symbol of the practicality of his philosophy of peace, love and
unity and the authenticity of his incessant preaching that he is determined to
mould a society positively tuned to the tenets of humanness.' What was curious about the editorial was that it made no reference to a virulent attack Moi
had just launched against the *Nation* and which it carried in its news columns.

Moi said:

> *Some of our local newspapers do not want peace in this country …*
> *especially the* Nation. *I have been watching this newspaper very*
> *carefully for a number of years. The editing of this newspaper is*
> *number one. It leads all the other newspapers. But its intention is evil.*
> *We are not against it criticising but what they do underground is of*
> *great concern. I would have liked to mention their names but I will*
> *not do it today, I'll spare them. But if they continue doing the same*
> *thing I'll name them, because if trouble breaks out in this country,*
> *they will run away but many of you* wananchi *will remain here*
> *because you have no passport.*

Apart from his impression that the *Nation* was still being edited by expatriates, Moi gave no indication of exactly what he was angry about. The editors
thought they knew. Two weeks earlier, an instruction by the President's press
chief, Lee Njiru, had been resisted at Nation House, causing Moi himself to
get on the phone and accuse the newspaper of being 'Kenya's enemy number
one'. When Njiru telephoned, Mbugguss refused to take the call and it was
picked up by news editor Mutegi Njau. Njiru said the President wanted stories about corruption allegations against cabinet minister Elijah Mwangale

to be killed. The fiery Njau protested angrily that the stories were balanced and included Mwangale's own comments. Njiru was adamant. Njau passed the phone to Wangethi Mwangi, by then the *Daily Nation* managing editor, who told Njiru that it would be difficult to drop the stories since Mwangale had been mentioned at almost every public meeting that day.

Within minutes Moi was on the line, accusing the *Nation* of blowing up anti-government stories and playing down favourable ones. 'That was when I tried acting like a tough editor', Mwangi recalled ruefully. 'He accused us of being unpatriotic and an opposition newspaper. He said I should realise that if ever there was chaos in Kenya I would not be spared, I would be a victim with my family like everybody else. He meant it in general terms, me as a Kenyan not an individual, but it was very scary coming from the head of state.' Mwangi explained the technical difficulties and said the paper was not trying to bring down the government, simply to write about an individual minister accused of corruption. Moi said some *Nation* journalists were paid to write certain stories. Mwangi said the *Nation* staff were patriots and he was unaware of any such payments. However, he killed the page one lead and other Mwangale-related stories, and ran comments from the President, in effect quashing further debate on Mwangale. Next day, Moi called Mwangi direct and said the *Nation* was doing a good job; its only problem was its 'attitude of mind'.

Notwithstanding Mwangi's eventual submission, that an editor had the temerity to argue with the President was a minor sensation at Nation House. Mwangi said, 'There was an inquisition to find out what transpired between me and the President, whether I had insulted him or been disrespectful to him and I got clear instructions that if he called again, I should get hold of the chairman or the MD and I should not engage him in argument.' Mwangi did, in fact, argue with the President again. When Moi called at a later date and accused *Nation* staffers of acting in the Kikuyu interest, Mwangi protested that the younger generation of Kikuyus were not tribally minded, and that he, for instance, considered himself a Kenyan first, a Nairobian second and a Kikuyu third. Moi took the point and the evidence of several editors was that Moi was amenable to reasoned argument. Instant capitulation had long been the preferred option, however, and all the evidence suggests this simply made things harder for the newsroom. Philip Ochieng recalled that when he was editor of KANU's *Kenya Times* he would often argue with Moi: 'He would listen and think and he could be persuaded. He was not so bad as the people surrounding him. The *Nation* got into problems partly by not arguing.'

After the public Madaraka Day blast, Ekirapa sought a meeting with Moi, and on his way in encountered an angry Njiru. The President's media chief described the *Nation* as 'like a very beautiful coffin with something less beautiful inside'. Moi referred to unrest in the region and to attacks on him by the older generation of Kikuyus. Ekirapa, not himself a Kikuyu, took this as an allusion to the preponderance of Kikuyus in the *Nation* newsroom, and said this was partly because Philip Ochieng took a number of non-Kikuyu staffers with him when he left to edit the *Kenya Times*. As to the undesirables on the paper, Moi said in fact he had no names. He stressed, 'We are not Americans, we have a different understanding of the role of the press.' When Ekirapa spoke of the effect of attacking 800 workers 'who consider you their father', Moi fell silent. There was no specific conclusion, but it was obvious Moi was surrounded by people ready to drop poison in the presidential ear.

Except for sedition cases incurred in the course of reporters' duties, no *Nation* employee was ever charged, much less convicted, of any act of disloyalty to the Republic of Kenya or the head of state. Nor was any conspiracy ever unearthed at Nation House that would remotely support accusations of lack of patriotism or working for foreign interests. However, the paper crucially failed to respond to the President's vague Madaraka Day charges, leaving itself open to suspicion that there might be some truth in them, according to the long-held proposition in law *qui tacet consentere* (he who remains silent, consents). This silence may have led Kalonzo Musyoka to assume the newspaper would be easy meat when he opened a bitter campaign against it four weeks later.

In Parliament on 28 June, Deputy Speaker Musyoka moved that 'in accordance with the provisions of Standing Order number 170, this House resolves that representatives of the *Nation* group of newspapers be excluded from the Press Gallery for an indefinite period'. Musyoka, who was also KANU's organising secretary, then led MPs in a comprehensive denunciation of the *Nation*, its policies and its employees. Some 32 separate allegations from various members included the following: The group had underworld connections and international espionage links and sent journalists to St Petersburg for training in how to subvert Kenya; it highlighted corruption to discourage investment and belittled the country's achievements; a four-man 'tribal advisory council' recommended staff promotions; it gave all its reports to the Associated Press which twisted them for foreign distribution; it wrote cynical articles which scandalised MPs; the *Nation* was owned by the Ismaili community of Shia Muslims and half of its cover price was pocketed by the Aga Khan, who was hostile to Kenya; it harboured dissidents, lacked patriotism, tried to cause chaos and set up an investigation unit aimed at maligning leaders. It should be forced to change its name.

The onslaught was deftly orchestrated, with two speakers called from each province. Joseph Odindo, then with the *Kenya Times*, recalled that 'Kalonzo would come to our office in the evenings during the debate and tell us this or that is going to happen tomorrow and we knew it was going to be our lead story'. Many MPs sought to settle old scores, and the House as a whole revealed a surprising ignorance of media institutions and practices. Much of the debate was couched in scarcely disguised racist terms aimed at Kikuyus and Ismailis. *Finance* magazine described an assembly 'filled with emotion, anger, hate and exasperation', and said, 'It would appear that most of the MPs were driven by personal vendettas rather than substantive reasoning … the sweeping accusations could have been levelled against any other publication.'

Many of the accusations, such as foreign spying, were simply preposterous, while others amounted to wild rhetoric and personal opinion. Lack of patriotism, for instance, seemed to mean failure to support KANU. Specific allegations frequently crumbled under scrutiny. Assistant Information Minister Shariff Nassir accused the *Nation* of misreporting a speech he made in Parliament seven days earlier, but *Hansard* proved the story was accurate. As to Ismaili 'ownership' of the *Nation*, the group was majority Kenyan-owned, the Aga Khan's shareholding having been reduced to 45 per cent the previous year; no Ismaili had ever held a management position at the *Nation*. One allegation said KSh2.25 of the KSh4.50 cover price 'finds its way to Geneva or France, where the Aga Khan resides'. In fact, the net profit margin per copy was 22 cents, most of which was reinvested; in the 1988 financial year, 63 per cent of profits after tax were ploughed back through capital investment. Energy Minister Nicholas Biwott accused the *Nation* of misreporting a speech he made at the Turkwell Gorge hydro-electric project. The report actually appeared in the *Kenya Times*. Minister of State Johnstone Makau accused the *Nation* of carrying photographs of exiled dissidents after Moi's amnesty declaration. It published no such photographs. Ojwang K'Ombudo said the *Nation* reported his contribution at a harambee as KSh2,000 when it was KSh116,000. The *Nation* did publish such a report, but it came from the government's Kenya News Agency and was also published by the *Kenya Times*. K'Ombudo did not complain at the time.

The MPs' sense of humour seemed to be at fault in other instances. When Wahome Mutahi wrote a satirical piece about the sub-division of Karen-Langata plots, Musyoka denounced it as 'laughing at Kenyans'. And when Muthui Mwai's 'The Week in Parliament' column suggested that the standard of debate had taken a nosedive, the deputy speaker declared that this scandalised members. What is more likely to have offended Musyoka was Muthui's reference to MPs playing it safe and asking innocuous questions. 'If the freedom to speak freely, to expose wrongdoing in society and to criticise does not exist in Parliament, it is not likely to exist elsewhere in the community', Muthui declared. Information Minister Waruru Kanja called for caution from MPs and praised the Aga Khan for his role in Kenya. But the House voted overwhelmingly to ban the *Nation* – and Kanja was sacked before the year was out.

The day after the debate ended, the boards of NPP and NNL published a joint holding statement which affirmed loyalty to the President and to KANU, expressed serious concern about the allegations made in Parliament and announced they would inquire into them. The company promptly contacted two law firms, one of which subsequently reported in unlawyerly language that 'what the Members said was libellous garbage'. It added, 'The contributions fall below the standard one would expect members of a reasonable National Assembly to maintain. They all abused the powers and privileges which the National Assembly (Powers and Privileges) Act has conferred upon them.' The opinion recommended a rebuttal that should be 'well-reasoned both as regards facts and law couched in temperate language'. Otherwise, 'some readers will construe silence to be an admission of the truth of the allegations'.

At least three MPs had personal reasons to attack the *Nation*. In moving the motion, Musyoka referred to the unfair dismissal of an unnamed *Nation* manager. The company believed this to be Elias M. Musyoka, a relative of the deputy speaker, who was terminated as personnel manager for 'inadequate performance'. (He was also a political activist, which the company frowned upon.) Johnstone Makau said he had been interviewed for the post of MD at the *Nation*, but had rejected the offer because the paper was 'racialistic'. Old-timers recalled that Makau was indeed interviewed for an executive position and failed the interview. (Makau declared during the debate that 'no country can leave its print and electronic media free because of its influence, because it can destabilise the country'. He later became minister of information.) Shariff Nassir was keen to denigrate the *Nation* to save his political career. According to reports at the time, his attack on corruption in the civil service – the speech he later accused the *Nation* of misreporting – had not been received kindly in KANU's upper circles.

Interviews with senior editors suggest that the campaign was not so much personally motivated as a concerted effort to silence a newspaper which was showing signs of rebellion. Moves had been made against the three other areas from which discussion and debate arose – the Church, the Law Society and Parliament – and the *Nation* was visibly dominant in the last troublesome area, the media. Philip Ocheing said, 'The *Nation* was beginning to get out of the one-party mentality and become more critical. It started when KANU removed security of tenure from certain national offices and introduced queue-voting. The *Nation* began to take sides and become sympathetic to a burgeoning opposition and from that time, the government was against the *Nation*.' Kadhi agreed: 'That was a period when the *Nation* was beginning to behave like a true newspaper again. We were fought against politically not for our reporting but for ceasing to be the good boys, like Githii and to a certain extent every editor had been. It was orchestrated at State House not by little Musyoka.' Mbugguss said, 'They wanted to teach us a lesson for not toeing the line.' Wangethi Mwangi: 'The powers-that-be decided to take us head-on and find a way of bringing us to our knees.' Odindo believes there was also a tribal element: 'There was an anti-Kikuyu thing in the government which was extended to the *Nation*. KANU was playing the tribal card and the banning had a lot to do with that. Moi was using anti-Kikuyu feeling to harry people around.'

The removal from Parliament was painful. The VOK dropped any reference to the *Nation* from its daily review of the Press, and reporters found many senior civil servants and politicians suddenly inaccessible. A number of parastatals and local government authorities cancelled advertising, causing a significant drop in revenue, while sales slipped from 179,186 for January–June of 1989 to 156,924 for July–December, the lowest point for two years. Urgent action was essential at a high level, and within a week of the debate *Nation* editors had inspected reporters' notebooks, checked copy, tracked down sources, scoured opposition newspapers and parliamentary records, and prepared a detailed statement of rebuttal. Mistakenly, the board delayed publication. Ekirapa recalled, 'The more serious, legalistic-minded directors advised us not to answer immediately as we would appear confrontational. We should give it time, use a bit of diplomacy.' Ekirapa sought a meeting with President Moi and the Aga Khan wrote him a respectful but forthright five-page letter.

The principal shareholder described the attacks on his role in the *Nation* and his relationship with Kenya as untrue, offensive and personally insulting, and asked if they represented the true feeling of KANU and the government. He pointed out that the security authorities had never been able to provide evidence or names of any subversives at the newspaper, and he noted that the company's 800 Kenyan employees and 10,000 local share-holders would be hurt by falling circulation. 'If it is the wish of the government progressively to weaken the *Nation* or even to close it, then it would be better to state that intention clearly', he said. If not, then the attacks on the newspaper should be halted. The Aga Khan recalled his positive response to Moi's personal appeal for help in the 1976 ownership crisis and the *Nation's* support for him during the Change the Constitution campaign, and again in the 1982 coup attempt. He enclosed a copy of the board's draft rebuttal and offered to meet with Moi later in the month. There was no reply.

A well-founded suspicion at the time was that much of the animus shown towards the *Nation* sprang from a desire by some powerful politicians to take a controlling interest in the group, which they could not do as long as the Aga Khan retained his 45 per cent shareholding.[2] Nation House discussion of the government's hostility ranged beyond the Musyoka campaign to Moi's Madaraka Day outburst and the persistent threatening phone calls to the newsroom from State House. So seriously was the government's intimidation taken that at one point closure of the newspaper was seriously considered. Ekirapa spoke to virtually everybody who had influence in government, and once, when he was at Parliament Buildings to see the Speaker, he bumped into Musyoka. The begetter of the *Nation's* troubles was unrepentant. He accused the newspaper of carrying out a vendetta against him and threatened personally to sue.

When it became obvious that Moi had no intention of seeing the Aga Khan or Ekirapa, the rebuttal statement and a lengthy editorial were approved by the NPP and NNL boards, and finally published in the *Daily Nation* on Friday 8 September. Approval was not unanimous. NPP board member and Attorney-General-to-be Amos Wako announced that he wished to abstain. Said Ekirapa, 'Wako stood up to go. As he passed the Company Secretary, Tim Straker, he bent down and said, "Don't forget to record that I don't support the motion". I was very disappointed.' Wako had an office in the same building as Ekirapa, and after the meeting, Ekirapa walked over and remonstrated with him. All Wako would say was that the board decisions were taken by majority. What galled Ekirapa even more was that when the statements were published, Wako telephoned to congratulate him and said they should have been even stronger![3]

The two statements, drafted by Gerry Wilkinson, were masterly replies. The directors' rebuttal reproduced key elements from the editorial policy, restated the company's loyalty to the state and set out a series of crushing refutations of the parliamentary accusations. It disclosed Musyoka's kinship to the sacked employee, dispensed summarily with Nassir's self-serving charge of misreporting, explained the twinning arrangement with the *St Petersburg Times*, outlined how international news agencies such as the Associated Press operate and spelled out the ownership situation. The statement said it was difficult to respond to many other attacks because they involved a highly subjective use of the events reported. An elegantly argued editorial pointed out that the *Nation* had neither persistently misreported Parliament nor refused to correct any misreporting, while the extra-parliamentary charges were either untrue or matters of interpretation. The newspaper, therefore, had been accused and tried on extremely questionable evidence, and condemned without being given the right of reply. It suggested that if the *Nation* and *Taifa* lacked patriotism and sought to create social disorder, they would hardly be accepted by the 3 million Kenyans who read them every day.

The *Nation's* response put to rest any doubt among ordinary Kenyans as to its good intentions and the ban was lifted on 13 October when MPs returned from their recess, three-and-a-half months after its imposition. If anything, the affair enhanced the newspaper's reputation, but commercially it was a blow. The group's pre-tax profit for the year was £2,795,000, another record, but substantially lower than forecast, in part because of cancelled advertising. There was also the question of 30 per cent import duty on newsprint. While the *Nation* paid £1,304,000 in newsprint costs in 1989, 24 per cent more than in 1988, the *Kenya Times* was allowed to import its newsprint, together with equipment and spare parts, entirely free of tax. The party paper also received all the government advertising and tender announcements. This was a bad deal for the taxpayer, given that the *Nation* reached 2.3 million readers daily compared with 337,000 for the *Kenya Times*. The advertising rate on a cost-per-thousand-readers basis was 6.99 cents per column-centimetre in the *Nation* and 78.26 cents in the *Kenya Times*. It was this sort of misuse of public funds for political reasons that was soon to bring the government into serious conflict with Western aid-giving nations and international donors, as geopolitical changes began to sweep the globe.

## *Notes*

1.  *Three Days on the Cross* by Wahome Mutahi, East African Educational Publishers Ltd, Nairobi, 1991.

2.  A senior official at State House sought unsuccessfully, through Sir Eboo Pirbhai, to acquire substantial shares at the last offering. He did not disclose for whom he was acting.

3.  Wako's failure to join the battle against repression did not prevent the United Nations from appointing him its human rights envoy to East Timor in 1992, to inquire into Indonesian military attacks against civilians.

# Rise of
# Multipartyism

**8**

*Patiently endured as long as it seems beyond redress, a grievance comes to appear intolerable once the possibility of removing it crosses men's minds.*
French historian and political scientist Alexis de Tocqueville
(1805–59)

Ex-schoolteacher Daniel arap Moi was not dubbed the 'Professor of Politics' for nothing. Although calls for multipartyism in 1989 were few and muted, Moi was quick to see the threat which pluralism posed to the KANU hegemony. In May alone of that year, he referred to it three times at public meetings: 'Those yapping about multiparty politics are swimming in the high seas and seek to confuse the country's youth who have not even begun to swim on the edges of the lakes.' And, 'Multiparty advocates are tribalists surviving on borrowed ideas.' And, 'We are threatened that unless we do as we are told [introduce political reform], we risk losing friends and their financial aid.' Indeed, Moi had already set out his hard-line position in a book published in 1986 when discontent over his rule was gathering pace: 'I have great reservations against multiparty systems in Africa for, rather than promoting patriotism, they refuel political ethnicism and factionalism ... they proliferate ethnic alliances and sub-national factions in all facets of national life.'[1] It can be argued that events were to prove Moi correct as the opposition movement divided along tribal lines, but it would be naive to disregard KANU's role in making his predictions come true, not least in the promotion of ethnic conflict, which killed many hundreds of Kenyans and turned thousands more into refugees in their own country. A *Nation* journalist in Mombasa told the author, 'I was hardly aware of my tribe until the government started talking about ethnic this and ethnic that and tribal zones and KANU zones. I was also insulted to be told I was too ignorant and simple to understand multiparty politics and KANU was my *baba* and *mama.*'

The Kenya establishment already felt threatened by events in Eastern Europe, as Communism collapsed and single-party governments were thrown out. With the Soviet Union heading towards Balkanisation and the Cold War effectively over, the Western democracies moved to realign their policies. Massive aid to governments of developing countries to counter Soviet blandishments was no longer necessary, and British Foreign Minister Douglas Hurd declared, 'Aid must go where it can clearly do good. Countries tending towards pluralism, public accountability, respect for the rule of law, human rights and market principles should be encouraged. Those who persist in repressive policies, with corrupt management or with wasteful and discredited economic systems, should not expect us to support their folly.' Later in 1990, he elaborated, 'We will reward democratic governments and any political reform which leads to greater accountability and democracy. The corollary is that we should penalise particularly bad cases of repression and abuse of human rights. We are not only talking about freedom from poverty and hunger but freedom from the fear of torture and arbitrary arrest.' References to torture, arrest and repression must have caused disquiet in KANU's upper echelons, while 'pluralism' and 'political reform' doubtless provoked something close to panic.

On 3 May, US Ambassador Smith Hempstone told a Nairobi Rotary Club luncheon audience, 'A strong political tide is flowing in our Congress, which controls the purse-strings, to concentrate our economic assistance on those of the world's nations that nourish democratic institutions, defend human rights and practise multiparty politics.' The *Nation* front-paged the speech under the headline 'US mounts pressure for multiparties'. Hempstone described the reaction in his book *Rogue Ambassador*:[2] 'Kalonzo Musyoka huffed, "Don't dictate to us". Burudi Nabwera, Minister of State in the Office of the President, ordered the provincial administration to monitor my movements outside of Nairobi. Elijah Mwangale, the most ardent of the Moi toadies – in a speech at the coast he asserted that even the fish in the sea bowed down before the President – accused me of financially supporting the Kenyan dissidents, and the Kenya foreign office told me that Moi would not open the US trade fair in Nairobi.' Though in the event, he did.

Hempstone's speech was delivered on the same day that Charles Rubia and Kenneth Matiba returned to haunt those who rigged them out of Parliament in 1988. The two men issued a statement calling for repeal of

Article 2A of the constitution providing for a single-party state, for the dissolution of Parliament, for a limit on presidential tenure to two four-year terms and for a public referendum to decide the country's political future. Rubia and Matiba constituted a powerful new element in the forces of democratisation hitherto represented mainly by churchmen and lawyers. In fact, the first formal shot in the multiparty campaign had already been fired in a New Year's Day sermon by Presbyterian Reverend Timothy Njoya, who urged African leaders to re-examine their preference for the one-party system in light of the debacle in East Europe, and the overthrow and execution of Nicolae Ceausescu and his wife in Romania just a few days earlier. Anglican Bishop Henry Okullu urged repeal of 2A and protested that many Kenyans feared expressing views different from KANU's because they would be victimised. The *Nairobi Law Monthly* pressed for a widening of the debate in light of 'the bogey of tribalism and chaos which is whipped up by defenders of the one-party system'.

Some of the new oppositionists complained that the mainstream media were leaving the minnows to fight the battle for democracy, and it is true that the *Nation*, smarting from its brutal handling by Parliament and wary of the unconcealed hostility of the President and his party, did not rush headlong into the multiparty battle. However, its editors ran significant developments in such a way that their importance could not be overlooked, as in front-paging Hempstone's speech under a headline which pressed interpretation to the limit (though Hempstone did not object). The *Nation* did not editorialise on Njoya's New Year's Day sermon (it commented on Moi's New Year's Eve message), but it led the paper with Njoya and dropped Moi's speech below the fold. And for those with eyes to see, it carried an editorial-page article from its sister organisation in Europe, Compass News Features, about the changes in Europe. The headline read, 'New decade ushers in dramatic possibilities'.[3]

The government adopted the classic shoot-the-messenger response by launching a form of guerrilla warfare against the media which was to continue up to and beyond the next election in 1992. The true mindset of the Moi regime was demonstrated as far back as 1982 by the egregious G.G. Kariuki, who told Parliament, 'When I was in charge of the internal security of this country, I kept on saying that the country will be destroyed from the editorial boardrooms of the newspapers because that is the only place we have people who say what they want to say.' This seemed to imply two things: free expression would lead to national downfall; and the vast majority of Kenyans were not permitted to say what they wanted to say. In line with this thinking, small critical magazines that began to emerge in 1990 were confiscated regularly. Their printing machinery was sometimes disabled, editors were arrested, interrogated and periodically charged and detained. The national dailies were subjected to relentless verbal attacks from the President on down.

It was not just multipartyism that was worrying Moi at this time, but the sensational murder of Foreign Minister Robert Ouko. As with J.M. Kariuki 15 years earlier, the first that *Nation* readers knew about this drama was a headline on 16 February, 'Minister Ouko goes missing'. Next day, inside a black border, 'Ouko's burnt body found'. Ouko had been shot in the head and his charred body dumped in a field four miles from his home in western Kenya. Some reports said he had been driven away in a white car at 3.30 in the morning. News of the murder triggered massive anti-government demonstrations in Nairobi and Kisumu. Police and GSU units clashed with students, and witnesses reported that security forces fired both over and into the crowds, dragged drivers from their cars and beat women at bus stops with rifle butts. Contradictory official statements fuelled the belief that the killing was government-inspired, and Ouko's death was compared with the murders of Mboya, also a Luo, Kariuki and Pio Gama Pinto during Kenyatta's rule. For the first time, demonstrators publicly called on Moi to resign. Moving quickly, Moi called in a British police team led by Superintendent John Troon to investigate Ouko's murder, and announced a judicial investigation.

In an effort to take the heat out of the growing civil conflict, Moi ordered an immediate end to the multiparty debate, but found that Kenyans were no longer willing to be gagged. Bishop Okullu declared the debate could not be over since it had never started, and the *Nation* splashed a statement by a Roman Catholic bishop that was strongly critical of politicians agitating for preventive detention. Four archbishops and 14 bishops denounced queue-voting, official corruption and forced harambees, and decried the ascendancy of KANU over Parliament. The Catholic intervention made a particular impact since until then the church had been muted in its comments.

It was at this point that KANU set up a ten-man committee under Vice-President George Saitoti to review the party's electoral processes, taking pains to deny it had anything to do with the pressures for pluralism or criticisms of queue-voting. The committee toured the country and heard a large number of remarkably outspoken and unwelcome complaints that extended far beyond the modalities of the ruling party. One of the witnesses was Sir Michael Blundell, the liberal white leader at the time of independence but by then a farmer long out of politics, who decried the manhandling of Professor Wangari Maathai when she demonstrated against a proposal to erect a 62-storey KANU tower in Uhuru Park, Nairobi. The environmental crusader (and Nobel Prize-winner-to-be) was threatened, her office closed and her papers ransacked. Blundell noted, 'At the time of the Maathai episode, one of the best editors [Mbugguss] was grilled for three hours by the CID and police for publishing so many letters on the subject, to which he replied that they were the only letters he was getting.'[4] The review committee's findings were considered at a two-day KANU delegates' conference in December. Moi insisted that Kenya must remain a one-party state. But the secret ballot was restored for election nominations, and it was agreed that security of tenure be returned to judges, the attorney-general and the auditor-general. Moi also ordered an end to suspensions from the party.

Matiba and Rubia applied for a licence to explain multipartyism at a rally at the Kamukunji meeting ground, Nairobi, on 7 July. Predictably, it was refused and the two conceded that the meeting could not take place. However, Moi announced a 'plot by anti-government people' to have *wananchi* shot at Kamukunji and blame the police. This charge was met with eager calls by MPs for 'anti-government elements' to be detained without trial, and the signal for a crackdown was delivered by Moi in a long speech on 3 July which declared that state security was not negotiable. Anyone who wished to confuse freedom to express his views with licence to undermine state security would be dealt with 'by the full might of the law', he warned. Twenty-four hours later, the swoops began. Matiba was arrested at his office and Rubia was dragged from a committee meting at Muthaiga Club. Also picked up were Raila Odinga, and lawyers John Khaminwa, Mohammed Ibrahim and Gitobu Imanyara. Paul Muite went underground and Gibson Kamau Kuria fled to the American embassy and later into exile.

If the aim was to pre-empt any popular gatherings in the multiparty cause, it backfired spectacularly. Licence or no licence, thousands gathered at Kamukunji for an event that went down in history as *Saba Saba*, the seventh day of the seventh month, marked by the worst violence since the coup attempt eight years earlier. The leaderless crowd waved branches, flashed the two-finger salute, and called for the release of Matiba and Rubia. Hemmed in by security forces, with a police helicopter overhead, individuals began stoning police cars, then a mob surged out of the grounds towards the city centre, at which point the waiting GSU charged with tear gas and batons. Running battles spread throughout the city, and young men and the urban poor seized the chance to loot shops and steal from cars and people. At one point, ten men walked down Tom Mboya Street shouting at the security forces, *Watue! Watue!* (Kill us! Kill us!). The only permitted broadcaster, VOK, now the Kenya Broadcasting Corporation (KBC), blacked out the demonstrations on TV and radio, but the news spread anyway and violence exploded in at least six towns in Central Province, as well as in Kisumu and Nakuru. The rioting lasted three days.

It was by presidential edict that KBC had remained silent. But this time, at the *Nation*, the worm turned. Joe Kadhi recalled, 'I was the editor on duty that Saturday and I received a telephone call from Moi himself, who said, "I don't want that story [about the riots] in the paper". I did not have the courage to tell the reporters to stop writing because they had been on the streets dodging blows and bullets, they had torn clothes and broken cameras and they were enthusiastically writing the story. How could I tell them to stop?' Kadhi reached Njagi and Mbugguss by telephone:

> They told me, 'You are the man on the spot, the decision is yours.' As if that wasn't enough, I got a call from Ali Hafidh [by then Editor of the Standard], who said he had also been told by Moi not to use the story and he was thinking of using it as a filler. Fifteen minutes later, I got a call from Philip Ochieng, who was editor over at the Kenya Times. He said, 'I have been instructed to tell you not to use that story.' I was infuriated. OK, I had been told the decision was mine, so I decided to splash the story and run it long.

The *Sunday Nation* devoted half of its front page to a dramatic photograph of a burning minibus and carried the story over three pages, with two more pages of photographs by staffers Yahya Mohammed and Joseph Thuo. 'I didn't know if I was going to be fired next day, or worse, arrested', Kadhi said, 'but nothing happened. It was an international story, the number one item on all the wire services. It was a story that could not be suppressed.'

Officially, the government admitted to 20 deaths, though there were certainly more. At least 1,056 people were charged with riot-related offences such as looting and raising the two-finger multiparty salute. Moi blamed 'hooligans and drug addicts' and the *Nation* carried a cautious editorial which condemned violence, but noted that the outbreak had raised 'matters of great political significance'. From the United States came the first hint that Congress might freeze aid when the Kenyan ambassador was summoned for talks at the State Department in Washington DC. The Nordic countries and Britain expressed concern about the use of preventive detention. These warning signals went unheeded in Nairobi. Not only were the two VIP arrestees now formally gazetted as under preventive detention, the ever-vocal Musyoka called in Parliament for Matiba and Rubia to be put on trial. At the same sitting, Kirugi M'Mukindia pointed to *Nation* reporter Emman Omari in the Press gallery, 'smartly dressed and not limping', and said this showed he had not been battered in the riots as his newspaper claimed. The one-time *Taifa* journalist John Keen, now an assistant minister, produced a purported list of opposition shadow cabinet members that named George Mbugguss as shadow presidential press secretary. Mbugguss recalled, 'It was all over the radio and television and people shunned me for months. Those were the days like *1984*, you had to look behind you before you spoke, but I got a lot of support from *Nation* management. Albert [Ekirapa] took it very calmly and nothing happened in the end but it was very, very nasty at the time.' When Keen later quit the government and joined the opposition Democratic Party, he admitted he was given the list by Burudi Nabwera, then minister in charge of security. Keen said he believed the list 'was fashioned and drawn by the state to silence the opposition of the time'.

It seemed this extraordinary year could hardly yield more sensations, but on 15 August, the *Nation* pulled out its biggest typeface again to proclaim, 'Muge is dead'. The Anglican bishop, who had criticised KANU sharply and often, died instantly when his car was in collision with a truck as he drove home to Eldoret from a visit to Busia. What made the event exceptional was that Labour Minister Peter Okondo had given a warning that if Muge or Bishop Okullu went to Busia they would 'see fire and might not leave alive because they want to poison the minds of Busia people against the government'. Ambassador Hempstone recalled meeting Bishop Muge five days earlier and asking if he intended to make the Busia trip. Muge replied, 'Of course. Busia is within my see and its people are part of my flock.' Was he not afraid? 'Of course. There are murderers in Moi's government. But the Lord's will, not Peter Okondo's, be done.'[5] When a powerful minister and Moi confidante, Nicholas Biwott, attended a memorial service for the bishop at Eldoret, angry mourners forced him to leave with cries of 'We do not want you here'. Talk of yet another political assassination was widespread but no firm evidence emerged, and the truck driver was later convicted of dangerous driving. Okondo resigned but was reinstated in 1991.

John Troon of Scotland Yard completed a 110-day investigation into Ouko's murder and presented his report on 24 September. Reneging on an earlier promise by Moi, the government refused to publish it on grounds that it did not name the killers, and thus publication served no useful purpose. The conclusions of the report, which stated that Biwott and former internal security boss Hezekiah Oyugi had a case to answer, were finally published in Kenya in May 1999, along with an account of a Kenya police investigation which contradicted Troon's findings. It was water under the bridge by then since Troon had named the two men at the Ouko Commission of Inquiry, along with Nakuru District Commissioner Jonah Anguka as a peripheral suspect.

Kenya's *annus horribilis* tottered to an end with the banning of the *Nairobi Law Monthly*, the breaking of diplomatic relations with Norway for 'harbouring' dissident Koigi wa Wamwere (Norway promptly stopped its aid), and a KANU delegates' conference that affirmed the one-party system. A human rights organisation calculated that there were 68 prosecutions for sedition in Kenya between March and October of 1990 alone, including one for removing Moi's portrait from a wall and others for possessing copies of the London-based newsletter *Africa Confidential*. The Kenya shilling had depreciated in value (24 shillings against the dollar compared with 17 in 1986), inflation was running at 17–19 per cent (petrol alone rose 32 per cent in the year), and foreign exchange earnings from tea and coffee fell short of 1989. The *Nation* was as much a victim as anyone and saw its newsprint costs rise by 25 per cent, while the government continued to give its advertising to the *Kenya Times*, and to ban both the *Nation* and the *Standard* from advertising on radio and television. The *Nation* group in fact established a new pre-tax profit record – £2,905,746, a 7.7 per cent increase on 1989 – but this was 31 per cent under budget, and almost entirely due to a 10 per cent increase in advertising volume and record sales in the newsiest of years. The *Daily Nation* topped 230,000 at one point and the *Sunday Nation* 253,000. Average sales for the year were more than double those of the combined competition.

But all was not well in the newsroom. The *Nation's* regular run-ins with the government were usually the result of hostility from the authorities rather than editorial caprice or faulty reporting, but some senior journalists felt that the company did little to support them in these rows; indeed, that it loaded extra pressures onto editorial staff. Kadhi said, 'I think the government got to understand that whenever they and Moi attacked the *Nation*, our principals did not like it. A statement would come out from State House or from a minister and that made everybody shake in their boots. We made ourselves vulnerable by not fighting back.' Kadhi recalled editors being summoned to State House 'for a tongue-whipping', and added, 'Every time that happened we would not be asked to defend or substantiate our stories, we were asked to write memos explaining why we got insensitive to the regime's philosophy and why we were always antagonising the powers-that-be.'

There were also fears that the news agenda was being politicised in the cause of individual politicians. Some senior people were known to be close to men like Kenneth Matiba, Njoroge Mungai, Njenga Karume, Kuria Kanyingi and Julius Kiano. 'Reporters were complaining that trivial activities like harambees had to be covered by senior guys because certain politicians were involved', Kadhi said. 'It created dissatisfaction. One non-editorial manager would come to the newsroom late at night to check on how any story involving Matiba was handled. He was not interested in what else was in the paper. Another wanted to find out about Dr Kiano.' Chege Mbititru said, 'The paper became politicised and tendentious', and Odindo recalled, 'There was a very strong feeling among the senior Luo journalists that they were disadvantaged because of their tribe. There was a feeling that there was a tribal cabal and policies were driven by tribal interests.' It would be wrong to suggest that the *Nation* became crudely propagandistic in any single person's cause, but some newsmen were fearful about editorial manipulation, the sort of thing then being demonstrated by the *Standard*.

Mohammed Warsama, news editor at the *Standard* before he joined *The EastAfrican*, explained in an interview:

> *You can push a politician or omit his enemy, you can kill or not kill a story, you can give it undue or reduced prominence. You can choose a wide picture so that 6,000 people seem like 100,000. There can be collusion between the reporter, the news desk and the chief sub. In 1990, when I was a senior sub at the* Standard, *there was a politician, Arthur Magugu, and all his functions were covered by the same guy, even on his day off. Magugu would call the desk and ask for him to cover his functions. Then the copy would go to the chief sub and he would say, 'Yes, this should be page-three lead.' We used to joke that the page-three lead was reserved for Magugu.*

During the first week of September 1991, the atmosphere in Nation House was tense. The gossip was of sweeping change at a high editorial level and preparations were made for a strike following a rumour that an expatriate was being brought in to run things. On the contrary, *Daily Nation* managing editor Wangethi Mwangi was the new group managing editor, and associate editor Tom Mshindi was named ME of the daily; production editor Bernard Nderitu and *Sunday Nation* managing editor Justin Macharia swapped jobs; the veterans Mbugguss and Kadhi were retired. Mbugguss was shocked and hurt ('I got no warning, I thought I was ill-treated'), but went on to a lively second career as editor of *The People*, a newspaper funded by Kenneth Matiba. Kadhi went about improving his academic status, and with two degrees under his belt became a lecturer in journalism to university students in Nairobi and the USA. Ekirapa had long considered Mwangi possessed editor potential. He was apolitical and non-tribalist, technically assured, cool under fire, did not play favourites and, though no one would ever admit it, had earned widespread admiration by arguing with Moi on the telephone. He was, however, less assured than he appeared. He said in an interview:

> *I wasn't mentally prepared and the appointment gave me the shakes. For a week, I couldn't sleep soundly. I kept wondering how I was going to manage those calls from Albert Ekirapa and the President and his ministers. And then the staff, my classmates at college many of them, would they accept me as their senior, having grown up with them? But Ekirapa told me I was being foolish and I gained the confidence of the newsroom when I showed I could hold the paper together. I formed a good relationship with the chairman. I was never politically directed by management but I would share sensitive stories with them and this often paid off in editorial terms.*

The first major test of Mwangi's fibre came when he received a series of calls from a KANU politician who had a reputation for compromising reporters. Mwangi said:

> *He had deep pockets. He had a habit of picking up a reporter and photographer and driving them to Moi's constituency, Baringo, to donate to some development project of the President and then you would have a picture of him smiling and holding a big wad of notes on page one. I decided to keep my distance from him and I refused to take his calls. But he persisted and I realised I would eventually have to talk to him so I listened. He said, 'I've just been with so-and-so and he sends his greetings and I told him I was trying to meet you. We are under extreme pressure from our enemies within KANU and I would like to explore how you could help us.' I agreed to meet him at the Hilton Hotel.*

*We were alone in the bar except for the waiters. He gave me his spiel about his problems and I said he should write a statement and send it to us and if we thought it had merit, we would publish it. He said that was good enough and we talked about ten more minutes and I said I had to go. Then the guy dips his hand into his inside pocket and pulls out an envelope and says, 'I realise these are hard times and I thought I should make a small donation just in case you have a harambee project.' I said, 'Wait a minute. I came here trusting you wanted to talk about something I could help you with. I didn't expect you to insult my intelligence by trying to compromise me.' Roughly, those were my words. I said, 'I have no harambees. If I do have a harambee and I feel I want to ask you to donate, I will.' He said, 'I'm sorry, I'm sorry' and put the money back in his pocket. I don't even know how much it was. As I walked out I made up my mind that I would make every effort to ensure that the only coverage that man received in the* Nation *would be when he died and that he would no longer get the coverage he was used to and I would instruct my editors that whoever was assigned to cover any activities he might be involved in was pulled out and somebody else sent in his place and that I wanted to see every story that was ever written about him. We never spoke together again.*[6]

Years later, Mwangi was able to state:

*The greatest change in the* Nation *has been in ridding itself of all the political influences that you tended once to associate with the paper – politicians, government ministers, even religious figures who tried to control the contents of the paper. They would telephone and ask for prominence for their speeches, or could you suppress a story or sanitise it, or they would call to know what their enemies had said at some meeting. All that has gone. We don't feel beholden to any politician or any group. Now we lampoon the President in our cartoons every day, we criticise his policies and those of his ministers, we are able to take powerful people head-on.*

But in the earliest years of the 1990s such freedom was no more than a pious hope, and the *Nation* sustained the most vitriolic attacks in its history from a government and its allies fighting a desperate rearguard action against pluralism and its threat to continued KANU rule.

Opposition to Moi's rule began to attract support across a broad front, which finally cohered in August with the formation of the Forum for the Restoration of Democracy (FORD), a political movement, not a party, since these were still illegal. The founders of FORD were the veteran campaigners Oginga Odinga, Martin Shikuku and Masinde Muliro, and the movement attracted a powerful range of anti-KANU heavyweights in Matiba and Rubia, lawyers Paul Muite, Gitobu Imanyara, James Orengo, Pheroze Nowrojee, John Khaminwa and Mohammed Ibrahim. They also counted Odinga's son, Raila, a former mayor of Nairobi – Andrew Ngumba, the powerful Ahmed Bamhariz of Mombasa and trade unionist Dennis Akumu. KANU responded by striking Muliro, Shikuku and Bamhariz from the party rolls, explaining that this was not expulsion (outlawed by Moi) but deregistration. On the same day, Philip Ochieng was sacked as editor of the *Kenya Times*. British media mogul Robert Maxwell had put money and a British manager into the paper and it was selling nearly 50,000, the best it was ever to achieve. But Ochieng said, 'One of the reasons I was in trouble was that though I often wrote commentaries criticising the opposition, I gave them a lot of coverage in the news pages, describing what they did, and the government did not like that.'

A new pressure point for the government was the conditionality of aid. Kenya was looking for $1 billion over the next two years, and if the West's demands for liberalisation were to be taken at face value this huge sum was in jeopardy. Donors had long been aware of the misuse of both private and official development assistance. At one point, Japan had 14 ventures in Kenya, but by 1991 these were down to two. The most notorious foreign deal was the Turkwell Gorge hydroelectric project. VP and Finance Minister George Saitoti signed an agreement in 1986 with a consortium of Paris banks to finance construction of a dam at more than double the sum on offer by international tender. A confidential report by A. Kratz, the Kenya representative on the then European Commission, stated, 'The Kenyan government officials who are involved in the project are fully aware of the disadvantages of the French deal ... but they accepted it because of high personal advantages.' For many years thereafter, foreign donors refused to put money into the energy sector.

The government could not have been surprised when the Paris Consultative Group of donor nations decided in late November to delay a decision on Kenya's $1 billion request for six months. The group made it clear it wanted to see progress in economic and political reform. Moi promptly announced that his government was committed to 'a new era of openness and accountability', and then stunned delegates to a KANU conference by declaring, in a massive climbdown, that Article 2A of the constitution should be repealed to permit the registration of other political parties. Legislation was promptly taken to Parliament and passed on 10 December. Before the end of the year, five ministers, including the former Vice-President Mwai Kibaki, resigned and went into opposition.

It was at this time that a sinister new development emerged that was to have bloody and long-lasting effects on the country, with 1,500 people dead, 300,000 displaced and tribal relations in some areas poisoned for years. What was initially described as cattle rustling soon became land clashes, then tribal clashes, until finally the *Nation* gave it the correct description – ethnic cleansing, based on the violent campaign in the former Yugoslavia to establish sovereign states on the basis of ethnic exclusivity. The long and blood-spattered Kenyan version was heralded by an inside-page lead story in the *Nation* of 2 November, 'Two dead in Nandi property dispute'. Correspondent Tom Matoke reported that a woman had been burned to death and a man shot dead by police at Meteitei Farm on 31 October, when a group that wanted the farm tenants evicted attacked with bows and arrows and set houses on fire. It was the prototype for hundreds of similar stories over the next four years. The key to the attack was contained in a speech made a few weeks earlier by MP Joseph Misoi, who said that a *majimbo* constitution for regional self-government had been drafted, and if the proponents of multipartyism continued their efforts, it would be tabled in the House and 'outsiders' in the Rift Valley (Kikuyus and Luos, that is) would be required to return to their motherlands.

The violence quickly escalated, spreading from the Rift Valley, where large numbers of Kikuyus bought land in the 1960s and 1970s, to Western and Nyanza provinces, where bands of warriors attacked farms belonging to the Luhya, Luo and Kikuyu, all groups which broadly supported the opposition. Witnesses reported that the attackers were often dressed in red or black T-shirts, their faces streaked with clay, like initiation candidates; they were armed with pangas, bows and arrows and sometimes spears. Although there were occasional, disorganised counter-attacks, the word 'clashes' was clearly a misnomer, since the violence invariably consisted of one side attacking and the other fleeing. In her book, *The Ukimwi Road*, Irish travel writer Dervla Murphy described a scene she witnessed near the Kenya shore of Lake Victoria:

*A bar stood at a junction 12 miles from Sondu and I was about to enter it when two open-backed lorries came at speed from the Kisumu*

*direction, halted and disgorged scores of warriors (or graduates?).*
*These were clad in animal skins and armed with bows and arrows*
*and formidable six-foot-long, broad-bladed spears. For an instant I*
*felt afraid. Then the men loped away, off the road into the maize*
*fields, moving silently and purposefully. Turning back to the bar, I saw*
*a small, slim young Luo in the doorway, staring at the vanishing*
*warriors. 'Who are these people?' I asked. The young man blinked and*
*moistened his lips and hesitated. Then he said, 'I didn't see them.'*[7]

Quickly recognising the significance of the so-called land clashes, the
*Nation* promoted the story to page-one lead status and carried pictures of
the homeless victims, thus placing the problem squarely in the national
spotlight. The *Standard's* coverage was 'very patchy', its training editor and
a former *Nation* sub-editor, Colin MacBeth, recalled. The *Standard's* Kisii
correspondent, Peter Makori, heard from a woman on a bus that violence
had erupted in Molo. Unable to check because the area was sealed off, he
filed the story. It was either erroneous gossip or a plant, and Makori and
three editors were charged with sedition. The charges were later dropped.
The *Nation's* reputation for accurate coverage was seriously damaged
when a reporter quoted an American human rights investigator as saying
she had counted between 365 and 1,000 bodies in Molo, an absurd figure.
She protested that the reporter had got it wrong and the government
denied it, too, and the *Nation* hurriedly backtracked. The paper also
pressed too far with a report that a government helicopter was used to
transport warriors. In fact, the craft had been used by a high official to take
guests to his daughter's wedding. What made covering the conflict difficult
was the lack of co-operation by the security authorities and restrictions on
the reporters' movements.

Mounting pressure from the opposition and from church groups eventually forced Moi to authorise an official investigation into the violence, and,
between May and September of 1992, a 12-member Parliamentary Select
Committee headed by Coast MP Kennedy Kiliku met 43 times in Parliament
and in the clash areas. Although made up entirely of KANU members, the
committee produced an unexpectedly critical report which adversely mentioned six cabinet members including Saitoti, Biwott, Ntimama and
Kipkalia Kones. The report said government officials had paid the warriors
to kill people and burn houses, and government vehicles transported the
assailants. It recommended action against officials who encouraged or participated in the violence. In testimony before the Akiwumi Commission,

*The 16-storey Nation Centre, designed by Danish architect Henning Larsen, which became the newspaper's new home in 1992.*

*End of an era; President Kenyatta's 1978 funeral*

*KANU chief J.J. Kamotho being helped from the US embassy where he was meeting diplomats when the terrorist bomb went off in 1998. He recovered from his injuries*

*A distraught woman at a Kiamba church, where 30 people burned to death in violence that followed the 2007 election*

*Cars are wrecked and fires rage in the Kibera slum in Nairobi*

*Watched by mediator Kofi Annan, President Kibaki and Prime Minister Odinga sign the 2008 peace agreement*

*Kenyans celebrate as news breaks that a peace agreement has been reached*

another investigation of the violence in 1999, Kiliku said some politicians contributed to the violence by 'rumour-mongering, incitement and conducting their public duties along tribal lines'.

A 1995 report by Human Rights Watch, *Slaughter Among Neighbours*, charged that 'the clashes were deliberately instigated and manipulated by KANU politicians who were eager to retain their power in the face of mounting internal and external pressure for change in government. Those alleged to be directing the violence and the attackers themselves enjoyed legal and political immunity.' The National Council of Churches of Kenya said much the same: 'These clashes were and are politically motivated … to achieve through violence what was not achieved in the political platform.' Human Rights Watch set out a series of motives: 'To prove the government's assertion that multiparty politics would lead to tribal chaos, to punish ethnic groups perceived to support the political opposition, to terrorise non-Kalenjins and non-Maasais to leave the Rift Valley Province and allow Kalenjins and Maasais to take over the land.' Government critics believed the aim in the Rift Valley was to remove enough anti-government Kikuyus from the province to ensure that Moi received at least 25 per cent of the vote in the next election. (Constitutionally, a president was required to win at least a quarter of the votes in five of the country's eight provinces.)

At the long-running Ouko inquiry, the *Nation* reported a week of sensational stories which gave it circulation figures that remain a record to this day (335,000). In short order, readers scanned these headlines: 'Biwott, Oyugi chief suspects'; 'Biwott sacked'; 'Troon details bid to conceal murder'; 'Biwott, Oyugi arrested'; and finally, 'Moi stops Ouko probe'. Denied publication of the suspicions set out in his written report, Troon voiced them frankly on the witness stand: 'I suspect Mr Oyugi and Mr Biwott have some knowledge of or involvement in the death of Dr Ouko.' His evidence was intended to link the murder to Ouko's determination to expose corruption involving some cabinet members, and to a personal dispute with Biwott during a state visit to Washington by Moi the month before Ouko died. Moi sacked Biwott, his industry minister and closest ally, and he and Oyugi were taken into custody. A witness reported that the two men took their detention at GSU headquarters badly: 'Oyugi was falling apart, wearing a long pullover with holes in it, unshaven, brushing away tears. Biwott looked seriously worried.' Not so Biwott's feisty Israeli wife, Honey, who let it be known that the police would answer to her if anything happened to her husband and warning that if he went down, he would not go down alone. But when the *Nation* got a call through to Mrs Biwott, the reporter found the ex-minister was already enjoying the comforts of home, freed after a brief detention. Abruptly, Moi then announced an end to the inquiry and a *Nation* editorial expressed the wan hope that the truth about Ouko's killing would emerge in a court of law. Biwott and Oyugi and some lesser lights were released for lack of evidence. Nakuru District Commissioner Anguka was tried for Ouko's murder but was acquitted. Troon described him as a sacrificial lamb.

In the emerging political landscape, the strength of FORD was that it cut across ethnic divisions and united Kikuyus, Luos and many Luhyas in a single organisation. Its top leaders were politically powerful in their own right, and the second echelon contained a large number of government critics who were intellectuals but not of the ivory tower sort – they were veterans of Kenya's street-fighting politics. FORD had the tacit support of most churches and human rights organisations, and was regarded hopefully by Western embassies. Above all, it excited many Kenyans with the prospect of change and rebirth. Over the last ten years, the country had slipped remorselessly in almost all categories of national performance. The *World Human Rights Guide* for 1992 gave Kenya a rights rating of 46 out of 100, the same as embattled Uganda and 12 points fewer than it achieved in 1983. The *Guide* said, 'Authority is ensured by close surveillance and arrests of opponents, Press restrictions and control of broadcasting.'[8] Capital held by Kenyans abroad rocketed from $200 million in 1982 to $2.6 billion in 1991, and foreign and domestic investment was minimal. Government expenditure was increasing by 20 per cent a year, most of it going on salaries for the bloated civil service (ghost workers were estimated at more than 85,000). Hopelessly inefficient parastatals accounted for a fifth of the country's gross domestic product (GDP). Waged employment was increasing by 2.5 per cent a year, but the labour force by 6.5 per cent. Infant mortality rose over the decade from 85 per 1,000 live births to 111, and per capita income dropped from $380 per year to $370.

When FORD held a licensed rally at Kamukunji in January 1992, the first since the return to a multiparties system, it seemed that a new era might have dawned. A breathless *Sunday Nation* story declared, 'An estimated half a million supercharged FORD supporters yesterday attended the most spectacular and electrifying public rally in Kenya's history. It was a spectacle to behold, as surprising in the crushing turnout as it was orderly and enthusiastic. It was as if Kenya in microcosm went to the historic Kamukunji grounds.' Cautious voices in the *Nation* thought this sort of overheated prose transgressed the rules of objectivity, but the reporters argued that they were simply reflecting the euphoria of the crowd. Oginga Odinga, address-ing his first political rally in 22 years, condemned 'the ills committed over the last 15 years by the KANU government' and warned that 'Moi is going to do his best to frustrate Kenyans in having a freely-elected government'. KANU was shocked by the size of the opposition support, and its secretary-general, Joseph Kamotho, commented sourly that 90 per cent of those attending were curious youths not old enough to vote. 'KANU is still very popular', he declared stoutly.

In the first use of an opinion poll since 1960, the *Nation* reported that 79 per cent of the 1,080 Kenyans interviewed believed they were worse off than ten years ago, and that the main reason was mismanagement and corruption by the government. Eighty-five per cent of respondents considered the gov-ernment had performed badly in reducing corruption, 75 per cent thought it had performed badly in managing the economy and 70 per cent gave it a 'bad' rating in protecting people's rights. An overwhelming 93 per cent named multipartyism as their preferred system of government. The *Nation* and the *Standard* continued to highlight tribal conflict, the former declaring that 'the clashes are widely perceived to be politically engineered'. An edito-rial said, 'The so-called ethnic clashes are not the creation of the Press, they are the creation of politicians and the government must be held responsible.'

The benefits of multiparty democracy.

The small magazines went even further, astonishing Kenyans with headlines such as 'Moi knows Ouko's killers' and 'Moi must go!' Pius Nyamora's *Society* magazine enraged the establishment by naming the reviled American ambassador, Smith Hempstone, as Man of the Year.

This surge in free expression prompted the sudden introduction of a motion in Parliament to curb 'media irresponsibility' by establishing a Press Complaints Commission with powers to punish errant newspapers. A few days later, Wangethi Mwangi was picked up by two police officers from his home at 7 am and questioned for four hours at CID headquarters about the *Nation's* coverage of riots in Kisumu. The *Standard's* Mitch Odero and Joe Ngugi were also questioned. The parliamentary motion was passed on 25 March, but an amendment deleted the reference to the complaints commission on grounds that it might include people with views contrary to those of the government. The move nevertheless sent shivers through the Press establishment, which saw it as a back-door attempt to reintroduce the controversial Section 2A of the national constitution providing for a single-party state.

The move in Parliament put the media on the defensive and the question that preoccupied editors once again was, How far can we go? The *Nation* had its editorial policy and guidelines, but they were not written to cover a uniquely problematical story which confronted Mwangi in March. A group of mothers of political prisoners went on public hunger strike in Nairobi's Uhuru Park, demanding the release of their sons. They sang and prayed in an area that became known as Freedom Corner. When the government decided that this visible demonstration of opposition had gone on too long, it sent in three squads of policemen with batons and tear gas. Back in Nairobi by then, travel writer Murphy had joined the women out of curiosity. She wrote, 'Without warning, the sitting crowd was charged and I could hear all round me the sickening thud of wooden staves on innocent backs. Twice I was struck hard across the shoulders and we all fled in panic.'[9] Then the women, in a stunning symbolic gesture, stripped naked.

Mwangi recalled:

> *We had pictures but the* Nation *had a very strong policy against obscene or titillating material. On the other hand, the women's gesture was the ultimate form of protest in the African tradition and the photographs perfectly captured the strength of their protest. What bothered me was that I was looking at the bare breasts of women old enough to be my mother. I consulted with Albert Ekirapa and we decided to telephone around and get some opinions. I spoke to my*

*father and to Archbishop Manasses Kuria of the Anglican Church and*
*Albert called up some other elders. The archbishop said that a woman*
*baring her nakedness symbolised the highest form of protest against*
*injustice and the Kenyan public would see it in that light and he*
*believed there would be no hostility if we published the pictures.*
*Ekirapa got similar replies. The photos were so dramatic they summed*
*up the entire story and by the time we went to press I was sure there*
*would be no negative reaction.*

Mwangi used one masked photograph of a naked woman on page one and
another inside. 'There was no hostile response', he said. 'People saw it for
what it was, a political statement that needed to be made, the issue itself
demanded it.'

In a year in which parliamentary and presidential elections were due, the
anxiety of the KANU chiefs was plain to see, although early signs of a split
in the opposition should have reassured them that in Kenya unpopularity
need not translate into electoral defeat. Mwai Kibaki decided, when he quit
the government, to bypass FORD and form his own group, the Democratic
Party of Kenya. This not only deprived the main opposition force of essential Kikuyu support, but split the Kikuyus themselves between Kibaki and
Kenneth Matiba, or geographically between Nyeri and Murang'a. Matiba
had been in London receiving treatment for strokes he suffered during his
ten months in detention, brought on, his supporters said, by the withhold-
ing of medication by his jailers. He had gradually recovered the use of his
limbs, but it was widely rumoured that he could no longer read or write with
any comfort. When news of his return from London circulated, huge crowds
flocked to the airport and gave him a frenzied welcome. Significantly, however, the crowd was almost entirely Kikuyu and contained few oppositionists from other tribes. Both Oginga Odinga and Matiba made it clear they
wanted the presidency, and the last chance of a compromise opposition candidate disappeared when the Luhya veteran Masinde Muliro died in July.
Inevitably, in August, FORD split into two parties – FORD Asili (FORD
Original), headed by Matiba with Shikuku's support, and FORD Kenya, led
by Odinga and backed by Paul Muite among others. Thus, long before an
election date was announced, the opposition sowed the seeds of its own
defeat, with Kibaki, Matiba and Odinga threatening to split the opposition
vote for president, while only Moi would stand for KANU. This was an
encouraging prospect for the ruling party but the KANU bosses were taking
no chances, and embarked upon the most ruthless and intimidating election

campaign in the country's history. The *Nation*, firmly perceived as an enemy of KANU, was an early target.

In the vanguard of the assault was Youth for KANU '92, or 'YK92' as it became known, led by Cyrus Jirongo, whose animus against the *Nation* appeared to stem from a series of articles exposing a shady KSh1.2 billion ($16 million) land transfer deal he set up with the National Social Security Fund (NSSF). YK92 became notorious as a vote-buying machine and the KSh500 note quickly became known as 'a Jirongo'. Widespread practices were the purchase by KANU agents of opposition identity and voters' cards, as well as straightforward bribing of candidates and voters. Opposition leaders advised, 'Take the money but vote for us.' FORD Kenya, the best organised of the opposition parties, claimed that the government printed huge amounts of cash to oil the wheels of the KANU campaign, and the US embassy confirmed that the money supply leaped by nearly 40 per cent in the pre-election period. The result of the over-supply was 100 per cent inflation, which reduced low-income Kenyans to the poverty level. John Githongo wrote:

> *I recall housewives gazing stunned at the increased prices and leaving items at supermarket checkouts because they had not brought enough money. The government's efforts to mop up the excess liquidity meant extremely high interest rates and this led to bailiffs repossessing goods from people who could no longer service their loans. Many middle-class Kenyans took second jobs. The infamous YK92 handed out copious amounts of printed money, assisting the process of our impoverishment.*

Jirongo's brief seemed to include smearing the *Nation* with charges of tribalism and weakening its editorial strength by buying individual journalists. On 1 October, publicity chairman Pyman Onyango led a small group of demonstrators to the *Nation's* Mombasa office and set fire to a copy of the *Sunday Nation* while chanting, 'Burn the Satan, Burn the Satan.' He accused the paper of recruiting along tribal lines. Two days later, similar charges were made at a harambee at Bungoma, where a youth party official challenged the *Nation* to publish its staff roll and Elijah Mwangale accused the editor of conniving with Kikuyus to 'finish' the Luhyas. On 5 October, the *Kenya Times* quoted yet another YK92 activist as suggesting the paper was part of the Democratic Party, and on 8 October the *Kenya Times* and KBC gave massive coverage to the simultaneous resignations of four non-Kikuyu

*Nation* journalists in Nairobi, followed by two stringers at the coast and two in Western Province. KBC carried the story for three straight days on both radio and television, and the party organ offered an analysis of 'ethnic bias' in the newsroom. In a page-one rebuttal, the *Nation* pointed out that two of the Nairobi staffers had not spoken to the government media and the third gave an interview but made no mention of tribalism. The fourth, William Omoga, had been seeking to persuade colleagues to resign so as to make true his prediction that six other newsmen were about to leave. Like the Parliament ban of 1989, the crusade was politically motivated, the editorial said: 'The ultimate objective in this elaborate scheme involving massive funds is to destabilise the *Nation* group of newspapers.'

The beleaguered ME of the daily, Tom Mshindi, recalled:

> *The guys they targeted were mainly Luhyas. Jirongo was a Luhya so he found it easier to go after them. Omoga was a Luo on our sports desk and he was convinced of their cause. He believed the* Nation *was a tribal paper and that he was not going to make it as a Luo. He didn't like his editors, he didn't like the GME. They offered 40 thousand shillings [$520] to correspondents out in Kisumu and Kakamega to quit and one guy ended up getting about 400,000 shillings [$5,250] and the promise of a house in Nairobi. Whether he got the house, I don't know. It was all engineered by YK92 with the active assistance of KANU.*

Mshindi, a Kisii, said three approaches were made to lure him away: 'The campaign did not hurt the paper in operational terms since the people they took were not key people, but it did reinforce the lie the government was pushing that we were an opposition newspaper and wanted to bring down Moi. People used to wonder how I managed as a non-Kikuyu senior manager. I told them, "What these people are saying is simply not true".' Ekirapa described the campaign as a 'very frightening development' and said he protested in writing to the attorney-general.

On 3 November, the election date was announced (7 December, later postponed to 29 December), and a pamphlet began circulating in Nairobi entitled, *A Newspaper that Serves 24 per cent*, authored by Youth for Unity and Patriotism. The title was clearly a gloss on the *Nation* slogan, 'The newspaper that serves the nation', and the percentage was a reference to the estimated proportion of Kikuyus in the population. The authors were clearly journalists working for YK92. The entire pamphlet appeared in the

*Kenya Times,* complete with typos. It revealed considerable inside knowledge of *Nation* staff and operations such as the times of editorial conferences and who participated, and it carried an organogram of the management structure with names, titles and tribes. It stated that 22 of the top 37 managers were Kikuyu and all four editors attending the 6 pm deadline conference which mapped out the front page were Kikuyus. The two best-read columnists, Mshindi and Associate Editor Kwendo Opanga, were not Kikuyus; 'obviously these two gentlemen are used as a front', the pamphlet said, while the chairman Ekirapa, also a non-Kikuyu, was either a party to Kikuyu hegemony or just a figurehead or both. The pamphlet charged that 'this newspaper group has hired people, 30 of them, to steal documents from government offices which will be used in its campaign against ardent KANU supporters' – apparently a reference to the *Nation's* use of documents in exposing Jirongo's NSSF deal. The pamphlet took a routine swipe at the Aga Khan and foreign ownership, and declared that 'the *Nation* stands out as the epitome of all that is antithetical to democracy'.

That YK92 had intelligence lines into the *Nation* is incontestable. What the plotters did not know was that Mwangi had his own mole in the enemy camp reporting on the man who coordinated the anti-*Nation* campaign:

> *He says he has a complete network at the* Nation, *including messengers, drivers, library assistants, computer systems staffers and editorial. He says proudly that his network is drawn from all tribes and that his reach extends to rotary [the printing hall], where he saw to it that there were complications that made the paper late on two days on the weekend of November 8 and 9. He takes special pride in having secured a job for the daughter of one of the Kikuyu drivers and of periodically giving an envelope to another Kikuyu driver. He says he often employs the services of [X], a former employee now working at a hospital. [X] is increasingly to be seen in the* Nation *library, apparently conducting private research but mostly holding whispered conversations with staff from various departments. The organiser says he has 'not yet' got to telephone or mail intercepts but he has swift access to files, memos and computer queues, however confidential. If he really wants something he says he will target an employee and offer him or her their gross annual salary and it works wonders. He talks freely about his role, which he says includes intensive surveillance of top managers, the GME and the MD being people he watches*

*personally while YK operatives with training in surveillance watch the rest. He describes the daily routine of the GME [Mwangi] as very narrow and predictable, saying he proceeds mostly from his home to the office and back and often stops at his mother's house in Kaloleni. He describes the GME as boring and says he has no style and is a tribalist. About the MD [Peter Chadwick, a Briton], he says he has no Africa experience and is being used. He says the ME [Mshindi] is a good guy but thoroughly confused and unreliable. Of the assistant news editor [the beret-wearing and combat-booted Catherine Gicheru], he says, 'She is a total bitch.'*

Mwangi's informant was told that the YK92 campaign started not as a result of the Jirongo exposé, but after the *Nation* reported that Catholic bishops had gone to State House and confronted 'Heavy D' (Moi) on a number of issues: 'He also talks of a meeting at Kitale at which the President urged YK92's seniormost operatives to look into the matter of the tribal setup at the *Nation*.'

However risible some of the boasts, such as YK92 running trained surveillance agents, much of the information rang true, and Ekirapa told a 3 December board meeting, 'Many attempts have been made at disrupting our operations. This has been a very scaring experience and security has been stepped up.' Peter Chadwick remembered the press breakdown:

*The production manager found that a delicate little part had been removed and our security officer instructed two of his men to follow a certain suspect around. He soon left. There were a lot of dirty tricks. We got mysterious faxes without an originating address carrying false information. We fell for one and then didn't print any more. We assumed they were all done by Special Branch.*

Pressure was also applied from the highest level and it was during the heat of the campaign that Mwangi got a call from Moi. In a memorandum, the GME stated, 'The President telephoned me shortly after 9 o' clock this morning and in a very angry tone launched into a monologue of accusations against me and the newspaper. He asked why we would wish to destroy the country through lies and fabricated stories.' Moi said it was neither the Kalenjin people nor KANU who started the clashes, but tribalists. He himself was not a tribalist and the young people should get their priorities right. Mwangi went on, 'I told him I was not a tribalist, that I was born and bred in Nairobi and that I think more like a Kenyan than a Kikuyu. He said he was glad to hear this but he suspected there were people within the *Nation* who slanted stories to promote their tribal interests.' During the conversation, Moi made only one specific complaint – that the *Nation* had published a story purportedly from the ministry of foreign affairs criticising KANU secretary-general Kamotho. The story was published by the *Standard*, not the *Nation*.

YK92 was only one weapon KANU employed in this dirty election. Another was a regular package of stories entitled 'KANU briefs' in the *Kenya Times*, which became notorious for its attacks on opposition figures and their families, on newsmen, defectors from KANU and indeed anyone thought remotely to threaten the regime's election chances. It flouted just about every rule of ethics, racial and religious harmony and good taste. When Philip Ochieng occupied the editorial chair at the *Kenya Times*, he had shown little restraint in pursuing the KANU agenda, in particular by attacking Ambassador Hempstone, the government's hate figure of that period. It was under Ochieng that the *Kenya Times* carried the immortal headline, 'Shut Up Mr Ambassador', and described Hempstone as a vagrant, the epitome of the Ugly American, an out-and-out enemy of Kenya and an international diplomatic terrorist. In *Rogue Ambassador*, Hempstone, himself a former journalist, noted that 'Ochieng had been a managing editor at the *Nation*, a good paper, before becoming editor of the *Kenya Times*, a bad one. Clearly, he valued truth or he would not have used it so sparingly.' Less diplomatically, when he bumped into Ochieng at a cocktail party, Hempstone told the *Kenya Times* editor he was 'as full of shit as a nine-pound canary'.

Ochieng argued that as a known party newspaper, the *Kenya Times* was fully entitled to campaign in the KANU cause. It was the intemperance of his language and the tendentious and sometimes plain inaccurate nature of the reporting that undermined his stance. But it is hard to imagine Ochieng presiding over the anti-*Nation* campaign or the deluge of vituperation, dissimulation, innuendo and scandal-mongering that masqueraded as political campaign reporting twice a week in the *Kenya Times* after he left. Coverage appeared first on 4 July 1992, collected together under the title, 'KANU news: A roundup of party activities'. It was reformatted a week later as 'KANU briefs' (though the stories in total often spread across three or four pages of the newspaper), together with a column of shorts, 'Points to ponder', by Jogoo (the cockerel, KANU's symbol). There were no name bylines and the stories were rarely about KANU, but targeted a wide range of its critics. Accusations against oppositionists included charges that one was a British spy in colonial days, another a freemason, one slept with his son's wife, a drunken woman activist beat her husband, Oginga Odinga was an atheist pretending to be a Christian, and the assassin of Pio Gama Pinto was roving Nairobi as a member of the Democratic Party.

Four men were responsible for 'KANU briefs': three journalists and an academic. 'These guys were vicious', Mshindi said. 'They hatched the idea somewhere underground in the Kenyatta International Conference Centre', which housed KANU headquarters. 'They had access to CID files and personnel files and wrote very vicious things about people.' Mshindi was asked twice in 1992 by the *Kenya Times* chairman, Jared Kangwana, to join that paper but refused: 'They were very keen to get rid of anyone who was a key man at the *Nation* and not a Kikuyu so as to support their tribal-paper claim and particularly anyone who was critical of them, as I was through my column ['Barbs and Bouquets'].'[10]

Conscious of being under hostile scrutiny as never before, the *Nation* planned its election coverage with meticulous care. A central desk was set up and duties allotted to reporters in every constituency. Staffers and stringers were lectured on ethics, reporting and presentation: equal space to the major parties, no subjective language, no preferential cropping of pictures, tape recorders to be used and tapes retained, no hospitality from candidates, special scrutiny of captions and headlines. Extra copy-takers were rostered and a lawyer placed on standby. Issues, not personalities, should be the order of the day; the parties would be invited to set forth their programmes and leaders to submit to interviews. Specialist commentators would be harnessed to write on important areas of expertise. Election advertising would be vetted by the GME. The *Nation* would be strictly non-partisan, its editorial stance predicated upon the need for free and fair elections on a level playing field. In the event, the newspaper proved far more enthusiastic about issues than the candidates, who mostly preferred character assassination and pork-barrel politics. None of the major party leaders responded to requests for interviews, prompting Mwangi to carry a story to this effect and list the questions they would have been asked. The newsroom was forced to scalp party manifestos to present their policies to the public.

The *Nation* nevertheless parcelled out its campaign coverage conscientiously, and between 1 and 30 December, Moi got 29 headline mentions, Kibaki 25, Matiba 22 and Odinga 16. Its close and sustained coverage of the Electoral Commission of Kenya, tasked to organise the poll, prevented it from blatantly favouring KANU, as in the past, and by reporting violence (it ran 32 violence stories between October and the election) the *Nation* made the election observers aware of partiality by the security forces. A successful editorial innovation was 'Election platform', which offered substantial space to ordinary readers to highlight issues and offer solutions. This proved extremely successful, and the quality of contributions, many from non-political professionals, was usually higher than the politicians' speeches on the news pages. Each constituency was examined in detail, there were explanations of the voting procedures and lists of where to vote. But any hopes that the paper's strenuously non-partisan efforts would be recognised by the politicians were dashed on Nomination Day, 14 December, when Moi declared, 'The *Nation* has now resolved to support the Democratic Party. The *Nation* is a tribal paper and is now supporting a tribal party.' George Anyona accused the paper of a 'biased, hostile and malicious campaign' against his small party, the Kenya Social Congress. Since the *Nation* was also accused of supporting FORD Kenya and FORD Asili, the complaints seemed only to support the newspaper's claim to being independent.

The first large-scale multiparty election since 1963 pitted a united but often unpopular KANU against a divided opposition with the inevitable result, a win by Moi and his party. But the results in many areas reflected antipathy to KANU leaders from local officials to MPs and ministers. In the presidential poll, Moi won 36.3 per cent of the vote, Matiba 26 per cent, Kibaki 19.5 per cent and Odinga 17.5 per cent. Had the opposition presented a single candidate, he would have beaten Moi by more than a million votes in a poll of 5.3 million. Since Moi also received a minimum of 25 per cent of votes in five of the eight provinces, he was sworn in for a further term. In the Parliamentary elections, KANU took 100 of the 188 elective seats, while FORD Kenya and FORD Asili won 31 each and the Democratic Party 23. The President was constitutionally entitled to nominate 12 MPs, bringing KANU's tally to 112 out of 200. The minor parties got three seats. Vote-splitting cost the opposition seats in the Parliamentary elections, too, where balloting was along ethnic lines. FORD Kenya swept the board in Odinga's Nyanza homeland, while FORD Asili and the Democratic Party shared Central Province, and KANU was virtually swept out of Nairobi, where socio-economic issues predominated. Among the KANU faces the electorate indicated they were tired of seeing were *Nation* critics Kamotho, Mwangale and Nabwera.

## *Notes*

1.  *Kenya African Nationalism: Nyayo Philosophy and Principles* by Daniel T. arap Moi, Macmillan, London, 1986.

2. *Rogue Ambassador: An African Memoir* by Smith Hempstone, University of the South Press, Sewanee, Tennessee, USA, 1997.

3. Compass News Features was funded by the Aga Khan and managed by this writer in a project which aimed to bring news of the developing nations to the Western world. Based first in Luxembourg and later in London, the agency secured a niche in many newsrooms, but eventually fell victim to the global spread of communications technology.

4. Some reports said there was also to be a seven-storey bronze statue of Moi in Uhuru Park, which had been commissioned in Italy. Supported by pressure from Western environmentalists and the US government, Wangari Maathai's campaign was successful and the party high-rise was never built.

5. *Rogue Ambassador.*

6. As with the national concept of harambees as fund-raisers, ordinary Kenyans would often stage their own harambees to meet extraordinary expenses such as university fees, or to pay for a wedding or funeral.

7. *The Ukimwi Road* by Dervla Murphy, John Murray (Publishers) Ltd, London, 1993.

8. *World Human Rights Guide* by Charles Humana, Oxford University Press, Oxford, 1992.

9. *The Ukimwi Road.*

10. Mshindi left the *Nation* in 1999 to join the United Nations and was succeeded as ME at the *Daily Nation* by Joseph Odindo from *The EastAfrican.* Mshindi worked for the UN in New York and Nigeria before returning to Kenya to become chief executive officer of the *Standard* group. In 2009, after a period as managing director of Monitor Publications in Uganda, he was appointed managing director of Nation Newspapers Division.

# Move into Broadcasting

*A free press is not a privilege but an organic necessity in a great society.*

US columnist Walter Lippmann (1889–1974)

That the titles of the *Nation's* founding companies were East African Newspapers Limited and East African Printers and Publishers Limited sent a clear signal of the Aga Khan's regional intentions, and the early issues of the *Nation* regularly set Kenyan developments in an East African context. In 1970, when a five-year development programme was discussed at an EAP&P board meeting, the Aga Khan said he wished to see 'at least one prestige publication of high quality circulating throughout East Africa'. In 1986, a Paris-based director reported after a visit to Nairobi, 'I have continued to push the concept of the *Nation* becoming a major regional newspaper through editionising and eventual satellite printing', adding, however, that 'appreciation of this concept is very slow in coming'.

Early efforts to extend the *Nation's* reach into Tanzania and Uganda were blown off course when the *Uganda Nation* and *Mwafrika* of Tanzania were folded for commercial reasons. Thereafter, these two countries received early editions of the Kenya paper which contained a modicum of regional news. Although sales were often healthy, supplies were erratic. Periodic bouts of inter-government hostility resulted in frequent border closures. Distribution in Uganda became impossible when that country collapsed into bloody anarchy under the murderous rule of Milton Obote and Idi Amin respectively. There is a story that Amin personally hammered a notice on the *Nation* office door in Kampala, declaring, 'This newspaper is closed.' The author has been unable to authenticate the report, but certainly being in the news business was fraught with danger. In 1973, a Kenyan teleprinter operator with the *Nation's* associated company Uganda African Newspapers was murdered, apparently for buying a car from an Asian who was leaving under Amin's wholesale expulsion order. In 1977, the tottering East African Community finally collapsed and the concept of an integrated region of co-operating nations faded.

It was only with the accession to power of Yoweri Museveni in Uganda and warmer relations between Kenya and Tanzania that regular distribution resumed to the two countries. When Ekirapa visited Uganda in September 1990, the *Nation* was selling 2,700 copies a day in Kampala. He told a board meeting that he found the new government tolerant of criticism. Compared with Kenya, where the official attitude to independent media remained hostile, Uganda and Tanzania began to look like viable markets again. Accordingly, the author of this book was asked to investigate how the *Nation* footprint could be planted firmly across the region. Senior executives favoured a strategy of separate editions for the two countries: the basic Kenya edition with four localised pages. However, since the *Nation* was already producing two editions (Coast and City) and planning a third for Western Kenya, close examination suggested that two further editions with eight page-changes per night would be an editorial and production nightmare.

The concept of a single edition covering both countries and perhaps titled *East African Nation* became the basis for in-house debate and wide-ranging research, led by marketing manager Jerry Okungu. Thinking turned to a separate new product altogether, a weekly rather than a daily, an upmarket compact whose bottom line would be quality. Thus was *The EastAfrican* conceived. The title choice proved contentious. Critics considered it needed a noun, *The East African Journal* perhaps or *The East African Gazette*, while reformers pointed to *The Sowetan, The Australian* and *The Scotsman* as precedents. Cover prices were set for each country, space rented and staff hired for fully fledged bureaus in Kampala, Dar es Salaam and, because it was to be the site of the East African Co-operation, the East African Community's successor, in Arusha, Tanzania, too. This was the group's most significant editorial development in many years, the first major new product since the birth of the *Nation*.

With Joseph Odindo, a former chief sub-editor of the *Daily Nation*, at the helm, issue 0001 of *The EastAfrican* was a revelation. Almost all of the region's tabloids were based on the *Nation* formula; indeed, on Bierman's 1960 design of a dramatic page one, and an editorial page which boxed the leader alongside a political cartoon and the top news feature. Now here was a tabloid of small headlines and broad columns, the op-ed space two pages deeper into the paper and horizontal editorials without a box-rule in sight. There were no advertisements on page one, not even ear pieces; portrait photographs were shot on camera – and reshot and reshot – so that all the heads were the same size; and rule-offs encapsulated major stories. Trendily, the features section was named Part 2 (confusing some readers, who wondered if they had missed Part 1). The new product was proof of Michael Curtis' argument that a tabloid newspaper could be handsome, authoritative and indisputably upmarket at the same time. Above all, its meticulous apportionment of stories disarmed Ugandans and Tanzanians who had predicted a Kenya-dominated news agenda.

Mohammed Warsama, who joined *The EastAfrican* in a senior position shortly after its launch, said, 'My feeling was that it was totally different to any paper I had ever worked on. Odindo had a very clear vision of the sort of paper he wanted. It was so professional, such demand for precision and accuracy. It was as if I was learning my job all over again. For the first time, I talked to journalists who said they wouldn't work on *The EastAfrican* because it was too demanding. I was there a full year without hearing a serious complaint about inaccuracy in a story.' Some 18 months after the launch, an International Press Institute report on the world media said, 'One of the best, if not the best, of regional newspapers in sub-Saharan Africa is *The EastAfrican*, providing readers with sober incisive news of issues and events. Such a newspaper is far ahead of the political leadership of the region. *The EastAfrican* is proof that commerce, travel, the environment and culture tie the region together logically.' Odindo achieved his vision of an issue-led journal of record with a bias towards business, but it was a hard sell in a region dominated by politics and personalities, and building circulation proved an arduous task. The ME was encouraged when the Aga Khan, visiting his Nairobi operations, assured him, 'Quality is not easy to sell.' *The EastAfrican* nonetheless moved into profit within two years and after five years it was selling around 30,000, half in Kenya, the rest split evenly between Uganda and Tanzania.

The years between the 1992 and 1997 elections saw extraordinary growth in the *Nation* group, involving a move into new headquarters, upgrading of pre-press technology, launch of *The EastAfrican*, construction of a press hall and installation of state-of-the-art presses, entry to the Internet and the launch of three websites, and, finally and crucially, expanding into the electronic media. Turnover increased from KSh957 million ($14 million) in 1993 to KSh2.1 billion ($33 million) in 1997. Profit before tax went up from KSh106 million ($1.5 million) in 1993 to KSh418 million ($6.6 million) in

1997. Shareholders' funds rose from KSh529 million ($7.7 million) in 1993 to KSh1.2 billion ($19 million) in 1997. Capital expenditure topped KSh665 million ($12 million) in 1996, the year of the new press, against an average KSh93 million ($1.6 million) for the other four years. From the perspective of the turbulent multiparty struggle years, these were extraordinary achievements.

The group marked the multiparty era by finally moving out of its decrepit headquarters at scruffy Nation House. Accommodation that was neat, clean, conveniently central and adequate for its staff in 1960 had long been bursting at the seams, with desks crowded together, partitions erected and dismantled, toilets overflowing and the noise level somewhere close to a jumbo jet on take-off. Training editor Hitchcock remembered arriving in 1982 and being shown his 'office', a cubbyhole which formerly housed the telephone operator and his switchboard: 'It was near the loo. I looked out on an alleyway. There was almost no air. If I opened the window I was covered in dust and it was so hot I had to struggle to stay awake in the afternoons. I fought for a blind to keep off the sun but never got one and I put up a tatty piece of rag for a curtain. Eventually, they put me in another cubicle which was a bit larger, but it was still a cubicle and still airless.'

The newspapers' new home was the custom-built 17-storey Nation Centre on Kimathi Street, in the centre of town. Designed by a Danish architect, Henning Larsen, the building had a curved façade of black and white horizontal stripes topped by two circular towers, bisected by a red mast starting above the canopied entrance. The black and white were said to represent a printed newspaper or a zebra's stripes, and the mast to be a Maasai spear or a representation of a broadcast aerial. Two jutting windows high on the façade gave the impression of eyes in an African mask. For the first time in three decades, all of the group's departments were housed under one roof, with the exception of circulation, which remained at its distribution centre in Tom Mboya Street. The new building was owned by Industrial Promotion Building Ltd (IPB), an affiliate of the Aga Khan Fund for Economic Development (AKFED) in which the *Nation* had a 20 per cent interest. The newspapers took four floors in the new building in 1992 and the fitting-out budget was KSh80 million ($2.2 million). Rent costs increased from KSh2 million ($55,000) per year at Nation House to KSh20 million ($555,000), but the extra space delighted the staff. By 1994, the Centre was 100 per cent occupied and the *Nation's* share in IPB contributed significantly to group profits. Prestige tenants included the Nairobi Stock Exchange and the financial institution Diamond Trust Bank. The new building was a distinctive addition to Nairobi's architectural repository, a marked departure from the soaring glass towers like the Lonrho building, and if it did not please all the city's aesthetes, *Nation* people were happy to work in a spacious, bright, air-conditioned, noise-controlled ambience with plenty of toilets. Unusually, for a building of such importance, Nation Centre never had a formal opening. It was felt that to invite President Moi at a time when the media were suffering persistent state harassment would send the wrong signal to staff and public.

The move to Nation Centre had a knock-on effect which took the company into a new era of technology. Systems manager Nick Chitty recalled:

> *It was strange how the place seemed to mushroom. More people came aboard and soon we were short of terminals. A decision was taken to get a fourth Central Processing Unit and go for full-page makeup, with news, ads, images and graphics all on the page and no more cut-and-paste. We also decided it was time to network Nairobi with the bureaus, which we had been talking about for years. We linked to Mombasa first, then Kampala and Dar es Salaam, then Kisumu in Western Kenya and, about a year later, upcountry places such as Nakuru and Nyeri and, of course, Arusha. All their copy came straight into the computer along with the international wire services and we got rid of the Telex room.* The EastAfrican *was the catalyst for all of that.*

On the national scene, the government's priority was to win back the foreign aid it lost in November 1991. Economic reforms were announced, including an anti-inflation budget, a tight monetary policy, retrenchment in the civil service and moves to clean up the parastatals. Persuaded that Moi and his new team were making serious attempts to stem corruption and control government finances, foreign donors meeting in Paris in November 1993 agreed to make $850 million available to Kenya over a 12-month period. It was a generous decision considering that a financial scandal had exploded just a few months earlier, which made the rest of Kenya's extensive corruption look like petty theft.

The Goldenberg Affair entered the nation's psyche as a byword for the ruthless looting of public funds. In essence, Goldenberg International Ltd, a trading company set up by a Nairobi businessman, Kamlesh Pattni, was accused of colluding with government officials to export non-existent gold and diamonds, and claim export compensation to cover fluctuating exchange rates, not just the normal 20 per cent but a special 35 per cent figure approved by the then Finance Minister, George Saitoti. The first snippets about Goldenberg appeared in a *Nation* article by business editor Peter Warutere. But it was when the daily paper published an eight-part exposé by freelance writer Sarah Elderkin that the massive scale of the fraud became apparent. Setting its origins in 1987, Elderkin said the original plan was to receive compensation for genuine gold exports (freelance miners in Kenya produced about 100 kilos a year). At a 35 per cent top-up, there was a fortune to be made. But then the conspirators wondered, 'what if, in some cases, they only *pretended* to export gold, filling in all the right export forms but never actually buying the gold, let alone sending it out of the country? All they would have to do was make sure the relevant officials got substantial bribes. And to make it even better, what if they added diamonds?' Elderkin quoted a letter she had seen from Pattni to Saitoti stating that 'diamonds … are in large supplies here in Kenya'. In fact, Kenya has no diamonds.

Remorselessly, in minute detail supported by letters and documents, Elderkin's stories exposed malfeasance by officials in the Treasury, the Central Bank and a raft of private banks, the Customs Department, the Mines Department and a number of ministries. Robert Shaw, a Kenya-born businessman, *Sunday Nation* columnist and political activist, said, 'So many people were implicated or beneficiaries they probably ran into hundreds – MPs, permanent secretaries, former PS's, ministers, many, many people. It was a masterpiece of fraud. They had all the right paperwork, the right rubber stamps, the right reference numbers.' Elderkin recalled:

> It was a story that required weeks spent poring over papers and much thought and leaps of imagination to figure out how the facts fitted together. It was mostly painstaking research. Many of the documents were already in the public domain but no one had taken the trouble to figure out what they were all about and follow the clues they offered. People I talked to were fearful and meetings were discreet.

Shaw said, 'I believe it was the most impressive and successful thing the *Nation* ever did and Wangethi Mwangi's enthusiasm was key.' Mwangi recalled, 'The first person I spoke to was Mr Ekirapa. I let him read the stuff Sarah had put together and we decided to get Reg Sampson, our libel lawyer, to look at the articles, so I got Reg and Sarah to sit together and they worked on them and when they were through, I had no more editing to do.

That was it. We ran them.' The impact was explosive, sales figures soared and Goldenberg became the hottest topic in town. Saitoti reacted angrily and called a press conference after the first article to deny any involvement. He said he was not a mere clerk to check routine documents and charged that the accusations were part of a widespread conspiracy to bring down the government.

Goldenberg is Kenya's largest economic crime, though the precise cost to the taxpayer remains uncertain. Newspapers routinely referred to 'the KSh68 billion Goldenberg scandal', which would translate to $1.3 billion, using an average exchange rate for 1992 and 1993, when most transactions took place. Elderkin said an arrangement Pattni finalised with the government in 1990 was to export gold and jewellery worth $50 million (then KSh1.8 billion) a year, producing $17 million annually in export compensation. A much-quoted figure of phoney exports to Switzerland and Dubai was $600 million, 35 per cent of which would be $210 million. When Pattni was eventually charged, he and three officials from the Central Bank and the Treasury were accused of defrauding the state of KSh5.8 billion ($111 million).

The proceeds were not entirely for individuals' personal gain but also to finance KANU's 1992 election campaign, and the effect on the national economy was devastating. The Kenya shilling was devalued so often that by 1994 it had lost more than 60 per cent of its pre-Goldenberg value; interest rates increased five-fold from 14 per cent to over 70 per cent; inflation rates and prices trebled; a number of banks collapsed and companies shut down. A journalist who knows Pattni said:

> *He was a cash cow. A person would go to the powers-that-be and they would give him a note and he would go to Pattni's office and get his cut. This was Goldenberg money. He became so powerful he told me he could see the head of state any time. He also told me that when the new Governor of the Central Bank, Micah Cheserem, called him in to investigate his affairs, Pattni said, 'You don't know who you are talking to' and walked out.*

In 1999, Nassir Ibrahim Ali, a business rival of Pattni holding Canadian and Pakistani passports, swore an affidavit tying Moi to Goldenberg. He said Pattni and Moi's personal aide, Julius Kulei, visited him in Dubai in April and June of 1992, and sought his help in contacting Middle East heads of state to solicit funds to finance the forthcoming Kenya election campaign. A letter that Ali produced, purportedly from Moi, said the funds were to maintain stability in Kenya, where there were 'certain forces who would like to create disturbances'. Ali said he arranged a $200 million line of credit for the government guaranteed by Saitoti and the then Central Bank Governor, Eric Kotut, but Pattni and Kulei declined because they wanted dollars in cash. 'I have no doubt that the VP and the then Governor were under the instructions of President Moi to transact with Mr Pattni and Goldenberg International Limited', Ali told reporters in Nairobi on 19 July 1999. Four days later he was deported. Ali was the supposed recipient of Goldenberg's exports to Dubai in 1992 and 1993, which documents put at KSh15.3 billion ($288 million). He said he received no such consignments. The purported recipients of exports to Switzerland proved to be non-existent when the *Nation* investigated.

Elderkin said her series made such a massive impact because 'for the first time it offered proof of a sensational financial scandal involving very senior persons, just the kind of thing people had suspected was happening but could never quite put their finger on'. When she wrote her stories, Elderkin had left the *Weekly Review* after many years as managing editor and, like Robert Shaw, who worked closely on the articles, was involved in politics with the opposition FORD Kenya.[1] Saitoti denounced them both at his Press conference and Elderkin said, 'I heard later that immigration officers had visited the *Nation* and other places looking for me, presumably for deportation, but I am a Kenya citizen. I was working for Oginga Odinga at the time and he became anxious for my safety. After four of the articles had run, and at Odinga's insistence, I left the country for a month's holiday.'

If the government felt the Goldenberg accusations did not permit it to haul the *Nation* before Parliament again, it pressed its anti-media campaign with enthusiastic malice, in particular against independent magazines such as *Society* and *Finance*, as well as a new publication by Peter Warutere, *Economic Review*. Using the powers that the *Nation* had warned against back in 1960, police confiscated thousands of copies of *Finance* and disabled machinery at Fotoform, which printed the magazine. When the publisher, Njehu Gatabaki, moved to Colourprint, police arrested the owner and beat his workers. Gatabaki announced, 'I cannot publish any more. The government will not give me a chance.' Soon afterwards, *Society* went the same route. Publisher Pius Nyamora, his wife Loyce, and staff members had been subjected to constant arrest and intimidation. Unable to find a printer to handle his magazine, lacking any advertising revenue and facing 50 libel suits, mostly from government, Nyamora called it a day and emigrated with his wife to the United States.

A quotation by the American satirist Art Buchwald was posted above the desk of *Nation* cartoonist Gado. It said, 'Dictators from the political left or right fear the political cartoonist more than they do the atomic bomb. No totalitarian government can afford to be ridiculed.' The *Nation* had carried political cartoons in its early days, but poking fun at government figures became a dangerous game. Kenyatta was never caricatured in the Press and to lampoon Moi was unthinkable. It was Gado's predecessor at the *Nation*, Paul Kalemba (pen-name Madd) who broke the taboo at the behest of Nyamora. Kalemba said in an interview:

> *I was with the* Nation *for five years, up to the end of 1991, and in all that time, I never once drew Moi although the* Nation *was much more open than other papers and I did the government ministers and VIPs. Then all during 1992 in the run-up to the December election, cartoonists were trying to put Moi into their cartoons. We were hiding him, giving him a hat, using shadows. Then Nyamora said, 'Yes, go ahead.'*

On 2 November, the colour cover of *Society* showed Moi in running shorts taking a short-cut inside an athletics track while the other presidential contenders puffed around the legal lanes. Kalemba recalled, 'Nyamora disappeared for the whole day. He didn't go to the office. He would call me and say, "Have they come yet?" Nothing happened. Not a whisper. This was the cartoon that opened the floodgates.' Days later, the *Nation* published a Gado cartoon showing Moi with a walking stick asking for five more years in office. The head of state became fair game on the political battlefield, within the culturally accepted limits for elders and holders of high office. Shattering the cartoon taboo was a significant advance towards demystifying the presidency.

Gado, a Tanzanian (real name Godfrey Mwampembwa), was hired straight from art school in Dar es Salaam. What his fans liked was the genially caustic eye he applied to the socio-political scene, classically in his representation of an incident involving the US ambassador after Hempstone, a large lady named Aurelia Brazeal. On one visit upcountry, in contravention of all diplomatic niceties, she was stopped and ordered to report to a police station. Inside a ramshackle building, Gado showed a diminutive police inspector in patched trousers looking up defiantly at the towering envoy and declaring, 'Brazil! I don't care if you come from America.'

When parties visiting Nation Centre were asked if there was anyone they would like to meet, the answer was invariably 'Gado and Watchman'. At about the time that Madd left the *Nation*, feature writer Wahome Mutahi took his popular 'Whispers' column temporarily to the *Standard* and *Nation* MD Peter Chadwick suggested a gossip column in its place. Training editor John Lawrence was given the task of writing one, but quickly concluded that gossip did not work in Kenya. What emerged over weeks of trial and error was a waspish, anecdotal column on *pro bono publico* lines that quickly became a hit. Written almost entirely from contributions by readers and leavened with black humour, it delighted ordinary Kenyans by battling on their behalf against a supine and uncaring public service, corrupt policemen, mendacious politicians, crooked businessmen, bad manners, bad driving, even bad taste. The column consisted of seven or eight brief items on the Letters page titled 'The Cutting Edge' by Watchman (the original 'Outside Edge' was discarded). Contributions arrived at the rate of 30–40 faxes and letters a day, and some PR officials confessed they dreaded opening the *Nation* for fear their companies would be mentioned. The column named erring individuals, businesses and organisations, and gave vehicle registration and police badge numbers. It came to terrify bureaucrats and a mention in the Edge usually led to the hasty reconnection of telephones and power supplies. When the column complained about the unavailability of good croissants in Nairobi, a bakery delivered a box of six within hours. The Watchman reported next day that he had accepted his first bribe and challenged the authorities to find the evidence. A newly arrived *Washington Post* correspondent asked to interview the columnist, saying, 'I have only been here six weeks and every dinner party I have been to has been talking about Watchman.' Extraordinarily, the Edge went for years without ever being successfully sued. However, an item published in 1999 led to an order for KSh10 million ($130,000) libel damages, an expensive lesson in not believing everything you are told.

'The Cutting Edge' generally addressed the concerns of the middle class, people who could afford telephones and cars and who constituted the bulk of the *Nation's* readership. These were not problems for the rich and powerful and the column rarely ventured into the political arena in a serious way. Thus it was a surprise when the first Watchman was summarily deported. Lawrence, 60, was picked up at the office by three immigration officials on 12 July 1994, served with an order stating that his continued presence in the country was 'contrary to the national interest' and taken to the airport. His wife, Dinny, was instructed to deliver travel documents, clothes and money. After eight hours incommunicado, Lawrence was put on an Olympic

Airways flight to Johannesburg and thence to Australia. There were stories that Lawrence had delivered some Edge-style witticisms about Kenyan politicians at Parklands Sports Club which were not appreciated by eaves-dropping immigration officials. Lawrence and his wife denied this and he attributed his expulsion to his bare-knuckles criticism of society's ills in the column. The Australian was the fifth *Nation* expatriate to be deported. Tony Dunn was expelled by Tanganyika in 1964 for his Zanzibar reporting. In 1965, a British editor of the women's pages, Mrs Sally Shapiro, was declared a prohibited immigrant. Mrs Shapiro said at the time that the reason was 'personal not political', but the fact that she had once worked for the Communist *Daily Worker* in London could not have endeared her to Kenyatta's government. In 1966, John Dumoga, on attachment to the *Nation*, was sent back to Ghana, apparently because of his condemnation of preventive detention in Kenya. In 1969, Mike Chester was thrown out, apparently as a makeweight for two *Standard* colleagues. The reason for Lawrence's expulsion has remained a mystery. When the *Nation* sought access to his immigration file, it had disappeared – just the sort of thing to make an item in 'The Cutting Edge'.

KANU was behaving as if multipartyism had never happened and seemed to see enemies everywhere. So Kenyans were not surprised when a new 'threat to national security' appeared in the form of the February 18 Movement, with its armed wing, the February Eighteen Resistance Army or FERA, allegedly led from Uganda by Brigadier John Odongo. FORD Kenya was making its political presence felt in Western Kenya and unsurprisingly this was the area where FERA was suddenly declared to flourish. Dozens of Kenyans were arrested and held. A man of 19 told Amnesty International he was stripped naked and beaten twice a day for two months.

The similarities with Mwakenya were striking: FERA held no press con-ferences, its office-holders were unknown and its existence depended entirely on the word of the Kenya government. As with Mwakenya, FERA suspects would be taken to court late in the day without lawyers, would con-fess and receive jail terms. A group of youths arrested in Bungoma, Western Kenya, were said to have been trained in Libya, but it was clear they had never heard of Libya. Kenya claimed that Odongo was leading armed raids across the border to overthrow the Moi government, but when *The EastAfrican* tracked him down in Kampala, they found a deluded fish-monger and second-hand clothes dealer. *The EastAfrican's* Charles Onyango-Obbo wrote, 'There are no independent eye-witness accounts of the existence of a FERA camp anywhere, nor of engagements with Kenya government forces. We are yet to hear of a battle FERA has fought and won or lost.' When a Siaya farmer appealed against a five-year sentence for FERA membership, Kenya High Court Justice B.K. Tanui released him and said, 'I cannot verify whether it has been established that there was a movement known as FERA.'

It was not only FERA. *Sunday Nation* columnist Kwendo Opanga calculated that between January 1994 and October 1995, Moi talked publicly about plots 16 times. He implicated Britain, Italy, Mozambique, South Africa, Rwanda, Burundi, Uganda and members of the Kenya opposition. At a rally in Nakuru, two men, a former opposition councillor and an ex-soldier, confessed to plotting to assassinate Moi at the instigation of the opposition. Moi promptly pardoned the two, a legal impossibility since they had not been charged. John Githongo talked to relatives and acquaintances who characterised the two men as beggars and liars, one of whom was due for a psychiatric check-up. As to the plot, Githongo wrote in his popular column in *The EastAfrican* that 'restaurant tables in Nairobi where it was discussed rocked with laughter'. The armoury with which they intended to overthrow the government was produced by police: two AK-47 assault rifles and 45 rounds of ammunition. Githongo declared, 'These kinds of stories are given prominence at times when the regime needs to distract Kenyans and the world community from more pressing matters. The rigging of the next election … is something that powerful people would rather we did not focus on.' Although Moi often said he knew the names of plotters, none was ever arrested. 'The fact that many of these alarming statements coming from the highest office in the land are not followed up in credible legal fashion diminishes the state of the office of the president and of the man who occupies it', Githongo wrote.[2]

Significant among opposition names was that of Richard Leakey, whom Moi linked to FERA. Leakey was a white, third-generation Kenyan and a world-renowned palaeontologist. He had dramatically reduced the poaching of ivory with a shoot-on-sight policy when he was Director of the Kenya Wildlife Service, then lost the job under pressure from KANU bigwigs who saw their financial interests in the wildlife parks threatened. There was nothing you could tell Leakey about corruption in Kenya and his decision to join some of KANU's toughest opponents in a new party, Safina (The Ark), clearly worried the powers-that-be. Terrified of a party that claimed to transcend racial as well as ethnic boundaries, which had an internationally recognised figure such as Leakey as its secretary-general and which contained a generation of highly educated Kenyans who held the national leadership in contempt, KANU launched a counter-attack, which started with vilification and climaxed in violence.

On 10 August 1995, a group of Safina officials and supporters travelled to Nakuru, north of Nairobi, to accompany lawyer and political activist Paul Muite to court, where he was charged with taking photographs of a police station. Safina had caught the imagination of the media and the group was accompanied by a large number of Kenyan and foreign reporters. All were set upon by KANU youth wingers, policemen in plain clothes and paid thugs wielding whips and clubs, and throwing rocks and eggs. Leakey, who wore two artificial legs after a light plane he was piloting mysteriously crashed, was pursued to his car and whipped repeatedly. The *Nation's* Nakuru bureau chief, Michael Njuguna, was attacked twice, robbed of KSh2,000 and his wrist watch, and ended up in hospital. A KTN reporter was beaten and his camera was stolen, and a *Standard* reporter was beaten until he could not walk. He crawled into a maize field and hid there until he was carried to hospital. Said BBC correspondent Louise Tunbridge, 'Thugs whipped and punched me, shouting, "Beat this BBC slut". I was scarred for life. I had my hair pulled and people were shouting *mzungu* [white]. There was a racist element because of Leakey.'

Tunbridge said in an interview, 'The powers-that-be at the very top were determined that Leakey and the others were going to be stopped, given a thorough hiding and frightened off. The planning on the ground would

*Richard Leakey's whipping at Nakuru gained world attention.*

have been done at the local level but that sort of thing doesn't happen unless the top people say, Yes, do it.' Leakey and Muite said the attack was organised by the government to associate Safina with violence and thus deny it registration as a political party. Although the government quickly realised that by registering many opposition parties it could split the anti-KANU vote, registration was refused to Safina until the eve of the 1997 election. The Nakuru attack heaped international condemnation on the Moi regime, as a photograph of the famed scientist showing the visible weals on his back flashed around the world.

The mid-1990s saw significant changes in the media. One of *The EastAfrican's* first stories reported that the *Standard* had hired four expatriates to capitalise on colour printing and push a more populist style: 'Recent editions demonstrate an evolution towards light and often shorter stories and a bolder visual presentation, punning headlines, multi-photo reportage, involvement of the newspaper itself in some stories and some magazine-style serials.' The story noted that the *Daily Nation* sold 163,487 copies a day during 1993 against 61,516 by the *Standard*, and it added that downmarket experiments had not proved successful in the past. The *Nation's* huge lead did not, however, remove a long-held sense of insecurity. When board members suggested that the *Standard's* presentation was better than the *Nation's*, Peter Chadwick replied that the *Standard* was being turned into 'a real tabloid' and the board must decide if the *Nation* should follow suit. The hint of exasperation was understandable since policy was 'upmarket', and at this point the *Nation* was selling more in Nairobi than the *Standard* was countrywide.

Under Lonrho, the *Standard* took care not to rock the political boat and an editorial executive recalled ruefully, 'The *Nation* did all sorts of things we wouldn't be allowed to do. You would never see the Goldenberg series in the *Standard*.' Colin MacBeth said, 'Sometimes we had super stories but then we would drop them, maybe because word came down from above. I was asked to pull stories quite late on in the run, good stories and they would just not appear. That was very irritating. Goldenberg was almost untouchable because of the interests involved. It was never investigated by us. It was off-limits, as was anything to do with Ketan Somaia (a businessman with close ties to government) and one or two other bigwigs. The *Standard's* coverage of the ethnic clashes was also very patchy.' At the same time, Lonrho paid decent pensions and salaries, and pressure on editorial performance was less than at the *Nation*. Thus more than a few hearts missed a beat in the *Standard's* Likoni Road offices when a story appeared in the *Nation* of 15

August 1995, quoting the London newsletter *African Analysis* as saying Lonrho planned to sell the paper to Mark Too, deputy chairman of Lonrho EA and a nephew of Moi. Within a week the sale was completed and Too became chairman of the *Standard.*

The buyers were said to be overseas interests and their identities were not revealed, but there was little doubt in media circles the new owners were identical or close to the topmost power. Gado suggested as much with a cartoon showing Too with a massive shadow looming over him, a common technique by Kenyan artists to suggest the presence of Moi.[3] Nick Russell recalled, 'There was great speculation at the *Standard* about who had bought the paper and what was going to happen and in fact nothing much happened until just before the election. The big guns came out from Britain, building up confidence that there was going to be no undue influence, then suddenly, Wap!' On election eve, 28 December 1997, the *Standard* carried a massive headline, 'Poll predicts huge Moi victory', and quoted the Public Universities Research Team as forecasting that 49 per cent of the presidential vote would go to Moi and 16 per cent to his nearest rival Mwai Kibaki. The polling organisation was unknown to Kenyans and actually submitted its research as a paid advertisement. On election day itself, the *Standard* went one better. It carried a large portrait of Moi and the headline, 'Why I need your vote'. The story said:

> *President Daniel arap Moi has made a passionate appeal to all Kenyans to vote for him today as president, considering his long dedicated service to the people ... President Moi was addressing a campaign rally at Sulmac in Naivasha where he was received by thousands of jubilant* wananchi. *By a massive show of hands, they promised to vote for him and for KANU parliamentary and civic candidates today.*

*Nation* staffers must have felt a whiff of apprehension that their newspaper now stood alone as a significant independent publisher.

The *Nation*, too, was under new leadership. The deft and subtle chairman Albert Ekirapa retired on 31 March 1994 after 20 years with the group, 17 of them in the top job. Wilfred Kiboro, MD of Nation Newspapers since February 1993, became Group MD, and long-serving board member Mareka Gecaga became non-executive chairman. Kiboro had spent 19 years in the oil industry before rising through Rank Xerox Kenya to become MD there. Gecaga had become the *Nation's* first African director back in 1960 and had been on the board ever since. On 12 October, Michael Curtis vacated his seat on the NNL board, severing his last official link with the group after 35 years. He donated the 20,000 shares he owned in NPP to the Nation Group Staff Investment Trust Fund. An in-house issue of the *Nation*, distributed at his farewell party in the Serena Hotel by a portly white man in a vendor's jacket, stated, 'It might be an exaggeration, but not much of one, to say that Michael Curtis created the *Nation* group of newspapers single-handed. Certainly it is impossible to pretend that his departure from it is anything other than the end of an era.' A message from the Aga Khan said, 'I acknowledge publicly and with gratitude my debt to Michael. He can look back with justifiable pride and great satisfaction at what has been accomplished.'

In a similar publication headlined '*Kwaheri* [Farewell] Albert', the Aga Khan acknowledged Ekirapa's many years as chief executive and chairman, and praised the dedication and skill which brought the group to the cusp of extraordinary commercial success. The pre-tax profit for 1994 was 137 per cent up on 1993, the 1995 figure was 23 per cent up on 1994, the 1996 figure was slightly down because of investment in a new press, but 1997 was 59 per cent up on 1996, reaching KSh417 million ($6.6 million). Kiboro charged energetically into a wide range of projects. At a cost of KSh750 million ($12 million), a 759-square-metre, two-storey press hall was built off the Mombasa Road on the outskirts of Nairobi and computer-controlled printing presses were installed capable of producing 60,000 copies per hour. President Moi pressed the button to start the great machines rolling and Kiboro demonstrated the advance in technology by presenting him, as he sat down to lunch, with a special issue *Nation* bearing a colour photo of his arrival an hour earlier.

The group sold its 41.3 per cent interest in Kenya Litho Ltd, traditionally a company of fluctuating performance, for KSh48 million ($900,000). Nation Carriers Ltd, which distributed the newspapers, became a 100 per cent subsidiary company and was relocated next to the printing plant. Aware that the communications company he was now leading was not communicating too well internally, Kiboro introduced Total Quality Management courses which were attended by everyone from messenger to MD. He also addressed the long-standing problem of broadcasting.

It was back in April 1961 when the first reference to the electronic media appeared in the company records. The Aga Khan wrote to Curtis, 'It will be essential to have a foot in the door when television comes to Kenya.'[4] Television arrived just 18 months later with an inauspicious opening ceremony in which Patrick Jubb, chief of the Kenya Broadcasting Corporation, hailed 'a new drama on the stage in Africa'. The drama followed immediately as the studio lost sound on the filmed messages of congratulation, including one from Jomo Kenyatta, forcing viewers to practise their lip-reading skills. 'That was bad luck', VIP guest Governor Renison remarked cheerily. Sitting on a leopard-skin sofa, newsman Tony Cullen and Major Ian Grimwood talked about 'game', Carol Raye interviewed Mrs Charles Rubia, wife of Nairobi's first black mayor, and Alex Mitchell conducted viewers round a Picasso exhibition at the Sorsbie Gallery. Unhappily, the films seemed to get mixed up, and the *Nation's* first TV critic, Kate Johnson, noted:

> At one point Grimwood and Cullen were seen high up in the trees of the game park with a lion at their feet and later we were treated to a dose of subliminal Picasso between the lions, the men and the game park. Viewers saw and heard a lot of Miss Raye and too little of Mrs Rubia. The Swahili headlines were very smoothly handled by Stephen Kikumu. The backgrounds needed only an aspidistra or two to complete the setting for a Laurel and Hardy film.

It was just about par for the course in TV's early days.

The arrival of Achieng Oneko as information minister swiftly put paid to the Aga Khan's early ambitions in broadcasting and the government increasingly monopolised the medium in its own interest. But the *Nation* kept its eye on TV and radio for the day the airwaves might be liberalised. In 1991, when the independent Kenya Television Network prepared to launch, Gerry Wilkinson, by then at the Aga Khan's Secretariat in France, enquired at a board meeting if this was the right time for NNL to revive its own plans. Stan Njagi suggested the company might at least apply for a licence. Year after year thereafter, the group's annual reports bemoaned the government's lack of response. Kiboro later recalled:

> The government was not willing to give us a licence nor to say why it would not give us a licence. We assumed it was because of our independent editorial line. Some people saw us as an opposition newspaper and there was a lot of discomfort as to what effect a Nation *radio or television station might have on those millions out there who heard only the official view from KBC. When I came aboard in 1993 I pushed very hard. I would write every other week to the Minister of Information about the status of our application. I would ask ministers at social functions. They would come up with all*

*kinds of excuses but never an official letter of acknowledgement. By the end of 1997, we were coming to the conclusion that the government was never going to give us a licence, so we decided to see if we could get other people to help us.*

The *Nation* had already bid unsuccessfully for KTN. The company was owned substantially by Transnational Bank, and the Central Bank was pressuring Transnational to get rid of its shares. Kiboro said, 'I went to see the chairman of KTN and said, "If this company is being sold, we would like to make a substantial offer". I wrote a formal letter making an offer. We never even got an acknowledgement and the next we heard, KTN was sold to the *Standard*.' The *Standard* group itself was already in the hands of its new owners and Kiboro said, 'The government had now allowed the *Standard* to enter the electronic media and this strengthened our case. We also knew that we had to get into broadcasting real quick.'

The *Nation's* solution was to buy a controlling interest in East Africa Television Network Ltd (EATN), which already had TV and radio licences. 'It was perfectly legal, but it was a naughty thing to do', Kiboro said. 'We were trying to get in through the back door because the government had stopped us going through the front door.' Kiboro called a Press conference and announced that the *Nation* was establishing a nationwide broadcasting service. The government reacted by cancelling EATN's licences on grounds there was a dispute between the two original directors of the company about the transfer of shares to the *Nation*. The newspaper went to court, challenging the action of the Ministry of Information and that of the Kenya Posts and Telecommunications Corporation (KPTC), which had withdrawn EATN's frequencies. There ensued a series of postponements, hearings, adjournments and objections. 'It was a merry-go-round of delay', Kiboro recalled. 'Everybody was working in high gear to stop the *Nation* group from broadcasting. We decided to use the case to show the injustice the *Nation* was being subjected to by the government, which by then was giving licences to anybody who applied – Capital Radio, Hilary Ng'weno at Stellavision, anybody other than the *Nation*.'

Finally, in May 1998, the *Nation* was awarded TV and radio licences, but for Nairobi only. 'This was a major disappointment', Kiboro said. 'Our intention was always to cover nationwide.' He decided nonetheless to seek the necessary frequencies but met new procrastination from KPTC: 'I went to see the President just before Christmas and I said, "The government gives us a licence but the Post Office denies us a frequency. I don't understand it". So the President picked up the phone and called the MD at the Post Office and two days later we get the frequency.' But the saga was not over:

> *They had neglected to give us the microwave link frequency to transmit the signal from Nation Centre to the transmitter site at Limuru. They were also asking us to set up our transmitter in Ngong after we had all the no-objection certificates for Limuru, a far better site. And finally we found that the frequencies were so weak the signal would not reach the city centre and TV would only get to Dagoretti Corner. We did not know if this was a sick joke or malice or incompetence, but it was a harrowing experience. We couldn't get straight answers, you call and they don't call back, you write and they don't reply.*

In his darkest hour came a ray of light:

> *The President called and said he had ordered that we be given other areas than we had applied for and this was music to my ears. We got radio-only licences for Mombasa, Nakuru and Kisumu and we started negotiating for frequencies for these areas, along with stronger frequencies for Nairobi. A timetable was set: radio broadcasting in Nairobi before the end of 1999 and television early in 2000, with radio operating to Mombasa, Nakuru and Kisumu later that year. Resolution of the EATN case would provide a vehicle for a national radio and television network.*[5]

At the height of these efforts, Kiboro explained why the campaign was so crucial: 'All over the world, there is media convergence and the division between print and electronic is becoming less distinct. We cannot afford not to be involved in multimedia.' The advertising spend, traditionally dominated by the print media, was turning to electronic broadcasting, and Kiboro said, 'We must share in that new revenue even while we are losing some of the share in the print media. Electronic and other multimedia applications like the Internet are really the future.'

Kenyans approached the 1997 general election with markedly less enthusiasm than in 1992. Although opposition in principle was now an accepted feature of the political scene, the anti-KANU ranks proved hopelessly divided by personal ambition and ethnic rivalry, and there seemed little prospect of an election changing the way the country was governed. *The*

*EastAfrican* wrote, 'The disillusionment bordering on contempt which the ordinary voter now regularly expresses for opposition groupings stems not so much from their failure to provide a united alternative voice in national affairs as from the naked ambition and limited vision this failure demonstrates. The policy of the average oppositionist can be summed up as follows: "The President must go and I must replace him".' Opportunistic ambition was reflected in the ease with which some opposition MPs were persuaded, in return for cash or other favours, to abandon their parties for KANU. A typical defector was Agnes Ndetei, who deserted the Democratic Party for KANU in February 1997. She said, 'KANU told me to defect so that Kibwezi (her constituency) could get electricity. I did just that and the promise was fulfilled.' The reporter asked was it not the government's responsibility to develop the whole country and did her action not cheapen her? She replied, 'The niceties of good governance and equity in development are just on paper. They are never practical on a continent where the party in power rules supreme.' The cynical Ndetei lost her seat a few months later when Charity Ngilu's Social Democratic Party swept the Ukambani region.

It was after the 1992 poll that brighter elements within the opposition realised that multiparty elections did not automatically bring democracy, and never would while the constitution concentrated so much power within the presidency. As the 1997 election approached, some opposition politi-

*The arrival of the broadcast media posed new problems for advocates of a free Press.*

cians were joined by students, churchmen, lawyers and civil groups in demanding that the government start talking constitutional reform, or face mass action and/or an election boycott. On 17 July, Moi conceded the need to establish a constitutional review commission and to talk with opposition parties. Discussions between opposition and KANU MPs began on August 28 and some reforms were agreed. In October, some ten political parties were registered, though three others were refused and police continued to break up some opposition rallies. The National Assembly passed legislation giving all parties equal access to state-owned media for electoral purposes, though this proved largely illusory. The government by now owned or controlled the *Kenya Times*, the *Standard*, KBC and KTN. Two KTN editors were suspended when they ran extended footage of police breaking up an opposition rally in Nairobi and beating spectators. The agreed reforms went nowhere near the root-and-branch constitutional changes the opposition wanted, and anyway came too late for some KANU opponents to organise their campaigns. Richard Leakey's Safina was not registered until 26 November, a month before the election.

On 13 April, with the election nine months in the future, Kiboro invited 13 senior news executives to his home to discuss coverage. He said there were reports of *Nation* people working for KANU for a fee at previous elections, and he warned that anyone found to be wrongfully involved would be dismissed. Each person present was publicly asked if he was engaged in anything that could embarrass the company or compromise its coverage. Each replied in the negative. A month later, coverage began with a series of constituency profiles. As in 1992, the *Nation* reminded staffers of their obligations as journalists and citizens. Each member of the editorial staff was handed a wad of documentation 'to ensure professional, independent and unbiased reporting in this pre-election period and during the General Election itself'. The package included the long-established and regularly revised policy guidelines and editorial objectives, and the *Nation's* own Code of Ethics, which formed the basis of a Code of Conduct drawn up by a press task force set up by the government to consider media conduct. A 16-point document on election coverage directed reporters to frame their questions around issues, quote both police and organisers on the size of crowds, eschew single-source stories and refuse all inducements, including rides in politicians' vehicles. When two coast correspondents were found to have taken money from a KANU official, Wangethi Mwangi suspended them and published their names. But embarrassment was to come when the election was a distant memory.

On 18 June 1998, the government's *Kenya Times*, ever keen to smear the *Nation*, published a story claiming that Kwendo Opanga, writer of a popular *Sunday Nation* column, 'The week that was', had worked for KANU on the 1992 election for KSh50,000 ($1,380) per week. It was claimed he contributed to the 'KANU Briefs' column and provided the tribal breakdown on Nation Centre. Opanga called a press conference and said he had been under intense pressure, as a non-Kikuyu, to quit the *Nation*, and had received a death threat from YK92. 'Never have I felt so insecure, so vulnerable', he said. Opanga said he told Mwangi and Ekirapa of these pressures and swore an affidavit before the company lawyers. Three people then asked him to join a KANU think-tank to articulate policy and to devise responses to the opposition. Others included four university professors, three journalists and a number of professionals. He agreed. Opanga said he was asked about *Nation* people, but he knew only those in editorial and he did not author the tribal chart. He was paid a fee, but it was not KSh50,000 a week. Three days after his news conference, Opanga resigned. A *Nation* statement said the company was not aware of his work for KANU: 'By dint of his actions, Mr Opanga breached the *Nation's* editorial policy and general regulations and he obviously could not continue in his position.' Opanga joined the *Standard*, rising in later years to editorial director.

Unlike 1992, the *Nation* was not seriously targeted at the 1997 election as a more confident KANU moved smoothly to capitalise on opposition disunity, ignoring a national picture of decay and decline. In July, the IMF suspended its KSh12.9 billion ($208 million) structural adjustment aid because of poor governance and corruption, including failure to move on the Goldenberg scandal. This sent financial markets into a tailspin and interest rates soaring. The crime rate rose and the government admitted that some 45 per cent of Kenyans now lived below the poverty line. Once again, the pre-election period was characterised by ethnic violence, in particular against upcountry people resident in Likoni and other coastal areas. At least 69 people were killed, and hundreds of thousands displaced and denied the opportunity of voting. The polling process itself was marred by intimidation and rigging. Moi did not get the 49 per cent predicted by the shadowy university researchers but 41 per cent, and Kibaki's predicted 16 per cent turned out to be 31 per cent. The other three major contenders (Matiba did not stand) mustered an aggregate 28 per cent, and since Moi received 25 per cent support in five provinces, he was declared elected. The parliamentary fight was much closer and KANU ended with 108 of the 210 elective seats, compared to 102 obtained by nine opposition parties. To the relief of the anti-KANU elements, this fell far short of the two-thirds majority needed to secure changes in the constitution. A reflection of Kenyans' feelings lay in the fortunes of cabinet members. Twelve out of 25 ministers were defeated.

## *Notes*

1.  The single flaw in the *Nation's* handling of the Goldenberg series was its initial failure to identify Sarah Elderkin as a FORD Kenya activist, thereby permitting government supporters to denounce the articles as opposition propaganda. The paper did later note her political activity.
2.  Githongo was recruited later at a high level by government to investigate corruption. His travails as a whistle-blower are outlined in Michela Wrong's account, *It's Our Turn to Eat* (Fourth Estate, London, 2009).
3.  The belief in media circles was that the *Standard* was owned 100 per cent by Moi, his son Gideon and close associate Julius Kulei. The three were also believed to own KTN.
4.  The *Nation's* eagerness was in marked contrast to the attitude of Bolton, who refused to carry television programme listings in the *Standard*.
5.  The EATN wrangle continued until 2006 when Lady Justice Mary Kasango threw out Mr Ahmed Jibril's claim to ownership, declaring, 'This case, perhaps more than any other, will stand in the annals of history as an example of how Kenya was once ruled by a clique of political elite and where that elite did not tolerate divergent views and as a consequence the media were effectively muffled by the denial of airwaves for broadcasting.'

# A New President

*Poverty still gores Kenyans like an angry buffalo; igno-*
*rance stands in their way like an elephant and diseases*
*swallow them like a python.*
                    Ugandan poet Okot P'Bitek (1931–82)

On 19 January 2001, the *Daily Nation* published the following front-page
story by Muniu Riunge:

*A heart-breaking tale of tragedy and one child's heroism emerged*
*yesterday after a baby girl and her three brothers were suddenly*
*orphaned and lost their home as well. The hero is the oldest brother,*
*Wambua, who is bravely trying to take care of the family when, aged*
*only 10, he is barely old enough to take care of himself.*

*The tragedy came when the children's mother, Mumbi Muli, who*
*was the family's sole breadwinner, fell seriously ill in their Nairobi*
*slum shack on Friday last week. Wambua, realising his baby sister*
*Patricia was also ill, took her by himself to Kenyatta National*
*Hospital where the two-month-old child was admitted suffering*
*from starvation.*

*But when Wambua returned home to the Mukuru Kwa Njenga*
*slum, he faced a terrible sight. His mother lay dead and his two*
*brothers, aged six and four, had been evicted from their home. Their*
*few belongings were piled outside in the mud. The landlord claimed*
*Ms Muli owed him three months' rent.*

*Stricken with grief and with nowhere else to turn, Wambua asked*
*kind-hearted neighbours to look after his brothers while he ran back*
*to Kenyatta Hospital to ask the matron for help. The matron allowed*

*Wambua to eat and sleep at the hospital for as long as baby Patricia needs treatment.*

*But now he fears the day she is discharged. Not only have they nowhere to go, but the neighbours caring for his brothers say they cannot afford to look after them much longer. They too are extremely poor and can barely manage to feed and clothe their own children. Meanwhile their mother's body lies at the city mortuary. No-one knows how other relatives can be traced and the neighbours are at a loss how the funeral should be arranged.*

This account of a small boy strapping his little sister to his back and walking 7 km across the city to save her life provoked a mixed wave of sympathy and outrage. Fleshing out the family story in subsequent issues, Riunge said Wambua's father had deserted them in Mwingi district near Kitui and his mother travelled to seek work in Nairobi, leaving the children with their grandfather. Wambua dropped out of school and worked as a herdboy. But he said the grandfather, 'who never liked us', tired of caring for them, so in February 2000 the boy put together KSh300, gathered his siblings and travelled to Nairobi. 'When our mother saw us, she was very happy as she had heard of our suffering in Kitui', he recalled. The family lived first in the massive Nairobi slum of Kibera then moved to Mukuru, another vast conglomeration of iron and cardboard just off the highway to Jomo Kenyatta International Airport. There they rented a shack for KSh600 per month. Wambua borrowed KSh100 from a neighbour to sell peanuts and was able to pay the money back. But the income soon went on *sukuma wiki* (a green vegetable akin to spinach) and maize for meals, kerosene for the lamp, milk for the baby and medication for his mother. He also travelled to a main-road bus stop to waylay his father, who was a *matatu* conductor. The boy asked for KSh20 but his father refused. 'At first he used to visit', Wambua recalled, 'but when my mother fell sick, he never visited us once'. As his mother's condition worsened, the landlord threatened to evict them, demanding to know why they had brought their mother to die in his house.[1]

The Wambua Muli case was evidence of the accelerated social and economic decline which began to grind down Kenyans, especially the poorest, at the turn of the millennium. In 1999, some 48 per cent lived below the poverty line, that is, on a dollar a day; by 2001, the figure was 56 per cent. An MP said that residents of Mutumu had resorted to donkeys for transport because some roads had not been re-graded since 1969. When a crime wave hit Nairobi, the latest of many, Kariuki Muiru wrote in a letter to the *Daily*

*Nation*, 'Kenyans are under siege from muggers, robbers, carjackers, rapists, land grabbers and rogue policemen ... the police force is seriously underpaid, poorly housed, scantily equipped, tribally structured, anti-meritocratic and pathetically corrupt.' A schoolboy was fined KSh500 for giving a packet of cigarettes to an inmate of Eldoret Prison. A street boy was killed by hawkers for stealing a sweet. A Christmas survey in Britain disclosed that each child got presents worth an average of £250. A Nairobi father told a foreign correspondent that the Christmas gifts he bought for his children were a large bottle of Coca-Cola and a packet of coloured balloons.

Since independence, poverty, ignorance and disease had been public enemies number one, two and three. That so little headway had been made against them was ascribed by the outspoken German Ambassador, Michael Gerdts, to mega corruption, lack of effective management and misuse of scarce resources. In a speech on 28 April 1999, he noted that Kenya had received government-to-government development assistance since independence of $15 billion, to which must be added many types of unofficial aid and private foreign investment. A graduate working in the ministry of health told the *Daily Nation*, 'There are civil servants here driving BMWs, yet their salaries are less than KSh7,000 ($93) per month. What miracles do they perform?' *The EastAfrican* reported that five senior officials of the National Bank of Kenya received salaries for seven years while under suspension.

Policemen with daily access to the public became the overlords of corrupt behaviour at a popular level, but the judiciary was close behind. An investigation by Appeal Court Judge Richard Kwach found evidence of incompetence, racketeering, neglect of duty, corruption and sexual harassment. As in the bureaucracy, so in the courts, the missing file became the key to decisions delayed, changed or never taken. Cartoonist Gado pictured a judge demanding, 'Bring me the Missing Files file.' To which the court clerk replies, 'I'm sorry, sir, it's missing.' Both Attorney-General Amos Wako and the then Chief Justice Zacchaeus Chesoni acknowledged the truth of Kwach's findings.[2] A significant factor in the judicial deterioration was the dubious quality of some chief justices. One court official remembers the proceedings before Chief Justice Kitili Mwendwa being interrupted by the arrival of the conductor from the learned judge's Machakos–Nairobi bus. The takings from the route had to be counted before the court could continue. Another chief justice, the Jamaican-born Cecil Miller, once ruled against a company with Rhodesian connections and later explained his reasons to a brother judge. Miller had been a young officer in Britain's Royal Air Force during World War II and entered a club in London where his presence was questioned by a white officer. He discovered this man was Ian Smith, later prime minister of Rhodesia. 'I have been waiting to get my own back on him ever since', the chief justice said.[3]

The media doggedly tracked down and exposed scandals. The *Nation's* investigative unit, started by Mwaura and reinstated under the dynamic Mutegi Njau, was expanded and given extra funding after a brainstorming meeting of executives at the Mount Kenya Safari Club in Nanyuki. The result was a series of outstanding exclusives: a scandal in title deeds at Murang'a; the forging of official documents in Nairobi; a deception under which the President unwittingly signed away 500 acres of Mount Kenya Forest. But the effect was like dropping a pebble in the Indian Ocean. Philip Ochieng wrote in the *Sunday Nation*, 'Ministers denounce corruption only in the generality, never the particular. To mention a concrete crime would force the mentioner to take a concrete action. Thus they condemn crime in theory but sanction it in practice.'

In fact, there was a sensational breakthrough on the corruption front in May 2000, when a parliamentary select committee, which had been investigating for two years, published a report naming dozens of ministers and officials and urging they be investigated. The report said corrupt officials in the provincial administration had defrauded the government of

*A common view of the police force...*

some $700 million in the past decade. It named VP George Saitoti in connection with the Goldenberg affair and said Nicholas Biwott, at that time minister for tourism, should also be questioned. Moi's son Philip was named in connection with the evasion of duty on six imported Mercedes-Benz automobiles. The newspapers eagerly published the report and the names, which they dubbed the List of Shame. The BBC report that day said Kenyans would not be surprised to see top public figures named, 'but they are sceptical that those high up on the ladder will ever have to pay for their alleged wrongdoing'. True enough, two months later in a rowdy session, KANU MPs supported by some opposition members voted to expunge the names from the report, effectively tearing up the List of Shame and ensuring protection for the named suspects. Declared a *Nation* editorial, 'Our leaders lacked the courage to take sides on good versus evil ... Parliament just gave the corrupt everywhere a new lease of life.'

Increasingly, over the years, power was devolved to the Office of the President. By 1999, it controlled 48 departments of government including defence, security, police and immigration, but also, bizarrely, wildlife management, the Government Chemist and the Presidential Music Commission. Kenya had 35 foreign missions, and when the donors suggested these be reduced to save money, the government concluded that all were necessary.

*...and of the judiciary.*

The main duty of ministers, along with parastatal heads, university chancellors, police chiefs and senior civil servants seemed to be greeting or farewelling Moi on his trips abroad. At least once, this caused serious embarrassment. The Japanese government was handing over a KSh2.1 billion ($28 million) forestry research complex. Technology Minister Dr Zachary Onyonka failed to appear and his deputy arrived hours late because he had been at Jomo Kenyatta International Airport welcoming home Moi. A furious Japanese Ambassador Shinsuka Horiuchi refused to hand over the keys to the permanent secretary and drove off with a squeal of tyres. The ceremony took place a day later in the minister's presence.

As the millennium moved to a close, the *Nation* group was a significant force in the life of the country. The ninth largest of 56 companies quoted on the Nairobi Stock Exchange, it was valued at some KSh4.9 billion ($81.8 million), with share capital and reserves of KSh1.4 billion ($23 million). Its payroll approached 1,000. To reflect its entry into broadcasting and to optimise its position within the corporate tax legislation, the group restructured and changed its name to Nation Media Group Ltd (NMG). A subsidiary company, Africa Broadcasting Ltd, set up to handle TV and radio, was merged into a divisional structure within NMG, along with Nation Newspapers Ltd and Nation Carriers Ltd. A sign of the group's strength was the launch of a KSh500 million ($6.6 million) commercial paper issue to finance the entry into broadcasting and planned print activity in Tanzania and Uganda, and to retire debts of KSh200 million ($2.6 million) incurred for new buildings and facilities. Chairman Gecaga said the initial capital outlay for the broadcasting project would be KSh300 million ($4 million).

With its new ownership evidently controlling news contents, the *Standard* tended to address non-controversial areas. One of its earlier successes had been a pioneer giveaway magazine, *Now*, which frightened the *Nation* by sharply pushing up circulation of the *Sunday Standard* until the magazine was discontinued because of costs. *Now* was reintroduced as *Entertainment Now*, a 16-page, all-cartoon book of ten colour strips for children, including Beryl The Peril, Bananaman, Billy Whizz and Winker Watson. The last-named strip, set in a private school named Greytowers, appeared caught in a time warp, with teachers wearing gowns and mortar boards and boys in short trousers. The weekend paper also carried a popular bumper-sized cartoon, Madd on Sunday, and the daily *Standard* regularly ran six comic strips, local and syndicated.

The *Nation* was also into the value-added game, with a special features section in every issue and a breezy, A3-sized colour magazine, *Saturday*.

The aim was to boost circulation which had been stagnating due to a lacklustre economy, the spread of new radio and television, and the switch of Kenneth Matiba's *People* newspaper from weekly to daily. The *Sunday Nation's* average sale for 1998 was 215,000, its best-ever yearly figure, but the *Daily Nation's* 170,000 and the two *Taifas'* 30,000-plus were more characteristic of a downward trend. The problem was global as other forms of media fought for the reader's attention. The *Nation* responded editorially to sagging circulation levels and to the challenge of radio and TV by re-examining its own approach to news. Said Mwangi, 'When I watch the TV evening news and I know I'm looking at tomorrow's main story, I try to nudge the story one step further. We try to be deeper, more analytical, better written and to carry same-day commentaries on the big event, written in-house.'

A serious test of the new way of thinking was posed by the bombing of the US embassy in Nairobi on Friday 7 August 1998. Terrorists linked to the Osama Bin Laden network blew up the embassy and two neighbouring buildings. Some 247 people were killed, 5,000 injured and scores buried alive under the pancaked masonry, the great majority of them Kenyans. A simultaneous but much less serious attack hit the US embassy in Dar es Salaam, these two outrages being forerunners of the 9/11 destruction of the Twin Towers in New York city in 2001, and subsequent deadly terrorism in Spain, Britain and elsewhere. What the *Nation* did was to harness its traditional strength in hard news to the one-step-further philosophy and embellish the job with a couple of world exclusives. It was a highly professional performance sustained over many days by reporters and photographers forced to shut out their personal feelings of shock and horror.

As the *Nation* took on the aspects of a national institution, it began to act like one. Kiboro's Total Quality Management and strategic planning brought a new openness to the organisation. Mwangi said:

> When I was managing editor of the daily, I knew very little about what went on in Albert Ekirapa's office. But things changed and all the executives became exposed to the full range of programmes the company was trying to develop. We started to bring in all the managing editors and the bureau chiefs and the people from Uganda and Tanzania to forward-plan our growth in the new media environment. You throw out a wish list, dream as much as you like, put forward projects, then prioritise them and set a time frame and find people to handle them.

The new, caring *Nation* sought to undermine the cynics on its own rolls by addressing pay issues and the perennial bugbear of provincial correspondents – those brave front-line troops who took the worst of the hostility from *Nation*-hating regime supporters. In *Nation* terminology, correspondents were untrained freelance reporters or stringers who were paid for their stories on a lineage basis; some worked out of *Nation* bureaus, some did not; some got retainers, some did not. In May 1999, a coast correspondent complained that he had worked for the group since 1980 and never made more than KSh6,000 ($80) per month; sometimes, he said, he spent KSh2,000 ($26) getting a story for which the *Nation* paid him KSh200 ($2.60). Correspondents down the years said they were treated as second-class citizens, and mostly they blamed the Nairobi mindset of senior editors who rarely visited outlying bureaus. A one-time Kisumu bureau chief said he begged George Mbugguss for an editorial car to cover his vast territory and was told, 'We'll buy you all *piki-pikis* [motorised scooters].' A joke, of course. But not to the correspondent who takes a *matatu* to a distant political rally, telephones his story from a scorching booth using his own money, then finds he has missed the last *matatu* home.

Several contributors complained they were routinely insulted by Nairobi's copy-takers, who took it upon themselves to act as editors and tell the correspondent when to end his story. Photo-stringers protested that they had to buy their own film and the company refused to pay for camera repairs. Pay scales for journalists were reviewed regularly with the KUJ; the rate for correspondents was not. Structured scales were introduced for staff journalists with a percentage increase from one grade to another. As for correspondents, human resources manager Bernard K. Njeru said payments ranged between KSh3,000 ($40) and KSh40,000 ($533) per month, based on a fixed rate of up to KSh1,500 ($20) per story or KSh30–40 per inch on lineage. Said Finance Director Richard Henry, 'There is no country in the world where the staff don't complain about their remuneration. Our decisions are taken by a grading committee and I think we are rigorous and fair.' Nevertheless, editorial remuneration remained a problem, and only a few years later the company was required to make further considerable adjustments to retain its best staff.

At the turn of the millennium, the group's financial picture looked healthy: turnover had increased steadily, from KSh1,896 million ($24.9 million) in 1996 to KSh3,023 million ($39.7 million) in 2000; group revenue rose by 23 per cent in 2000 to KSh3 billion ($394 million); the *Nation's* share of the advertising market was 59.8 per cent, against 31.2 per cent for the

*Standard;* circulations were holding up. Set-up costs were hurting the broadcasting division, however. At a time of severe power rationing, TV was costing the group KSh16.8 million ($221,052) a month, and there were panicky calls to reduce broadcasting hours or close down altogether. It was clear, however, that even though serious profit from television could be ten years in the future, there could be no going back on electronic broadcasting and the commitment to diversification. What particularly troubled Kiboro was the group's over-reliance on Kenya and on the newspapers, particularly the *Daily* and *Sunday Nation*, which contributed more than three-quarters of the group's income. A plan was developed to reduce dependence on the Kenyan market.

In September 2000, Hannington Awori took over as chairman of the group from the long-serving Mareka Gecaga and set out the new thinking: 'Media companies worldwide have increasingly diversified ... these developments have led to mergers, consolidations and alliances ... Nation Media Group, as it extends its regional interests, is keenly aware of these developments, from which it cannot afford to stand apart.' The next few years were to see an explosion of growth, with *Nation* executives racking up thousands of air miles as they negotiated to take NMG into new areas.

With the advent of the Internet, the *Nation* constructed its own website, and readers in New York and Washington could access the contents of the daily six hours before Nairobians were able to buy the paper. But the web version was even more widely scanned in Kenya and by the time of the 2002 elections it was getting more than a million hits a day. In 1998, seven years after applying, the *Nation* had secured radio and television licences for Nairobi, then radio licences for Mombasa, Nakuru and Kisumu. October 1999 saw the launch of Nation FM (radio), with Nation TV following it on air in December. Also in 1999, the group acquired the *Weekly Advertiser*, a free sheet distributing 50,000 copies, for KSh2.5 million ($32,900), and registered Nation Carriers as a courier company so it could carry parcels on its return journeys. In March 2000, negotiations were completed to acquire a 60 per cent holding in Monitor Publications Ltd of Uganda and that company then launched Monitor FM Radio, as well as a Luganda-language newspaper, *Ngoma*. In 2002, the group took 60 per cent equity in Mwananchi Communications and 49 per cent of Radio Uhuru Ltd of Tanzania. In November, a provincial weekly was started targeting Mombasa, *Coast Express*, the group's 12th title, and the Kenya authorities finally handed over licences and frequencies for radio and television nationally. It was a whirlwind of expansion, unprecedented for the *Nation* group.

Historically, the attitude to start-ups by the *Nation* was cautious. It took a long and painful eight years from launch in 1960 to turn a profit, and while the Kenyan economy was usually buoyant and dynamic, it was ever susceptible to downturns overseas and to political volatility at home. Company initiatives, however, told a positive story – first the newspapers, then radio and finally television reached their financial comfort zones, even if the electronic media were still struggling as the group's 50th birthday approached. Since no new product was without risk, the Aga Khan encouraged his executives to look at potential threats not in the short term but in light of their staying power, and management was counselled against knee-jerk reaction to new competition. An example was the *Star*, a Nairobi populist daily. It did not appear to pose a long-term risk, but Nation Centre launched a competitor anyway – the *Metro*. Though sales quickly outstripped the *Star*, an increasingly harsh economic climate posed insuperable problems for advertisement sales and the publication was eventually discontinued.

Politically, Kenya was experiencing something of a whirlwind too, the demand for constitutional change having become unstoppable after the 1997 election. Moi was by now officially barred from a new term as President, though many Kenyans suspected he would pull a rabbit out of the hat and return to office yet again. But in March 1999, Moi confirmed that he would step down at the 2002 election. Needless to say, this did not prevent him from seeking continued control of the political process. Ever the professor of politics, Moi forged a KANU alliance with Raila Odinga's Luo-dominated National Development Party (NDP) and in January 2001 appointed Odinga as minister of energy, thereby creating the first coalition government in Kenya's history. In November, Moi reshuffled his cabinet again in an apparent attempt to provide suitable candidates for his succession. Most eye-catching of these appointments was that of Uhuru Kenyatta, a son of the late President Jomo Kenyatta, aged just 35, as minister for local government. In March 2002, the NDP was dissolved and absorbed into KANU, despite opposition from some members of both parties. Odinga became secretary-general of KANU when the long-serving but rarely elected MP Joseph Kamotho withdrew upon seeing which way the wind was blowing. Moi had long been admired, even by his enemies, for his deft management of political and party matters, but in August 2002 he made a decision that would lead to his party's downfall: he publicly announced that he wanted Uhuru Kenyatta to be KANU's candidate for the presidency.

Outraged, several senior KANU members including Saitoti and Odinga announced they would seek the presidential nomination themselves, and formed the Rainbow Alliance to campaign within KANU for a democratic vote to select the party's candidate. Moi responded by sacking Saitoti, but soon afterwards, in protest at Moi's attempt to impose a successor, members of the Rainbow Alliance resigned from their posts in the government and from KANU, along with some 30 KANU MPs. In a massive blow to the ruling party, they boycotted the KANU conference that endorsed Uhuru's candidacy. It was widely believed that Moi was hoping to continue his influence through Uhuru. This seemed to be confirmed when the President, showing surprise at the negative reaction to his nomination, remarked, 'But the young man will listen.' Already in July, some 12 opposition parties had formed an electoral alliance: the National Alliance Party of Kenya, or NAK.

14 October was an epochal day in Kenyan history. At the same time as 4,500 members of the KANU national delegates' conference endorsed Uhuru Kenyatta as the party's presidential contender at the Kasarani meeting hall, across the city in Uhuru Park, the main groups opposing KANU announced a grand alliance before 10,000 cheering supporters. The Rainbow Alliance transformed itself into the Liberal Democratic Party and joined with NAK to form the National Rainbow Coalition, Narc, with veteran politician Mwai Kibaki as the sole opposition candidate for the presidency. Horrified KANU supporters realised they could lose an election for the first time as the daily newspapers front-paged a historic photograph of old friends and former enemies all sitting at the same table: Mwai Kibaki, Moody Awori, Charity Ngilu, George Saitoti, Kalonzo Musyoka, Raila Odinga, Simeon Nyachae, Kijana Wamalwa and Farah Maalim. 'The grand opposition alliance Kenyans have for 10 years yearned to liberate them from President Moi's and KANU's misrule is finally here', crowed *The People*.

As at past elections, Mwangi and the news desk planned meticulously for the big day, 27 December 2002. In the final weeks, the investigations desk ran stories of renewed looting of the NSSF, as well as the National Hospital Insurance Fund and the Kenyatta National Hospital, through deposits in the failed political bank, Euro Bank, which eventually collapsed owing $22.5 million to a range of parastatals. Robbing the NSSF was nothing new – it had been a feature of the 'dirty tricks' election of 1992 and reported by the *Nation* at the time. Typically, the fraud involved a plot of government land being sold to a political operative and then resold at a vastly inflated price to the NSSF. The profit was used to make political payments to swing the election, even though the scheme hugely increased the money supply and caused 100 per cent inflation. Nobody was ever charged or arrested. In 2002, the *Nation* also reported a rush by ministries to pay construction and public works invoices, some going back ten or more years, many of them in dispute and often related to unfinished and probably even fictitious projects. These funds were not apparently intended to shore up a faltering campaign, but were seen by many Kenyans as the establishment making a last-chance raid on the Treasury's coffers to fatten their individual accounts.

The remnants of the discredited KANU regime had every reason to be fearful. Although opposition leader Mwai Kibaki was injured in a car crash while campaigning and was sidelined for several weeks, the extraordinary spectacle of a united opposition excited Kenyans as never before. After a campaign that was comparatively free from violence, the anti-KANU forces secured an emphatic victory on both the presidential and legislative fronts. Kibaki won the presidency with 62.3 per cent of votes cast, against 31.3 per cent for KANU's Uhuru Kenyatta and 5.9 per cent for Simeon Nyachae of the FORD-People party. In the parliamentary elections, Narc won 125 of 210 available seats, KANU 64 and FORD-People 14. The remaining seven seats were shared among four minor parties. The electoral turnout was 56.1 per cent. Moi stepped down as promised and Kibaki was inaugurated on 30 December, an event which raised the hopes of many Kenyans sky-high – hopes that were in many cases to be brutally dashed.

## Notes

1. Wambua and his siblings were taken into care and educated by the SOS organisation.
2. Kwach himself was subsequently mentioned adversely in a report on judicial corruption and resigned. Chesoni was forced from the bench in 1985 when bankruptcy proceedings were issued against him over a debt of $412,000, but Moi brought him back to chair the Electoral Commission and later named him chief justice.
3. Miller's stability was seriously questioned after an incident in 1988 when he rushed from his chambers and took off his trousers in the High Court parking lot while screaming, '*Nyayo, nyayo*'. Police put him in a car and took him home.

# Expand and Diversify

*Corruption will now cease to be a way of life in Kenya...*
*There will be no sacred cows under my government.*
President Mwai Kibaki upon his inauguration as head of
state, 30 December 2002

With a new government in place and Kenyans bursting with hope and optimism, the Nation Media Group (NMG) examined its own position at the start of 2003. Indisputably the media leader in East Africa, the group reaped the benefits of an enthusiastic election campaign by breaking through the KSh4 billion ($52 million) turnover barrier for the first time, and with broadcast revenues finally improving, ended 2002 debt-free. But senior executives were concerned that 'pursuing other opportunities beyond our current area of operations', as board strategy required, would stretch human and financial resources to the limit and perhaps beyond it. In the event, NMG's determination to enter two crucial areas – new acquisitions and electronic broadcasting – received a boost from two heads of state. President Yoweri Museveni was concerned that Uganda's leading daily, *New Vision*, was effectively in his government's control and he invited the *Nation* to take it over. Consultations with government ministers, however, received a negative response – the cabinet did not want to see a takeover when elections were nearing – so the Kenyans turned to *New Vision's* opponent.

In 1999, Monitor Publications Ltd (MPL) of Uganda, publisher of a feisty but cash-strapped tabloid, *The Monitor*, was valued by an international auditing company at $1 million, which some considered high since it had made losses in 1997 and 1998. But a Ugandan politician offered $2 million for 30 per cent of the company, and the Times Media Group of South Africa bid $4 million for 100 per cent. NMG decided to negotiate up to

$1.2 million for 60 per cent, with a further half a million for working capital requirements. In March 2000, NMG duly acquired its 60 per cent and in June injected $450,000, with $300,000 from the other shareholders to redeem bank loans and provide working capital. The group reserved four out of eight seats on the board and named Dr Martin Aliker, formerly a Minister of State for Foreign Affairs in the Uganda government, as chairman. MPL's first monthly contribution to the bottom line was KSh800,000 ($10,500).

*The Monitor* had a history unlike any other in the region. In 1992, six Ugandan journalists were working for *Weekly Topic*, a centre-left crusading journal which they made so successful that its owners were offered jobs by President Yoweri Museveni. As a result, the publishers pressured the writers to take a softer line on the government, which the news team resisted. When the editor, Wafula Oguttu, was taken off editorial duties and named manager of special projects – actually supervising the building of an office block – he quit and five senior men walked out with him: Charles Onyango-Obbo, Kevin Aliro, Richard Tebere, David Ouma and Jimmy Serugo. They decided to produce a newspaper of their own. A friend offered a vacant basement in his office building. It was filled with broken furniture and the staffers pulled out drawers and used them as stools. Eager interns from *Weekly Topic* volunteered their help and, lacking space sellers, journalists went from shop to shop seeking advertising. Staffers agreed to go without pay in the first month to establish some working capital while discussions focussed on a title. An early favourite was *The Flame*, but this was rejected as too socialist, and *The Monitor*, with its hints of a watchdog role, was chosen instead. When the first weekly issue appeared, reporters and sub-editors personally hawked it on the streets and a BBC journalist helped to distribute copies in her battered Land Rover. In a country hungering for an alternative viewpoint, the paper was sensationally successful, and with the second issue it became the highest selling independent newspaper in Ugandan history.

However, nothing prepared the founding six for the hostility they would face from Museveni and his ministers. Uganda by then boasted several independent newspapers which were occasionally critical of the government, but these publications were owned by business tycoons, churches or political parties, who could be pressured to bring their editors to heel. The *Monitor* men had no such shield and were exposed to the full force of government rage whenever the paper ran critical comment. In an unprecedented move, Museveni banned all government departments and affiliated institutions from advertising in the *Monitor*. With the paper scarcely a year old, the financial loss was painful and the knock-on effect was devastating: fearful private advertisers also stopped buying space. For months, the 16-page paper carried only a single quarter-page advertisement – for machetes, from a company owned by a sympathetic ex-journalist. Fearing the government's next step might be to move against the paper's landlord and its commercial printer, Oguttu and co. instituted an austerity regime, capping pay raises and benefits so that the company could build its own office block and buy its own press. Galvanised by the success of the *Monitor* with the public – by the end of 1995 it was coming out three times a week – the journalists went on a land-buying spree and started building an office block; staking the land and building as collateral, they got a hefty loan from a development bank and bought a new colour press from India. On 11 November 1996, the press was commissioned and the *Monitor* went to seven-day production with a Sunday edition. It was the first Ugandan newspaper to computerise (1993), the first African paper outside of South Africa to introduce an Internet edition (1994) and the first in Uganda to print full colour (1996). But government did not let up and began pressurising the company on legal and financial grounds, with Managing Editor Onyango-Obbo and writer Andrew Mwenda persistently targeted on usually specious grounds. The government advertising ban lost its bite as economic liberalisation squeezed the state sector, but with a staff of 100, newsprint problems and the cash flow slowing, the founders concluded that the only way the company would survive would be to spread the risk. Accordingly, negotiations began with the *Nation* in 1999. Nairobi executives were well aware of the parlous situation of MPL, but they believed the link-up was a good fit for both sides.

Keenly aware that radio was the prime medium for news and entertainment in Uganda,[1] the first major venture of the newly infused MPL was to launch a radio station, Monitor FM 93.3, in April 2001. It won a starting audience share of 2 per cent against 11 per cent for the top station, but only added to the financial difficulties, losing some $13,000 per month in the early days.

That a Kenyan group with a reputation for editorial caution should acquire a controversial newspaper run by young firebrands openly opposed to President Museveni and his government surprised many. The feeling in Nairobi, however, was that the *Nation's* reputation for objectivity would transfer naturally to the *Monitor*, adding coolness and stability to its mix of idealism and energy. When it came to politics, the slogan would be 'Praise where praise is due, criticism where criticism is necessary'. The policy enabled the BBC to describe the *Monitor* in later years as 'Uganda's leading independent newspaper'. But as in Kenya, the powers-that-be had difficulty distinguishing between an independent stance and an anti-government one, and the paper felt the full force of authoritarian rule on 10 October 2002, when operations were peremptorily shut down. Government security men locked and sealed the premises, and confiscated computers, disks, tapes, documents and mobile phones. It seems the military was angered by a story claiming that an army helicopter had been shot down by rebels of the Lord's Resistance Army, who had been fighting Museveni's forces in the north of Uganda for 16 years. The story, which was also carried by the Associated Press, was the latest in a number of reports on the army's failure to defeat the rebels and the government declared the paper would remain closed until it apologised. Frank Nyakairu, author of the story, Onyango-Obbo and news editor Wanyama Wangah were charged with publishing false news and information prejudicial to national security. Top *Nation* executives took the first available flights to Kampala and seven days later the *Monitor* returned to the streets. It carried a carefully worded apology but did not retract the story, arguing that to do so would prejudice the case against the accused journalists.

Amnesty International condemned the office raid as 'intimidation and harassment', and Human Rights Watch reported that the temporary closure had 'a chilling effect' on free speech in Uganda. The belief among Ugandan journalists was that the *Monitor's* persistent reporting of the conflict in the north had aroused personal acrimony against certain editors, pre-eminently Onyango-Obbo. The managing editor reflected later, 'I appeared in court more than 150 times for the helicopter and other cases. Increasingly, it was not about the *Monitor*, it was about me and the President's government. My troubles were taking their toll on my family and my mother was ill from the stress.' NMG declined to move against Onyango-Obbo under government pressure and he feared this would prompt action to remove him from the newspaper by killing or maiming him. 'It was clearly no longer tenable that I should stay at the *Monitor*', he said. After long internal discussions, it was agreed that Onyango-Obbo would turn over his ME responsibilities to David Ouma and take up a new post as Convergence and Syndication Editor in Nairobi. Inevitably, this was seen by some journalists as caving in to Museveni, but the company and Onyango-Obbo himself felt there was no alternative.

Whatever the agonies inflicted on Nairobi's executives by its Ugandan acquisition, NMG firmly believed that diversification within the East African region offered 'the strongest prospects for profitable future growth', and began investigating options in Tanzania. Once again, a head of state played a role. President Benjamin Mkapa, himself a former journalist who once sought a job with the *Nation* group, let it be known at the highest levels of NMG that he feared his country was being 'torn up' by a corrupt and incompetent media. Would the *Nation* consider bringing quality journalism to Tanzania? Discussions started with the *Business Times* to publish an English-language daily and a Kiswahili weekly or daily, but these got nowhere and the Nairobi negotiators moved on to Mwananchi Communications Ltd (MCL). This company was owned by two individuals who published three titles in Kiswahili and held a 51 per cent interest in Radio Uhuru, in which the ruling Chama Cha Mapinduzi (CCM) political party was also a shareholder. The international auditors Price Waterhouse Coopers valued total print and radio assets at $800,000, and NMG offered $960,000 including goodwill. Agreements were subsequently signed for 60 per cent equity in MCL and 49 per cent in Radio Uhuru, with 11 per cent for the original MCL owners. The media assets acquired were a Kiswahili daily and Sunday newspaper, *Mwananchi*, and a twice-weekly sports paper, *Mwanaspoti*, plus Radio Uhuru, which broadcast in Dar es Salaam, Mwanza and Arusha. NMG registered the title the *Citizen* for an intended English-language daily.

The first effect of the purchase was a marked increase in capital costs, including $375,000 for a printing press located in Australia which would be split between the *Monitor* in Kampala and *Mwananchi* in Dar es Salaam. Because MCL and Radio Uhuru were tenants in the CCM party building, an uneasy situation for an independent newspaper, plans were laid to move with the new press to premises near the airport. Mr Ali Mufuruki, chairman of the Infotech Investment Group based in Tanzania, was appointed chairman of the boards of MCL and Radio Uhuru. Recruitment started for all departments, but this proved problematic in a country with limited local talent and steeped in a highly politicised, socialist and Kiswahili-based culture. It was clear that human resources would need to be drafted in from outside, and a Kenyan, David Waweru, then working for *New Vision* in Uganda, was named as general manager.

Diversification into East Africa fitted two ways: national leaders wanted to introduce NMG's skills and status into their home-grown media (and had issued open invitations in private talks), while the group was eager to support new moves towards the regionalism it had long espoused. The East African Federation had died, partly as a result of the cold war – Tanzania leaning to China, Kenya to the West – and partly through unresolved national ambitions. It had since become clear that some individual states in the region, deprived of resources by the ending of the cold war, were scarcely viable, and that a new five-nation grouping of Kenya, Tanzania, Uganda, Rwanda and Burundi involving 150 million people could prove a significant player on the African scene. While there were clearly many dangers, such as the European Community's development as a two-tier body, *Nation* executives believed that the idea of turning the East African Community into a full federation with a federal president was more than talk. A major role of the media would be to sustain the drive for togetherness, and when President Paul Kagame invited NMG to invest in Rwanda the group saw this as an appropriate next step. A Nairobi delegation promptly travelled to Kigali to meet with the head of state and discussions took place on modalities. All this geographical muscle-flexing at Nation Centre inevitably led to questions whether the group could move on a yet larger scale and become the African media for Africa.

Back in Nairobi, expansion rolled on. The *Nation* website, redesigned to carry breaking news, brought in a useful KSh1 million ($13,000) per month on banner advertisements alone, as hits climbed from 950,000 per day in September 2002 past the 2.5 million mark. It was, boasted an online profile, 'the most visited website in East and Central Africa'. Cyber experts worked on further revenue-generating projects such as a weekly e-newsletter, online versions of obituaries and classified notices, and a news subscription service to international clientele via SMS. The *Nation Business Directory* was restarted and exceeded its revenue targets, but the *Weekly Advertiser* free-sheet, aimed at small businesses which could not afford space in the big papers, was wobbly. A regional (provincial) paper had long been under discussion and in November 2002, *Coast Express* weekly was brought to the market. If it was a success, consideration would be given to a similar publication for Central Kenya. At this point, NMG ran 12 print titles, three radio stations and a television station, and employed more than a thousand staff. The *Daily* and *Sunday Nation* were redesigned, and a relaunch was planned for *Taifa Leo* to target a younger audience and shed its image as a paper for people who could not read English. In a dull and stagnant market, sales of the two flagship papers stayed around 168,000 and 230,000 respectively, but Kenyans always responded to big political news, and when Moi sacked VP Saitoti the daily's sales topped 250,000. *The EastAfrican* was performing patchily on the circulation front at around 26,000, but seemed immune from economic chill factors – a supplement on Rwanda brought in $40,000.

After the election described by independent observers as 'free, fair, peaceful and transparent', hundreds of thousands of Kenyans flocked to Uhuru Park in Nairobi on Monday 30 December 2002 to witness the presidential inauguration of Emilio Mwai Kibaki and the end of nearly 40 years of KANU rule. Confined to a wheelchair after his car crash, with his bare toes poking through the plaster sheath on an injured leg, Kibaki, 71, recited the oath of office while Moi sat to his right, stoically enduring jeers and boos from sections of the crowd. Kibaki did not spare his predecessor, referring to 'years of misrule and ineptitude', an era when government was run by road-side declarations and the whims of individuals, resulting in grave consequences even to the present day. There would be no witch-hunt, he promised, but he declared, 'The era of "anything goes" is gone forever. Corruption will now cease to be a way of life in Kenya …there will be no sacred cows in my government.' In addition to constitutional change promised in the Narc manifesto, Kibaki pledged a series of sweeping reforms, including free primary education, better health care and a stronger economy. He also declared, 'The authority of Parliament and the independence of the judiciary will be restored and enhanced. We want to bring back due process, accountability and transparency in public office.' The mood in the park was euphoric, but onlookers reported handfuls of earth were thrown at Moi's car after he made his handover remarks.[2]

The first year of the new era was a political whirlwind. Kibaki formed a cabinet with Michael Kijana Wamalwa as Vice-President, Raila Odinga as minister of roads and public works, and the great survivor, George Saitoti, as minister of education. He appointed a commission of inquiry into the Goldenberg affair and a parliamentary select committee was established to re-investigate the 1999 murder of Robert Ouko. Steps were initiated to revive the Kenya Co-operative Creamery, enabling farmers to find a new quick outlet for their milk. A long-awaited constitutional review conference opened in April, and in May the Anti-Corruption and Economic Crimes Act came into effect, reinforcing the status of the Kenya Anti-Corruption Commission. Kibaki suffered a setback in August with the death of Wamalwa, who had been a moderating influence in high politics. There was pressure to appoint Odinga to the post, but Kibaki named another Luhya, Moody Awori, brother to Hannington, the NMG chairman.

One of the new government's first actions was to open a state torture chamber for public viewing. Towering over central Nairobi, the 24 ochre-coloured floors of Nyayo House, named for the Moi era, accommodated mostly mundane offices of the state bureaucracy. But as most Kenyans well knew, from 1983 to 1996 citizens seemed regularly to fall from the upper floors, while the subterranean levels were used to incarcerate and interrogate government opponents. Some 2,000 victims were believed to have passed through the cells during Moi's 24-year rule, though no figures are available as to prisoner numbers or deaths. Now in 2003, visitors, including former occupants, walked from the basement car park into a dark corridor that led to 14 cells, each about two yards square. Water pipes, hoses and pieces of broken chairs used to beat prisoners still littered the floor. Joe Njoroge, 35, said he spent five weeks in the cells in 1990 accused of belonging to Mwakenya. 'The floor was under water so I used to sit like this', he said, squatting in the corner of Cell 2. 'I was naked all the time. Every morning the guards would bring a hose and blast water at me. I did not know if it was night or day and they would bring me breakfast in the evening to confuse me.' Kibaki promised, 'Never again shall the people of Kenya endure such injustice at the hands of their own government.' A civil rights group, People Against Torture, applauded the government's action, but pointed out that nobody had been arrested and some torturers were actually appointed to the new government.[3]

The new government's most popular decision – indeed the single most popular decision by any government for many years – came when the President fulfilled his promise of free primary education for all. An extra 1.5 million pupils, some as old as 18 or 20, rushed to join the country's 18,000 public primary schools and some rolls doubled. One Nairobi school went from 461 students to 930 with four first-grade classes of 60 each, though classes of 100 were not exceptional. Up to eight children shared a single textbook. The Kenya National Union of Teachers counted 250,000 members, but at least 60,000 more teachers were needed. Saitoti estimated the immediate cost of the programme to be $97 million, with another $137 million needed to see it through the fiscal year of 2003/4. The state gave schools KSh1,020 ($13) per child, but often headmasters could not pay their electricity bills, and computers stood idle in those schools lucky enough to have them. Opec donated $13.7 million and Unicef promised $2.5 million. Negotiations started with the World Bank for a massive handout, realised within two years, of some KSh1.8 billion ($23 million). By 2004, some 7.4 million children were receiving free primary education and the transition to secondary school edged up to 30 per cent.

Almost as astounding to Kenyans as free education was a swift move against the tarnished judiciary. In 2002, an investigating panel of five Commonwealth judges had reported evidence of nepotism, favouritism, political interference and incompetence at all levels of the system. Chief Justice Bernard Chunga, a Moi favourite, rubbished the report as far-fetched, untrue and in bad taste. The system, he said, 'is not weak, not at the cross-roads and suffers no rot'. But nine months later, Chunga resigned when Kibaki appointed a tribunal to investigate his alleged complicity in torture and inhuman treatment of Mwakenya suspects, and in October 2003, the Kenya Anti-Corruption Commission published an explosive report demonstrating how corruption had infiltrated all levels of the justice system. The investigation, headed by Justice Aaron Ringera, reported that bribery was rampant, and prices ran from KSh15 million ($197,000) for an Appeal Court judge to KSh1.6 million ($21,000) for a High Court judge, to KSh4,000 ($52) for a magistrate. You could be cleared of murder or robbery with violence, both hanging offences, for as little as KSh40,000 ($520), while KSh19,000 ($250) would get you off a rape charge. Innocent people who could not raise bribe money were condemned and one judge estimated that at least 20 per cent of convicts were wrongly imprisoned. In civil cases, judges expected 10–30 per cent of any award. The report accused six judges out of 11 in the Appeal Court, 17 High Court judges out of 36, and 82 magistrates out of 254, that is, about half of all judges and a third of magistrates. Two disciplinary tribunals were set up and, within days, 21 of the judges opted to take retirement, plus benefits of between KSh5 million ($66,000) and KSh10 million ($131,000). All 82 magistrates were dismissed. However, seven judges opted to challenge the allegations against them and by early 2007 three had been cleared. In one case, the tribunal denounced the evidence as 'a concoction of rumours laced with hearsay'.

Marked changes at social level saw the new government move to rid Nairobi streets of child beggars and vendors, and to bring discipline to the roads. For the *matatus*, transport minister John Michuki introduced seat belts, governors setting speed limits at 50 mph (80 kph), and restrictions on the number of passengers; each vehicle had to carry a painted strip showing route and ownership details. Similar rules were set for buses.[4]

Thus early into its term, Kibaki's administration was redeeming some of the coalition's election promises, though others – 150,000 houses in the first year, 500,000 new jobs and a new constitution in 100 days – were clearly not going to happen any time soon. For a brief time, however, the nation seemed united and the authoritarian grip relaxed – few shops bothered to carry the regulation photograph of the head of state and Kibaki's image did not appear on banknotes. To the exasperation of Wangethi Mwangi, a groundswell of criticism became audible, including from some of his own staffers, that the *Nation* was giving Narc an easy ride. Mwangi said in an interview:

> *What happened was the* Standard *did a 180-degree turn when Narc came to power and in people's minds came to occupy the position that*

*the Nation had occupied. This volte face was no surprise to us considering the Standard's ownership in fact we expected it. For our part, we were not out to oppose for the sake of opposing. We simply felt, here was a new government come to power on a popular platform and we wanted to give it a chance to see how far it could go. This was not because of any sympathies we had for Narc but because it was the decent thing to do.*

Mwangi added, 'We are an independent paper but the difference between a critical paper and an independent one is difficult to get across. It is sad that a newspaper is only seen as good if it is critical. Being independent does not just mean attacking the government. There are other criteria, like the quality of its journalism and how well it keeps citizens informed.'

Of course, the government's honeymoon period could not last forever and Kenyans' hopes waned with the exposure of new high-level corruption. In December 2004, the US government banned Nicholas Biwott from entering the United States as 'a person engaged in or benefiting from corruption'. Nine months later, the British government barred Kibaki's transport minister, Chris Murangaru, until recently holder of the powerful security portfolio, because of his 'character, conduct and associations'. The USA followed suit three months later. Murangaru denied the graft implications and raged that he would sue. An online poll in the *Daily Nation* asked if the travel ban on Murangaru was fair. The Yes vote was 71.8 per cent, against 28.2 per cent for No. But Murangaru retained his seat in the cabinet.

The continued failure to move against corrupt individuals provoked from British High Commissioner Sir Edward Clay an outburst so stinging that it enraged government leaders. In a Nairobi speech to business leaders in July 2004, he said the names of honest ministers and senior officials would fit on the back of a postage stamp. Noting that fraud and theft accounted for about 8 per cent of Kenya's GDP, he said:

*We never expected corruption to be vanquished overnight. We all recognised that some would be carried over to the new era. We hoped it would not be rammed in our faces, but it has. Evidently the practitioners now in government have the arrogance, greed and perhaps a sense of panic to lead them to eat like gluttons. They can hardly expect us not to care when their gluttony causes them to vomit all over our shoes.*

One of the items prompting Clay's assault was a massive KSh50 billion ($700 million) scandal, which came to dog the Kibaki regime as Goldenberg did Moi's. Indeed, there were eerie similarities between the two. In 2003, Anglo Leasing and Finance was awarded a KSh2.7 billion ($37 million) contract to supply secure passport equipment previously valued at $12 million. The company turned out not to exist, though there was an agent in Liverpool, a small property company owned by Mrs Sudha Ruparell, a Kenyan Asian whose family had close ties with the Moi regime and was active in security contracting. Justice Minister Kiraitu Murungi said the arrangement had been inherited from the previous regime; it was now cancelled, he said, describing it as 'the scandal that never was'. But the auditor general said that while negotiations began under the old regime, Narc continued the deal, and MP Maoka Maore claimed in Parliament that the lowest tender had been KSh936 million ($12 million). Payment was approved by the Treasury without reference to Parliament. 'Someone at the Immigration Department pocketed a whopping $25 million', Maore said. Kenyans began to realise that, as Goldenberg money was made from non-existent gold and diamonds, with Anglo Leasing the profits came from phantom companies.

The bill for looting during the Moi regime was commonly set at $3–4 billion (KSh228–304 billion) – enough to pay for primary schooling for every Kenyan child for ten years – and Narc busily advised the people it was working hard to recoup their money. At least KSh87 billion ($1.1 billion) was known to be stashed abroad, representing some proceeds from the Goldenberg fraud, the sale of grabbed land and mismanagement of state corporations. After a year, investigators reported that they had located more than KSh76 billion ($1 billion) in assets, real estate and cash in Switzerland, Monaco, North America and the Cayman Islands. But two years later an assistant minister forlornly told Parliament that no money had been recovered, while the search had cost KSh20 million ($263,000). The government, he said, had underestimated the capacity of the looters to hide their ill-gotten gains.

In February 2005, Sir Edward Clay handed to Kibaki a dossier he said contained evidence of 20 corrupt public procurement deals which had cost Kenya KSh40 billion ($526 million). The frauds set out by his office included the dubious purchase of patrol ships for the Kenyan Navy in the Seychelles, a computerisation tender for the Kenya Airports Authority, a controversial loan repayment deal by the Kenya Pipeline Company, as well as the Anglo Leasing scandal. All of the cases involved Narc people at some level. The government bought space in newspapers to declare that the Kenya Anti-Corruption Commission (KACC) knew all about the 20 cases, 11 of which had been procured by the Moi regime anyway. In a speech to journalists, Clay declared, 'Many stones remain unturned … many, many stones … and the beacon of hope that the Narc government promised is almost extinguished.' He was supported by US Ambassador William Bellamy: 'Corruption in Kenya is not a matter of *kitu kidogo* (something small) or a few ministers skimming off commissions. It is big enough to cause macro-economic distortions. Every Kenyan labouring to feed his family, educate his children, care for a family member suffering from Aids or simply avoid getting hacked to death in the mounting wave of violence sweeping the country is a victim of today's corruption.'

As Western diplomats were going public with their anger, Kenya's reformers were stunned by the sudden resignation of John Githongo, the country's first-ever permanent secretary for governance and ethics, a Kibaki appointment which had delighted proponents of clean government. The one-time columnist for *The EastAfrican* and former head of Transparency International (TI) in Kenya had 'made powerful people very unhappy', said Gladwell Otieno, who succeeded Githongo at TI in Nairobi. 'He tried to break up networks which were plundering national coffers. This is not the sort of work that endears you to people in high places.' Githongo made his announcement in London where he fled after receiving death threats. He explained that senior government people told him to drop his probe into Anglo Leasing: 'I was told to leave this matter alone, let sleeping dogs lie, what I was doing was dangerous to my physical security.' Convinced he had found only the tip of an iceberg, Githongo retired to Oxford University and began compiling a massive dossier which he sent to Kibaki and to the Kenya Anti Corruption Commission in November 2005. When there was no response, he leaked the dossier to the *Nation* and declared, 'Anglo Leasing is real and not imagined. It is a fraudulent series of 18 contracts amounting to over 50 billion shillings that remain unresolved. It implicates the VP [Moody Awori] and other senior members of the government.' These included, importantly, the then finance minister, David Mwiraria, and former transport minister, Chris Murangaru. 'It is indisputable that on September 8, 2003, the VP approved the passport deal', declared Githongo. 'On October 2, 2003, Mr Mwiraria did the same.' Githongo said Murungi, then the minister for justice and constitutional affairs, told him profits would be used to fund the referendum and general election campaigns being managed by Mr Murangaru. He said he had informed Kibaki throughout of his findings. But the only action taken was to use public money to issue clearance statements. All the accused persons adamantly proclaimed their innocence.

Githongo said at one point in his investigations KACC chief Aaron Ringera told him there would be no Anglo Leasing prosecutions before the 2007 election, if ever. Kenyans were not surprised therefore when the KACC gazetted a notice in January 2007 saying it found no evidence of offences with regard to the Anglo Leasing contracts, and therefore recommended closure. Githongo recalled saying in an earlier interview, 'KANU handed us a skunk and we took it home as a pet. Not only did we assume the dubious transactions of the past, we used the same corrupt model to create our own shady deals. It is disingenuous to blame the person you took the skunk from for the fact that these days you smell.' In its annual survey, TI said the average city dweller in Kenya paid 17 bribes per month and named Kenya among the most corrupt countries in the world – 144th out of 159 nations. Uganda was ranked at 117 and Tanzania 88.

High corruption was certainly gnawing at society's underpinnings, but for the average Kenyan, poverty, crime and violence were the visible enemies. Simmering public anger exploded when MPs blocked the national

*John Githongo faces his problems.*

budget to force an increase in their travel allowances from KSh82 ($1.1) to KSh150 ($2.1) per kilometre, backdated ten months. This meant an MP could earn KSh850,000 ($12,000) per month in tax-free salary, with allowances, and the *Daily Nation* denounced the lawmakers' 'callous stance' as a 'total disgrace' at a time of famine and flooding. When, eight months later, Parliament moved to increase President Kibaki's salary from KSh700,000 ($9,900) to KSh3.2 million ($45,525) per month – more than the President of the USA – the outrage was such that Kibaki hurriedly declined the raise in favour of 'other priority projects'.

People seemed to be aggressive and resentful of each other. In one incident, four gangsters hijacked a truck that was distributing French beans to a market in Kirinyaga and drove off with KSh150,000 ($1,970). The vehicle stuck in the mud and the four men fled on foot with villagers in pursuit. After seven kilometres, the mob caught up with the robbers and slit their throats one by one. Said a police officer, 'They slaughtered them like goats.' Under death announcements, the *Daily Nation* published a photograph of a schoolboy and a notice from his family stating, 'We regret to announce the death of Daniel Njoroge Ngigi through brutal murder.' Who would murder a schoolboy? The same people who raped a toddler? Who stripped a woman on the street who dared to wear trousers? On the day the boy's murder was revealed, Kabete MP Paul Muite urged the government to 'accept that the current situation is a national emergency'. He was speaking at Kiambu where 16 people had been killed in a series of robberies and assaults. Nominated MP Ms Njoki Ndung'u referred to a police figure of 2,308 rapes in 2004, but claimed the true number was closer to 16,000. Introducing her Sexual Offences Bill in Parliament, she demanded chemical castration for repeat rapists. Khelef Khalifa, of the National Commission on Human Rights, charged that police were involved in as much as 75 per cent of crime, either by taking part, renting out their guns, doing reconnaissance for criminals or turning a blind eye. 'We all accept that the police force is the most corrupt institution in the country', he said.

Fears of insecurity stemming from the Twin Towers catastrophe in New York, and fuelled by sporadic terrorist incidents in Kenya, led to the IPI cancelling its annual world congress scheduled for Nairobi in 2004. Sensational as all this was, global terrorism, like high-level corruption, seemed remote from the average Kenyan, and a *Daily Nation* columnist commented, 'Kenyans have more to fear from local criminals than from the occasional terrorist.'

Three national issues on which Narc had promised decisive action were Ouko, Goldenberg and the constitution. Efforts to investigate the 1990 murder of the former foreign minister had proved inconclusive. Moi set up a Commission of Inquiry under the then Chief Justice, Evans Gicheru, but abruptly disbanded it a year later just before Hezekiah Oyugi, a former chief of internal security, was scheduled to give evidence. The separate investigation by British detective John Troon had concluded that Ouko had been murdered, and that Oyugi, who was in the minister's compound that night, and Biwott should be further questioned. When Kibaki's 15-member Parliamentary Select Committee began public hearings in December 2003, Moi and Biwott were summoned, but Moi refused to appear, sending a lawyer instead. Biwott did make an acrimonious appearance but refused to answer questions. The probe team travelled to London and held hearings at the Kenya High Commission, where Troon said Ouko was murdered because he was probably about to expose corruption by ministers, and his killers were paid KSh8 million ($105,000). He said Moi had blocked his efforts to interview Biwott. Fourteen people were named in the course of inquiries including Biwott and Saitoti. Ouko's brother, Eston Barrack Mbajah, gave evidence in Nairobi. He claimed that Moi offered him a post in the cabinet, money and houses if he would call for a halt to the investigations. When he refused, he was detained by police and tortured. He fled to the United States, only returning after Moi's government lost power.

On 12 May 2005, the parliamentary committee issued its findings. It recommended that ministers Biwott and Saitoti and a State House controller in the Moi years, Ibrahim Kiptanui, be investigated. 'The committee has considered carefully the adverse evidence against Hon Biwott and find he was involved either directly or indirectly in the disappearance and murder of Dr Ouko', the report said. It added, 'The committee is of the considered view that the misconstrued perception by the Kenyan leadership that Dr Ouko was seeking foreign support to accede to the presidency would be sufficiently supported as a motive to the cause of his death.' Several key witnesses in the investigations had died, some in mysterious circumstances, and the committee recommended that their bodies be exhumed to determine the causes of their deaths. The committee's recommendations were not implemented, Saitoti continued to serve in Kibaki's cabinet and no move was made against Biwott.

The Commission of Inquiry into the abuse of the government's export compensation scheme, the Goldenberg affair, heard evidence that the dubious foreign exchange transactions, made with the complicity of Central Bank officials, numbered in their thousands, while the Central Bank made multi-million dollar payments to private banks linked to Pattni or Goldenberg. The scam, which started with illegal export subsidies, later widened to involve foreign currency certificates, spot and forward contracts, cheque kiting and outright theft. The inquiry, headed by Judge Samuel Bosire, sat for 296 days at a cost of KSh400 million ($5.7 million). Its report on 3 February 2006 recommended that Saitoti should face 'appropriate criminal charges' and Moi should be further investigated because he could not have been 'completely unaware' of the fraud. The report declared Pattni 'the principal player' and said 'a lot of money was salted out of the country', and named 70 other people for further investigation. Saitoti resigned as education minister, but was reinstated by Kibaki after nine months when a constitutional court ruled that he could not be charged because he had simply followed accepted procedures. Twenty Kenyans were prohibited from leaving the country and ordered to surrender their weapons. They included Philip and Gideon Moi, Pattni, Saitoti and former High Central Bank and government officials. Moi, receiving famine relief food for his Kabarak area, said he knew nothing of the Goldenberg transactions. In March 2006, Pattni and six others appeared in court charged with plotting to steal from the Treasury and abuse of office. Attorney-General Wako recommended that the chief justice consider overturning Saitoti's exemption from prosecution, and other suspects claimed they should be allowed to go free on the same grounds. In a bizarre career, Pattni spent many periods in and out of prison, renounced Hinduism for Christianity and named himself Paul, and became chairman of the Kenya National Democratic Alliance, a political party.

The constitution proved by far the trickiest of Kibaki's promised reforms. His election pledge of a new document within 100 days of coming to power quickly began to look like a pipe dream, as inter-party and civil bickering began and the drafting process kept being postponed. A Constitutional Review Conference opened at the Bomas of Kenya conference centre in April 2003, but divisions over the proposal for a prime minister led to a stormy split between Odinga's Liberal Democratic Party (LDP) and the National Alliance of Kenya (NAK), threatening the ruling coalition. Eventually, some 629 impatient delegates hammered out what became known as the Bomas Draft, which provided for a reduction in the President's authority and the installation of an executive prime minister after the next election in 2007. The draft was passed in March 2004. But Kibaki's supporters wanted to keep a strong presidency and stormed out of the meeting, calling for a referendum on contentious issues. In July 2005, the Kibaki forces won a crucial vote in Parliament, giving them powers to alter the document. Attorney-General Amos Wako got to work and swiftly produced an amended version, the Wako Draft, which retained the premiership but with considerably diluted powers. The re-engineered constitution sparked riots in Nairobi and an organised opposition group emerged, including seven of Kibaki's own cabinet members. Led by Odinga and environment minister Kalonzo Musyoka, this faction joined with KANU under Uhuru Kenyatta, and some religious leaders and civil rights groups.

A referendum on the Wako Draft was announced for 21 November 2005. The No group campaigned under the symbol of the orange against Kibaki's Yes campaigners, represented by a banana. The contentious issues centred on executive authority and land reform. Many Kenyans, aware of the damage visited on their country by the imperial presidencies of Kenyatta and Moi, wanted to introduce a strong restraining figure as head of government, a prime minister with power to choose the cabinet. The Wako constitution continued the status quo, with a president as head of both state and government. The draft proposed a land commission to prevent officials from dishing out acreages to cronies, while also barring foreigners from owning land. It provided for redistribution of land in certain cases. This stirred anxiety among owners of large tracts, especially in the fertile Rift Valley, and among those Maasai people who received their land under colonial arrangements.

The 12-week referendum campaign cost nine lives in sporadic rioting and split the nation along tribal lines. The result was an emphatic rejection of the Wako draft: 57 per cent No against 43 per cent Yes. Six of the eight provinces rejected the constitution in a reflection of ethnic affiliations, with Odinga's Luo people and the Kalenjin overwhelmingly voting No, while Kibaki's Kikuyu community backed him with 92 per cent of the vote in Central Province. Many Kenyans saw the vote as a referendum on Kibaki's record in office and used the occasion to condemn him. Three years earlier, he had promised free primary education, an end to corruption and a new constitution, and had provided only one of the three. It was widely accepted that Odinga's support for Kibaki as coalition leader back in 2002 had been conditional upon his future appointment as an executive prime minister, and the failure of this development was seen, certainly by his own people, as a betrayal by Kibaki. Looking sombre in a television broadcast, Kibaki declared that 'my government will respect the will of the people'. But the vote was a huge personal and political setback, and in a move unprecedented in Kenya, Kibaki sacked his entire cabinet. In mid-2006, an investigating committee headed by career diplomat Bethuel Kiplagat reported that Kenyans still wanted a new constitution. But urgency dwindled as election fever began to grip.

The political parties moved to reinvent themselves, and individuals formed tactical alliances in a crowded field jostling for power. When Kibaki announced his new cabinet, it contained none of the leading politicians who stood against him on the constitution. Eleven of his new invitees promptly refused the offer of ministerial posts. With no Raila men aboard, the Rainbow coalition was pronounced dead. The opposition Orange Democratic Movement became the ODM-Kenya, and a new Narc emerged – Narc Kenya – which Kibaki supported at a distance and which quickly won three by-elections. Opinion polls reflected Kenyans' changing preferences. In April 2006, Kalonzo Musyoka was heavily favoured for president with 34 per cent of the vote, against 22 per cent for Kibaki and 15 per cent for Uhuru Kenyatta of KANU. The next month, a poll gave Musyoka 23 per cent, against 22 per cent for Kibaki and 17 per cent for Raila. However, by March 2007, according to a Steadman International survey, Kibaki's popularity had soared to 51 per cent, with Raila on 17 per cent and Musyoka on 14 per cent. A month later, the International Republican Institute produced a similar scenario: Kibaki 44.3 per cent, Odinga 18.7 per cent, Musyoka 15.3 per cent. Clearly the combined vote of oppositionists would seriously challenge Kibaki, but everything hinged on whether the opposition remained united behind one candidate or split in the traditional Kenya way.

Kibaki was widely attacked for the failures of his administration, but some commentators were more sympathetic. From Moi, said one, he had inherited dysfunctional institutions, a destroyed infrastructure and a severely compromised environment. The *Nation's* Onyango-Obbo, writing as a Ugandan, pointed out that Kenya was one of only two black African countries not to have political prisoners, while Kibaki had demystified the presidency, discouraged frequent political rallies and did not fix the referendum in his favour. The state of fear had gone, as witnessed by the refusal of ministers to join his cabinet, something unheard of under Moi.

Back at Nation Centre, NMG chief Kiboro faced a crowded agenda. The Aga Khan transferred his 23.9 million personal shares in the group, representing 44.73 per cent ownership, to the Aga Khan Fun for Economic Development (AKFED). This organisation, incorporated in Switzerland, was built on the idea of import substitution, then moved to exploiting natural resources and more recently infrastructural projects. AKFED had been restructured to include a division, Media Promotion Services, under which NMG would fall, with Lee Huebner, former publisher of the *International Herald Tribune* and an NMG board member, as Director of Media. The shares transfer worried some editors who feared a loss of independence and conflict with AKFED's commercial objectives. Would AKFED be involved in the running of the group, they asked, and how would the changeover affect them? Years after the transfer, most executives said their work had not been affected. Said Mwangi, 'The only thing I've noticed is their representatives' presence at the annual review meetings. There is no pressure.'

The decision to move under the AKFED umbrella was no whim. It stemmed from concerns about the long-term future of the group, eventually without the Aga Khan, and involved two years of consultations and consideration. The principal shareholder became convinced that the group's future would best be assured by institutionalising what was previously his personal investment. Industrial Promotion Services (whose subsidiary Industrial Promotion Building Ltd was a substantial investor in the Nation Centre) and AKFED were seen as structures within which NMG could safely flourish, assured of protection for its quality and integrity. AKFED works in partnership with international organisations and governments to stimulate the private sectors of developing economies. The aim is to build high-performing institutions and sustain long-lasting development initiatives. The Fund operates widely in Africa, Central Asia and South Asia, with footprints ranging from the Kyrgyz Republic and Tajikistan to Bangladesh, Mali and the East African nations. Sectors include financial services, industry, tourism and aviation. A decision was taken that NMG would fit snugly into a new media services division and, backed by other strong entities in the Fund, would share and benefit from their mutual experience.

A major challenge for Kiboro was to get Nation Broadcasting out of the red. The broadcasting division's loss at the end of October 2003 was KSh43 million ($565,000), but radio and television had been rolled out nationally during the year and received a favourable reception. A year later, things were better again, but the loss was still a hefty KSh22.5 million ($296,000) and long-standing problems clearly needed to be solved. A new man at the top took on the challenge – Ian Fernandes, born and raised in Kenya, with a degree in electronic engineering and IT from the University of Nairobi. Fernandes worked for the *Standard* for 11 years, first overseeing production of the newspaper and later also as managing director of KTN. There he took a company that was in receivership and turned it into the number one television station in the country. He thought he knew exactly where Nation TV was failing.

In an interview for this book, Fernandes said, 'Three things needed immediate attention – news, imagery and programming. In Kenya, news drives television. People see their politicians in the news and believe they can be their saviour. They rely on news – and on God – to help them through their woes.' Unhappy with the content, presentation and consistency of bulletins, Fernandes poached six top-line operatives from rival stations, news managers with good contacts and political insights, whose move not only boosted Nation TV but weakened its opponents. Crew assignments and briefings were improved, as was story packaging. Although news drove the industry, it was entertainment that occupied by far the greater part of the day, and, because the *Nation* was known as a serious newspaper, Fernandes felt this image undermined the lighter priorities of the television and radio services. He also did not like the TV logo, which contained a shield: 'The shield is for Europeans, we Kenyans do not need to be reminded that we are Africans.' Thirdly, programming at Nation TV had foundered following the departure of an acquisitions manager, and KTN swiftly stepped in and bought many hours of serials and features.

By now, television in Kenya was fully commercial and aggressively competitive, and the days of KBC domination were over. For years, the state-funded KBC was the only station with a national reach, officially an arm of development but effectively a propaganda tool of the government; it set the editorial agenda (leading every news bulletin with the activities of the President) and it determined the market rate for advertising. Once the other stations went national, however, KBC ran into trouble. The government promised to service its enormous debt but not its running costs; for day-to-day operations, it was on its own. But KTN was a major challenge and smaller new stations were making their presence felt. With at least 3 million television sets in Kenya and a technological revolution sweeping the world, Fernandes supervised digital updating – tape-cutting became a thing of the past – and a new world reach in programming. In Kenya, the viewer could switch through the channels and get just about everything that was available in the USA or UK, plus some channels that were not available on free-to-air stations there.

Figures for NMG's broadcast arms began to look healthier: NBD reported a 35 per cent increase in turnover for 2004 against 2003; TV advertising income for the first quarter of 2005 was 25 per cent better than the comparable period of 2004, and Nation FM grew its revenue by 17 per cent. Fernandes' concentration on the news product was rewarded by ratings putting Nation TV in top spot for both the 7 pm and 9 pm news bulletins. All this was encouraging, but Fernandes believed television and radio needed radical rebranding and plans for a relaunch were set in motion. In June 2005,

Nation TV changed its name to NTV, got rid of the shield and introduced new anchors and fresh news sets, and in August, Nation FM was relaunched as Easy FM. The results were impressive. NTV shot to the top of the rankings with a national viewership of 32 per cent, against KTN's 28 per cent and 16 per cent for KBC. With three English-language and one Kiswahili news bulletin per day, the news audience was the highest the station ever achieved. The new radio's listening figure rose to 16 per cent, second only to Kiss FM on 22 per cent. By November, both stations were recording all-time high revenue returns, with NTV doing KSh37 million ($486,000) for the month (previous high was KSh28 million, $368,000), and Easy FM bringing in KSh16.5 million ($217,000). NTV coverage of the constitution referendum was hailed as exceptional as the station stayed on air for 24-hour coverage of voting, analysis and results, the latter presented graphically by means of a virtual set. The *Financial Times* correspondent described the performance as 'comparable to any in the First World'.

Major problem areas for Kiboro lay with the newer acquisitions. In Dar es Salaam, Radio Uhuru was causing embarrassment on two fronts: it was losing KSh1 million ($13,000) per month and it remained associated in the minds of Tanzanians with the ruling CCM party. In a decisive move, Kiboro and the board discontinued broadcasts, retrenched staff and sold off equipment for $150,000, with the proviso that the station could be reactivated at a later date. The same perception, aided by the appointment of two local directors, was held in regard to *Mwananchi* newspapers, which were seen as a mouthpiece of the government. NMG, with its cherished tradition of independence, hoped to banish this perception with its new English-language newspaper, the *Citizen*. Unhappily, the first issue on 16 September 2004 front-paged a picture of the President with his message of welcome, and this served only to underline belief in a link to government. Senior editorial and management staff were parachuted in from Nairobi and Joachim Buwembo, the editor, was a Ugandan, causing resentment among patriotic Tanzanians. The handling of national politics became a minefield, and negative reporting on presidential candidate Salim Salim brought a libel suit and the removal of the managing editor. The paper was selling only 3,500 copies per day. It was fair to note, however, that in a Kiswahili-oriented market where educated journalistic talent was hard to find, the *Citizen* helped to raise the benchmark in other English-language papers, whose standards were embarrassingly low. Editorial executives were not alone in thinking that Tanzania's elevation of Kiswahili over English at the behest of its poet-President Julius Nyerere (who translated Shakespeare's *Julius*

*Caesar* into Swahili in his student days) was another retrograde result of the Arusha Declaration and an anachronism in the modern world.

In June 2005, the Tanzanian government peremptorily deported six seconded *Nation* Kenyans – four journalists including the editorial chief of the Tanzanian operation, Mutuma Mathiu, plus the advertising manager and an accountant – on grounds they were working without valid permits. The expulsions meant only four expatriates remained in the resource-needy company. In Nairobi, the assistant minister of foreign affairs, Moses Wetang'ula, said the Kenyans had been expelled because of business rivalry. But the belief in Dar es Salaam was that they were victims of Tanzanian internal politics connected to pressures over the Salim Salim affair. Painstakingly, the Nairobi executives worked to restructure, and by 2007 the chief executive was able to state cautiously that in Dar es Salaam, 'we are on the right track'.

Kiboro's problems in Uganda were twofold: knocking the company into shape and handling political issues. The latter were by far the trickier. The former Uganda country manager of *The EastAfrican*, Conrad Nkutu, was hired from the *Standard* to be managing director of MPL and management was restructured. Moved from his ill-fated editorship of *The Citizen*, Joachim Buwembo was appointed as managing editor, along with new sub-editors and reporters. The company moved all its operations into its own premises in the Namuwongo suburb of Kampala and the new press was installed and commissioned. Monitor FM was relaunched as KFM and swiftly gained new popularity. As for overall performance, the company reported a loss of KSh10 million ($131,000) to the board's December 2004 meeting, but, having divested itself of peripheral loss-makers, MPL was moving in the right direction. If it wasn't for the politics…

The star of Ugandan print and radio journalism was the *Monitor's* political editor, Andrew Mwenda, 33, a blazing mixture of energy, erudition, stubbornness and bravery verging on foolhardiness. 'I would rather live on my feet in jail than on my knees out of it', he once said, a preference which President Museveni showed every sign of accommodating. On 10 August 2005, on his KFM show *Andrew Mwenda Live*, Mwenda suggested that Museveni's government deserved blame for the 30 July death of Sudanese Vice-President John Garang in a helicopter crash after leaving Uganda. They should not have let him take off at dusk in bad weather to fly over rebel territory, he said. The radio station was closed and Mwenda was arrested and charged with sedition. 'He must stop completely', said a furious Museveni.[5] In court, Mwenda said, 'I don't plead guilty to the offence. I was exercising my right to liberty and freedom of speech guaranteed by the constitution.' He was freed on bail of $500,000, but was soon in trouble again.

On 13 November, Mwenda wrote a story in the *Sunday Monitor* which said Museveni had offered the post of Chief of Defence Forces to his brother Major General Salim Saleh, but he declined and another officer was appointed. This was an innocuous story but the government reacted angrily, demanding a retraction and apology. The newspaper published the state's rebuttal in full, but Museveni turned the dispute into a crisis by declaring he would close the *Monitor* unless it sacked Mwenda. The reporter shared his sources with the NMG editorial committee and convinced the members of their veracity. They took the view that to buckle under to government pressure would render the newspaper defenceless against future demands. In an internal memorandum, Kiboro wrote, 'We cannot find any justification to terminate the services of an employee for telling the truth... Mr Mwenda's only crime appears to be publishing a story that has upset the President and the army ... if we were to give in to the government's demands, we would irredeemably lose our credibility in the marketplace and long term this would render us irrelevant.' The matter went to court but was suspended pending a ruling on the constitutionality of the charges. *Monitor* lawyers argued that as a result of a Constitutional Court ruling in Mwenda's and Onyango's 1997 case, journalists in Uganda could not be accused of printing 'false news'. Mwenda travelled to the USA for study.

The problems did not end there. After a long and painful struggle for a licence, NTV Uganda started television broadcasts on 18 December 2006, offering a new choice of documentaries and news bulletins in Luganda and English. The $4 million station was the most advanced in East Africa. Five weeks later, the channel was shut down by the Uganda Broadcasting Council, charging technical infractions. Three months and three days after the switch-off, on 30 April 2007, NTV Uganda returned to air following a Memorandum of Understanding that 'technical issues which resulted in its closure will be resolved amicably in a specified period'.

With 15 media products under its wing, NMG's market value in 2005 stood at some KSh13 billion ($171 million), and the group ranked sixth on the Nairobi Stock Exchange. Sales for 2004 were up 9 per cent on 2003 to KSh4.9 billion ($64 million) and the profit figure rose 6 per cent to KSh641 million ($8.4 million). The magazines arm, EA Magazines Ltd, was incorporated as a joint venture with Media 24 of South Africa, publishing *Drum* and *True Love*, NMG had bought the *Weekly Review* title for future revival.

NBD revenue increased by 35 per cent, and Nation Carriers brought in an extra 27 per cent and extended its operations to Tanzania. *Coast Express* was folded, *Taifa Leo* was redesigned and *The EastAfrican*, which had lost both sales and advertising, was relaunched. Chairman Awori outlined group strategy at the 26 May 2005 annual general meeting: 'To consolidate in East Africa and establish a firm foundation to pursue other opportunities beyond our current area of operations.' With a range of products, both print and electronic, growing numerically and geographically, there was clearly a need to review editorial structures and resources, as well as newsroom morale.

The Tanzanian nightmare had shown what could happen when lines of communication to the top were unclear and an editorial chief was expected to fulfil both a hands-on and an overseeing role. Wangethi Mwangi was a consummate journalist, but running everything from *True Love* to *Taifa Leo*, whilst acquainting himself with broadcast media and addressing news problems in two other countries, was not a practicable proposition. Accordingly, Mwangi was named to the new post of editorial director of NMG, with Joseph Odindo as group managing editor, and individual managing editors appointed or confirmed for the various newspapers. Eventually, the thinking was, a GME would be appointed in each country. Mwangi welcomed the changes: 'I no longer had to worry about missing commas or bad headlines. I had time talk to editors across the region, to sit with Odindo and work out policy guidelines, to talk with the television people and to read all the papers. It has given me time to operate more effectively in a wider field of play.' Mwangi brought new energies to bear on *The EastAfrican*, which seemed to have lost focus, with circulation dwindling to less than 19,000, and the *Sunday Nation*, which he believed should reflect its own personality and not sell simply as a seventh-day replica of the daily. He was also keen, as was Circulation Manager Neema Wamai, to have another try at a regional paper, applying lessons learned by the failure of *Coast Express*. She said, 'The need is there but it is a long-term investment and we have to wait for payback. Even if a regional paper cut into the sales of the daily, the money would still be going into our pocket. If somebody else does that paper, we lose.'

To secure his ambitions, Mwangi needed a stable and loyal staff; and here there was a problem. As *Nation* MD Dennis Aluanga explained, 'For years, journalists in Kenya had only two real options, the *Nation* or the *Standard*, but then public relations exploded in this country and our people left in droves to become PR and media communications managers. This was hardly surprising, since we paid very poorly compared to other professions yet demanded the highest qualifications – at least a degree.' Other journalists joined the opposition when offered an attractive job title, along with a little more money. Said Mwangi, 'We realised we were under-compensating our people, so we went to the board and made a strong case and a salary review for the whole company was put in place. We ended up spending an extra Sh80 million [$1.05 million] to raise salaries to a proper level.' Average monthly pay for reporters and sub-editors shot up to KSh62,500 ($820), which compared to KSh55,000 ($720) for a company accountant and KSh41,500 ($545) for an accounts assistant. Some lower-paid workers found their wages doubled; higher up, the increases were around 40–50 per cent. It worked. The group's labour turnover figure of 6 per cent in 2003 dropped to under 1 per cent, and Mwangi said, 'We began luring back some of our valued defectors.' What's more, a policy was adopted of an annual pay review.

The thinking behind the group's diversify-and-spread strategy was well grounded: worldwide, people were losing the newspaper-reading habit and Kenya was no exception; if the print bedrock of the group was threatened, action must be taken to build in new areas. Neema Wamai gave an example: 'Nestlé are a Swiss company with a small home market, but they are one of the biggest companies in the world because they realised that if they stayed within their market, they would only go so far. Here, our papers have 70 per cent market share so the only way we will grow substantially is by getting out and diversifying.' But as Ian Fernandes had already found in television, incomers invariably had problems with local cultures. Said Wamai, 'The South Africans made that mistake when they rushed into Kenya to invest. They set up everything the way they would back home and two years down the line, they wonder why they failed. One of the reasons we have struggled in Tanzania and Uganda is that transplanting the Kenya way does not work. Imagine how much harder this will be if we move into other countries, say the Francophone ones. We don't even speak their language.'

The dream of a footprint elsewhere in Africa was not a new one for the *Nation*. Back in its earliest days, the Aga Khan spoke of flying papers to the Congo, Burundi, Rwanda and Central Africa. Even after the painful retrenchment from Tanzania and Uganda in 1963, he held to the conviction that his company had a future far beyond its borders. In 1967, when the *Daily Nation* was seven years old and still selling barely 30,000 copies, he wrote to an aide, 'I am convinced that in the years ahead, we are going to have to expand our operations in Africa, either printing in Ethiopia or Zambia or sending our papers there.' Nearly four decades later, greater

Africa was back on the agenda, still an enticing prospect. Said Aluanga, 'We have to take a position as the most authoritative media about Africa. This means we have to operate physically outside of our current areas. We must carve out a niche as experts on Africa. We have the commitment and the ongoing interest which other large groups like CNN and South African-based, non-African publishers do not.' The spearhead of attack probably would be newspapers rather than television, and the target areas would be English-speaking countries ahead of Francophone and Portuguese-interest areas. Money was available to finance new ventures; the problem was people. A business development unit was set up and began researching prospects across Africa.

Becoming 'the media of Africa for Africa', a phrase now much heard at Nation Centre, implied the provision of serious journalism at the highest level of performance by experts in their field. A School of Journalism and Media Studies of the Aga Khan University (AKU) to be established in East Africa would provide the necessary academic capacity; stories on topics such as health, the economy, religion and government would be written, not by generalists but by specialists, and would focus not on personalities but issues. AKU, occupying a pivotal place within the Aga Khan Development Network, was chartered in 1983 as Pakistan's first private university. Already, it offered outreach programmes in East Africa and London, with base institutions in Karachi of a medical college, school of nursing, a teaching hospital and an institute for educational development. The university operated on a non-denominational basis and boasted a 44 per cent faculty apportionment to women. The Aga Khan's interests in media, education and development coalesced with his commissioning in 2007 of a study for a journalism faculty, with special focus on the developing world. In 2008, the University trustees accepted recommendations by a Thinking Group for, initially, a master's degree programme in journalism, to be followed by more academic media arts, management and entrepreneurship courses. Based initially in Nairobi to benefit from the presence of the Nation group, the School would serve the broad arc of countries around the Indian Ocean; its eventual base would be Arusha, Tanzania, co-located with the Faculty of Arts and Sciences and other graduate professional schools. The creation of a high-profile intellectual forum to lead research on media issues through the Internet was a central plank of the plan. An AKU statement said it was 'concern for the absence of strong, self-reliant, media-related cultures in much of the developing world' that animated discussions: 'The entire project was inspired by a confidence that, through the education of a professional cadre of able and responsible media leaders, such a programme could have a significant impact on social progress in the developing world.'[6]

Kiboro saw the need for expansion: 'Our shareholders are keen that NMG should become a significant player on the African continent. We see the group as being among the top five media companies in Africa and we cannot do that by staying in this region.' He recalled:

> *We started having strategy meetings ten years ago and I was looking at the minutes of one we had at the Mount Kenya Safari Club. We said then we would like to be a Sh5 billion-turnover company with a billion shillings on the bottom line. It seemed like a dream because our turnover was hardly a billion. Now that has happened and those figures have been achieved. We said at the time we wanted to be a multi-media company but we were not even in radio and television then and we did not truly understand the implications. Now we really are an international organisation with a very strong presence in the region and ambitions beyond.*

As for the future, Kiboro saw it like this: 'The Nation Media Group in the next 10 to 15 years will not resemble anything like we are today but will be a truly multinational organisation working in many countries in Africa and not only across various media platforms but in other areas we have not even imagined.'

In November 2006, after 11 years as Chief Executive Officer, Kiboro retired and was succeeded by Linus W. Gitahi, 44, who joined from GlaxoSmithKline. Six months later, Hannington Awori retired after seven years as group chairman and 18 years on the board. Financially, the recent years were particularly successful as the company's market capitalisation increased five-fold to KSh17.2 billion ($257 million). In the five years to 2006, revenues increased from KSh3.5 billion ($49.9 million) to KSh6.3 billion ($85 million) and pre-tax profits breached KSh1 billion ($14 million) for the first time. The broadcast division was finally adding to the bottom line, growing its revenue by 35 per cent in 2006–7, the website counted a record 5.4 million hits during the referendum campaign, and even Tanzania had good news with Mwananchi Communications revenues doubled and losses halved. CEO Gitahi, addressing his first investors' meeting, noted that a new venture had been launched, *Business Daily*, while the flagship papers enjoyed 75 per cent of market share: 'The company will now look to duplicate this success across Africa with its vision to be the media of Africa for Africa.'

## *Notes*

1.  By the end of 2002, Uganda had 62 radio stations, 23 of them in Kampala.
2.  In his biography, *The Mediator*, published in 2006, the Army commander at the time, Lt. Gen. Lazaro Sumbeiywo, revealed that terrified officials of the Ministry of Public Works refused to assist with the handover ceremony, fearing reprisals if KANU retained power. The military took charge and hired a private contractor to build the ramp needed to wheel Kibaki onto the stage.
3.  One who narrowly escaped death at Nyayo House was the Kenya-born international civil servant Salim Lone, who became head of communications for the United Nations in New York. Falling foul of Moi, Lone was stripped of his nationality and fled Kenya in 1983. He returned in the 1990s, but was arrested and led to the roof of Nyayo House. He was only rescued when UN officials were tipped off by his two teenage sons who had been left unsupervised in his hotel.
4.  The reforms did not last. Three years later, *Nation* writer Peter Kimani spent a day travelling by *matatu* and reported that seat belts were not being used, crews were not in uniform, drivers were speeding, the vehicles were overcrowded, and few carried the yellow strip and destinations. Road deaths which had dropped by 25 per cent to 2,250 were back to 3,000 a year, or 30 a day.
5.  An element of lese *majeste* in Mwenda's programme probably angered the President as much as it tickled listeners. After playing an excerpt from remarks by Museveni ('I have seen this young boy, Mwenda … he must stop … these newspapers must stop … I am the elected leader of Uganda and have the ultimate mandate to run its affairs'), Mwenda shot back: 'If he closes the news paper and I am out of a job, I will seek his job.'
6.  At its widest remit, the AKU Media School would seek to raise ethical, management and journalistic standards in East Africa and beyond, educating not only journalists but the totality of the industry, owners included. These other aims were set forth: to address the needs of the overwhelmingly rural sectors of developing countries, harnessing appropriate technologies to reach far-flung populations; to embrace the duty of social responsibility and play a national role in preventing conflict and in developing democracy; to establish close links with Nation Newspapers and thus assist students to develop the skills and integrity crucial in their profession.

# CHAPTER 12 | Torn by Violence

*The love of liberty is the love of others; the love of power is the love of ourselves.*

William Hazlitt, English essayist, 1778–1830

Horse-trading in the run-up to the general election of 27 December 2007 brought a line-up of three principal candidates for President: Mwai Kibaki, Raila Odinga and Kalonzo Musyoka; and two dominant parties: Kibaki's Party of National Unity (PNU) and Odinga's Orange Democratic Movement (ODM). In ethnic terms, frankly unavoidable in any consideration of Kenyan politics, the Kikuyu, Embu and Meru backed the PNU, while the ODM gained total support from Odinga's Luos, as well as Moi's Kalenjin community and some Luhyas.[1] The campaign period was peaceful by Kenyan standards, but the nomination process was marred by widespread clashes, accusations of fraud and logistical problems. 'This year's nominations must rank among the worst ever', the *Nation* thundered. 'We witnessed dishonesty, fraud, open rigging, outright theft and utter incompetence.'

The national economy was doing well, regularly posting growth rates of more than 6 per cent, but the poorest Kenyans continued to struggle on a dollar a day and opinion polls began to reflect a consistent, if narrow, preference for Odinga over Kibaki, with Musyoka a distant third. Odinga's supporters charged Kibaki with betraying his Inauguration Day promise that 'corruption will now cease to be a way of life in Kenya'. A report by the BBC said, 'Despite President Kibaki's pledge to tackle corruption, some donors estimated that up to $1 billion had been lost to graft between 2002 and 2005.' Kibaki was further accused of failing to provide the 500,000 jobs he had promised and of breaking a pledge to offer Odinga the post of prime minister. Kibaki's men countered by pointing to a surging GDP, country-wide stability and unprecedented freedom of speech and the Press.

Twenty-four hours after the polls closed, it was clear Kibaki's men were in trouble, with voters throwing out more than half of the 32-member cabinet, including such heavyweights as Vice-President Moody Awori, Mutahi Kagwe, Njenga Karume, David Mwiraria and Simeon Nyachae, as well as the 'Total Man' Nicholas Biwott. Three sons of ex-President Moi – Gideon, Jonathan and Raymond – all failed to win in the Rift Valley. This was significant for two reasons: Moi's word had been law in the province for years; and he had thrown in his lot with the PNU. The ODM was outpolling the PNU two-to-one for Parliament and in the presidential race in early returns, and, with more than half the ballots counted, Kibaki trailed Odinga by 700,000 votes. Many felt this was a margin that was impossible to make up, though several heavily populated constituencies had not reported at this time. Then came a series of unexplained delays that sent tensions soaring across the country. With almost 90 per cent of the votes counted, officials suddenly declared that Odinga's lead was down to 38,000 votes, an announcement that triggered frenzied claims by Kibaki's opponents that the election was being rigged right there and then. On 30 December 2007, Electoral Commission chairman Samuel Kivuitu appeared at the heavily-guarded

*The almost permanently disunited opposition.*

Kenyatta International Conference Centre in Nairobi to announce the final result. In a brawling atmosphere of hysteria and panic, Kivuitu's words were shouted down by ODM activists and riot police took him under their protection. Protesting journalists and observers were pushed outside, and Kivuitu, speaking only to the state broadcaster, KBC, announced the official final tally. Kibaki, he said, had polled 4,584,721 votes to Odinga's 4,352,993, with Musyoka polling 879,903. Kibaki was sworn in as president so hurriedly that there was no band to play the National Anthem and no foreign diplomats were present.

What ensued was the gravest humanitarian, political and economic crisis in the country's post-independence history, involving violence such as Kenyans had never known and which most did not believe possible. It caused an estimated 1,200 deaths, the displacement of anything between 350,000 and 600,000 people, with about 6,000 ending up as refugees in neighbouring Uganda. One business leader estimated damage to the economy would total $3.6 billion when all the bills were in. The violence came in three waves. Even before Kivuitu's announcement, rioting flared in Odinga's strongholds in Western Kenya and in poor areas of Nairobi and Mombasa, when furious Luos became convinced they were being cheated of power. Quickly, an ethnic factor became evident, and smoke and flames billowed from Kikuyu homes and businesses torched by rampaging mobs in the Rift Valley and Nairobi's notorious Kibera slum, located in Odinga's parliamentary constituency. Finally, came reprisal attacks against non-Kikuyus in parts of Rift Valley, Central Kenya and Nairobi, and suddenly there were camps of displaced people in places like Limuru and the capital. Although triggered directly by politics, the clashes exposed long-simmering anger over power, land and the distribution of wealth. The depth of the fury was illustrated by the burning alive of some 30 people, many of them children, in the mud-and-wattle Kenya Assemblies of God church in Kiamba, just outside of Eldoret.

The *Sunday Monitor* of Uganda told the story in a vivid interview with one of the survivors, Mrs Lucy Wangui, a refugee in a border camp at Malaba, Uganda. 'There were rumours all over that should Kibaki win, the Kikuyu would not sleep in their houses', she said. 'On December 31, we got information that we were to be targets of a Kalenjin militia and we decided that the Kikuyu men should defend us while we women and children would lock ourselves in the church. We were about 150 and we believed they would respect a church.' The assault came at 8 am on New Year's Day 2008 from a force of men with pangas and bows and arrows, who far outnumbered the

Kikuyu defenders. 'There were many many attackers and I peeped through a crack and saw them overpower and kill our husbands', Mrs Wangui said. 'Then they came with petrol in cans and poured it all round the church and the little ones started collapsing because of the smoke.' Other reports said the besiegers stuffed gasoline-soaked mattresses and dried maize stalks through the windows, and one woman said when a child escaped, she saw an attacker pick him up and throw him back into the flames. This may have been an accurate observation or a distorted version of an incident reported by Samuel Mwangi, who rushed to the church to try to protect it. He told Reuters he saw a woman break out of the church with a baby tied to her back, but the wrap holding the baby caught fire and the child fell back into the flames. 'The mother ran away with her hair burning, she was screaming', Mwangi said.

Mrs Wangui said she owed her life to a man she thinks was a Kalenjin married to a Kikuyu woman, who opened an exit from the church: 'People were choking with the smoke when the door was opened. It was too small for all of us but I struggled through, gripping the hands of my two children, and we started to flee. It was then I saw a man running with an arrow sticking out of his back and I realised it was my husband, Joseph. He fell down and three men chasing him chopped him into pieces.' That night Mrs Wangui and her children were taken in and hidden by a non-Kikuyu friend. When the violence died down, she returned to the burnt-out church and found and buried her husband. Then the fatherless family boarded a truck to Malaba, joining 2,000 other displaced persons.

The church burning, reflecting the worst horrors of the Rwandan genocide, made front-page news across the world, but it was not the only incident of its type. In Naivasha on 24 January, a marauding gang proclaiming allegiance to the PNU torched a house on the Kabati estate with 14 people inside. A police spokesman said, 'It appears the attackers locked them in and set them ablaze.' Odinga denounced 'a murderous, evil act'. On the Nairobi highway into Naivasha, one man, apparently a Luo, was pulled out of a *matatu* bound for Western Kenya and clubbed to death. In the town itself gangs fought running battles. A reporter counted ten bodies (six burned and four hacked to death), an Internet cafe looted and burned, and computers thrown into the street; 300 terrified locals camped at a police station and a prison. In Kisumu, police said a mob blocked the highway and attempted to set ablaze 47 oil tankers destined for Uganda. When a *Nation* reporter visited the Nyanza Provincial General Hospital, he counted 19 bodies on the floor, all with gunshot wounds, indicating they were shot by police, since the gangs generally did not have firearms. After three weeks of violence, police said 510 people had died, of whom 356, or 70 per cent, were in the Rift Valley, and 621 properties were destroyed. Fifty-four people died in Western province, 51 in Nairobi, 39 in Nyanza and ten at the Coast. Eighty-seven were killed 'during police intervention but not necessarily shot by police', a spokesman said. Blood-soaked January saw the murders of three famous athletes and three politicians. Lucas Sang, a Kalenjin Olympic runner, was stoned to death near Eldoret after being mistaken for a Kikuyu, marathoner Wesley Ngetich Kimutai was shot with an arrow in Trans Mara District, and former basketball international Donald Odanga was hit by a stray police bullet. An independent councillor, G.G. Njuguna Ngengi, was hacked to death at Kuresoi while trying to broker a peace agreement, and two newly elected ODM MPs lost their lives – Malitus 'Mugabe' Were, shot dead on his driveway in Nairobi, and David Kimutai Too, shot by a police-man in Eldoret.

For days, angry Kenyans looted and burned, and television crews from round the world hastened to observe the descent into murderous mayhem of a country hitherto regarded as a rare rock of stability in turbulent Africa. Alarmed by vivid daily film of the violence, the government abruptly imposed a ban on live broadcasting. This order was respected only in part, but fuelled public suspicions that the local media were blacking out stories. No such restrictions affected foreign journalists, and Canadian TV reporter Arno Kopecky reported from the riot-torn Nairobi slums of Mathare and Kibera: 'Politics fly out of the window and a delighted sort of rage takes over.' In chaotic and lawless conditions, there was hyperbole, too, as some reporters sought sensationalism over balance. Perhaps it was too dull to report that not all the expected trouble spots exploded. Parts even of volatile Kibera did not witness a rock being thrown, and most of the Mathare and Kawangware slums were peaceful. Many stories emerged later of city slum-dwellers and Rift Valley residents hiding neighbours and fugi-tives. However, where it erupted, violence was pitiless. In Kibera, for instance, a petrol station belonging to a nationally known rally driver, Patrick Njiru, exploded in an enormous fireball, and young men and women sharpened their pangas on the gravel and chanted 'No Raila, no peace'. Angry children, many of them drunk, surrounded journalists, spit-ting and shouting 'Tell them'. Outside the deserted city centre, young men climbed up billboards and ripped down Odinga posters. Reporters who flew by helicopter over the Rift Valley saw roadblocks every few hundred yards manned by youths with rocks and crude weapons – 30 checkpoints were spotted on the 30-kilometre stretch between Burnt Forest and Eldoret; smoke rose from burning fields and homesteads, and the lush countryside was spotted with what looked like dark shadows – in fact, the ashes of hundreds of torched houses; in some places every home was burned, while a neighbouring area remained untouched. A Red Cross official said, 'Our 48 branches put contingency plans in place but no-one imagined the worst-case scenario we have now.' He said in some areas even Red Cross workers with emblems on their jackets were challenged to declare their ethnicity. At the stock exchange in Nairobi, share prices plummeted and tea and coffee auctions were postponed. The capital emptied by 8 pm and, without vendors or buyers and with the roads out of Nairobi closed, the *Daily Nation* printed under 100,000 copies per day. Food and fuel prices shot up, and fear-filled families fled to secure areas or across the borders into Uganda and Tanzania. 'It is unbelievable this is happening in Kenya', said Eva Mwai, chief executive of the national St John Ambulance, helping coordinate food distribution to displaced persons at the international trade fair grounds in Nairobi. 'What hurts me is that the politicians have food, security and money while the common people are suffering.' Declared the *Daily Nation* desperately, 'This madness cannot be allowed to go on.'

In fact, peace moves were afoot. In a joint statement, British Foreign Minister David Miliband and US Secretary of State Condoleezza Rice called for the cessation of violence and 'an intensive political and legal process' to end the crisis. African Union chairman John Kufuor of Ghana arrived to mediate, but the Kenyan protagonists took a hard line. Odinga declared he would not negotiate with Kibaki unless he resigned, while the PNU declared the crisis was merely a local problem and they could handle it. International pressure was building, however, and US Assistant Secretary of State Jendayi Frazer flew in. On 5 January, she made it known that Kibaki was willing to form a government of national unity, but three days later, fresh anger erupted when Kibaki announced a partial cabinet of 17 ministers, with failed presidential candidate Kalonzo Musyoka as Vice-President. The *Nation* said Kibaki's move would be seen as 'a sign of bad faith' and that it could 'poison the atmosphere'. The USA 'expressed its displeasure'. Parliament opened with the ODM taking the opposition benches – despite a threat to sit on the government side – and Odinga in the seat of leader of the opposition. Street violence continued in many areas and 22 people were reported killed in a three-day ODM protest ending on 18 January. In Kibera, a train was looted by hungry slum-dwellers. The main hope for peace, the former UN secretary-general Kofi Annan, arrived on 22 January and took over negotiations from Kufuor. Two days later, with the ex-UN chief in the chair, Kibaki and Odinga met and shook hands publicly for the first time since the election. Annan called the meeting 'very encouraging' and 'the first step toward a peaceful solution'.

But the country was still a tinderbox ready to blaze at any ill-judged move and, when MP Melitus Were was shot dead by a policeman on an Eldoret street, violence erupted again. Annan called for an end to 'the downward spiral into chaos'. Preparatory talks between designated negotiators began on 29 January and on 1 February, Annan announced that the two sides had agreed on an agenda for formal discussions to target violence, humanitarian distress, the political crisis and historical injustices, including land. Touted avenues of reform included a new election, power-sharing in an interim government, root-and-branch reform of the constitution and the electoral process, and a public inquiry into the conduct of the election. However, the negotiations stuttered as two deeply suspicious parties postured and shadow-boxed for advantage. Above all loomed the question of responsibility and, by inference, impunity: To what extent were the outbreaks spontaneous and how far were they planned? And if they were planned, who planned them and how should the perpetrators be dealt with? Furthermore, was the violence fuelled by a preliminary hate campaign? In a decisive move, the government set up two judicial commissions: one led by retired South African judge Johann Kriegler, to investigate the electoral process, the other chaired by Kenyan judge Philip Waki, to inquire into the post-election violence.

Waki's team considered claims such as those made to the Associated Press in January by human rights official Muthoni Wanyeki that much of the violence was the work of militias paid by politicians. 'Our investigations indicate [the violence] seems to be organised militia activity, directed and well-organised', she told the AP. Attackers, she claimed, were paid KSh500 ($7) for a burning and KSh1,000 ($15) for a death: 'Training areas have been identified and some of the people from whom they get money have been identified.' Odinga's spokesman, Salim Lone, said the charges of payment were 'wild propaganda', but added, 'I cannot categorically say that no politician is doing that [paying militias].' The BBC claimed government officials met with members of Mungiki, a feared Kikuyu organisation of thugs and gangsters, at State House and instructed them to cause mayhem in Nakuru and Naivasha, while ordering police to stand aside. Government spokesman Alfred Mutua denounced the report as 'preposterous, baseless and unfounded lies'. The New York-based Human Rights Watch reported that attacks on Kikuyus were organised by local leaders, as were reprisals by

Kikuyus. A report, *Ballots to Bullets*, based on the testimonies of about 200 witnesses, quoted a Kalenjin leader: '[The elders] said that if there is any sign that Kibaki is winning, then the war should break. They were coaching the young people how to go on the war.' Delays in the counting of votes and rigging rumours sparked the first attacks against Kikuyus. But Human Rights Watch found no evidence directly implicating the top ODM leadership. The report also quoted a young Kikuyu involved in reprisal attacks against Luos in Naivasha as saying, 'This was not done by ordinary citizens, it was arranged by people with money, they bought the jobless like me. We need something to eat.' According to witnesses claiming affiliation to Mungiki, local businessmen and politicians met at a Nakuru hotel on 24 January, after which the previously quiet town was hit by violence.

Stoking the election temperature were posters, leaflets, e-mails and mobile phone messages, such as an anonymous text circulated widely in mid-January which called on Kikuyus to list the names and addresses of Luos and Kalenjins, and the location of their children's schools. The *Daily Nation* reported that the severed hand of a man who had been murdered near Mombasa was found grasping a message ordering two communities to vacate the region. Also spotted on the Internet was a document, dated 8 September 2007, purporting to be from high ODM officials setting out election strategy, and referring to an anti-Kikuyu crusade and a strategy for violence. This eight-page document was known to the mainstream media but never apparently used.[2] Most strident of all were statements and songs broadcast on vernacular radio stations. The role of Kigali's Radio–Television Libre des Mille Collines in inciting people to slaughter their neighbours was reflected in language that was sometimes subtle and obscure, other times blatantly provocative. 'Vernacular radio stations played a role in the escalation of violence', said Caesar Handa, chief executive of Strategic Research, whose company was contracted by the United Nations to monitor the run-up to the election. 'There was a lot of hate speech, sometimes thinly veiled – the vernacular stations have perfected the art.' Handa singled out stations whose call-in shows included references to the need for 'people of the milk' (pastorialists) to 'get rid of weeds' (groups seen as settlers). Other broadcasters played songs about beasts from the West (of Kenya), while others sang about the leadership of baboons.

Politicians, though slow to rein in their own foot soldiers, were quick to load blame onto the broadcasters. 'The violence after the announcement of the polls was due to polarity in the media, especially the vernacular media which were turned into political tools', charged Information Minister Samuel Poghisio. The government seized the opportunity to announce a formal review of the media's performance, a move that was fiercely resisted by the independent regulatory authority the – Media Council of Kenya. In an article in the *Nation*, chairman Wachira Waruru pointed out that the Council was already auditing the media's conduct as required by its duty to promote professional standards. What's more, it needed no lessons in conduct from a government which had raided a publishing house, imposed an illegal ban on live broadcasting and threatened to disband the Media Council because of its independent stance, he said. The BBC World Service Trust argued that the performance of the local stations was the product of a chaotic regulatory policy and the lack of training, especially of talk-show hosts. Most of the stations were set up as commercial entertainment vehicles and struggled to mediate complex and angry debates, it said.

The Kenya National Commission on Human Rights (KNCHR) expressed concern about pre-election rhetoric by some politicians, including Mutahi Kagwe, who, it said, had compared Odinga to Idi Amin and Hitler. The rights group recalled that it tried to sue MPs for using hate speech at the time of the 2005 referendum, but the attorney-general terminated the case. And before the election, MPs rejected legislation to incriminate hate speech on grounds it would curtail their freedom of expression. KNCHR argued that 'when action is not taken against people who openly make statements which are inflammatory, they will keep doing it', creating a culture of impunity. It was just this question, crime and punishment, that was to cast a baleful shadow over the future of the nation.

When full-scale peace talks started in Nairobi, the *Nation* declared that mediation must succeed 'because the result of failure would be too terrible to contemplate'. Kibaki and Odinga 'must recognise that they are making a decision not on who gets to enjoy the trappings of power but on the survival of Kenya'. It was now starkly clear that the only way Kenya could realistically be governed, given its inescapable ethnic divisions, was by sharing power. 'First past the post', whereby communities accessed the fruits of office on a turn-by-turn basis, implied a willingness by the leading party to hand over the spoils upon electoral defeat – a surrender most Kenya's politicians proved incapable of making. Thus some form of coalition was the fundamental requirement of the negotiations. Such was the fury over the election, however, that the question of electoral fraud demanded priority attention. Many thousands of Kenyans still burned with resentment, believing they had been cheated of victory. Because the presidential result gave Kibaki a tiny margin of 230,000 votes out of a total 10 million, any malpractices could easily have changed the outcome. Opposition suspicions were supported by a wide range of domestic and international observers who questioned why results were delayed for more than a day at a time when Odinga was leading, why thousands seemed to have voted in the presidential poll but not for an MP, and why some results were different when announced nationally to when they were released locally. PNU officials adhered to the line that if there were discrepancies they were the result of inefficiency not fraud.

Ms Koki Muli, head of the Institute for Education and Democracy, said in some areas there were as many as 50,000 more votes in the presidential ballot than in the parliamentary one. 'People vote for their local man', she said, 'they don't just turn up and vote only for the president'. The European Union observer mission reported 'serious inconsistencies' and inflated national results. ECK chief Kivuitu came in for relentless criticism. He admitted there had been 'some problems' in the vote counting, noting that in one constituency the turnout was 115 per cent. Later, astonishingly, he conceded he had been pressured into declaring Kibaki the winner and was not sure who really won. Four commissioners said they were told to inflate numbers. Writing in the *Nation*, High Court advocate Donald B. Kipkorir declared that Kivuitu 'deliberately misled the world and subverted the law', and should undo his mistakes by retracting the result and ordering a recount. The irony here is that Kivuitu had been trusted and liked by journalists and by independent bodies, who had canvassed strongly for his reappointment as chairman in good time for the election – a move Kibaki acceded to only on 12 November. This followed the President's unilateral appointment of five new commissioners, a move oppositionists said infringed the 1997 Inter-Parties Parliamentary Group (IPPG) agreement that they be consulted on such appointments. There was dismay and puzzlement that the hitherto independent Kivuitu appeared weak and indecisive at a crucial juncture. What angered the losers even more was the government's bland assertion that election disputes should be referred to the courts in the normal way. With the independence of the judiciary in serious doubt, no opposition activists would ever take this route.

It became clear at subsequent forums that neither a recount nor a new election were feasible amidst continuing anger and insecurity, and thus the election Commission of Inquiry (Kriegler plus six commissioners – four Kenyans, a Tanzanian and an Argentine) was appointed and held open hearings across the country. Evidence adduced in the regions often proved a microcosm of national allegations. In Voi, for example, the leader of a lobby group charged that the provincial administration in Taita-Taveta, from the DC to chiefs' assistants, acted illegally on behalf of the PNU. Richard

Mwangeka, of the Opinion Leaders lobby, claimed that chiefs bribed voters with relief food, that a senior administrator cast two votes for Kibaki in the Voi constituency though he was not registered to vote in the area, that a box with votes pre-marked for Kibaki was found at Ikanga village but the man with the box was later released. Mr Hamisi Omar said Coast politicians influenced voters by issuing them title deeds during the campaign. Two witnesses urged that powers to appoint members of the Electoral Commission should be taken from the president and given to an independent body because, one ODM councillor said, 'they sing their master's song'. When a Kwale council officer, Immanuel Mbandi, complained that the inquiry was 'just a ploy to hoodwink Kenyans', Justice Kriegler vowed that his report would not be left to gather dust on the shelf of a government office. 'I understand your anger and passion', he said. 'It is going to be a long uphill journey for Kenyans. The solution may not come from this commission. Not even a constitutional review will change the situation. But a good electoral process is a good foundation.'

A week into the peace talks, the internal security minister in the new cabinet, George Saitoti, lifted a ban on rallies, but it was clear that deep divisions remained about how a coalition government would work and what would be the responsibilities of any prime ministerial appointee. Squabbling negotiators blew hot and cold through the month of February, and the East African Community said the crisis was having a negative effect on the regional economy; Condoleezza Rice flew in from Washington and declared that an agreement should already have been reached. Talks were moved to a secret location and a clearly frustrated Annan requested a complete news blackout. Onlookers feared the negotiators were stuck at the level of party politics, unable to raise their sights and craft what the *Nation* characterised as 'a new dispensation that guarantees justice and equity to all communities ... that tackles our scandalously unequal distribution of wealth and deals a final blow to our winner-takes-all politics'. Odinga returned to a hard-line stance and demanded Kibaki resign – then relented; Kibaki announced that he was prepared to share power and the PNU accepted the post of an executive prime minister – but then talks stalled over the extent of his powers. The rivals were also split over cabinet positions and whether a new election would be called if a coalition collapsed. Annan said he felt like 'a prisoner of peace', unable to get an agreement but unable to leave Kenya, and both sides complained of unfair pressures from media reports of supposed deals. A *Sunday Nation* survey showed that 61.3 per cent of Kenyans supported a grand coalition and there was widespread exasperation at the delays in the negotiations. Annan, finding that he could make more progress when he talked to Kibaki and Odinga directly than in the broader forum, cajoled the two into a face-to-face meeting. Five hours later agreement was reached, and a historic peace document was signed by the two men on 28 February 2008.

Under the National Accord and Reconciliation Act, the parties agreed to form a grand coalition government led by a prime minister empowered to 'coordinate and supervise government affairs' in which cabinet posts would be apportioned equally. The office of prime minister went to the leader of the majority party in Parliament, in this case Odinga, whose ODM held 102 seats against the PNU's 46, though some 61 MPs, otherwise aligned, were thought to be in the PNU camp against only half-a-dozen extras for the ODM. Crucially, the agreement provided that the prime minister – whose role was likened to a headmaster overseeing cabinet affairs – could only be dismissed by Parliament, not the President. The agreement also provided for two deputy prime ministers, one from each of the major parties. On 11 March, Parliament unanimously passed the Constitution of Kenya (Amendment) Bill, and MPs agreed plans to set up a Truth and Reconciliation Commission to expose injustice and begin the healing process. Discussions on long-term reform of land ownership, the economy and the constitution remained to be tackled. Kibaki exulted, 'Kenya has room for all of us.' Annan said, 'We want to return to the old Kenya – stable, peaceful, prosperous and welcoming.' Odinga expressed hopes for a new constitution within a year and fresh elections in two, though the government later indicated July 2009 would be the earliest date for a referendum on a new constitution. Even that was to prove too optimistic.

On a popular level, the agreement was widely welcomed, with thousands dancing in the streets in Odinga's home town of Kisumu. Said the *Nation*, 'Signing that deal, with the concessions each has made, stands as a true mark of leadership and patriotism.' But it warned that the two sides must be ready to cohabit for a full five-year term to give Kenya a chance to recover and move forward. 'The country is still divided and the peace is only skin-deep', it said. True, many Kenyans, especially among the masses of internal refugees, were cautious. A mother of four, whose husband died in the notorious Kiamba church blaze, said, 'It's become a habit of saying peace, peace, then after the peace we see flames of fire.' An unemployed Kikuyu youth, in a displacement camp for 20,000 on the outskirts of Eldoret, told the BBC, 'I don't imagine I'm going to stay with a person who stole my cloth and burned my house because he's still my enemy.'

Kofi Annan warmly acknowledged the *Nation's* role in mobilising the forces of civil society in the cause of peace. Although such elements tended to become visible only in a crisis, their presence represented a new capacity in Kenyan society. The media reflected this movement and eventually the politicians, too, came to recognise it. The *Nation*, for its part, urged Annan to regard journalists as friends and to work with the power of the Press in the search for an enduring peace.

Back in Nairobi, all the talk was of ministerial portfolios. Civic societies called for a lean team with untainted personalities, something that was never going to happen. The government argued that the cabinet had to be large to be properly inclusive, and spokesman Mutua said, 'No price is too high for our country to ensure the healing and stability that will ensure peace and spur the economy.' The opposition charged Kibaki was reserving important portfolios such as finance, energy and justice for his own people, and ODM secretary-general Anyang' Nyong'o said no agreement could be achieved 'until the PNU fully recognises the 50–50 power-sharing arrangement and the principle of portfolio balance'. After private meetings between Kibaki and Odinga, a huge cabinet of 42 ministers (21 for each party) and 52 assistant ministers was announced, though the ODM still complained it had been given the weaker posts. Odinga was formally named prime minister and Uhuru Kenyatta (PNU) and Musalia Mudavadi (ODM) as deputy prime ministers. What horrified Kenyans was the cost to the country of the biggest ministerial team in its history, requiring 42 permanent secretaries and their staffs, two limousines for each minister and one for each assistant minister, plus drivers and bodyguards. Kenyan politicians are among the best paid in the world and experts estimated that salaries alone would cost the taxpayer $1.5 million a month, plus benefits such as travel allowances, health insurance, rural homes, even club memberships. One Western source calculated that bonuses were worth $13 million a year, or enough to build 50 new schools. The *Daily Telegraph* in London said Kenya might find it difficult to secure donor funds to resettle refugees – for which it was seeking $484 million – and to rebuild infrastructure when almost half of its 222 MPs were ministers or assistant ministers. The paper said that of Kenya's annual budget of $10.5 billion, more than $8.4 billion would be consumed by government running costs, leaving only $2.1 billion for roads, schools and hospitals. Two weeks later, Finance Minister Amos Kimunya told Parliament he needed to find another $300 million to pay for the expanded cabinet and might be forced to shift funding from vital programmes such as resettlement.

Costs apart, the quality of some chosen ministers dismayed Kenyans, and Macharia Gaitho in the *Nation* wrote a coruscating denunciation of political opportunism and lack of vision. 'A monstrosity of a bloated cabinet was one of the things many of us grudgingly accepted as the price for a return to peace', he said. 'But I suspect that for the political classes, return to normalcy is also about re-establishing opportunities for official looting and plunder.' The unveiling of the coalition team was not so much a 'Come, let us reason together' moment as a 'Come, let us eat together' moment. Kibaki, he said, had added old allies who had absolutely no value, while Odinga was happy to bring aboard some of the most disreputable faces of the Moi kleptocracy:'Looking at the mugshots in the paper, all I saw was a gallery of rogues … Goldenberg and Anglo Leasing are in coalition.' Gaitho said, with such a disreputable cast in charge, 'we might as well bring in the Mafia to run the country'. He urged that ministers be restricted to ceremonial duties and a professional civil service be trained up to do the job.

With a cabinet, however tainted, in place and serious violence ended, politicians confronted the urgent challenges of re-homing hundreds of thousands of displaced persons and punishing the men of violence. Ahead, under National Dialogue and Reconciliation efforts, lay the tasks of rewriting the constitution, procuring land and electoral reforms, cleaning up the police and judiciary, and dealing with economic inequality. Meanwhile, the *Nation* evaluated its own performance on the biggest story in its history. It was clear that in espousing a 'peace above all' policy, the company had made desperate efforts to calm passions and encourage reconciliation. On 3 January, the *Nation* and the *Standard* ran front-page editorials with the same headline, 'Save our beloved country', which denounced politicians as responsible for the violence and for failing to come up with a quick solution. Independent TV stations repeated the 'Save Our Country' call. The risk inherent in the 'peace first' approach was that, in choosing not to publish all the facts, the *Nation's* editorial decisions and thus its stance as an independent communicator were laid open to question. A fact-finding mission by three international bodies – Reporters Without Borders, International Media Support and Article 19 – reported that the early media efforts to keep things calm were undermined when the government clamped its ban on live coverage. Papers and broadcasters responded by reporting facts, figures and statements, but nothing likely to provoke disorder, and often appeared flabby and weak-kneed to the reader. The ban was only spasmodically obeyed before being lifted on 4 February and journalists claimed its only effect had been to worsen relations with the government.

Of more concern for the *Nation* were charges of political tendentiousness, that it failed to take a moral stance because it supported the PNU. NMG had long presented itself as a champion of justice and democracy, a crusader against corruption and a defender of the downtrodden, but now confronted the question: Had these core values become in practice mere abstract ideas? Among the specific charges were that the rigging of the election became evident at an early stage, but NMG did not investigate the fraud nor denounce the obvious culprits – indeed, it stated surprisingly in an editorial on 31 December that 'it is not for us to say whether the allegations [of fraud] were true or not'. Editors later conceded the infelicitous nature of this phrase, but argued that it probably would not have been used in calmer times. A widely disbursed allegation which angered *Nation* executives was that the company suppressed its own vote-tallying feature on television at a crucial point in the election returns. Declared Group Editorial Director Wangethi Mwangi, 'That is simply not true. The system did substantially break down but we had no reason to suppress any information because at that point we were relaying ECK results that were widely available anyway.'

Other charges:

- *When trouble broke out, the* Nation *blamed both sides, hiding behind its policy of independence to avoid taking a principled position. Mwangi declared, 'Taking sides would have been dangerously divisive.'*
- *The newspaper failed seriously to investigate the post-election violence, including the role of the police. Mwangi responded, 'This was something our reporters tried but which proved virtually impossible to achieve.'*
- *Reports and omissions reflected preference for the Kikuyu cause, for instance, a non-political Nairobi businessman told this writer bluntly, 'It is well known the election was rigged but there was hardly any critical comment of the PNU from* Nation. *People like Kibaki, Kenyatta and Martha Karua are never criticised, presumably because they belong to the same ethnic group as NMG management.' Mwangi: 'It is notable that the Kikuyu establishment accused* Nation *of being pro-ODM and our editors and reporters were targeted with blood-chilling threats from the Mungiki sect. We had ugly altercations with party hacks from both sides seeking to influence our political coverage.'*

A Kenyan lawyer based in Geneva, Sisule F. Musungu, concluded in an early analysis that the national media reduced the election dispute to a duel between Kibaki and Odinga. The director of IQsensato, a development think tank, Musungu charged that editors failed to play democratic watch-dog and to provide credible information on the disputed numbers. 'Why did the *Daily Nation* website suddenly withdraw figures posted on 30 December?', he asked. 'Did the media cave in to threats and intimidation?' Not so, said Mwangi: 'There had simply been no new data for nearly 24 hours.' Not everybody deplored media inaction, however. At a June sitting in Voi of Justice Kriegler's election commission, a religious leader, Mohammed Washalla Abdi, said the media had chosen to be 'referees and players' at the same time. The chairman of the Taita-Taveta branch of the Supreme Council of Kenya Muslims said, 'Even before the final tallies had been announced, some media houses had already been giving out results, commentaries and biased opinions, which ended up misleading Kenyans.'

Beyond the election and the violence, the *Nation's* handling of the peace talks was faulted as lopsided and inconsistent. When the PNU sought initially to shoot down the idea of a coalition, the daily carried an editorial on university education, a decision which one director characterised as 'a total copout'. Another complaint referred to a general absence of editorial robustness and a retreat into neutrality, which editors seemed to think was the same thing as editorial independence. The Nairobi businessman said, 'At first, the PNU stance was rigid and unethical and the *Nation* should have been more forceful in condemning this dishonourable behaviour, but there were only mild rebukes and even then, the ODM were equally blamed.' There was concern that most of the strong writing which did appear was in commentaries and opinion pieces rather than in editorials boldly stating the company's view. Accusation of pro-PNU bias appeared to be supported by a Western embassy's survey of pre-election coverage which showed *Nation* giving 54 per cent to the PNU against 29 per cent to ODM, though the *Standard's* figures were remarkably similar – 53 per cent and 30 per cent, respectively. It is normal, too, that the government party makes the running when the opposition can only respond and thus garners the lion's share of space. Nevertheless, mobile phone texts criss-crossed Nairobi calling for a boycott of the company's newspapers.

The international media mission found some senior journalists agreeing that they failed their watchdog responsibilities by not investigating the rigging charges.[3] Both the *Nation's* Macharia Gaitho and Kwendo Opanga of the *Standard* said writers were haunted by the grim role of the media in the Rwanda genocide and obsessed by the fear of making things worse. Gaitho believed they had behaved responsibly, but wondered if in doing so they had hidden the truth. This issue, he said, was fiercely debated inside the company. Many experts made the point that Kenyan journalists had never experienced so grave a crisis and, not knowing how to handle it, retreated into self-censorship. Physical fear was also a factor and a KTN editor admitted the station was afraid to broadcast all the news it had in case of reprisals against staff. David Makali, director of the Media Institute, said it was fear of attack that prevented newspapers from setting up probe teams. He believed the media should have defied the broadcast ban outright, but editors and owners came under great pressure and played down some stories while not reporting others. Preaching peace and reconciliation was the job of priests and politicians, he said – a conclusion backed by the fact-finders. Their report declared, 'Preaching is not a journalist's main job. The alleged fraud in the election was clearly an urgent matter … but in the interests of public order [journalists] deliberately chose to ignore it, while thousands of Kenyans poured into the streets in search of truth and justice.' The report urged the media to investigate and offer the public maximum insight into its election and post-election crisis, to strengthen its system of self-regulation, and to set up a fund to train journalists in investigative reporting and self-protection in conditions of violence.

In early February, the Aga Khan made one of his rare interventions, urging NMG to re-establish itself as a 'trustee for democracy'. Editors, he said, should suggest ways that a value system be installed, addressing issues of inequality and outlawing all forms of violence. Editorials should call for the setting up of technical ministries protected from politics, and a solution to the dysfunctional relationship between the executive and parliament, so that the economy could be managed in an apolitical way.

The *Nation* did eventually find its footing, and by mid-February was delivering some strong editorials and commentaries. When the PNU quibbled about the powers of a prime minister, arguing they should come within the provisions of the current constitution, the paper showed its claws. 'To insist on this argument is to obstruct the search for a political settlement with legalisms, even as the country squirms with pain', an editorial said. The constitution had already been amended 37 times and could certainly be changed again to accommodate the new requirement, it declared. Writing in the same issue, Lucy Oriang expressed disappointment in Kibaki's leadership – he had proved to be no Nelson Mandela as many hoped – but she believed he could yet aspire to greatness: 'He is the man in charge, he chose to be president, he cannot delegate the responsibility. This is no longer about who's right and who's wrong; it is about rising above petty and self-defeating ambitions and doing what's right for Kenya.' Denouncing obsessions with the constitution, she demanded, 'Don't get imprisoned by rules as Kenya burns to the ground.'

The return of editorial self-confidence came late, however, and the *Nation's* early failure to condemn electoral theft lingered. One source close to NMG, who asked not to be named, said:

> *We did not foresee these problems and we were not equipped to handle them, we lost the confidence of readers with our infamous editorial of December 31 which failed to acknowledge that there was electoral fraud against the ODM, and we failed to bring the leadership to book for letting these things happen. Internally, we seemed to be divided and to lack courage.*

Seeing the damage wreaked by these failures dismayed staffers who had laboured loyally over the years to build the *Nation's* good name in the face of much government harassment and intimidation. Anger, condemnation and recrimination split editors and managers. NMG became a microcosm of polarised Kenya. Outside threats were made against MD Linus Gitahi and leading journalists, including Gaitho, Joseph Odindo and NTV political interviewer Julie Gichuru. Blog contributors, often from the diaspora, repeatedly returned to the Kikuyu hegemony charge, listing the preponderance of Kikuyus in management. One probable reason for the *Nation's* undue hesitancy was the absence of a chairman since Hannington Awori's retirement a year ago. NMG moved to repair some of the damage at its 18 March board meeting when Dr Martin Aliker, the Ugandan chairman of Monitor Publications, was elected to succeed Awori. At the same time, Wilfred Kiboro left the board's editorial committee. Aliker's choice was presented as an appropriate step for an enterprise, which not only had strong regional connections but was planning to enter the West African market.

Defending its stance in the early days of the crisis, the company said its first duty had been to helicopter employees out of danger areas such as Eldoret, Kisii and Kericho – some reporters had received death threats and were still having counselling months later. AKFED sent its head of security to Nairobi to advise on safety measures. Management admitted imposing censorship, particularly on political advertorials, but stressed this was to prevent further flare-ups, though it was debatable if this tactic always succeeded. 'Some of these advertorials were full of hate-mongering which could easily have exacerbated the problem and we had to pore over every detail to ensure copy was safe to publish', Mwangi said. Certainly, reports of violence against a particular community were sometimes followed by retributive attacks; on the other hand, an internal *Nation* memo stated that 'graphic coverage of the violence appears to have prompted calls to end the violence and submit to mediation efforts'.

In a series of soul-searching post-mortems, editorial chiefs, managers and directors explored areas of vulnerability or ambiguity, including the perception of NMG as Kikuyu-heavy. The company said this charge was simply not true and decided to expand the list of named department heads which the *Nation* carried daily, to demonstrate its multi-ethnic nature. It also considered methods by which it could redress the tribal misperception. To counter the belief, widely held in western Kenya and Nyanza, that the papers supported the PNU, the company considered creating the position of ombudsman, who would be a link with the public without influence from management or directors. Reflecting ethnic divisions within the group, one meeting heard that some directors had taken issue directly with journalists over particular articles. Directors were reminded that it was the board's responsibility to protect journalists. For their part, some board members complained that their suggestions were sometimes met with disdain by management.

Major concerns focussed on future editorial performance. Although the *Nation* had long promoted its Editorial Policy Guidelines and Objectives and the Editorial Procedure Manuals, which all journalists were supposed to follow, these seemed to be inadequate in a crisis. For instance, policy prohibited the naming of tribes in situations of conflict, but reports on attackers and victims using the usual euphemisms were considered by readers to be pointless or absurd – especially since family names could usually identify the ethnic connection. In his column 'What others say', Charles Onyango-Obbo described phrases such as 'a certain community in western Kenya' as 'the politically correct but disembowelled language of the day'. It was decided that the guidelines would be rewritten to give practical definitions to issues of justice, democracy and pluralism, and the discretionary authority granted to editors would be reviewed. To guide all this, the company agreed to establish a resident editorial board, essentially a sub-committee to the standing Editorial Board Committee, which would focus on policy issues as opposed to operational matters dealt with at the thrice-daily editorial conferences. The initial proposal was that the group editorial director and the heads of news divisions would sit on the board, with the chief executive officer as an ex-officio member.

The financial effects of the crisis on the group, as on the rest of Kenya, were severe. Normally at election time the *Daily Nation* would sell more than 300,000 copies; this time, with streets deserted and no vendors, it sold no more than 80,000. With little advertising, average pagination fell from 72 to 40 pages. Two new products launched in 2007, the serious *Business Daily* and the popular *Daily Metro*, managed to come out regularly, but sales were minimal. Nairobi became a ghost city after 8 pm and the Nairobi Stock Exchange index slumped, with NMG trading only 6,000 shares on 1 January. An internal report on 2 January said, 'There has been a collapse of business activity, food is running out, petrol is in short supply, there are queues outside supermarkets.' Mombasa port ground to a halt, trucks on the crucial road route to Kampala were frequently blocked, sending food and petrol prices soaring in landlocked Uganda, and even Dar es Salaam port was affected. The World Bank estimated that an extra 5 million Kenyans may have been pitched into poverty by the election crisis, and the BBC reported that the dislocation of farm workers meant crops were rotting in the fields, while prices of potatoes, onions and tomatoes nearly doubled. Wheat, rice and maize soared, too, after granaries and farms were set on fire, forcing the government to import 3 million bags of maize. With inflation running at 26.6 per cent, hundreds demonstrated in Nairobi demanding a cut in the cost of staples. Police dispersed the crowd with tear gas. The *Nation* reported that by late May insurers had received claims totalling KSh1.2 billion ($18.7 million) for property destruction. It said thousands of Kenyans were drowning in debt, unable to repay monies taken before the violence through unsecured loans and easy credit. The $900 million tourist business was savaged, and in January and February hotels reported single-digit occupancy. But the figures rose after the peace accord and by Easter many coast hotels were fully booked, mostly by locals or East Europeans. Safaricom, East Africa's most profitable company, sold 10 billion shares in Kenya's biggest ever stock market flotation and the stock soared 45 per cent. The sale was oversubscribed by more than 500 per cent; a sign, analysts said, that investor confidence was returning. However, independent economist David Ndii predicted that the 6.1 per cent growth rate Kenya recorded in 2007 would drop by 2 to 3 per cent.

The return of political stability and a tentative security dragged the *Nation* group out of the catastrophic depths of January, and, when the mid-March Board meeting came round, Linus Gitahi was able to announce a 39 per cent increase in pre-tax profits to KSh1.6 billion ($24.8 million), though this was largely on the back of the strong regional economy in 2007 before the elections. Gitahi reported that group turnover was up by 21 per cent to KSh7.7 billion ($119 million) and he announced an intended split of 2:1 for the company's shares trading at an average KSh325 ($5). The board recommended a final dividend of KSh10.50 per share, up from KSh6 in 2006. The CEO noted that a new division, Nation Digital, had been launched and said the group expected to do well despite the violence. 'The signing of the peace accord ushers in renewed investor confidence', he said. 'We expect the economy to recover and gradually achieve last year's pre-election growth rate.'

Meanwhile, the fact-finders began to report to the nation. In August 2008, the Kenya National Human Rights Commission released details of its investigation into the violence, naming 200 people, including seven sitting PNU and ODM cabinet ministers, as organisers, facilitators or perpetrators. Five clergymen, eight senior administrators and 13 MPs were also listed. The Waki Commission declined to accept the report as evidence, but the *Nation* carried interviews with some of those named and the report was later posted on the Internet. Soon afterwards the Kriegler Commission handed over its report. It said Kenyans would never know who won the 2007 election because 'the conduct was so materially defective that it is impossible to establish true or reliable results'. The Commission said there was no evidence that the ECK rigged the result in favour of Kibaki or anyone else. The electoral crisis was due to systemic dysfunction of the entire system and the ECK should be overhauled or replaced. Tom Mshindi spoke for many when his *Nation* column said, 'It is not in this country's interest now to know who the winner or loser was as that would only reopen wounds.' What concerned Kenyans was whether the government would act on the Commissions' reports or whether they would be shelved as so often in the past.

Looking to the future, the government turned to two crucial problems: resettling the displaced, and punishing the men of violence. Hundreds of thousands of homeless Kenyans were camped in tented cities that stretched as far as the eye could see. The logistical and financial difficulties were considerable, but the memories of neighbour turning violently on neighbour posed psychological problems that seemed insuperable. Nearly six months after they fled, 50 Kikuyu families tried to return to their homes in the Rift Valley, but, when they started to unload their possessions, their Kalenjin former neighbours turned against them. Said Samuel Njuguna, 'They were coming close to us and they started screaming and shouting, "We will kill you, go back where you came from".' A local pastor said his church would be burned if the families left their possessions there, and the group returned to their camp in Eldoret. The *Nation* quoted Andia Visa, writing in the *Guardian* of London about the days when her family travelled from

Mombasa once a year to western Kenya to visit her grandparents. 'The idea of Kenya belonging to all Kenyans and Kenyans having the right to live where they like is dead', she wrote. 'Will we ever again be able to look each other in the eyes, to suppress the knowledge of the things we have done and are capable of doing to each other? Will we all retreat to the safety of our ethnic enclaves?' A thoughtful editorial in the *Nation* made the point that some displaced persons had been burned out two or three times in successive waves of political violence since the early 1990s, and it would take more than government promises to persuade them to return: 'These people will not be reconciled by the presence of armed policemen or through diktat from above. What is required is grassroots engagement, bringing together the people themselves and their leaders at village and township level to talk about their differences and agree to live in peace.' Unhappily, this element was missing from the resettlement process, the paper said.

The crucial question of amnesty threatened to undermine the fragile solidarity of the coalition. Odinga argued that most of the 15,000 being held for election violence were small-fry victims of a partisan police force and should be released, while Kibaki said not even minor malefactors were above the law. The bigger question concerned the leaders in the shadows. Among the public there was little doubt that some of those who organised and funded the clashes were sitting in the government, on both sides. Amnesty International described this as 'the elephant in the room', and pointed out that both ODM and PNU negotiators had promised Kofi Annan they would 'identify, investigate and prosecute perpetrators' of violence. It was up to Kibaki to ensure that the inciters of violence, including those in the police and their own ranks and not just the foot soldiers, should face justice. Odinga, for his part, should use his executive powers to ensure the police and justice system worked fairly. 'If politicians do not rise above their partisan interests, the country's history of impunity, corruption and violence will become its future', Amnesty said. A *Nation* editorial argued forcefully that Kenyans who burned and killed other Kenyans 'are murderers and arsonists. There can be no amnesty for that type.' But it supported a solution proposed by the Kenya National Commission on Human Rights that offenders should be sorted into two groups. Those involved in rioting and protesting should be forgiven after confessing their deeds and providing any information which they might have about the organisers. Those suspected of murder, arson and perpetrating serious violence should be prosecuted. Further, every killing by a policeman should be independently investigated and, if necessary, followed by a trial. Columnist Gaitho said neither side enjoyed a totality of right, and, by quarrelling in public, Kibaki and Odinga were portraying their coalition government as a dysfunctional organism destined to abort. 'Kenyans are desperate to see their coalition survive', he said. 'They know the consequence of failure could be meltdown', with Kenya joining other African hellholes such as Somalia and Liberia. He called on the politicians to settle the issue in the cabinet room.

Deep into 2009, more than a year after the power-sharing agreement was signed, there had been little movement on critical issues. Peace broker Kofi Annan accused the coalition leaders of 'losing momentum' in delivering reforms and failing to face up to the big decisions needed to bring change. Government supporters argued that there had been wildly unrealistic expectations for the new arrangement and at least the coalition had remained intact. Critics pointed out that with two big political blocks sharing power there was barely an opposition in Parliament, and meanwhile there were new accusations of corruption against both major parties. Areas where Kenyans expected urgent action to prevent the 2008 violence ever recurring included land reform, constitutional change, judicial cleansing and moves to reduce ethnic tensions, including trials for senior figures suspected of war crimes. Few of these areas had proved susceptible to dynamic movement, and Annan's team extended its original targets and urged the men of power to extra efforts. The good news was that Kenya was at peace; the crucial objective was to keep it that way. A country abounding in talent and boasting the biggest economy in East Africa had much to be optimistic about. Internationally, it had earned praise for its leadership role in the Somali and Sudanese peace processes; confidence in security quickly returned and tourism bounced back to become the best hard currency earner after horticulture and tea; the economy began to show its traditional buoyancy. A veteran foreign observer of the political scene remarked, 'Kenyans have an enormous capacity to forgive.' Harnessing such goodwill was clearly the key to enduring peace, providing the politicians had the vision to see it.

The *Nation*, for its part, though bruised by the post-election experience, had its own vision for the future. Anchored in a belief that civil society had a unique role to play in developing societies, convinced that Kenya's future lay in dynamic co-operation with neighbour states and buoyed by the confidence reflected in invitations at the highest level to expand beyond its borders, the group laid plans to mark its 50th anniversary in March 2010. Wilfred Kiboro returned as Chairman in succession to Dr. Martin Aliker and Joseph Odindo took over the editorial reins on the retirement of Wangethi Mwangi. Armed with a new maturity and unquestioned status, no ambition appeared too small as editors and managers positioned all of Africa and every type of media in their sights. The next 50 years looked like being as interesting as the first.

## *Notes*

1. Traditionally, the Kenya media have treated ethnic-political affiliations with kid gloves, eschewing the naming of names although the connections were clear to all. Stemming from the focus on nation-building in the early days of independence (when the word 'tribe', for instance, was replaced by 'community'), these policies led to a meaningless sort of double-speak that convinced nobody. One effect of the clashes was to prompt the *Nation* to review its policy in this area.

2. The document was headed 'Executive Brief on the Positioning and Marketing of the Orange Democratic Movement and the People's President – Hon. Raila Odinga'. It named a five-member 'core strategy team' headed by Peter A. Nyong'o and outlined 'a strategy for overcoming the odds and delivering the presidency to Hon. Raila Odinga and ODM in the December elections'. This included support for a 'Kikuyu alienation' campaign and under 'Ethnic Tensions/Violence as a Last Resort', the use of ODM agents 'to engineer ethnic tensions in target areas'.

3. After the election, the *Nation* investigated the rigging claims in depth and collected a wide range of data, including what it believed was the true result; however, a decision was taken not to publish this story for fear that it would derail the peace process and re-ignite tribal warfare.

# Did We Do Our Best?

Managing a quality newspaper requires an enduring mix of talent, integrity and sound judgment. Running the *Nation* through years of political and economic turbulence called for near-superhuman qualities from those at the top. The occupant of the editorial chair in particular had to contend with the commercial requirements of the ownership, hostility from successive governments, the demands of an intelligent, aspiring staff and the daily scrutiny of a highly politicised readership – all this whilst guiding the paper faithfully by its founding slogan, 'The truth shall make you free'. Imprisonment, personal violence, blackmail, bribery and disinformation are not problems which normally appear on the docket of a Western editor; for many *Nation* employees they were inescapable constituents of the working life. Recalled Wilfred Kiboro, 'What was a terrible shock when I joined in 1993 was how the newspaper was regarded by people in authority – as unpatriotic, suspect, an enemy of the people. It had never occurred to me that I might ever do anything remotely unpatriotic so this attitude was a big shock. I was nervous, my family was worried and I put in strong security at home.' It is unsurprising that not all editors down the decades were able to cope.

A fundamental paradox was rooted in the group's foundation. The Aga Khan came to hold severe opinions about the media stemming from his painful personal exposure, as an international personality in Europe, to a prying tabloid press. In a 1961 letter to Nairobi, he set out these strictures: 'No happy-go-lucky reporting, no intimate details of who did what to whom after a late night.' But his main concern was the cultural ignorance of young European journalists who had never been to Africa, and the risk of misunderstanding traditional values in such areas as polygamy, nudity and worship. He did not want British writers making mistakes that their African counterparts would not make. It was the young Aga Khan's visits to developing countries around 1957 which made it clear to him that there was a desperate need for responsible and independent media – as young Kenyan nationalists like Tom Mboya kept reminding him. Reflecting 25 years later on his decision to back their requests for a voice in the independence debate, he said, 'It seemed to me that there should be one or two media establishments in that part of the world which could report completely, responsibly and seriously on the constitutional moves, political structures, economic and social evolution and objectives that were on the minds of African leaders at the time.' Thereafter, almost all of the *Nation's* public problems stemmed from the belief of those young leaders that a newspaper should be an arm of nation-building and a cheer-leader for government, and the *Nation's* reluctance to fill such a role.

'Did we do our best?' is a question that conscientious editors address in their more pensive moments. A long-serving officer of the company, dejected by the state of Kenya many years after he joined the *Nation*, asked in a personal memo, 'Should we be held partly responsible, as the leading independent media, for the hardships that have been foisted upon Kenyans in recent years by thoroughly corrupt regimes? Have we been timid for the sake of a peaceful life when we should have taken a stand?'

From its birth, the *Nation* demonstrated a courageous commitment to multiparty democracy and freedom of the individual. Immediately after independence, Mboya started a campaign for one-party rule and the *Standard* supported him. The *Nation* argued that without an opposition party, democratic institutions would be undermined. During the three-year existence of the Kenya People's Union, Oginga Odinga's party was subjected to relentlessly hostile treatment from the *Standard* and the government-controlled VOK radio. The *Nation* frowned on Odinga's socialist views, but argued fiercely for the party's right to exist. In 1968, Odinga accused the Kenyatta government of altering the constitution for reasons of political expediency and this provoked outraged demands for the KPU to be banned. The *Nation* defied the trend, saying Odinga's opinions should be considered in the context of an adversarial political system and any action against him should be within the law. An editorial thundered, 'The present administration has no right to legislate for a one-party state or tie the hands of posterity on the question.' The *Nation's* dislike for leftist politics ran fierce and deep, but the paper demonstrated an obstinate belief that a multi-party system was the bedrock of democracy and declared so tirelessly during the dangerous Kenyatta years.

The paper was equally stubborn in defence of human rights. Even before independence, it battled alone against colonial laws restricting freedom of expression and it fought single-handedly again in 1966 when the sinister Preservation of Public Security Bill was introduced. It is easy to underestimate George Githii's courage in taking the fight to the establishment and Michael Curtis' far-sightedness in backing him. This, remember, was just three years after independence, when most Kenyans still passionately supported their government and President, and when criticism was seen as disloyal if not treasonable. A decade later, the *Nation* defended the constitution against factional subversion and resisted attempts to subvert its own organisation in that faction's cause. In 1982, in markedly more repressive circumstances, it denounced a constitutional amendment making Kenya a *de jure* one-party state, and demanded that dissident opinions and constitutional freedoms be respected. And when the coup attempt was launched, it rallied support for Daniel arap Moi as the legally elected head of state.

The first serious brush with Moi came after Oginga Odinga was barred from fighting a by-election at Bondo in 1979 and Rodrigues wrote his 'Time for magnanimity' editorial condemning the ban as unconstitutional and undemocratic. At a time of creeping but visible repression, the editorial was considered daring, and Amnesty International was not alone in considering the subsequent roundup of the *Nation* Six as a delayed reprisal. The arrest of the entire editorial leadership of a newspaper was unprecedented and a milestone on the road to dictatorship. Not at its worst had Kenyatta's government shown such contempt for Press freedom. A government statement that accused the *Nation* of setting itself up as an opposition party was unwittingly accurate, for Moi's iron-fisted leadership was turning the *Nation* into a lone public voice against oppression. An emasculated Parliament had abdicated its responsibilities and its debates were empty rituals. A political role fell willy-nilly on the only newspaper willing to speak out, even if it spoke in increasingly cautious tones. Looking back on those years, Joe Kadhi conceded that editors 'became butchers of important national stories which were only heard on the BBC, never read in our newspapers'.

Parliament debated the *Nation* on four separate occasions in 1989, a tactic intended to intimidate editors, frighten off advertisers and raise suspicions about the motives of its writers. It was during the debate which led to disbarment from Parliament that the Kikuyu canard – that the *Nation* was run by Kikuyus in the Kikuyu interest – was introduced, an extremely damaging accusation against any newspaper in a multi-ethnic society. By then, however, the pressures for pluralism were gathering internally and internationally, and the turning point in the battle for freedom to speak and write came in 1991 when the *Nation*, and this time the *Standard*, too, defied Moi's direct orders to suppress news of the FORD rally at Kamukunji.

It would be dishonest not to acknowledge the *Nation's* occasional descent into sycophancy, its periods of calculated silence and its propensity to turn a blind eye. In a London interview with this writer in early research for this book, human rights activist Njonjo Mue used words that proved uncannily prophetic when he suggested the *Nation* sometimes equivocated when it should have led. Referring to the 1997 poll, he said:

> *I read a number of irritating, almost patronising, editorials calling on all sides to come together and eschew violence and so on, instead of taking a real stand, not for a particular party but on the side of justice and respect for human rights. In countries where the political opposition is undeveloped, the media find themselves being pushed into that vacuum, not to play a blatant opposition role but to set out the issues clearly for public debate. I felt the* Nation *did not play the role it might have.*

It could be argued that the newspaper's performance at the disgraceful 1988 'queuing election' had been demonstrably worse. It ignored flagrant rigging and abuse of the democratic system, and consigned defence of *wananchi's* rights to lawyers and churchmen. This, however, was the era of the Mwakenya terror, when *Nation* journalists were followed, detained and spied upon, and one of them, Wahome Mutahi, was jailed and tortured. With personal survival an issue, it was not surprising that self-censorship became an accomplished art. Periodically, when it felt over-exposed, the *Nation* would deploy oblique methods to criticise the government, such as using readers' letters or carrying articles from foreign newspapers. From a later perspective, banning the *Nation* seemed inconceivable, but the late 1980s and early 1990s were precarious times. Libel actions were a constant threat, particularly with a pliant and cowed judiciary, and over the years the *Nation* paid out many millions of Kenya shillings for news reports that would have passed without comment in a developed democracy.

Some of the *Nation's* troubles lay squarely on its own head – such as care-lessness about facts, skewed headlines, tendentious misreporting and on occasions too cosy a relationship with the men of power. Choosing to ignore the first Parliamentary blast of 1989 was probably wrong, too, since it seemed only to provoke KANU further. Most painful was accepting the loss of Joe Rodrigues, arguably the best hands-on editor the newspaper ever had, at the behest of government. Many bitter words have been spent on this episode but veterans say the *Nation* had no choice, the government was harassing the paper on a daily basis and clearly intended to bring it to a halt if Rodrigues stayed. There was also an anti-Asian element in the campaign. An insider from the era said, 'Joe was not sacrificed by the *Nation*, he was put to the wall by the government.'

The coming of pluralism reduced pressures on the media, if only by spreading the risk, but if editors thought the 2002 Kibaki administration would demonstrate a more enlightened attitude, they were deeply disappointed. Commented executive Dennis Aluanga, 'The hostility of government and the possibility of media restrictions remained a dark cloud. We were absolutely wrong in thinking a change of government would mean change in that area.' The US media-monitoring organisation Freedom House found that during 2004 only two countries registered a negative shift in Press freedom – Kenya and Pakistan – down from the Partly Free category to Not Free. The reasons: isolated cases of harassment, arrests and beatings of journalists. In the same year, Reporters Without Borders issued Press-freedom rankings which dropped Kenya from 82nd among 167 countries to 109th place. It was Githii who pointed out that governments take over newspapers, newspapers do not take over governments. But the urge for control proved as strong under Narc as under Moi. Monthly media briefings promised by Kibaki at the start of his term never materialised and the appointment of ex-newsmen to high government positions did nothing for Press relations. The *Sunday Standard*, *Kenya Times*, *Citizen Weekly*, Hope FM, Citizen Radio and KISS FM all felt the government's wrath, while the *Nation* received a personal night-time visit from the First Lady, who expressed her anger about the newspaper in unbridled terms. On 2 March 2006, armed and hooded police stormed the *Standard* offices, disabled the presses, burned newspapers, confiscated computers and shut down KTN. Interior Minister John Michuki claimed the raid was to protect state security. 'If you rattle a snake, you must be prepared to be bitten by it', he said. It was the first time a Kenya government had shut down a major media company and the IPI named Kenya among 23 countries found to stifle media freedom. In the face of international condemnation, Kibaki said Michuki would remain in his cabinet and, though the *Standard* was back on the streets the next day, six weeks later the government withdrew its lucrative advertising.

Senior journalists are adamant that this kind of creeping intimidation was not a factor in their performance at the 2007 election, since they had suffered harassment from information ministers and their flunkies over many years. The *Nation's* hesitant and lopsided coverage of the poll and the violence stemmed, they insisted, from fears that they could be putting lives at risk. A statement from Editorial Director Mwangi said:

> *This was a nightmare none of us had ever envisaged, the most painful experience of our careers. The opinion polls said it would be a very tight election. The atmosphere was polarised as never before and we were bombarded with accusations of bias from activists on all sides. The primary challenge to our gatekeepers was to maintain even-handedness and fair play and this we strove desperately to do. It is true that when the fire blazed, we started preaching peace. Could we have done differently? I do not think so. As journalists our traditional role as dispassionate witnesses can be stretched to absurd lengths. If I see a house burning, do I simply call in the story or help to put the fire out? Is there not a point at which unimpeachable objectivity costs us our humanity? A cry for help is a cry for help. Kenya was crying for help and we could not ignore that cry.*

In assessing the *Nation's* performance in the battle for good government, consideration must be given to the sheer length of the conflict. Over the years, as many institutions became unstable and corrupt, the *Nation* came to carry more weight than would a newspaper in the liberal democracies. Involuntarily, it acquired a power and influence that gave it unusual presence on the national scene. There were three factors. First, it grew to dominate the print market and was thus important to players in the political game. With the addition of a broadcast division, this influence became even stronger. The second reason was the trust and credibility the newspaper built up after nailing its colours to the African majority mast in 1960. A third factor is the existence of a constitutional acknowledgement of Press freedom, which, though frequently spurned by the state, has always offered the media a legal basis for resistance.

Thus in consistency and longevity, the Nation group of newspapers stands comparison with any Kenya institution and rates far higher than any of its media competitors. Whereas some lawyers and human rights activists joined the fight late in the day when abuses were so evident that they cried out for condemnation, the *Nation* was in the front line from the twilight of colonial rule. It backed early independence and the release of Kenyatta, and under John Bierman it campaigned against the repressive media legislation of 1960; it cautioned Kenya's first opposition party, KADU, against dissolving itself to give KANU a monopoly of power; it defended the KPU as a disagreeable but legitimate political institution; it opposed preventive detention and one-party rule. In the transition to democracy, it drew attention to the unjust trials of political dissidents in the mid-1980s, to the abuses of power which sprang from unaccountable government, and to the erosion of constitutional and Parliamentary authority as KANU grew ever stronger. By focussing insistently on the wave of ethnic violence beyond Nairobi, the *Nation* directed a spotlight on the government's role and the plight of internal refugees. Throughout its history, the group exposed corruption: Coffee Board finagling in the early 1960s; the massive Goldenberg scam of 1993; thefts of huge tracts of Karura Forest in 1999; the resurgence of fraud and graft under the new regime.

Could the *Nation* have done more? Undoubtedly – there is always room for heroes! Could it have done more given the often intolerable pressures of the day? That is a harder question and it would be an unforgiving critic who would condemn beleaguered troops for decisions taken in the heat of battle. One thing that 50 years of pressure bequeathed to the paper's editors and managers was a wider perspective for the next half-century. It was this vision the Aga Khan began to set out following the restoration of peace in Kenya – in the first place, a growing role for civil society and a duty upon the media to mobilise it. There seemed little doubt that Kofi Annan's belief in the importance of this unsung sector and the *Nation's* support in marshalling these forces responded to popular aspirations and helped resolve Kenya's post-election violence. To protect the forces of reason against the fissiparous tendencies of tribalism would be a key editorial responsibility in the new dispensation. Looking back over many years in which the major concern was survival, NMG now found itself enjoying a new status and maturity. Being invited into Uganda, Tanzania and Rwanda by their heads of state was not only recognition of this status, but also in a wider sense a pointer to a new shape for East Africa. Whereas the Cold War had virtually strangled the old East African Federation, those pressures disappeared with the collapse of Communism. Now the way was open to an enlarged East African Community, not simply as an economic force but as the engine for political federation with all the strengths of a five-nation entity.

Clearly a media group with such a vision required concomitant action on the ground and an Africa Media division was set up charged with turning NMG into 'the Media of Africa for Africa', as well as for Africans in the diaspora, a growing and wealthy sector. Heading the initiative, Charles

Onyango-Obbo, the group's media convergence specialist, saw the shrinkage of newspapers around the world as an opportunity to provide the coverage they could no longer afford. Plans were laid for an Africa news portal, an Africa newspaper pullout, a pan-African magazine, *Africa Review*, and eventually a 24-hour TV channel dedicated to African news. The digital division targeted being the undisputed leader in the market by 2011. Initiatives included a social website, Zuqka, a hybrid of Facebook and citizen journalism; improved news and sports delivery, including stock prices and Sudoku puzzles, to the mobile phone; and e-papers delivering group content online. A cautionary note in a planning paper warned that 'the only hurdle NMG has to overcome to be the main voice on Africa in the emerging world concerns intellectual resources.' It is there that editors believe the Aga Khan University's planned School of Media and Communications in East Africa could help. It would be the first new private sector regional university in East Africa and would aim at securing a privileged relationship with NMG, providing specialist experts in all fields.

As in most newspapers, tensions emerged periodically among the board of directors, managers and journalists. If the board's occasional unease was partly the result of some erratic decisions by headstrong editors, the newsroom looked askance at the favoured remedy – editorial boards or committees. Rightly or wrongly, they saw a tendency to assume that, whenever the government clashed with the newspaper, the journalists were blamed. As for editorial committees, they felt that, however helpful they might be long term, instant decisions had to be taken by the editor on the spot. Ever nervous about the paper's stance, senior journalists were assured that it was not the policy of the board or NMG to stand up for the government. Privately, editors were told, 'We never set up to be opposition in nature.' The divide between opposition and independence was always a complex one, particularly in Africa. Because the *Nation* traditionally asked governments tough questions, exposed corruption and wrote forthright editorials, it was seen by many readers as *ipso facto* anti-government. This was a perception as unwelcome to NMG as a popular belief that it unwaveringly supported the government would have been. Neither was correct, neither was nuanced, and the fact that three heads of state invited the *Nation* into their countries appeared to reflect a confidence in the company's even-handedness.

Over the years the *Nation*, its founder and staff were accused of justabout every sin in the canon and many outside it: racism, tribalism, nepotism, tendentiousness, partiality, dishonesty, gender bias, parsimony, ill will, disloyalty, lack of patriotism, illiteracy, misreporting, misspelling and costing too much money. But most staffers have heard a reader say, 'We know the truth will be in the *Nation*.' The fact is newspapers are denounced constantly, often unfairly, most particularly by governments. The day the challenges stop is the day the *Nation* should start worrying.

# Index